ADVANCE PRAISE FOR *OFF SCRIPT*

"An eye-opening trip behind the political scene demonstrating how showbiz helped money wreck our political landscape. If you enjoy the TV show *Veep*, you'll enjoy this book."

—Kirkus Reviews

"Josh King knows what he is talking about when it comes to political messages because he was there, painting with ingenuity many of our most enduring images from the great canvasses of American politics and the U.S. presidency. In *Off Script*, Josh gives us an unprecedented and candid, fun look behind the scenes at the creative processes that have shaped the reputations of some of the most important political figures of our times."

—*Don Baer, White House Chief Speechwriter, 1994–95, and White House Communications Director, 1995–98*

"In the middle of a campaign, right at its core, are the major-league concierges, the people who can pick the right route, find the perfect setting, the best optics and the spot where a candidate can flourish while the press can find its way to a semi-good place to eat and drink. It's a full-time, full-focus job that comes complete with hilarity, heartache, worry, weariness and the constant realization that what you do or don't do can mean a good or a bad day for the candidate. Ladies and gentlemen, boys and girls, Josh King opens a window on the world of the tireless advance men and women who make any campaign work."

—*Mike Barnicle, MSNBC political analyst and columnist for* The Daily Beast

"Politics is show business for ugly people. Josh King is the master of making political events look pretty. *Off Script* shows you how a master advance man works his magic."

—*Paul Begala, Senior Strategist, Clinton-Gore Campaign, and CNN Contributor*

"Ever wonder what happens in a presidential campaign when the cameras are off, the doors are closed and no one's looking? Find out in *Off Script*, a guide to the messy, ugly and sometimes poignant world of political stagecraft by one of the best practitioners in the business."

—*Jay Carney, White House Press Secretary*
to President Barack Obama, 2011–2014,
and former Washington bureau chief
for Time *magazine*

"Discreetly leading the way in every campaign are the advance men and women who literally set the stage. Josh King, a Jedi master of that profession, vividly brings the image makers out of the shadows in *Off Script*."

—*Mark Halperin, Managing Editor, Bloomberg Politics*

"In *Off Script*, Josh King takes us on a guided tour of the theater of politics as we rarely see it: from the other side of the proscenium, all the way backstage, and even into the performer's dressing rooms. For those seeking to decode the power of image in the age of optics in our politics, King's book is a must-read."

—*John Heilemann, co-author of* Game Change *and*
Double Down *and co-host of Bloomberg TV's*
With All Due Respect *and Showtime's* The Circus

"Josh King captures a truth in politics—our candidates need stage management on a grand scale to be elected and re-elected. Many gifted advance people have ushered leaders into power, but more importantly many have driven them back into private life. But King's real insight is that in critical moments it's up to the candidates to perform on the political stage or to simply know enough to not put on the funny hat. A great read for anyone who wonders how the political sausage is made."

—*Joe Lockhart, White House Press Secretary*
to President Bill Clinton, 1998–2000

"Josh King is one of the most creative political visual artists of our time. He understands how image, picture, and content come together as one to communicate the messages that America sees and hears as it considers its national leaders. What could be more timely as we embark on a national election to pick our next president?"

—*Mike McCurry, White House Press Secretary, 1995–1998*

"Presidential politics is theater at the highest level. Successful events are huge productions that require master stagecraft. Josh King is the Wizard of Oz of presidential advance. In *Off Script,* King pulls back the curtain to reveal the stories and secrets behind the making and sometimes breaking of presidents."

—*Mark McKinnon, co-creator and co-executive producer of Showtime's* The Circus, *and former chief media advisor to George W. Bush and John McCain*

"Do you love the wicked brilliance of campaign stagecraft and the gilded lies that come with being a politician? Not as much as Josh King does. *Off Script* will show you why it's an art form."

—*Brad Meltzer, best-selling author of* The President's Shadow

"Josh King has written a zippy, snazzy book about the inner workings of American politics and the thankless work performed by idealistic grunts who get no credit when things go well and all the blame when they go badly."

—*John Podhoretz, author of* Hell of a Ride: Backstage at the White House Follies 1989–1993, *editor of* Commentary, *and columnist for the* New York Post

"Advance men (and women) are the wildest characters in most political campaigns, in my experience generally a mix of well-organized and half-crazy. In a rollicking ride though the last nearly three decades of presidential campaigns, Josh King chronicles some of the low and high moments created by, inflicted upon, or suffered through by the political wizards of stagecraft and appearance, presidential campaign advance teams. Quite a read!"

—*Karl Rove, Deputy Chief of Staff and Senior Advisor to President George W. Bush and author of* Courage and Consequence *and* The Triumph of William McKinley

"Josh King has been at the top of the campaign game for more than 20 years—and *Off Script* takes us behind the scenes to show what works, what doesn't and why. A must-read for anyone who works on—or just loves—the presidential trail."

—*George Stephanopoulos, Chief Anchor of* ABC News, *co-host of* Good Morning America *and host of* This Week

OFF
SCRIPT

OFF
SCRIPT

AN ADVANCE MAN'S GUIDE TO
WHITE HOUSE STAGECRAFT,
CAMPAIGN SPECTACLE,
AND POLITICAL SUICIDE

JOSH KING

Former White House Director of
Production for Presidential Events
and Creator and Host of *Polioptics—
The Theater of Politics* on SiriusXM
Satellite Radio, 2011–2014

St. Martin's Press
New York

www.stmartins.com

Design by Letra Libre, Inc.

Library of Congress Cataloging-in-Publication Data

Names: King, Josh (Joshua), author.

Title: Off script : an advance man's guide to White House stagecraft, campaign spectacle, and political suicide / Josh King.

Description: New York : St. Martin's Press, 2016.

Identifiers: LCCN 2015045855| ISBN 9781137280060 (hardback) | ISBN 9781466878921 (e-book)

Subjects: LCSH: Communication in politics—United States. | Mass media—Political aspects—United States. | Presidents—Press coverage—United States. | Political campaigns—United States—Press coverage. | Presidents—United States—Election—Press coverage. | United States—Politics and government—1989– | BISAC: POLITICAL SCIENCE / Government / Executive Branch.

Classification: LCC JA85.2.U6 K48 2016 | DDC 320.97301/4—dc23

LC record available at http://lccn.loc.gov/2015045855

Our books may be purchased in bulk for promotional, educational, or business use. Please contact your local bookseller or the Macmillan Corporate and Premium Sales Department at 1-800-221-7945, extension 5442, or by e-mail at MacmillanSpecialMarkets@macmillan.com.

First Edition: April 2016

10 9 8 7 6 5 4 3 2 1

To the stewards, scribes and sentries of the spectacle: the advance people of every political stripe in every political era; the journalists who cover the candidates and tell their stories; and the military and law enforcement personnel who safeguard our presidents and those they govern.

"It is not the critic who counts; not the man who points out how the strong man stumbles, or where the doer of deeds could have done them better. The credit belongs to the man who is actually in the arena, whose face is marred by dust and sweat and blood; who strives valiantly; who errs, who comes short again and again, because there is no effort without error and shortcoming; but who does actually strive to do the deeds; who knows great enthusiasms, the great devotions; who spends himself in a worthy cause; who at the best knows in the end the triumph of high achievement, and who at the worst, if he fails, at least fails while daring greatly, so that his place shall never be with those cold and timid souls who neither know victory nor defeat."

—Theodore Roosevelt,
excerpt from the speech
"Citizenship in a Republic,"
delivered at the Sorbonne in
Paris, France, April, 23, 1910

CONTENTS

PART THREE

THE VANILLA PRESIDENCY, 2009–2017

*Eight pages of black and white photographs
appear between pages 120 and 121.*

 **PREFACE** ★ ★ ★

THE AMERICAN SPECTACLE

The scene was so perfect it had to have an advance man's fingerprints on it.

In a 2016 Iowa Democratic debate moderated by CNN's John King, three candidates for president of the United States stood at podiums in a town hall format. The combatants and their ringmaster were surrounded on all sides by potential caucus-goers arrayed in five tiers of choral seating, creating a bowl effect. The manufactured setting was purpose-built for television, with a wall of human faces in soft focus as a backdrop. Televised debates—political theater—had come a long way since Nixon v. Kennedy in 1960.

But for the debaters, 2016 was as claustrophobic as 1960, if not more so. Their every physical and verbal tic was under intense microscopic scrutiny from the audience, both live and on television.

In visual makeup, the 2016 scene mirrored the 1992 debate between Bill Clinton, Ross Perot and George H. W. Bush at the Robbins Field House at the University of Richmond. As those three men sparred, Bush stole a glance at his watch, the gesture caught on camera and reigniting a narrative about a patrician detached from his people. *Only ten more minutes of this crap,* Bush thought to himself. "You look at your watch and they say he shouldn't have any business running for president," he would say later.[1]

The 2016 Iowa exchange also echoed the first debate in 2000 at UMass-Boston, where Al Gore's persistent sighing during George W. Bush's answers was amplified by a hot mic, and a split screen more common for tennis matches that stole peeks at Gore's eye rolls while Bush gave his answers all conspired to spoil the vice president's night. Gore's grunts, groans and grimaces regularly rank among the top ten cringe-worthy moments in debate history. Jon Stewart of *The Daily Show* called the performance "sigh language."[2]

The 2016 Iowa encounter did its predecessors one better. John King wrestled haplessly with the candidates to steer the direction of the dialogue. Ignoring him, they squabbled over women's rights and wage inequality with rehearsed one-liners and poll-tested rebuttals, making mincemeat of the agreed-upon rules. The crowd, interrupting with applause when each blow landed above (or below) the belt, became a live jury.

At the New Hampshire headquarters of one candidate, his astonished volunteers watched, open-mouthed, in frozen silence. His spouse, there to rally the pizza-fueled troops, couldn't stomach the bombast and walked out, trailed by a biographer who had been shadowing her that day. In ABC's TV studio, George Stephanopoulos prepared to weigh in with comment along with strategists Matthew Dowd and Donna Brazile. On MSNBC, Lester Holt got ready to cover the action.

With real newsmen, pundits and talking heads saying exactly what they always say when reacting to real political theater, the scene was so true to life that a casual viewer couldn't be faulted for thinking it real. The truth, however, was that it was all fake: fake candidates, fake caucusgoers, fake set, fake questions—but real journalists—all following a made-up script and delivering their lines to perfection.

The pitch-perfect scene unfolded in "Chapter 37" of the Netflix series *House of Cards,* created by real-life former advance man and the show's executive producer Beau Willimon. It was the eleventh episode of the show's third season, in which President Frank Underwood fought for his political life in the 2016 campaign against former solicitor general Heather Dunbar and Congresswoman Jackie Sharp. For the thirty-six episodes that preceded "Chapter 37," Willimon's viewers had been treated to all the trappings of office, backroom deals, campaign events, media manipulations and the associated triumphs and pitfalls of running for president.

The daily humiliations and degradations visited upon Underwood, Dunbar and Sharp ring true to keen-eyed followers of American politics over the last thirty years during the Age of Optics, where playing to camera and creating compelling imagery forces candidates far from their comfort zones.

Future *House of Cards* storylines on humbling candidacies could borrow liberally from a series of glaring mishaps on the public stage in the Age of Optics. An unwarlike candidate rides in a tank. A seventy-three-year-old candidate falls from stage. An eco-conscious candidate canoes down a river deepened by a carefully timed water release. A gung-ho candidate lands on an aircraft carrier. A pugnacious candidate screams on-screen. A candidate with an aristocratic manner sets out for an afternoon of windsurfing in flower-patterned board shorts. A war hero candidate speaks in front of a gag-inducing green backdrop. A businessman candidate sings a patriotic song off-key.

Each of these moments happened in sequential presidential campaigns from 1988 to 2012, courting political suicide for the man in front of the lens. While each gaffe was damaging in the immediately following news cycles, three of them lived extended second lives as lethal attack ads aired by their opponents. Through advertising, news video, newspaper photos or social media contagion, visual backfires have a powerful way of hoisting candidates by their own petard.

Given the long history of death by stagecraft, the perils of political production can threaten even the real 2016 front-runners until the final votes are cast.

As First Lady Claire Underwood, played by Robin Wright, exits the headquarters toward her awaiting limo, the trailing biographer, Tom Yates, played by Paul Sparks, asks why she's leaving while her husband still struts and frets his hour upon the stage.

Weighing on the beleaguered woman is not just the circus of the debate but also the demeaning depths to which she must sink to help the president rise in the polls, including parading door-to-door with a flock of photographers in tow and dyeing her hair to conform to the preference of focus groups, among a checklist of other indignities.

Claire answers her biographer contemptuously. "It's all spectacle," she says.

 **PROLOGUE**

THE TROPHY PRESIDENT

There is a parable, told and retold across a quarter century, involving a prohibition on politicians wearing headgear in public. Calvin Coolidge was once photographed in a full Indian headdress, making him look like Big-Chief-in-a-business suit and forcing the president to defend his decision to don the feathered crown. John F. Kennedy famously swore off a top hat at his 1961 inauguration, the thinking went, to ensure that his youthful mane distinguished him visually from an embalmed generation of leaders.

Like all parables, the superficial meaning of the presidential hat ban belies a deeper instruction: it warns of the perils of portraying someone you're not. The tenuous balance between who a public figure seems to be versus who they actually are is measured every day in American politics. Untidy advance work, a hot mic, an unguarded selfie or a misplaced prop can easily alter the equilibrium.

A real-life reminder of the cautionary parable took place in the East Room of the White House in the spring of 2013. In the pedagogy of Professor Barack Obama, a man renowned for his self-discipline and stripping the drama from public office, he called the lesson "Politics 101." For everyone else, it's called "Dukakis and the Tank."

The president drew his lesson from a September 1988 campaign event in Sterling Heights, Michigan, during which the Democratic nominee that year, Governor Michael Dukakis of Massachusetts, took a ride in an M1A1 Abrams Main Battle Tank wearing an oversized helmet with his name prominently stenciled above the visor. The resulting video from the foray became one of the most famous attack ads of all time, inaugurating, in thirty seconds of airtime, the Age of Optics.

A quarter century later, in the East Room, the president found himself in a similar position to Dukakis. A crowd was gathered. The press was assembled. Cameras were rolling. And an imminent decision on whether or not to slide a helmet over his head was about to be rendered. For his audience at the White House, it was going to be a teachable moment.

By virtue of their 28–21 overtime victory over the Air Force Academy Falcons and their 17–13 victory over the Army Black Knights during the 2012 regular college football season, the Midshipmen of the U.S. Naval Academy recaptured, after two elusive seasons, the Commander-in-Chief's Trophy, the accolade for the best record among the military academy rivalry. The trophy, whose three silver-plated footballs look like cannonballs stacked at the ready, had been held by the Air Force for two successive seasons, largely due to the pinpoint passing of quarterback Tim Jefferson.

The Midshipmen were arrayed on choral risers behind President Obama, much like the counterfeit Iowa debate audience stood behind John King in *House of Cards*.

Prior to the Air Force mini-streak, it was Navy's honor to hold the coveted trophy in a glass case for seven straight seasons in Bancroft Hall, the Midshipmen's dormitory at Annapolis. The 170-pound trophy, named for the U.S. president, was first awarded in 1972, providing a moment of national pride for the military during the Nixon years. In the years since, successive presidents regularly bestowed the honor on the winning team, either at the stadium at the end of the season or, once the punishing bruises of the gridiron campaign concluded, at a ceremonial event at the White House.

Handing out trophies to victorious teams in the East Room, under Gilbert Stuart's Lansdowne portrait of the first commander in chief, George Washington, should be one of the unadulterated joys of office, a brief respite during days when presidents shuttle from room to room and crisis to crisis. These ceremonies happen with regularity, following Super Bowls, Stanley Cups, World Series, NBA Finals and a host of other professional, intercollegiate and Olympian efforts. They also allow the president's communications team to stage events that invite rare bipartisan comity and front-page photography for the cities, towns and campuses that the victors call home. I helped to orchestrate many of them when I worked in the White House from 1993 to 1997.

In a typical gesture by the visiting champions, and to capture a memorable moment for photographers present, the team captain will bestow upon the president a customized relic of the athletic campaign. It could be a jersey with the president's name embroidered on the back or, in the case of these Midshipmen, a tricked-out football helmet adorned with the iconic Navy anchor in blue with an interwoven gold chain.

These keepsakes often reference other aspects of the awardee's legacy. A jersey given to Barack Obama, for example, may have the number 08 on it, pointing to the year of his election. In this instance, the helmet bore the number 44, Obama's numerical place in the pantheon of U.S. leaders. Eventually, all but the most treasured of these tributes end up behind exhibit glass or in storage at the presidential libraries of the recipients, another shard of history consigned to the perpetual safekeeping of the United States government.

In the East Room during Navy's visit, pride filled the faces of the Middies. The president, too, seemed happy, if only from the momentary reprieve of the weight of his office. Nearing the hundredth day of his second term, President Obama felt that weight heavily. Questions lingered over his handling of the attack at the U.S. Consulate in Benghazi; calls grew for action against Assad's regime in Syria; doubts persisted after the massacre at Sandy Hook Elementary School that the president could influence passage of even modest legislation requiring universal background checks on handgun purchases. Fifteen minutes with the Navy football team offered a break when such weighty matters could simmer briefly on the back burner.

When handed his new protective headwear by Midshipmen Bo Snelson and Brye French, Obama graciously accepted it and examined the equipment, looking it over from all angles, wondering, perhaps, whether it would fit his greying head.

"All right," he said, "that's the official Navy helmet, fitted for me! Pretty sharp, huh?"

A voice from off-camera suggested that Obama put the helmet on, seconded by a murmur of approval from the team and the gathered audience in the East Room.

It seemed like the perfect photo op, a picture that would certainly earn placement on the front page of the next day's edition of *Stars and Stripes* and *Navy Times*. It would live on as an inspiration for future classes of midshipmen in Annapolis, including those who would defend the Commander-in-Chief's Trophy the following season, and take its rightful place in the annals of collegiate football history.

Obama knew instinctively, however, that the image had a better chance of living in the Hall of Political Infamy, the immediate focus of a thousand toxic tweets and retweets, fodder for his enemies who could ascribe to the image, whether through caption, Photoshop or creative video editing, any matter of negative metaphor. The cruelest use of a doctored version of the image might carry a racial overtone, as was the case with many other Obama shots coursing through the Internet. As the father of two young girls, he wouldn't let this happen on his watch.

"Here's the general rule," said President Obama to the disappointed gathering. "You don't put stuff on your head if you're president. That's Politics 101. You never look good wearing something on your head."[1]

In offering the audience an impromptu course in stagecraft—Politics 101, as he called it—President Obama was recalling a long-established campaign taboo and sharing an established maxim of political survival. While few in the East Room made the immediate connection, Obama was rekindling memories of Dukakis's watershed moment from Sterling Heights, forever ingrained in the minds of campaign operatives and consultants from Washington to Hollywood as the most disastrous image-making moment in political campaign history.

For that reason, this most routine of White House events earned a spot on *NBC Nightly News* that evening. Reflecting on Obama's demurral, with video of the East Room event dissolving into a still image of the infamous moment in Sterling Heights, anchor Brian Williams reminded his audience of roughly 8 million viewers of what I knew all too well: "The example that comes very quickly to mind, Michael Dukakis and the tank; it has haunted politicians for generations ever since."[2]

 **INTRODUCTION**

POLITICS 101

Dukakis and the tank. The image has certainly haunted me, as it has most advance men or women at some point entrusted—for a few hours or even a few minutes—with protecting the image of a politician or presidential candidate. That's what advance people do during elections, as well as in the years in between: travel ahead of their principal, laying out plans for successful visits, ones marked by memorable images and, hopefully, free of embarrassing screw-ups.

It doesn't always turn out that way. The potholes of politics, in ways large and small, can upend a campaign and the political careers of those involved. As novice advance people are always admonished: *you're only as good as your last event.*

In and of themselves, moments like Dukakis and the tank cannot single-handedly doom a campaign. Only a pattern of missteps will kill off a candidacy. But images, and how they snake through traditional and social media, edited, cropped and contextualized to fit new stories and angles, do the most long-term damage when they align with an evolving *narrative* of the candidate's persona.

The linkage is even more combustible when connected to military service and simmering questions over a person's temperament to serve as commander in chief. Of our forty-four presidents, only twelve, including Bill Clinton and Barack Obama, had no record of military service. And yet one of the dozen, Franklin Roosevelt, was, in the minds of many, our greatest wartime president.

In 1988, Dukakis might have wished for some of Roosevelt's command residue to attach itself to him. After all, Dukakis had served in uniform, unlike Clinton and Obama. Leaving Swarthmore in 1955, he was drafted into the Army and sent to Korea, where he served for sixteen months of his two-year hitch. But his service, contrasted to his opponent that year, Vice President George H. W. Bush, didn't result in career-defining aerial combat and rescue at sea after being shot down over the Pacific in World War II.

Dukakis, at five-foot-eight, also didn't look like a warrior in 1988. He had long since traded his fatigues for a business suit, methodically ascending the ranks of local politics. As governor, he earned a reputation as a competent administrator, stewarding over an extended period of economic vitality—the "Massachusetts Miracle," he liked to call it. Another problem for Dukakis in 1988 arose from his policies while in office, which invited a "liberal" label and, worse, a "soft on defense" tag. To counter the branding, his campaign and advance teams worked exhaustively in the summer and fall that year to offer substance, create events and provide imagery to alter the politically fraught attributes.

One of those events was the September 13, 1988, visit to General Dynamics, maker of the M1A1 Abrams Tank, the battlefield workhorse of the conventional deterrent against the Soviet Union. The visit was staged in Michigan, another battleground of sorts. It wasn't the dividing line of the Iron Curtain, but unclaimed territory whose spoils offered twenty electoral votes to the winner. Dukakis would fight a pitched battle with Bush for them. Every move in Michigan, especially every filmed moment, might have an impact on the election.

I worked for Governor Dukakis that summer and fall, joining his campaign following the ill-fated effort of Illinois senator Paul Simon on whose short coattails I rode after graduating from Swarthmore a year earlier. In my first few years of college and in high school before that, I identified with Republicans, less through ideology than the emotional reaction of a young man growing up during the end of the Cold War to the image of commander in chief embodied by Ronald Reagan.

Reagan, on the cover of *Time* magazine, standing toe-to-toe with Mikhail Gorbachev in Geneva and Reykjavik. Reagan, with Defense Secretary Caspar Weinberger, rebuilding the Navy toward the 600-ship level. Reagan, presiding over the restoration of the Statue of Liberty at its centennial in 1986. These were the images—choreographed as they were—that struck a chord with me in my teens, adding to a strong patriotic streak instilled by growing up in the cradle of the American Revolution outside of Boston.

Through my eyes, *Time*'s photos of Reagan, captured by photojournalists like Diana Walker and Dirck Halstead, were linked directly to a long line of presidential imagery beginning with Emanuel Gottlieb Leutze's oil painting of *Washington Crossing the Delaware*. Also included in my mental collage were Alexander Gardner's collodions of Lincoln at Antietam with George McClellan, FDR touring wartime factories and John Kennedy, binoculars in his hands, watching early launches of the U.S. manned space program.

Commanding the armed forces, from the Situation Room to the forward deployments, comes with the office. As Michael Deaver, Reagan's deputy chief of staff, reminded me when I got to the White House in 1993, these moments are also loaded with symbolism. If you study them closely—angles, lighting and composition—*Time*'s photos by Walker and Halstead offer textbook instruction on how to chisel symbolism to a high gloss. In the back of my mind, as far back as high school and those pictures of Reagan, was a sense that crafting campaign imagery with a powerful and persuasive embedded message can rise to an art form— a dark art form, perhaps, but an art form nonetheless.

I came to Simon's campaign in June 1987. I did menial tasks in campaign headquarters but listened intently to tales of advance men and women returning from the road. They were knights of a sort, and I wanted to serve alongside them. My knowledge of the highways and byways of New Hampshire, a product of my upbringing in those parts, qualified me to move to Manchester as their apprentice. Moving from Simon's campaign to Dukakis's, I continued my education as a national advance man.

Mitchell Schwartz, Andrew Frank and Steve Barr, swaggering advance men who learned their craft on Walter Mondale's campaign against Reagan in 1984, served as my role models. They were the Democrats' answer to Deaver during that summer of 1988, and they taught me well. Schwartz was a lead advance man brimming with self-confidence, swarthy machismo and quick humor. Frank was a "site guy" with an artist's eye for design. Barr had spent part of 1984 planning the cross-country journey of the Olympic Torch to Los Angeles and was an expert in conjuring large, seemingly spontaneous crowds from nowhere.

I have been an advance man all my life, even long after I left government. It is a role that has brought me all over the world, and there are few better jobs on the planet. It takes a special kind of person—creative, detail-oriented and fast on your feet—to make the most of public moments while avoiding catastrophe. These skills never leave you, nor does the weird ability to look at the front page of a newspaper and be able to deconstruct all the elements, on both sides of the lens, that brought it to life. If nothing else, it makes watching the news an interactive experience.

This is a book about the spectacle of running for, and serving as, president of the United States. Creating the spectacle is what advance people do, but they don't do it alone. Spectacle sells. It sells television ads between the segments of newscasts. It sells display ads in newspapers. It sells banner ads on websites. Some publications, like the *Economist* and the *New Yorker,* traditionally don't traffic in visuals, preferring to allow thousands of words to tell the story. And yet, even those long-form pieces are laden with imagery. The first few paragraphs of a *New Yorker* story usually paint a mental picture for the reader. Pictures, real or mental, form an enduring impression. There is an implicit partnership between political strategists and professional storytellers around the simple fact that spectacle sells.

The more compelling a front-page picture, the quicker it flies off a newsstand. Crisp color tells a story more impactfully than pixelated black and white. *USA Today,* a newspaper brought to life by color ink, made its debut on September 15, 1982, at the beginning of the Reagan era. Al Neuharth's vision of a full-color newspaper, punctuated by a large photo on the front page, changed newspaper publishing forever. The *New York Times* finally added color to page 1 in 1997, followed by the *Washington Post* in 1999.

Time, Newsweek and *U.S. News & World Report,* staples of middle-class weekly reading for decades, delivered color to millions of American doorsteps, helping subscribers form opinions through the emotional tug of composition. On television, the replacement of videotape for film in the 1980s enhanced and quickened the pace of visual storytelling by allowing correspondents, cameramen and sound engineers to capture events unfolding in the field, edit it in a nearby truck or temporary "filing center" and transmit it to newsrooms via a satellite dish. From that point forward, campaign spectacle became an increasingly valuable commodity to be harvested. Daily dramas on the campaign trail could become evening entertainment, and drive viewership, on the news. In the process, political correspondents became celebrities.

In addition to staging a spectacle in front of the lens during presidential campaigns, advance teams go to extraordinary lengths to make the lives of reporters, producers, cameramen and photographers easier in many ways. The teams spend days on the road arranging planes and buses for transportation and securing banquet halls or temporary tents to serve as filing centers in close proximity to the political action. They stock these centers with tables and chairs, power outlets, phone lines and Wi-Fi Internet service. They even order banquet-style cuisine, billing all of the costs back to the news organizations who have signed up to attend the event. While both sides are often loath to admit it, in many ways, the work of a candidate's staff and the press assigned to cover a candidate is a symbiotic, mutually dependent partnership.

But sometimes an event goes awry, and a feeding frenzy ensues. The best laid plans of candidates and staff can fall apart in seconds as the press corps, willing partners a minute ago, bare their competitive teeth and feast on errors when campaigns go off script. In 2016, digital photos can reach the Internet in seconds, compared to hours in earlier days when film had to be couriered, processed, edited and moved on the wire.

Sometimes, too, the calamity unfolds more slowly but more lethally, the magnitude of the mistake emerging only when magnified by an eager opponent.

In every presidential campaign since 1988, at least one image has taken on a life of its own. While we'll have to wait until the end of the 2016 race to determine which images, if any, are fatal, there is always one that wreaks widespread damage. Working backward, in 2012, Mitt Romney's singing in Florida became a devastating TV ad for Barack Obama. In 2008, John McCain's bad backdrops exposed his flaws against an impregnable marketing machine. In 2004, John Kerry's windsurfing voyage off Nantucket was redeployed against him with effective and humorous precision. In 2000, Al Gore went canoeing in New Hampshire on a glorious summer day, but an advance team misstep turned it into a debacle. In 1996, Bob Dole fell off a stage in Chico, California, reinforcing perceptions that he was too old to be president. In 1992, George H. W. Bush watched a supermarket scanner in action and was deemed by the *New York Times* to be "amazed" by it, adding to his reputation, unfair as it might have been, as an out-of-touch WASP.[1]

And in 1988, the spectacle of running for president entered a new era when Michael Dukakis rode in the Abrams tank wearing a helmet too big for his head, thus inaugurating the Age of Optics. It was a colossal mistake of campaign strategy and advance work that played out precisely at a time when the fight over image became a daily battle and the packaging of political spectacle on television became a highly saleable product.

Ever since, that moment in Sterling Heights has been the prism through which campaign stagecraft is judged, with the mortifying moments befalling Bush, Dole, Gore, Kerry, McCain and Romney graded on that scale. It is no different in 2016. Even now, barely a day goes by without a Twitter reference to "Dukakis and the tank." It has lived on in the Age of Optics, in the minds of many who follow politics, as the worst political event in history.

PART ONE

THE WORST POLITICAL
EVENT IN HISTORY

THE ADVANCE MAN

DUKAKIS'S RUNNING MATE

Matt Bennett, a twenty-three-year-old advance man from Syracuse, New York, didn't enlist in the 1988 Dukakis presidential campaign with ambitions to oversee the worst political event in history. Despite modest misgivings about what his assignment held in store, only in hindsight could the gangly, khaki-clad operative form a fuller perspective on the catastrophe that lay in store on his watch. Advance people, as much as they try to anticipate disaster when serving a presidential candidate, can't foretell the future.

And even if he could smell doom for the event itself, as Bennett thought he might, who would listen to the warnings of a fresh-faced young man just off a plane in Detroit?

In the summer of 1988, Mike Dukakis looked well positioned to wrest the White House from the Republicans who had held onto presidential power for sixteen of the previous twenty years. One task before him was selecting a running mate. Among the names floated for the short list were Bob Graham of Florida, John Glenn of Ohio, Sam Nunn of Georgia, Tom Foley of Washington, and Lloyd Bentsen of Texas.

Picking a vice-presidential running mate is a process first cloaked in secrecy and then bathed in marketing. Part beauty contest and part background check, it is also the first decision-making "test" of a party's nominee. On July 13, 1988, Dukakis announced that Senator Lloyd Bentsen, a bomber pilot in World War II, would be his wingman, reprising the Massachusetts-Texas axis of the 1960 Democratic ticket. "Jack Kennedy and Lyndon Johnson beat the Republican incumbent vice president in 1960," Dukakis said, referring to Richard Nixon and his running mate, Henry Cabot Lodge, at a rally at Faneuil Hall, Bentsen beaming at his side. "And Mike Dukakis and Lloyd Bentsen are going to beat him in 1988."[1]

But that summer the Republican Party was also putting someone on Dukakis's ticket. Their choice was clear. His name was Willie Horton.

Horton, of South Carolina by way of the Northeastern Correctional Center in Concord, Massachusetts, was not on Dukakis campaign chairman Paul Brountas's vetting list. A convicted murderer, Horton was serving a life sentence when he was released on June 6, 1986, as part of a weekend furlough program put in place for Massachusetts inmates but didn't return from his hiatus. Instead, ten months later, he raped a woman in Maryland and beat her fiancé to a pulp before being captured by the Prince George's County Police Department. Maryland refused to extradite Horton to Massachusetts out of fear he might be furloughed again.

The awareness campaign for "Candidate Horton"—the slowly building linkage between a convicted criminal and a presidential candidate—began in the primary season but reached a crescendo on October 13 at the second presidential debate between Bush and Dukakis, moderated by Bernard Shaw of CNN at UCLA's Pauley Pavilion in Los Angeles. Some 67.3 million people watched at home, making it the fourth most-watched debate in history.[2] It was the year that the Commission on Presidential Debates, or CPD, debuted as presidential debate sponsor, taking over for the League of Women Voters.

The CPD brought with it a striking, made-for-television set that endures to this day. The candidates stand at identical podiums on a bright red carpet installed for the event. They appear before a royal blue backdrop, a "hard wall" like those that once flattered the anchormen on news programs, framing them against a strong, flat color. In the hard wall, hard to see by those watching at home, is a hole through which a TV camera takes "reverse shots" of the moderators without distracting the viewer. Above the candidates rests a graphic depiction of a bald eagle alighting on a shield of the Stars and Stripes. In the eagle's beak billows a ribbon that proclaims, in all capitals, "THE UNION AND THE CONSTITUTION FOREVER." The old League of Women Voters debate sets simply used a draped curtain as a backdrop.

In addition to marketing itself with these words and icons of strength and nostalgia, the CPD also catered to the vanity of the candidates. Vice President Bush, at six-foot-two, and Governor Dukakis, half a foot

shorter, represented the widest height differential in any presidential campaign in the twentieth century. To make Dukakis look roughly the same
height as Bush, the floor beneath his podium was elevated by a three-inch
riser underneath the red carpet. Always a keen observer of the visual in
politics, Maureen Dowd wrote in the *New York Times,* "When [Dukakis]
stepped off of [the riser], the six-inch difference in height between the
men looked suddenly dramatic."[3]

Following their walk-out on stage, the pre-debate handshake allowed
the audience to momentarily take the measure—literally—of the combatants, but the tale of the tape soon gave way to a jab below the belt. Surprisingly, it came not from one of the fighters but from the ref. The debate's
moderator, Bernard Shaw of CNN, was a man in a hurry. As soon as the
clock struck 6:00 p.m. in Los Angeles and the red tally light blinked atop
the camera, Shaw took aim at one of Dukakis's most vulnerable spots.

"For the next ninety minutes we will be questioning the candidates
following a format designed and agreed to by representatives of the two
campaigns. However, there are no restrictions on the questions that my
colleagues and I can ask this evening, and the candidates have no prior
knowledge of our questions," Shaw warned. "By agreement between the
candidates, the first question goes to Governor Dukakis. You have two
minutes to respond. Governor, if Kitty Dukakis were raped and murdered, would you favor an irrevocable death penalty for the killer?"[4]

Willie Horton's name was never mentioned, but the consequence of
his grisly case was applied in the most personal way to the Democratic
nominee in the first thirty seconds of the debate.

I was in the audience that night in L.A. and had barely found my
seat when Shaw's first question flew across Dukakis's plate. There was
an audible gasp from the Democrats seated in the rows in front of and
behind my vantage point. *Bernie, a curveball for the first pitch,* I thought
to myself. The moment called for a little hitch in Dukakis's swing, but
the pitch was eminently hittable. Handled well, it could be a home run.

Instead, Dukakis's response was the rhetorical equivalent of the
thump of a strike landing untouched in the catcher's mitt. "No, I don't,
Bernard," Dukakis said. "And I think you know that I've opposed the
death penalty during all of my life. I don't see any evidence that it's a deterrent, and I think there are better and more effective ways to deal with
violent crime. We've done so in my own state."

While Shaw's ghoulish scenario envisioned a heinous crime committed against the governor's spouse, Dukakis's clinical response comprised

44 milquetoast words, followed by 319 more of boilerplate rhetoric on drugs, including his familiar refrain, "We have work to do to fight a real war, not a phony war, against drugs," before his lips stopped moving. Slumped in my seat at the Pauley Pavilion, I couldn't believe the exchange I'd just heard.

Horton's story had been gaining traction since it first appeared in a Massachusetts newspaper, the *Lawrence Eagle-Tribune,* in a series of articles beginning in 1987. It was picked up by one of Dukakis's Democratic rivals, Senator Al Gore, who used the failures of the Massachusetts furlough program to score political points before the New York primary. But it was Lee Atwater, Vice President Bush's campaign manager, who used Horton and furloughs to kneecap his opponent. Atwater told a Republican gathering, "By the time we're finished, they're going to wonder whether Willie Horton is Dukakis's running mate."[5]

Vice President Bush started making oblique references to the case in his stump speech, and Atwater spent time that summer observing voters' reactions when they heard the basics of the Horton story. He noted how quickly their opinions turned negative toward the Democrat when it was suggested that there was a link between the rap sheet of the paroled murderer and a governor promulgating liberal policies.

On September 21, an independently produced ad from the National Security Political Action Committee called "Weekend Passes" hit the airwaves. The ad, produced by Larry McCarthy, was simple but brutal, a combination of words on the screen and narrated copy edited together with still photos of Bush and Dukakis. The ad also featured Horton's mug shot, designed to shock. The spot was taken off the air on October 4, replaced by one directly from the Bush-Quayle campaign, called "Revolving Door."[6]

"Revolving Door," more stylized and cinematically menacing than its predecessor, delivered an anti-Dukakis message similar to "Weekend Passes," leaving out the Horton mug shot but adding in a subtle pulsing score that, in movies, might signal imminent danger for women walking down dark alleys. Those sounds were mixed with images of prison guards and twenty male inmates passing through a chain-link gate. One of the prisoners, an African American, is the only one to make eye contact with the camera as he passes through the revolving door.

Dukakis never forgave himself for failing to respond to his enemies' early efforts to define him. "Houston had a homicide rate four times the homicide rate of Boston," he said many years later about a major city in Vice President Bush's home state. "It was inexcusable that I let him get away with this. But I did."[7]

WHILE DUKAKIS SLEPT

The governor had reason to think that he could play nice that summer, well before the debate in Los Angeles. He was pictured in news footage looking carefree, lounging on the lawn of his father-in-law's home in the Berkshires after capturing his party's nomination at the Democratic Convention in Atlanta. As he started his vacation at the end of July, a Gallup poll gave him a 55 percent to 38 percent advantage over Bush. With a lead like that he could afford to relax, but Dukakis's staff was uneasy about the mounting attacks and the muted response.

In the White House briefing room in early August, President Reagan, readying for his own summer vacation, joked about Dukakis, saying, "I'm not going to pick on an invalid" in response to unsubstantiated rumors that the governor had undergone treatment for depression. Strip away the Reagan wit and you're left with a sitting U.S. president suggesting a potential successor suffers from mental illness. Dukakis brushed it off. "We all occasionally misspeak," he said. "I'm a very healthy guy."[8]

In California, at the end of the month, Bush needled Dukakis for a 1977 veto of a bill that imposed fines on teachers for not leading classes in the Pledge of Allegiance. Dukakis's rationale rested on a 1943 Supreme Court decision, *West Virginia Board of Education v. Barnette,* but the vice president ridiculed him, saying, "What is it about the Pledge of Allegiance that upsets him so much?"[9] The pledge attack opened a wound that didn't heal fast.

Later, in an interview with a Blackfoot, Idaho, radio station, Republican senator Steve Symms hinted at the existence of photos of Kitty Dukakis, the candidate's wife, burning an American flag at a 1960s anti-war demonstration.[10] The description of such an image, even if it couldn't be produced as evidence, started more rumors buzzing.

At least Mrs. Dukakis fought back. "There couldn't be such a photograph because there was never any such incident. It's outrageous. It didn't happen," she said angrily.[11] Mrs. Dukakis's anger notwithstanding, the chatter about Willie Horton, Reagan's quip, the commotion over the pledge and rumored flag burning struck a chord among voters.

Despite the attacks, Dukakis turned the other cheek and decreed that August was time for him to return visibly to the role of governor of the Commonwealth, nurturing his "Massachusetts Miracle" state programs to keep them ripe for the fall campaign to come. Putting his national campaign temporarily aside, his statehouse staff organized official events in Springfield, Greenfield and other western Massachusetts towns.

Dukakis campaign press secretary Mark Gearan was a native of Gardner, Massachusetts, one of the stops along the tour. "When we left Atlanta at the convention," he told me, "we were seventeen or eighteen points ahead. We were very excited, imagining D.C. And then August, because of the commitment to running the state, really put us way behind."[12] The Berkshires, with its country inns and antique galleries set behind white picket fences, make for bucolic vacations, but spending time there with a soundtrack fed by the summer home of the Boston Symphony Orchestra at Tanglewood was a massive time suck for a national campaign in an election year. The press following Dukakis, Gearan remembers, was "bored."[13]

Ignoring the directive for campaign staff to lie low while the governor was on state business, Gearan tagged along on the trip to his hometown of Gardner and tried to take command of the media logistics of the tour. Directing the traveling press bus onto Fairmont Avenue, where his mother lived, Gearan assumed the role of advance man. "Robin Toner [a dean of the political press corps] filed from my house," he remembered. He then took Michael Kelly, another media big shot, to the home of Mrs. Tannen next door. "I remember knocking on the door and saying, 'This is the *L.A. Times.*' It was crazy."[14] In proper advance work, filing centers should be well-organized work spaces, not a free-for-all at private homes on a residential street, but Gearan did what he could to improvise.

As the Dukakis tour of towns in Western Massachusetts consumed valuable days in August, the governor's supporters began to get antsy. "They have two weeks to turn the campaign around," Massachusetts congressman Barney Frank said publicly.[15] The Olympic Games in Seoul would begin September 17, much later than usual for a Summer Olympics, diverting attention from domestic politics for two weeks during the height of election season. While August passed at a snail's pace, September would become a race against time. Every day preceding the lighting of the Olympic Cauldron in Seoul was precious.

Dukakis knew he was in trouble. He brought back John Sasso, his exiled campaign manager, and inserted him into a new role as vice chairman. Sasso had resigned a year earlier as campaign manager after admitting that he had leaked a videotape showing Delaware senator Joe Biden appropriating lines from British Labour leader Neal Kinnock. But Dukakis needed his alter-ego back, as well as a shot in the arm, and his new vice chairman immediately commenced planning for a series of high-profile events in battleground states to portray the governor as a strong prospective commander in chief. "Bringing John back added a lot of energy and confidence," Gearan told me. "We needed him, because the campaign wasn't working."[16] The first order of business was what's known in politics as a "theme week" to commence right after Labor Day.

Sasso would become "an ambassador to the candidate," as E. J. Dionne noted campaign aides saying in a report for the *New York Times*—the new vice chairman serving to bridge a communication gap between Dukakis and his staff.[17] Among the plans Sasso put in place was the Reagan-style strategy of selling a consistent message, spanning several days, with each day serving as a variation on the theme. In campaigns, if you're not creating the message, the message is created for you. One of these "theme weeks," scheduled for mid-September, was designed to show Dukakis's command of national defense issues on a trip that would span five states in three days.

On Monday, September 12, the governor would give a speech in Carpenters' Hall in Philadelphia, site of the First Continental Congress. He would then fly to Cincinnati to tour a General Electric plant that built jet engines for the Air Force. On Tuesday, September 13, he would speak at the Council on Foreign Relations in Chicago, followed by a visit to a General Dynamics facility outside Detroit. There, he would be briefed on the M1A1 tank and speak to defense workers. The tour would then move on to Washington, D.C., for a policy address at Georgetown and a rally in Annapolis before returning to Boston on Wednesday night.

If all went well, the September national defense week would provide a new cloak of machismo for Dukakis, a triumphal return for Sasso and Reagan-style images for the press.

DEATH MARCH

Over more than a quarter century, a simplified chronology of the political death of Michael Dukakis has taken root. It begins with the August

attacks as the start of the fatal slide. The governor's clinical response to
Bernie Shaw at the October 13 debate, three weeks before Election Day,
is pegged as the final nail driven into the candidate's coffin. But it takes
more than one nail to bury a presidential candidate. First, the coffin must
be built. Then the corpse must be attired for the afterlife. Finally, a funeral must be held.

The specter of political interment that Barack Obama lectured about
to the Navy Midshipmen in 2013 is what Dukakis should have sensed in
1988 when, on September 13, his limousine arrived at General Dynamics
Land Systems.

That limousine was his hearse. That motorcade from Detroit Metro
Airport was his funeral procession. The General Dynamics facility was
his graveyard. The governor's awaiting casket took the form of a decommissioned M1A1, temporarily taken out of active Army service to serve
as a political prop. The tank, a twelve-foot-long, sixty-plus-ton behemoth
designed to counter a Soviet ground attack across the European frontier,
was a tight fit for four passengers but had more than enough legroom to
fit a single political corpse.

Dukakis's funeral attire was an unbecoming set of grey coveralls supplied to shield his business suit from the tank's belching engines. The
coveralls also satisfied a safety requirement, providing a set of orange
straps stitched behind the shoulders to allow rescue crews to extract the
wearer from a disabled or, worse, burning tank if the shit hit the fan.

On Dukakis's head, completing the funereal ensemble, sat a tank
commander's helmet. The helmet was requisite for a full-speed tank ride,
and a built-in speaker and microphone in the helmet allowed Dukakis to
hear above the M1A1's turbine engines as his guide told him about the
tank and to ask questions in response. Emblazoned across the brow was
a black-on-white label that reminded viewers of the stenciled call sign of
Tom Cruise's Pete "Maverick" Mitchell in the 1986 movie *Top Gun*. This
label did not say "Maverick." It said "Mike Dukakis."

The funeral would be televised.

Sam Donaldson of ABC, Bruce Morton of CBS and Chris Wallace
of NBC—together the conduits of moving images from the campaign's
traveling road show into the living rooms of American voters—offered
the requiem. The three correspondents didn't know it at the time, but the
footage their crews shot would, within a month, serve as the documentary
underpinning for one of the most devastating political advertisements of
all time.

TELLING WAR STORIES

Professionals in any endeavor, from fishermen to football heroes, gather with those of like minds at local watering holes and swap "war stories," some true, others embellished with a dose of drama. When I grabbed a stool at a New York City tavern in the fall of 2012 with my old friend Matt Bennett, no exaggeration was needed as he recalled, one more time, his ordeal as the site advance man for Dukakis in Sterling Heights.

But Matt went a step further. He shared with me, days after we met for beers, a treasure from his political archives: his quarter-century-old journal, typed out on six single-spaced dot matrix pages, that told his tale of being assigned by the Dukakis scheduling staff to travel to Michigan along with trip lead Paul Holtzman and press lead Neal Flieger. His mission, outlined in the journal, was to help the fifty-four-year-old Massachusetts governor attack, head on, a major liability: uneasiness among voters over his readiness to serve as commander in chief.

"There is always an issue, as there was much later with Bill Clinton, as to whether a governor has foreign policy experience. At that stage, Vice President Bush did have a lot of foreign policy experience," Madeleine Albright told me during a 2013 interview.[18] Albright, the secretary of state under Bill Clinton, was in 1988 a senior advisor to Dukakis and among those in the governor's entourage accompanying him to Sterling Heights, an eyewitness to the train wreck that Matt Bennett had spent five days on the ground setting up.

To read Bennett's narrative is to enter a time warp, arriving in an America where the July 25 issue of *Time* featured Dukakis and Bentsen on the cover as "The Odd Couple," and the August 29 cover showed George H. W. Bush and Dan Quayle beside the headline "The Quayle Factor." Although *Die Hard* and *Who Framed Roger Rabbit?* filled theaters that summer, the best spectacle was the fight for a White House up for grabs, the first race without an incumbent since 1968. The best seat to watch the spectacle unfold was on the road as an advance person.

In those days, a young advance operative could drink for free at the bar of the candidate's hotel, running up a tab on a reporter's expense account after a day on the road, talking freely about campaign theatrics. A story, rich in color, would show up a few days later under the byline of R. W. Apple Jr. or David S. Broder, its seeds sown in the bar, its sources shielded from readers. Information exchanged in such a way had no fingerprints.

"'Go to Detroit,'" Bennett remembers his simple orders, "'and we'll tell you what you're doing.' As was often the case, they didn't know exactly what they wanted us to do until we got there, so they put us in the wrong place."[19] The first task of an advance person is to ensure his team is properly housed. Before learning any of the specifics of their mission, they moved from a downtown hotel to lodgings in Macomb County, a suburb rich in Reagan Democrats that Dukakis needed to attract. When more detailed orders came in—put Dukakis in a tank—Bennett knew it was no ordinary assignment and wrestled with his own still-evolving views, having written his senior thesis at the University of Pennsylvania on the dangers of the military-industrial complex.

Bennett would have to deal with that conflict, but he operated on a long leash. His bosses in Boston were 700 miles away, tethering him only by SkyPager, without the emailed site photos that are used these days to micromanage trips. On "Game Day" back then, when the candidate arrived on site, there were only three network newscasts and CNN to worry about, along with local press, wire service and newspaper reporters and photographers who still comprised the rough makeup of "the Boys on the Bus." Most assignments from Boston Bennett could handle with ease, able to produce a camera-ready event before packing his bags for his next stop.

Sterling Heights was different. He had a sense, as soon as it was over, of its historic implications. As if he needed any reminding, one of Dukakis's traveling aides approached him as the entourage prepared to leave the site in the motorcade. "Nice event, Matt," the aide said. "It may have cost us the election, but beside that, it was great."[20]

It would take decades for Bennett to live the event down. After that ignominious start, he has earned the distinction, after more than a quarter century in Washington, as one of that town's most pragmatic voices on the fragile and fractured politics of gun control. When Adam Lanza fatally shot twenty children and six adult staff members at the Sandy Hook Elementary School on December 14, 2012, the sad work of moving from immediate grief to practical activism among the victims' families became a task made for Bennett and his decades of political training. While Bennett became close with the victims' families, as a centrist at heart he understood the reluctance of many people to support strict gun legislation.

Bennett did not earn his moderate stature overnight. That level of maturity would take time to develop. In 1988 Bennett was, like me, among scores of newly minted advance people traveling the country and producing events, focusing on the next city, the next task, learning the ropes of political stagecraft and making a mark on a historic campaign.

Advance people migrate from state to state in national elections with two primary missions: make the candidate look good on camera, and don't piss off the locals. A mostly young clique, advance teams don't always wear well when they descend on a tight-knit community. But in 1988, fresh out of college, Bennett's buttoned-down looks and WASP-ish bearing made him more presentable than most in his cohort. This was a benefit when working with corporate hosts whose sites beckon visiting presidential candidates.

Advance people, who spend all hours at their event sites during days of walk-throughs, want to remain close to these sites, preferring to roll out of bed and commune with the stage they're trying to create. With his assignment now clear, the new lodgings for his team worked much better for easy access to the facilities at General Dynamics Land Systems.

THE HOGWARTS OF ADVANCE

Michigan was a place that "Boston," shorthand for Dukakis Headquarters at 105 Chauncy Street, would send Dukakis, time and again, in pursuit of its twenty electoral votes. Within the state, Macomb County, where the General Dynamics facility was located, was prime hunting ground for white working-class voters who deserted Jimmy Carter in 1980 but might be brought back into the fold. There was almost no scenario drawn up for a Dukakis victory that didn't include retaking the Wolverine State, and results from polling places near General Dynamics could spell the difference in a close election.

My first outing as a Dukakis advance man also came in Detroit, after attending the campaign's "advance school" at the Sheraton Tara Hotel in Framingham, Massachusetts, where we practiced the art of staging an airport rally in an empty parking lot. Scoring an invitation to advance school—a presidential campaign's form of "basic training"—was the political equivalent of an admission to Hogwarts, but the two-day seminar turned out scores of site people and press advance trainees instead of apprentice wizards.

With that initiation, Detroit would bookend about a dozen advance trips I made around the country in the summer and fall of 1988. For a kid out of college, there wasn't a headier experience than calling "Boston" from a pay phone for your orders and picking up a prepaid plane ticket at the airline counter at the airport. They'd send you an overnight package with a rental car voucher, a hotel reservation and a wad of "campaign drafts," blank checks with a ceiling denomination backed up by the campaign's bank account. The checks could be written for any purpose and, in the hands of nomadic young operatives roaming the nation, were prone to misuse. Along with a duffel bag of tools to produce a small rock concert and enough cunning to deliver a good picture, the overnight package was the equivalent of Harry Potter's wand and broomstick. Our education in practical advance continued wherever the next plane landed across the country.

There is no college course in advance work—it needs to be learned hands-on. While no textbook has been written on it, Jerry Bruno, the burly Kennedy advance man, penned a 1971 memoir, *The Advance Man,* written with Jeff Greenfield, which I found in a used book warehouse and adopted as my bible. It starts out in the summer of 1963, when Kennedy aide Kenny O'Donnell enlists Bruno for a life on the road beginning with the western states that JFK might not get to visit during the following campaign year. In Bruno's telling, JFK bursts into a meeting between him and O'Donnell with a simple instruction: "I want the crowds," the president said. "I want the crowds to be there."[21]

O'Donnell became Bruno's mentor, and Bruno mentored the next generation of advance people. Almost every war story of an advance career begins with tutelage from an elder statesman of the trade. My favorite teacher was Mort Engelberg, a Hollywood producer from Memphis whose first exposure to politics came through a government PR effort to photograph LBJ's War on Poverty. He later earned his fortune producing films like the *Smokey and the Bandit* series, which allowed him to bring his cinematic sensibilities to the campaign trail.

Mort wore the same uniform as an advance man every day I saw him on the road and in the decades since, when I would visit him in his Hollywood Hills bungalow. I've never known how many fraying blue button-down shirts or pairs of rumbled khakis he owns, but that was his daily mufti. Beneath an ageless shock of orangeish hair, he would grudgingly wrap a madras tie through his collar and drape a too-small blue blazer over his shoulders for Game Day when his turn came to lead a trip.

In the earliest months of Governor Bill Clinton's campaign in 1991, Mort, along with campaign aide Bruce Lindsey and an Arkansas State Trooper, were Clinton's only road companions. With a sensibility that helped him see how Burt Reynolds would appeal to Middle America from behind the wheel of a black 1977 Pontiac Trans-Am (the three *Smokey* films have earned a combined gross of more than $300 million at the box office),[22] Mort applied the same thinking to Clinton's image. Along with his friend Harry Thomason, Mort helped to develop the cross-country bus tour concept that brought the *Smokey and the Bandit* ethos to politics and became the gold standard of campaign road trips ever since.

Combining Mort's teaching with what I learned from Michael Deaver's work for Ronald Reagan, I developed a few tricks that earned memorable imagery for my candidate. The first was finding the right lighting. If you position the candidate properly, the sun can flatter him, but too many shadows across his face can make him look dead. The second was building movement into event choreography. It was better to let a candidate move before the camera—the confident stride translating well on video and in pictures—than position him like a marble statue in front of a blue drape. The third was production design and choosing the right props. The right accents on stage can be a magnet for favorable photos.

The fourth and most important thing Mort taught me was complete devotion to perfecting "the shot." There are many types of shots, in cinema and in politics, that help tell a candidate's story. The "wide shot" establishes the setting—a big crowd in a small town, for example. The "medium shot" links the candidate with other people—women or police officers behind him always conveys an appealing message. The "tight shot" shows the passion on the candidate's face and drives the message home. The tight shot is often enhanced by tiny-type words strategically positioned on a backdrop behind the candidate that only a TV camera, zoomed-in on the speaker, can see clearly and transmit to living rooms. These words, crafted for quick consumption, serve as a bumper sticker for a viewing audience. My trick here, put to use long before it became common at major events and red carpet premieres, was a form of the "step and repeat" pattern on a backdrop, ensuring that every angle that a TV camera recorded at an event carried our succinct call to action. We called them "message ears."

Finally, the "cutaway shot" comes from behind, over the candidate's shoulder, to show the expanse of the throng before him. A great cutaway shot filled with exuberant faces stretching to the horizon screams *momentum*. With effective use of each of these shots mastered, trained disciples of Mort Engelberg and other masters became as much motion picture directors as political advance people. The end result, properly executed, was a two-minute movie packaged as a news report from one of the networks.

A trademark of my advance work was obsessing over drawing exactly what I envisioned on Game Day. While most advance people drew "site diagrams" on the fly, I took detailed measurements with a distance wheel and used a rifle scope that I purchased with campaign drafts to approximate the "tight shot," dictating exactly where I would position network TV cameras to record my event. In the evening, I would storyboard the drama in pencil elevations and map every inch of the site on graph paper with ruler and protractor to engineer my political architecture. Geometry is the math of success in advance work. Computation of area tells how many people can fit into a site, perimeter defines security, tangents lay out a candidate's route through a crowd, and angles determine how an event can be photographed.

These were some of my rules of advance, applying mostly to site advance people, the job Matt Bennett had at Sterling Heights. Advance people who specialize in other disciplines have their own set of tricks, passed down from generation to generation to those in the next campaign. They keep getting better at their craft, and the media keeps consuming it. At the same time, campaigns get more adept at distributing these images themselves through official photographers, videographers and social media specialists. As news organizations cut back on their own image-gathering resources, they're more prone to knit campaign or government-produced imagery into their publications and shows.

In each four-year cycle, campaigns try to put the rules on paper. These "advance manuals" appropriate liberally from preceding efforts and are Xeroxed and sent to the young operatives of the road. Assembling my lessons from three presidential campaigns, I wrote two tracts—*Notes for Advance Teams* and *Creating Visuals and Presidential-Style Communications*—which helped advance people plan events for Al Gore in 2000, John Kerry in 2004 and Barack Obama in 2008.[23] In the last decade, some other White House advance manuals have found their way onto the Internet, revealing a bit too much of the behind-the-scenes stagecraft and crowd management techniques. As a result, the era of the widely distributed advance manual may have run its course.

I still have a copy of the 1988 Dukakis advance manual. Chapter 1 reviews "The Qualities of a Good Advance Person."

"A political visit needs an advance person just as an orchestra needs a conductor," the manual reads. "You are the diplomatic liaison between local hosts competing for the candidate's time and his or her staff, who must conserve energy and time." The qualities for good advance people, it notes, include "stay[ing] cool, always portraying confidence and calm competence. The fuel of campaigns is enthusiasm and, more often than you expect, you'll be working with enthusiastic amateurs. They will look upon you as a pro in your craft. Put the job first. Let others blow their cool. Your job is to think clearly."[24]

Unwritten in the manual but part of "thinking clearly" is the necessity to possess an internal radar for avoiding unflattering visuals. Andy Frank was one of the campaign's best site guys, but he ran afoul of Boston for putting the governor in a hard hat and coveralls on a visit to the Donaldson Mine Company's shaft 350 feet below the West Virginia countryside. "Although he looked somewhat uncomfortable in his mining gear," wrote David Rosenbaum in the *New York Times,* "the Governor, who is intrigued by technology, apparently enjoyed his tour."[25] Boston didn't look favorably on stories that put Dukakis out of his element.

Frank had violated a cardinal rule of the Dukakis Advance Team: keep headwear off the candidate. Joyce Carrier, the campaign's director of advance, told me, "Beside the fact that he didn't look good in them, you could just never imagine him with a hat on. He didn't do any sports. He didn't play golf. You couldn't even imagine him in a hat, so putting him in one didn't fit with his personality."[26] The unwavering guidance for advance people was that headwear given to the governor could be appreciatively received and cheerfully waved on stage, but should not, under any circumstances, rest on his head.

As the Dukakis advance manual instructed, the advance man's goal is "to assure that the candidate can communicate the best and most appropriate message in the best possible way."[27] Affinity with the plight of coal miners might have been a good message for Dukakis, but wearing a hard hat wasn't the "best possible way" to convey it.

TEAM DETROIT

To deliver "the best and most appropriate message," advance teams descend on a city four to seven days before a candidate arrives. A team typically has six core members, often backed up by "seconds," younger team members dispatched for a training trip before they too are sent out by headquarters to form the core of a future squad.

The "lead advance," often a veteran of past campaigns, commands the overall visit. The "site advance" is the visual producer of the crew and responsible for the theatrics. The "press advance" ensures that reporters can file their stories no matter where the event happens. The "crowd advance" uses any means necessary to build a human throng to convey the appearance of campaign momentum—a great cutaway shot is a sure sign that a team had a crack crowd person assigned to it. The "motorcade advance" rents cars and recruits drivers to get the entourage from Point A to Point B, supplementing the armored vehicles driven by the Secret Service. When a candidate ends his day in the team's city, the "RON" (it stands for "Remain Overnight") handles hotel and rooming logistics.

When advance teams click well, they remain packaged, sent from city to city to repeat their road show about once a week. They work sixteen-hour days and use the remaining eight for swapping war stories or, when all else fails, sleeping. At the height of a national campaign, eighteen or more advance teams operate simultaneously around the country. Staffing at that level will power three stops a day for six days before the cycle repeats. Double that for a vice presidential candidate, and quadruple it for two national nominees operating simultaneously, and you have close to eighty separate advance teams working at full tilt at any one time in the final three months of a presidential campaign.

Such an army in the field is a lot to track for any scheduling and advance operation at headquarters. If a junior member of one of the teams raises a red flag—as Matt Bennett would do in Sterling Heights—there's limited bandwidth with which to heed the warnings and act on them.

The team that gathered in Sterling Heights in September 1988 was seasoned from a long primary campaign that started in 1987, but they hadn't worked together before they got to Michigan. With their trip coming shortly after Labor Day, they were also rusty from sitting on the sidelines during the governor's idle summer. Holtzman, the team lead, graduated from Harvard in 1983 and Yale Law in 1987, great training for sensitive negotiations with local officials and union chiefs. He was a few years older than those under his charge and thus would be expected to serve the role of "the grownup" that every advance team needs when dealing with campaign headquarters. Flieger, the press lead, had impressed traveling Dukakis staffers during the governor's visits to Capitol Hill, where he worked for the House Radio-Television Correspondents'

Gallery. With a booming voice and broad shoulders, he knew how the media operated—they liked him and he liked them—but he could also keep unruly reporters in line during an event.

While Holtzman was delayed en route to Detroit, Bennett maintained communications with headquarters. New details of the trip were passed down to him according to the campaign's chain of command—from senior management to the scheduling and advance office and ultimately to the advance team. With the trip now set, the person manning the campaign's "scheduling desk" for that day assumes operational control over the advance team, thus becoming the headquarters version of an air traffic controller. The "desk" for the Sterling Heights visit was Katie Whalen, who became Bennett's link to Boston.

"I got on the phone to Katie to find out what was up," Bennett wrote. "The plan was to have the Governor ride in a tank, and then give a 'strong on defense' speech to the General Dy workers."[28] The directive was simple, but the task was extraordinary. The tank ride—a Reaganesque visual to buttress Dukakis's readiness to lead the country into war—would be the icing on the cake.

Bennett saw his mission clearly as headquarters' strategy to get the campaign back on track. After the tank ride, he would position more tanks for a speech backdrop at General Dynamics and hand out mini U.S. flags for exuberant union members in the cutaway shot. With these ingredients for the planned visuals, Bennett was good to go, though he wasn't happy about it. There was a lot of hard work ahead to make the visit come off right. Done well, Dukakis would look to all Americans like the next commander in chief. Done poorly, he might look like a buffoon.

TWO

PLAYING WITH FIREPOWER

STRONG ON DEFENSE

The political road taking Mike Dukakis to "national defense" week, and Matt Bennett's tank, detoured at the Knights of Columbus Hall in Derry, New Hampshire, on Sunday, February 14, 1988, two days before the First-in-the-Nation Primary. Dukakis had placed third in the Iowa Caucus behind Dick Gephardt and Paul Simon, but he returned to New England with a comfortable lead in the state neighboring his own.

I was working for Simon at the time. Our hopes had been pinned on Iowa, but the caucus-goers didn't deliver. In New Hampshire, I began watching Dukakis more closely, sensing he had the name recognition and money to endure early setbacks and emerge as the front-runner. My own future as an advance man would depend on ultimately joining his team.

Dukakis would eventually win New Hampshire with 36 percent of the vote, almost doubling Gephardt's tally.[1] His lead in the closing days of the race allowed him to pivot to issues that would be top-of-mind for southern voters, the next key battleground. Fourteen states would go to the polls for "Super Tuesday" on March 6. Facing contests in Texas, Florida, Tennessee, Louisiana, Oklahoma, Mississippi, Kentucky, Alabama and Georgia, among others, Dukakis and his staff knew that these states were home to military bases housing millions of soldiers, sailors, airmen and their families, and military assembly lines and shipyards filled with defense workers.

The speech to the Knights of Columbus in Derry was billed to the media as "Renewing America's Strength: A Foreign Policy for the 1990s,"[2] in which Dukakis did his best to draw a line in the sand close to where James Monroe had drawn it with the Monroe Doctrine in 1823. In his remarks in Derry, Dukakis said, "As President, I will not hesitate to use force to defend our territory or our citizens or our vital interests; to meet our treaty commitments; and to respond to, or deter, terrorist attacks."[3] News reports noted that the governor used some construct of the word "strength" nearly thirty times during his speech.

Super Tuesday was also the last best hope for Dukakis's opponents. Al Gore, then thirty-nine, tried to salvage his fifth place in New Hampshire by going nuclear at stops in the South. "Governor Michael Dukakis does not have a single day of foreign policy experience," he said at one speech during a southern swing through Louisiana and Texas. "He said it would be perfectly all right with him for the Soviet Union to establish a client state on the mainland of the American continent. Now that reflects a lack of experience. After seven years of Ronald Reagan, do we want another President who doesn't know beans about foreign policy or what this country ought to be doing in the world?" Gore asked his audience.[4]

Dukakis responded in Atlanta, a city that had risen in prominence both from Jimmy Carter's presidency and as the headquarters of CNN, which Ted Turner launched in 1980. Turner opened CNN Center as the network's headquarters in 1987, and it quickly became a regular stop on the campaign. Dukakis arrived there the day after his New Hampshire victory to address a lunchtime crowd of 400 people. When asked by a reporter whether he thought Gore was the toughest Democrat on national defense, he responded, "I don't think he's the toughest. I don't think he's the toughest at all. I don't yield in toughness to Al Gore in any way, shape or manner."[5] Dukakis won six states on Super Tuesday, including Texas and Florida, the victories finally distancing him from the rest of the field.

When the battle returned north for the New York Primary on April 19, Dukakis grabbed 51 percent of the vote, with 37 percent for Jesse Jackson and 10 percent for Gore. Paraphrasing Frank Sinatra, the victor declared, "If we can make it here, we can make it anywhere."[6] With Gephardt and Simon on their last legs and Jackson on the verge of withdrawing, the campaign went through the motions of collecting delegates in the later primaries and caucuses to secure the nomination, ultimately returning to Atlanta for the Democratic Convention in July.

EYES ON THE OMNI

I flew down to Atlanta from Boston on Monday, July 18, for the start of the convention. By then, I had been working for Dukakis for a few months in his finance department after dusting myself off from the wreckage of the Simon campaign.

I checked into my room at the Hyatt Regency, eager to set foot on the floor of my first convention. With an all-access pre-convention credential, I walked into the Omni Arena, which had been transformed from the home of the Atlanta Hawks to a massive theater to stage political spectacle. It was, to my eye, gorgeous, and purpose-built for television, with materials that would sparkle for the cameras when the lights went on. Looking up into the rafters, I spied massive nets holding thousands of balloons ready to descend on the delegates when Dukakis formally accepted his party's nomination. The unique engineering of a timed balloon drop was something I had long sought to add to my repertoire of visual stunts, effective as they are to drive front-page coverage.

At the center of activity stood the podium, elevated twelve feet from the floor, where the convention's production designer, René Lagler, was surrounded by his blueprints of the Omni that mapped every camera angle in the house. A contingent of order-takers also enveloped Lagler to help him put finishing touches on the show. They tested a hydraulic lift that raised and lowered the podium to perfect height for each speaker, with glass teleprompter panels that rose magically from the floor. Secret doors allowed for grand entrances and exits by political celebrities. Another blueprint documented where each lighting truss would hang, where the lights would be targeted, and how much luminosity they would throw on the scene. It was a movie set. At that instant, I saw how political spectacles grew from Hollywood creativity, and Lagler was the magician who would bring it to life.

The Zurich-born Lagler wasn't the first person I would have expected to play a major role in shaping the image of American politicians, but it made perfect sense. He had won an Emmy for his design of the Academy Awards and was called into service to design the opening and closing ceremonies of the 1984 Olympic Games. He created the sets for TV specials for the likes of Frank Sinatra and Barbra Streisand and had also put his touch on Pope John Paul's mass at Yankee Stadium. When the Statue of Liberty needed a showpiece to celebrate its 100th anniversary and Mount Rushmore required a splashy setting to mark its fiftieth birthday, Lagler got the call.

Now, in Atlanta, Lagler was presiding over his newest creation: a stage that softly echoed in pastel colors the motif of the American flag—salmon for red, eggshell for white and azure for blue—the choices carefully selected for how they would translate on television. I leaned in to eavesdrop. I could learn a lot from this guy just by watching and listening to Lagler talk about not only color, but also camera angles, "jib cranes" and choreographed "blocking" of the politicians as they strode on set.

On the grandest stage of American politics, the national party conventions, Democrats have enlisted Hollywood talent since 1988, and they've consistently put on a better visual show than Republicans who, until recent years, relied more on political operatives than stage producers to plan, design and orchestrate their marquee shows. My path would cross again with Lagler's at the 1992 convention in New York, the Presidential Inaugural Gala in 1993 and the 1996 convention in Chicago, each time with my role in the show inching a little closer to the position of big event producer that artists like Lagler bring to the intersection of entertainment and politics.

I appreciated more and more the varied theatrical elements of production that go into political stagecraft. Every political event has elements that smack of Cecil B. DeMille. A stage built from lumber by craftsmen beat rented platforms any day. And arranging the crowd in such a way that the candidate must interact with them on a human scale increases the odds for a great picture. DeMille parted the Red Sea for Charlton Heston, and René Lagler would do the same for Dukakis.

I remained in Atlanta for the entirety of convention week, heading to the Omni each night to watch the big speeches. I saw Ann Richards, then the Texas state treasurer, bring down the house with her keynote address on Tuesday, July 19, that eviscerated Vice President Bush. "Poor George, he can't help it," she said. "He was born with a silver foot in his mouth."[7] Richards whipped up the partisans, taking shots at Reagan-era defense policies. "When we pay billions for planes that won't fly, billions for tanks that won't fire, and billions for systems that won't work," she bellowed, the delegates rising to their feet, "that old dog won't hunt."[8] Her rhetoric worked in the room and, for the moment, with the media, but her attacks emboldened the Republicans.

On Wednesday, July 20, I watched Arkansas governor Bill Clinton, putting in Dukakis's name for nomination, endure the low point of his rhetorical career. He was supposed to speak for fifteen minutes, but at the twenty-five-minute mark, it was hard to miss the image of thousands of overheated delegates fanning themselves with their Dukakis placards.

The producers wanted to get on with their tightly timed script, and from my vantage point, the production served Clinton poorly. They didn't seem to dim the arena lights when he spoke, a cue to the delegates to direct their attention to the podium. Instead, the house lights allowed TV cameras to cut to images of delegates chatting away amongst themselves. Watching replays of the speech, the chatter gives way to booing and, finally, cheering, as the forty-one-year-old Clinton finally says, at the thirty-three minute mark, "In closing . . ."[9]

Up in the broadcast booth, NBC's Tom Brokaw broke away from what Clinton was saying to offer his own analysis. "You're listening to the *lengthy* nomination speech of Governor William Clinton of Arkansas. . . . He's now seriously in overtime. He's only about halfway through his prepared text and he should have been done about five minutes ago because he was scheduled to go only twenty. We say all this—we're going to be here, we have to be here, until this proceeding is over—at the same time, they have to be aware of the television audience and whether or not it is staying with this lengthy speech and a recitation of a lot of the stuff we've been hearing the last couple of days," Brokaw told his viewers.[10]

To keep the viewers tuned in, Brokaw invited correspondent Chris Wallace, standing among the New Jersey delegation, to weigh in. "I can tell you that this place is just ready to explode, and I think they're long past the period, Tom, of listening to Governor Clinton," Wallace said from the floor as delegates used placards as megaphones to amplify their protests. "This has been very carefully planned, the idea that Bill Clinton would give a speech—a short speech, of about 15 minutes—listing Michael Dukakis's qualifications, talking about what kind of governor he's been and why he would be a good president . . . but it has gone on so long that he has completely lost this crowd," Wallace added.[11]

When the speech was finally over, TV producers and Clinton's close friends Harry Thomason and Linda Bloodworth-Thomason knew he needed damage control. They reached out to Freddy de Cordova, Johnny Carson's longtime producer, and asked if Clinton could come on *The Tonight Show* to make amends. As Thomason recounted the story for a PBS documentary, when Clinton flew to Burbank the next week, he was ready to go on stage with a trick up his sleeve. "Linda got a big hourglass," Thomason remembered, "and she gave Clinton the hourglass. And she said, 'When you walk out on the stage of *The Tonight Show,* and Carson is going to say, "How you doin', governor?," you're just going to pull this out and set it on the desk.'"[12]

The stunt worked, but not as planned. Spying Clinton holding the hourglass, de Cordova demanded he not use the prop. Instead, when Clinton sat down on Carson's set for the taping, Johnny used the same gag, but in reverse, producing his own hourglass from beneath his desk, the prop eliciting howls from the audience and the humbled guest, the first-ever example of the redeeming political firepower of late-night comedy.

In some ways, Clinton's poor showing in Atlanta let Dukakis exceed expectations when he took the stage on Thursday, July 21, the closing night of the convention. On ABC's *World News Tonight,* which preceded Dukakis's big speech later that evening, Peter Jennings reminded viewers as he introduced the first segment of his broadcast that "the battle with the Republicans is about to begin in earnest. From the moment that Dukakis begins his acceptance speech tonight, all of the party's best hopes, and worst fears, will be identified with him. He is about to get the kind of scrutiny that might make him long for the campaign as it's been up until now."[13]

The scrutiny was left to correspondent Sam Donaldson, to whom Jennings tossed for a report that typically precedes an evening of programming focused on a nominee's acceptance speech. "Like a prize fighter with his handlers inspecting the ring," Donaldson began, "the Democratic nominee went to the hall this morning to fiddle with the microphones, fiddle with the prompter and fine-tune tonight's big speech."[14]

With Donaldson reminding viewers that Dukakis was "no great orator," the piece cut to a sound bite from a Dukakis news conference that day. "Just before I left the hotel room," Dukakis said, "Kitty arrived from another wild round of appearances and interviews and she said, 'Have you got the speech in final form?' I said, 'It's pretty close to final,' and she said, 'Well, let me have it.' I said 'Okay,' and she went into the room. And then I went into the room to get my jacket. My wife was fast asleep on the bed."[15]

Donaldson closed his package by reiterating that Dukakis's "cadence is wrong. He sometimes swallows his words. His inflections are often off. Above all, he exhibits very little passion." Suggesting that maybe, this night, Dukakis could defy expectations, Donaldson hyped the drama to come. Echoing the campaign's hope, Donaldson predicted that "not only his wife, but everyone else, will stay awake."[16]

I was in the crowd at the Omni that night as the governor's cousin, Olympia Dukakis, an Oscar winner for her role in *Moonstruck,* introduced a video that she narrated from a car she drove through the governor's hometown of Brookline, Massachusetts. With Olympia leading us through her cousin's life, we saw him as a young boy, an athlete at Brookline High, a soldier in the army and through the early stages of his political career. She even brought us to the nominee's humble two-family home on Perry Street where, she reminded us, Michael mowed the lawn with his twenty-five-year-old manual mower. It was more evidence, if any were needed, of the governor's prudence and frugality, implying that these attributes would serve him well as president.

At 10:10 p.m., the video ended and the spotlight returned to Olympia at the podium as she narrated a closing stanza. Music swelled under her words and then took over from the speaker entirely. It was Neal Diamond's "Coming to America," the hit 1981 single from the soundtrack to the movie *The Jazz Singer,* the ultimate anthem of the immigrant experience.

The cameras pivoted from the stage to the back of the arena. There, led by his Secret Service detail and his "body man," staffer Nick Mitropoulos, Dukakis slowly made his way through the joyous crowd—the DeMille moment—shaking hands and being lifted, musically, by the rhythm of Diamond's song. The cinematic walk from the back of the house mirrored the path Ronald Reagan took each January when he was ushered by his own Secret Service detail through the House Floor to deliver the State of the Union Address, a moment as "presidential" as Dukakis would get in his campaign.

Walking through the crowd surrounded by a sea of placard-waving Democrats formed the four most triumphant minutes of Michael Dukakis's life. As Diamond's anthem wound down, all of the Stars and Stripes–themed Dukakis placards waved in unison as the nominee's father-in-law, Boston Pops conductor Harry Ellis Dickson, led the orchestra in the "1812 Overture." The usually stoic Dukakis basked in the extended ovations and smiled broadly, acknowledging the applause.

"I remember looking across at the Massachusetts delegation," Dukakis would say later. "It was kind of like the story of my life—just looking at people who had been with me from the time I was a young state representative and had campaigned so hard at the grassroots, and suddenly here we are."[17]

Defying the expectation-lowering comments of pundits, the speech was well-received. Dukakis's moment at the podium filled the front pages. Although it contained the buzz-killing line, "This election isn't about ideology. It's about competence," it allowed Dukakis to hit the key commander-in-chief themes, first voiced in Derry, New Hampshire, that his speechwriters believed would be crucial against Vice President Bush.

Dukakis told the TV audience, "My friends, the dream that began in Philadelphia 200 years ago; the spirit that survived that terrible winter at Valley Forge and triumphed on the beach at Normandy; the courage that looked Khrushchev in the eye during the Cuban Missile crisis—is as strong and as vibrant today as it has ever been."[18] When he finished, and thousands of balloons fell gently onto the convention floor, few could conclude anything other than that the convention, with all of its dramatic elements, had been a grand success.

TARGET PRACTICE

Unlike Bill Clinton and Al Gore in 1992, who exited their triumphant convention for a nine-state bus tour from New York City to St. Louis and the vote-rich Rust Belt states in between, the heights of Dukakis's oratory and excitement faded after Atlanta.

In August, to reinforce the defense theme launched in Derry, New Hampshire, Dukakis hit the road on a rare summer outing outside Massachusetts. On August 11, he traveled to McGuire Air Force Base in New Jersey and then on to Fort Dix, where the one-time "Private Dukakis" had been stationed in 1955 before being shipped off to Korea as a teletype operator.

At Fort Dix, he was reunited with fellow bunkmates Dominic Donato and Nick Antonicello for a tour of their old barracks, a visit that included target practice with an M-16, the Army's standard-issue rifle. To shield the moment from imagery, the hands-on weapons work was closed to the press. David Blomquist, a reporter for the Bergen County *Record* newspaper, wrote that "the governor's two friends wouldn't tell reporters whether Dukakis hit anything on the range, saying only that they all seemed 'a little rusty.'"[19]

A turn on a rifle range, even one invisible to cameras, is an essential ingredient for articles like Blomquist's. It was the same recipe used a month later in Sterling Heights. To give life to the dry substance of his defense proposals, and to make it into packages for the evening news, campaigns have to serve up what reporters call "color."

Creating "color"—the illuminating interstitial tissue of news reports—is a joint effort of the policy, communications, speechwriting and
scheduling departments of a campaign. The policy shop fleshes out a
stand. The communications shop turns it into a message. The speechwriting shop puts it into the candidate's voice. The scheduling shop finds
time in the candidate's day to sell it. The candidate then falls into the
awaiting arms of the advance team, tasked with finding a venue to buttress the message with color to accompany the story.

The first stop of that August trip was New York University in Manhattan where Dukakis, introduced by New York governor Mario Cuomo,
delivered a speech to an audience of about 300. Ben Bradlee Jr. of the
Boston Globe wrote that the speech "broke no new ground, but was an
effort by Dukakis to reassert his views on national defense in the wake of
two addresses on the subject by Vice President George Bush."[20]

Advocating for his "Conventional Defense Initiative" at NYU, Dukakis said, "Deterrence does not require the seemingly endless development of new and more expensive nuclear weapon systems—particularly
when, thanks to President Reagan and Secretary Gorbachev, we may have
the best opportunity in our lifetime to build a safer world, to cut strategic
arms by 50 percent or more."[21]

In the wings at NYU, the campaign's policy advisors were in spin
mode, providing amplifying comments to the reporters present to reinforce the governor's message. Senior Advisor Madeleine Albright, the future secretary of state during the Clinton years, said Dukakis is "going to
look at what the needs are. I know he wants to take a look at the Pentagon
books."[22] Deputy Issues Director Jim Steinberg, a future deputy secretary
of state for President Obama, said, "He was defining the quality of leadership that the American people are going to need for the challenges of the
next decade."[23] Both quotes made it into the major newspaper coverage
of the day.

Notwithstanding the spin, the Boys on the Bus seemed to yawn
through their reporting. "Dukakis received considerably more applause
when he arrived than after he spoke," Bob Drogin wrote for the *Los Angeles Times.*[24]

These were the dog days of August. Dukakis made it home from that
trip largely unscathed, and even when some press coverage got prickly, it
could be easily dismissed as coming when most voters were still on vacation and even fewer were focused on election news. Maybe the Dukakis
team could even learn from this early foray—they needed more media

ammo than some closed-press target practice. Within days, between August 15 and 18, Vice President Bush would headline the GOP Convention at the Louisiana Superdome in New Orleans. The heavy firepower would come out in the Big Easy, and Dukakis was still looking for his own big gun to match his opponent's arsenal.

QUAYLE HUNTING

The Republican Convention began curiously, and hopefully, from Boston's perspective. When Air Force Two landed in New Orleans, Vice President Bush whispered to President Reagan, there to greet him on the tarmac, that he had selected Indiana senator J. Danforth Quayle as his running mate.

Bush's selection surprised even members of his own senior staff. Jim Pinkerton, the director of research and a member of Bush's inner circle, remembered that his team played the role of unwitting decoy. "I had people's confidence such that they could lie to me and feel good about it," Pinkerton mused, "and so one of my duties was, in that time, to pull together sort of briefing books on all these vice presidential wannabe types. I now realize this was in the best CIA tradition. I was sort of the cutout, you do all this work, sit over there, it's like the entire mythical first army on Operation Fortitude on D-Day that's going to invade Calais, as opposed to Normandy."[25] The Pinkerton decoy worked.

The smart money was on Bob Dole, South Carolina governor Carroll Campbell or New Mexico senator Pete Domenici. One was a party elder who shared the national ticket with Gerald Ford in 1976; another was a mentor of campaign manager Lee Atwater; the third was a westerner with a Reagan-like bearing. Any of the three might do.

Instead, it was Quayle. Pinkerton's research team found itself flat-footed on the candidate's background, a scenario that would repeat itself twenty years later when John McCain asked Alaska governor Sarah Palin to join him on the ticket. Within hours, questions from the national press corps about Quayle's military service in the National Guard began to drown out the Republican's carefully crafted convention message.

Pinkerton told a campaign intern, Dylan Glen, to find the nearest bookstore to buy a copy of the *Almanac of American Politics*. "I started just reading," Pinkerton said. "We knew nothing about him. We knew nothing. That was probably an hour, like up to 4:30 in the afternoon. Six-thirty that night is Dan Rather clobbering him on the draft and everything like that—that was definitely a mess," Pinkerton recalled in an oral history for the Miller Center at the University of Virginia.[26]

As loud as the questions were about Quayle, and as unprepared as Bush's campaign was to deal with them, they didn't reverse a polling trend that took root during the Dukakis August siesta. While Dukakis enjoyed a seventeen-point lead after his convention, the tables turned after the Republicans left New Orleans. Thanks in part to the speechwriting of Peggy Noonan, a "kinder and gentler" George H. W. Bush asked voters to "read my lips" about no new taxes. They did, apparently, and a CBS News poll of 1,282 registered voters taken after the convention showed an advantage for the vice president, 46 percent to 40 percent.[27]

Dismissing the numbers, Tubby Harrison, Dukakis's pollster, said, "[Voters] may not yet have come to realize the meaning of choosing someone like Quayle. They may not yet be connecting it to Bush's judgment. We're waiting for the dust to settle."[28]

WHISPERING DEATH

While they waited for the dust to settle, members of the Dukakis campaign were also searching for their own big gun to counter the fusillade shot their way in New Orleans. What they found was the sixty-eight-ton mainstay of the U.S. conventional arsenal: the M1A1 Abrams Tank.

The M1A1, a marvel of modern warfare, stood in contrast to the Reagan-era infatuation with the "Strategic Defense Initiative" and its paradigm-shifting technology of a missile shield. Dialing back the imaginations of Pentagon planners to confront the real-life Soviet menace on the European frontier was exactly the wedge Dukakis needed if he was to make a dent in public perception that he was not a foreign policy heavyweight.

As Jim Steinberg told me, "From the time I arrived, there was an issue of how to develop Dukakis's credibility on foreign policy because, one, he had essentially no experience on that, with the exception of his Korean War experience and, two, he had early on staked out a number of positions which, to put it charitably, did not burnish the sense that this guy was going to be a strong and effective commander in chief."[29]

Dukakis's new stand on defense emerged ten months before his rendezvous with destiny in a helmet and coveralls. At the Dallas Democratic Forum on November 13, 1987, he unveiled his Conventional Defense Initiative, or CDI, to trump Reagan's SDI. "My top priority as president will be to improve our conventional defense," Dukakis told his audience, adding that, "We may not be able to make nuclear weapons obsolete, but a [CDI] might be able to make the current generation of Soviet tanks obsolete."[30]

An extension of this logic was putting Dukakis in a tank for a test ride. At this point, it was only an idea on file in Boston, but it had advocates. "The M1 tank was kind of the poster child of this because the Reagan administration had cut the production runs of the M1 tank and so it was possible to make the case that, despite the argument that the Republicans were strong on defense, they were actually short-changing the army and conventional weaponry," Steinberg told me, "and that is what suggested the tank plant as kind of the perfect symbol of the Dukakis approach to national security."[31] The Abrams tank became the heavyweight symbol to reverse public opinion.

The M1A1 was named after General Creighton Abrams, a famed World War II tank commander who led U.S. forces in Vietnam and became Army Chief of Staff. Twice earning the Distinguished Service Cross, Abrams had many admirers, including General George S. Patton, who said, "I'm supposed to be the best tank commander in the Army, but I have one peer—Abe Abrams. He's the world champion."[32] Fittingly, when the Army retired its fleet of M60 Patton tanks, its successor would be named for Abrams.

Equaling the weight of nine elephants, the Abrams first rolled off the assembly line in 1979 with over 9,000 units produced since then. If NATO couldn't match the Warsaw Pact in sheer numbers of tanks, its M1A1s would be better able to shoot on the run, using its superior speed to evade the numerically superior enemy. Powered by a 1,500-horsepower Honeywell turbine engine, making the Abrams run quieter than diesel predecessors, the Abrams earned the nickname "Whispering Death" from fans for its stealthy hunting and killing efficiency.

Motor Trend magazine, stacking up the aging M60 and the new M1A1 side by side, wrote that it was "as hell compares to heaven."[33] The tale of the tape spoke for itself: with its 750 horsepower diesel engine delivering top speeds of thirty miles per hour, the M60 had half the power and required twice the maintenance of the Abrams. Under the belly, the old tank's suspension system took eight times longer to fix than the M1A1. Using the cannon's laser sighting system, the Abrams could fire its 50 armor-piercing rounds at full speed of 70 mph. If the cannon had too much firepower, the Abrams could use its two 7.62 mm machine guns, for which it carried nearly 12,000 rounds, or the tank commander's

.50-caliber gun in the turret. "It is the Mercedes-Benz of battle tanks," reported *Motor Trend*.[34]

While his event in Sterling Heights would not test the extremities in which the M1A1 could excel, General Dynamics representatives were also quick to remind its VIP test drivers—including Matt Bennett during his advance work—that there were few scenarios, whether on land or in water up to seven feet, in which "Whispering Death" couldn't perform its mission.

ENGLAND TAKES UP ARMS

Gordon England, the General Dynamics executive who formally issued the fateful invitation to host Governor Dukakis, was a career engineer and an ardent fan of the Abrams. "We had lots of concern that Russian tanks could come across Europe," England told me, noting these Russian models were the same ones used by the Iraqis in Operation Desert Storm, the first time the M1A1 was actually used in combat. "We beefed up our systems and added armor in the Abrams. These were fantastic tanks. When Desert Storm happened, the Abrams absolutely dominated," England added proudly.[35]

England, a future secretary of the Navy under President George W. Bush, was no ordinary tank salesman, if one exists. He would be the perfect copilot for Dukakis's ride. Joining the company in 1966, he had climbed through the ranks of General Dynamics and was seen as an engineer with a rocket scientist pedigree (he was a veteran of NASA's Gemini Program) who could handle the company's toughest challenges. His bosses assigned him to move his family from Fort Worth to Sterling Heights to integrate Chrysler's Land Systems Division after General Dynamics acquired it, working through the many manufacturing and personnel challenges that had beset Chrysler when the automaker owned the division. He would need to oversee a complete overhaul of the division to right its course.

In August 1988, while Bush was introducing Dan Quayle onto the national stage, while the Dukakis campaign was grappling with its poll numbers and while Matt Bennett was an anonymous young man working his advance magic from city to city, England was knee-deep in the M1A1's production challenges. He brought from Fort Worth engineering techniques he had used at General Dynamics as director of avionics for the F-16 fighter, a workhorse of the U.S. Air Force and other customers around the world. If there was anyone who could turn the tank's fortunes around, it was Gordon England.

On the job in Sterling Heights for two years when the 1988 campaign revved into full gear, England identified the request by Dukakis to visit General Dynamics as an exercise in political one-upmanship, with Boston trying to beat Bush into the turret of a tank. "The way I remember that this came about is that, originally, Vice President Bush had planned to visit the tank plant," he told me, referring to the nearby Detroit Arsenal, owned by the Department of Defense, where the M1A1s were assembled piece by piece. According to England, planning for the Sterling Heights visit accelerated when the Dukakis campaign learned of Bush's interest to execute a similar event.[36]

John Eades, the Michigan state director for Dukakis, had the General Dynamics facility on a list of potential sites that his office prepared during the summer. Such a visit might resonate with Reagan Democrats, he reasoned, and he needed their support to win the state. He also knew that many defense workers who manned the tank's assembly lines were members of the United Auto Workers union local, with whom he had good relations. Still, Eades hoped that, when the time came for the candidate to devote more campaign days to the state, Boston would opt for venues like schools and hospitals more closely aligned with Dukakis's work as governor.

Eades's office called Land Systems to schedule a tour, a speech and test ride for the governor at the Detroit Arsenal. As England remembers, "I believe that [Bush's interest] got the attention of the Dukakis folks and then they decided, for embellishing his credentials on defense, he would also tour the tank plant." But as the Bush campaign also discovered, a political visit to a working government facility was off limits. "So, when that didn't work, I made the comment, 'You can always do this at our headquarters because we had a whole facility with tanks and we had a test track outside.'"[37]

Soon thereafter, Matt Bennett and Neal Flieger arrived at England's offices, thus beginning the drama that would soon unfold on the test track. "When they actually said, 'We'd like to come talk to you,' it became a serious activity," England remembered.[38]

England initially deferred to his bosses the honor of riding shotgun with Dukakis, but they kicked the honor back to him. "My view was we've got to do this. He could be president and you want to have a good relationship. Any corporation would respond if a candidate wanted to visit. Defense is a political process, so you need political support," he told me.[39]

England's insight was a simple lesson followed by defense contractors through decades of appropriations battles on Capitol Hill. To this day, political battles buffet tank production. Thirty years after Reagan's "Star Wars" became the faded star of Pentagon spending, the Abrams still roams the battlefield with new layers of steel, ceramic, plastic composite and Kevlar armor to thwart improvised explosive devises, and in a vastly different combat role than originally envisioned.

For his part, Don Gilleland, the clean-cut public relations chief for Land Systems, saw an enormous media opportunity with the Dukakis visit. The chance to bring the national press corps to Sterling Heights, where they would see the Abrams put through its paces, pleased the long-time military man, a veteran of Vietnam MIA repatriation operations.

Gordon England, too, recognized the goldmine before him, remembering, "You can be actually in the weapons system and be seen. It is dramatic—ninety tons of firepower. It's a logical place to showcase your interest in defense."[40] Deciding to move forward, England instructed Gilleland to work with the advance team to prepare for the event.

As August wound down and Americans returned from a Labor Day respite, skirmishes flared all over the political landscape. General Dynamics worried about incoming fire from Star Wars advocates. Republicans were attacking Dukakis over his readiness to serve as commander in chief. And the Dukakis camp fretted over how their candidate should show his mettle, even as the campaign's own leadership was divided on the topic. Everyone was playing with firepower, and the plan was about to explode.

THIS WHOLE IDEA STINKS

IN THE ARENA

Advance people think they know everything.

In Sterling Heights, Matt Bennett now found himself in direct negotiations about the tank ride with officials at General Dynamics while simultaneously taking direction from Boston about how to stage it. Everything about it made him squeamish. Given his druthers, he would have scrapped the stop and taken Dukakis to an auto plant for a classic assembly line shot with workers who made something other than weapons for a living.

The notion of telling headquarters to take their plan and shove it was something that many advance people, including me, dream about, and sometimes do.

Advance man Paul Meyer and I were assigned to stage a rally in a high school gym at an evening stop for a Clinton-Gore bus tour rumbling through Ocala, Florida, in October 1992. We hated the idea. Headquarters in Little Rock wanted to keep the event small to save money and dodge comparisons in the media with Bush and Quayle, who were attracting large crowds in the state. Even though Ocala, a haven for the thoroughbred horse set, was deeply rooted Republican territory and the Democrats were likely to lose Florida on Election Day, Paul and I thought we could do better.

For starters, we didn't want to be bored with our assignment during a five-night stay in central Florida. There was only so much time we could kill at Disney World. More than that, we were young men with something to prove to both "Little Rock" and "The Plane"—meaning the senior staff who traveled with Governor and Mrs. Clinton and would soon be selecting the permanent White House advance team, if the election went as we hoped. With only a few weeks left in the campaign, every stop was an audition in front of our present and, perhaps, future bosses. We had to show that we could think creatively and act resourcefully to put on a good show.

Despite pushback from headquarters, we made a strong argument against a small gymnasium event, which was a creative and risky bet in itself. Little Rock was three states away—out of sight, out of mind, we thought—but the Plane, which in Ocala would be "The Bus," would witness our work firsthand and see the opportunity to win votes and local press coverage the way we saw it. So Paul and I got to work raising money among local Clinton supporters to rent the Southeastern Livestock Pavilion, the 4,200-seat home of the Ocala Rodeo, and turn it into a boisterous after-dark jamboree. After all, if "the locals" demanded a bigger event, rather than the advance team, it was difficult for Little Rock to turn them down.

After a local country band warmed up the crowd, the Bus pulled into the middle of the dirt infield. It was another Cecil B. DeMille parting-the-Red-Sea moment, perfect for the local television cameras, a grand entrance if ever there was one. Through the windshield I could see Governor and Mrs. Clinton smiling ear to ear, overwhelmed by the enthusiastic outpouring in what was perceived as enemy territory. But the Clintons, shrouded by the reflections on the glass, were still largely invisible to the crowd at this point.

The bus became our main act, like a prized bull entering the ring of the rodeo, its blaring horn taking the place of the bull's flaring nostrils. The lack of easy egress for the bus gave the Secret Service fits. If a shot rang out and hell broke loose, the bus would be trapped in a sea of people. As a Plan B, the agents stashed a spare armored getaway limo behind the stage. Assuming the escape limo wasn't needed and the nighttime fest came off as planned, our scene would convince Floridians, especially the local press, that Clinton and Gore stood a fighting chance to take the Sunshine State.

Paul and I put to work every element that our agrarian setting had to offer. The cattle stalls abutting the arena became a makeshift—if malodorous—media filing center, allowing the reporters to work on their stories for the next day's papers. In another cattle pen, we created a set for a live CNN interview with Larry King, thinking we might convince them all to sit on milking stools for the hour-long show (they used canvas director's chairs instead). At the end of the long night, the crowd, the candidates and the press went home happy, reflected in beaming photos, positive headlines and grudging respect from conservative columnists in the next day's edition of the local newspaper.

Raising objections to authority doesn't always yield a positive outcome, however. In June 1996, at the annual G7 Summit held that year in Lyon, France, I was dispatched to help give the trip more colorful imagery than the summit planners had devised.

We started by bringing President Clinton to the medieval town of Pérouges—once a setting for the 1973 film *The Three Musketeers*—which sprang up in the fourteenth century on the strength of the local wine and weaving industries. In the center of the village, called the Place du Tilleuls, was a 200-year-old so-called Tree of Liberty that was planted soon after the French Revolution. It was a perfect backdrop and metaphor for the president's speech. The villagers loved it, and the scene, with tricolors hanging from the iron-balustered balconies ringing the square, recalled triumphant newsreel footage when U.S. forces liberated French towns in the closing months of World War II. *Mission accomplished*, I thought.

I should have declared my own victory then and there and gone quiet during the rest of the summit, but I couldn't resist trying to create a little more Gallic magic. I argued that the president's closing news conference should be held not in the summit's official press center, a temporary vinyl structure that was designed to support such events with ease, but rather by a serene pond in the Pavillon du Parc, a gorgeous botanical garden not far from the G-7 site at the convention center.

We might be only a few blocks away from the fully functional hub of global media, but by bringing Clinton to more pastoral surroundings, I felt we could create the impression for viewers back home that the president was really soaking in his old-world European surroundings. He could speak in front of a blue curtain anytime, but I wanted the image to clearly show that he was a man of the world. I made my case to the White House communications director, Don Baer, and the director of advance, Paige Reefe. Don and Paige backed me up, with reservations, but warned me not to screw up.

I didn't count on the weather, or the gnats.

It was approaching the height of summer in southern France. The air was still and the heat sweltering. The military personnel installing the president's sound system were sweating bullets as I watched them wrestle with the heavy equipment. The forecast for my late-afternoon pond-side scene called for a steady breeze that kept the air, and its inhabitants, moving. But in the hour before the news conference, the breeze was yet to materialize, and I noticed a swarm of gnats marshaling around the presidential podium—the Blue Goose, as it's known.

They seemed to be attracted to the microphone, the same spot where, in less than sixty minutes, Bill Clinton would address the White House Press Corps and take their questions. Improvising a solution, I walked into a local market and bought a can of something that looked like insect repellant with a French label on it. Returning to the event site, I sprayed a coat of the stuff on the podium. Only later did I learn it was insect killer, with the warning "do not get on hands or in eyes," written in fine print in the local dialect. They don't teach French in advance school.

The news conference started well enough. Clinton began his remarks with, "It's really beautiful, isn't it? The weather has certainly cooperated for our summit."[1] So far, so good. He seemed to be enjoying the change in scenery.

But there were dark political clouds overshadowing the gathering. Terrorists had just detonated a truck bomb outside the Khobar Towers in Dharan, Saudi Arabia, killing nineteen U.S. servicemen in addition to injuring hundreds of others, an incident that many thought might have been one of the first attacks by Al Qaeda. The president addressed questions on that topic, as well as others related to Bosnia, the Middle East and Russia. Changes in scenery, unfortunately, don't change the news.

On a domestic topic, CNN's Wolf Blitzer asked Clinton about a brewing scandal over a White House security officer who had requested files from the FBI on former government officials. It became known as "Filegate." The president at first seemed annoyed by the question and the issue, and no doubt he was, with it being put to him while he was conducting diplomacy on foreign soil and coming in the middle of an election year. But there was a smaller, more immediate problem to deal with. In fact, there were millions of them.

The swarm of gnats weren't repelled by my last-minute brew of insecticide, but rather attracted to it. They massed around Clinton's head, spinning themselves up into a visible cloud for the TV cameras. From my vantage point twenty yards away, I watched the crisis unfold but was powerless to fix it. As much as an advance man thinks he's on a movie set during an event, there's no way to yell "Cut!" once the president walks on stage.

To make matters worse, with the heat in Pavillon du Parc unabated and the hot movie lights we set up trained on the president's head to even out shadows created by the afternoon sun, Clinton was in the crosshairs. With all of the artificial lighting aimed at his forehead, he was sweating up a storm, far more than the assembled reporters. His hands, which had rested on the padded sides of the podium for the first part of the news conference, wiped beads of water from his brow as the inquest got intense over Filegate. In the process, the toxic substance I blanketed the podium with a few minutes earlier seeped into his eyes.

By the end of the news conference, Clinton's eyes were almost completely shut as he struggled to answer the remaining questions, like Rocky Balboa at the end of fifteen rounds with Apollo Creed. Dealing with tough questions on international and political issues would have been hard enough in the international press center. At the Pavillon du Parc, with swarming gnats, oppressive heat and poisoned eyes, it was almost torture.

After the last question, Clinton beelined to his limo without sending a glance back at me. The car took him to Air Force One where, I hoped, the medical staff would flush his eyes and restore them to working order without lasting harm. Don Baer was on the plane with him, and took a call in the air from Chief of Staff Leon Panetta who had watched the disastrous news conference live in the West Wing with political director Rahm Emanuel hovering nearby. "Don't even bother to come home," Panetta told Baer in a calm but cryptic monotone.[2] The next call Baer made was to me, with similar guidance.

A PIECE OF SHIT

After inspecting the proving grounds of General Dynamics Land Systems, the site of the proposed tank ride, Matt Bennett also didn't like his assignment from headquarters and tried to fight back.

He had been a Dukakis advance man for more than a year, his first job out of Penn, where he was a poli sci major. He was the son of David Bennett, a renowned Syracuse professor whose specialties were "political extremism in America," "twentieth-century American history" and "modern military history." A household like the Bennetts' was bound to produce a young man willing to question authority, and Matt played to type.

One thing young Bennett took to Boston upon graduation, in addition to a duffel bag of button-down shirts, was a copy of his senior thesis.

Echoing Dwight Eisenhower thirty years before, it warned of the dangers that the military-industrial complex posed to national interests. If that seemed to be an awkward resume for producing an event with a defense contractor, well, this was the Dukakis campaign.

A year into his advance career, Bennett harbored no illusions about the sometimes conflicting agendas of those in headquarters and their allies on different wings of the Democratic Party. Still, he soldiered on with the plan, starting with an obligatory meet-and-greet with Don Gilleland, the PR chief for Land Systems.

These initial courtesy appointments are perfunctory rituals between the host and the hosted. As they approached their first encounter, neither Bennett nor Gilleland knew that, 700 miles away at the Dukakis headquarters on Chauncy Street, an internal battle was heating up over their planned event, part of an increasingly desperate attempt to win the presidency. The prize had seemed in hand just six weeks earlier. Now it was up for grabs, and the ambitious events planned for the week of September 12 were intended to corral it once more.

The first page of the seventy-one-page Dukakis advance manual was devoted to Murphy's Law, more than any advance person would want to know, but less than each of them usually encountered during a week on the road. In all capitals, it reminded the young team, "IN ANY FIELD OF EN-DEAVOR, ANYTHING THAT CAN GO WRONG WILL GO WRONG AT THE WORST POSSIBLE MOMENT." In less exclamatory prose, page 10 of the manual said, "Close cooperation with the Scheduling/Advance Office in working out the schedule is essential; contact them at least four times a day; in any disagreements between you and Boston, Boston has the final authority."[3]

Bennett couldn't quarantine his doubts, no matter who had the final authority. Phone calls between him and Katie Whalen, his "desk" for the event and thus his umbilical cord to headquarters, became tense. Calling on his collegiate study, Bennett fashioned himself in his journal as a sort of Pentagon policy wonk with unique insight about the Army's mechanized weapon. "I informed Katie that the M1 tank is a piece of shit: it has been touted as the perfect all-terrain fighting vehicle, but it does poorly in mud and sand (your basic tank battle conditions); it guzzles an enormous amount of gas, making it difficult to use in protracted battles; its turbine engine runs very hot, making it very vulnerable to heat-seeking antitank missiles, etc., etc., and so forth. . . ." Bennett declared in his narrative.[4]

He didn't get far with his protests. "Not surprisingly, Katie didn't give a crap about what I thought, and I was told, in so many words, to shut up and do my job," Bennett wrote.[5] Reading Bennett's journal resonated with me. I had heard it all before. Having served as a scheduling desk in the White House, I routinely dealt with such anxiety from advance people, triaging it before elevating it to senior staff.

The authority of scheduling desks in HQ over advance people on the road often proved useful. With many events to manage each day, most issues that a desk dealt with solved themselves if given time. Those that lingered could go unnoticed in the maelstrom of a campaign trip as long as the press didn't notice. The tank ride might raise eyebrows if it backfired, but it might also be forgotten by the next news cycle. The slim risk of long-term damage was worth taking, the thinking went, for a front-page visual of Dukakis as strong on defense.

The blueprint for a Dukakis visit to Land Systems and accompanying tank ride rested in a dossier of potential Michigan stops maintained by the campaign's communications department. As Dukakis advance director Joyce Carrier told me, "We had stockpiled and vetted events for different subjects. We had been looking around for conventional defense events."[6] Land Systems was at the top of the file for events in Macomb County and was put on the schedule.

From his perch running the Michigan campaign for Dukakis, John Eades was caught in the middle and, like Bennett, conflicted over the event. A soft-spoken, hard-driving operative, he was an architect by profession. He had succumbed to the entreaties of his friend, Dukakis body man Nick Mitropoulos, to decamp from Ohio to Michigan with the mission of winning the state's twenty electoral votes. He wanted to win, but to achieve victory, he needed the candidate in his state and was wary of the accompanying optics that would result from some of the events on file.

Dukakis, Eades said, was "a moderate politically, but was perceived in Michigan as an Eastern, Massachusetts liberal. His problem was to move off that image to an every guy." It was a tall order. When Eades learned his candidate would be coming to Land Systems, he was wary of the venue and the message. As he said later, "All of a sudden, the campaign wanted to turn Mike Dukakis into a hawk who loves the military and wants to hug a tank. I didn't think having him riding around in a tank was believable or convincing or made him look strong on defense or a friend of the military."[7]

Michigan was too far away for Boston to hear the misgivings, vocal or muted, of Matt Bennett and John Eades. The political, issues and communications departments of the campaign, supported by its scheduling and advance operation, had been holding meetings about scoring a twofer: get the candidate to Macomb County and position him as a strong commander in chief. The impetus from those meetings wouldn't be derailed by a nervous advance man holed up in the Troy Hilton or a state director riding herd on his staff in Detroit and Lansing.

THE BATTLE OF BOSTON

The layers of security that Bennett was about to encounter as he walked from his rental car up to the door of Land Systems were mild compared to the layered agendas that Jim Steinberg and Madeleine Albright had navigated for a year to recast Dukakis from a governor with a firm grasp of local bureaucracy into a presidential nominee that voters would entrust with the keys to the U.S. arsenal.

Steinberg and Albright were playing foreign policy politics with a bad hand. Dukakis had served as a private in a U.S. detachment under U.N. command in Korea for sixteen months beginning in 1955, two years after fighting stopped between North and South. Service during the truce in Korea, honorable as it was, couldn't compare to the resume of his opponent, George H. W. Bush. The son of Prescott Bush, a U.S. senator from Connecticut, he might have found an easy route to avoid combat in World War II. But like John F. Kennedy, who marketed himself for the presidency from the pages of his heroic Navy record, Bush took on harrowing assignments as a young Navy aviator. His hairiest mission came on September 2, 1944, when his Grumman Avenger was downed by Japanese antiaircraft emplacements on the island of Chichijima about 150 miles north of Iwo Jima in the Pacific.

Had Private Dukakis only weighed his service against Lieutenant Bush, the scale would be lopsided but not insurmountable. But Bush had also served as a congressman from Texas, President Nixon's ambassador to the U.N. and President Ford's envoy to China to nurture the nascent Sino-American relationship. His final foreign policy credential, before being tapped as Ronald Reagan's running mate, was as CIA director, presiding over the agency during a tumultuous period in which Congress pressed its investigations over covert activities. If voters wanted a president with military service and foreign policy experience, the odds were decidedly in the vice president's favor.

The odds also favored Bush at the very location that Boston ordered Matt Bennett to prepare for a Dukakis visit. Bennett thought the plan would have been more palatable had Chrysler, a revered American auto manufacturer, still owned Land Systems, but General Dynamics was a pure-play defense contractor. The jobs it created were almost entirely dependent on work from the Pentagon. From top management to assembly-line workers, the Republican leaning was strong, as was the case in the rest of the military-industrial complex, where Reagan's legacy had a long tail. Taking all this into account, Bennett wrote, "With God and Neal Flieger as my witnesses, I said the following when told of the tank event: 'Katie, the fact is that this whole idea stinks.'"[8]

Like other college grads keeping watch on world affairs during the presidential election, Bennett whiffed change in the air from Moscow. On January 1, 1988, just as Dukakis and his challengers were battling in Iowa and New Hampshire, Mikhail Gorbachev launched perestroika in the Soviet Union. In March, mass demonstrations broke out in Bratislava against the socialist government in Czechoslovakia. In May, the Soviet Army began withdrawing from Afghanistan after eight years of fighting. And, later that month, President Reagan visited Moscow, addressing 600 students at Moscow State University.[9] Whoever succeeded Reagan would need to navigate the emerging new world order.

Dukakis's foreign policy team continued to try to shape their candidate's positioning around cost savings and bolstering the conventional arsenal. As Jim Steinberg described the strategy, Dukakis "would actually make the military stronger by not putting money into nuclear weapons and putting it into conventional weaponry." He noted that, during the Reagan era, production of the Abrams tank had decreased.[10] If Dukakis could successfully sell that case in front of defense workers in Sterling Heights, he might, against all odds, achieve his elusive twofer.

The August trip to McGuire Air Force Base and Fort Dix, augmented by the speech at NYU, had been a dry run. The September trip was a full-frontal assault. As Madeleine Albright told me, "If you have an organized campaign, you focus on certain themes for a period of time. We were involved in national security week, and the goal was to find interesting venues for identifying our candidate with some aspect of national security."[11] Once the interesting venues were found, the discussion turned to exactly what Dukakis could do on site to create an arresting visual for the news media.

Assembling the inputs was Mindy Lubber, Dukakis's director of scheduling, who had to square competing agendas with logistical reality. Lubber understood the forces at work to embolden the governor's image.

Dukakis, she said later, "had done good, smart things as governor, but for anybody running for president, you need to prove a whole set of credentials." As a state governor, she said, "You're not writing foreign policy for Iran or Iraq."[12]

Many of the inputs came from Washington. Sam Nunn of Georgia, who chaired the Senate Armed Services Committee, was a leading advocate for the candidate to step up his rhetoric on foreign policy. Senator Carl Levin of Michigan, another powerful Dukakis supporter on Capitol Hill, wanted to see Dukakis win his state's twenty electoral votes. He also wanted General Dynamics, a large employer of his constituents, to gain exposure in the national spotlight. An added benefit, beyond the perfect visual, was that a visit to a defense contractor could increase support for the candidate in the south and other conservative areas. The campaign hoped to check all of those distinct boxes with a single event.

Another Dukakis campaign bloc took a different view. They believed that talking up defense and foreign policy was futile against their better-qualified opponent. While Susan Estrich remembers that Nunn urged attacking "soft on defense" negatives head on, she had several conversations with Arkansas governor Bill Clinton, who advocated for the governor to play to his best assets. As Estrich put it, Clinton argued that if Dukakis "had walked into a school or hospital or job site, there was no hat he could have put on that would have gotten him in trouble, because he belonged."[13]

With Nunn on one side, Clinton on the other, and Albright and Steinberg in the middle, the battle continued from August into September, with Estrich trying to moderate the conflict. "We had a whole debate," she recalled. "Do you show up to events that will show more strength in the defense area or deal with the support gap by playing to your strengths—schools, health care, education and jobs—issues in which Dukakis had strong positions?" Estrich's gut view that Dukakis should remain in his comfort zone gradually gave way to the powerful voices filling the policy vacuum. "When you walk into a tank factory because the polls show that people have questions about your credibility and strength on national security, and you do something wrong, it will hurt you for life," she remembered thinking at the time.[14]

One factor that helped end the debate was the return of John Sasso as the campaign's vice chairman. Whether they would play it safe in schools and hospitals or attack their weak points head on, indecision was not an option. Ironing out the plans for defense week and telling Dukakis what needed to be done were duties that fit Sasso's sweet spot, but his return came at a cost. Alliances that had been established within Chauncy Street since his departure became frayed. In a news conference, Dukakis brushed off the concerns, saying, "I want the strongest team I can possibly get. John will be a very valuable addition to that team." In public, Estrich echoed the sentiment, telling reporters that "John Sasso is family," but it was an awkward time to be bringing a prodigal son back home.[15]

"When John came back, it was too late," Mindy Lubber said years later. "The change should have happened months earlier. In today's world, he wouldn't have been gone. The campaign would have been a different campaign," she said. Today, using video evidence to highlight an opponent's flaws, as Sasso had done to Joe Biden, is standard practice. "As much as Michael liked and respected Susan, it never clicked in the same way. As John came back in, so much was already in stone, so much was moving. There wasn't internal clarity of who was in charge here and there," Lubber added.[16]

The numbers didn't lie, no matter who was in charge. A national survey by the *Los Angeles Times* of 1,096 registered voters, taken between September 9 and September 11, the same weekend Matt Bennett was drawing up plans for the tank ride, reinforced Clinton's assessment of Dukakis's strengths. The poll showed Dukakis beat Bush better than five-to-one on the attribute of "cares about people like me." But the same survey also highlighted Nunn's concern about the candidate's Achilles' heel. On the tables stakes issue, "Which candidate do you think would do the best job of securing the national defense?," 54 percent said Bush while only 18 percent said Dukakis, a three-to-one advantage.[17]

TEST DRIVE

With his protests rebuffed over having Dukakis play Patton, Bennett soldiered on. Every day an advance person is on the road he rehearses, with increasing specificity, the exact steps that a candidate will take under his direction. These "walk-throughs" usually start with the operative pacing out the steps alone on Day 1, growing in crowd size as the day of the event approaches. On subsequent walk-throughs, dozens of onlookers are in tow, including the U.S. Secret Service and their counterparts from local law enforcement, often trading skeptical glances when the advance team introduces more moving parts to the plan.

For me, the more detailed I could make my site diagrams, and the more authority I could project in my voice, the less skeptical were those glances. Long before PowerPoint, I put my detailed drawings onto transparencies to project them onto the wall as the first item on the walkthrough, which helped my audience buy into the vision for an event before I put them through the paces.

For Bennett, before the large group walk-throughs started, he made peace with what might come on Game Day. He wrote in his journal, "From here on in, I swallowed my righteous indignation and had a blast with a fantasy site."[18] And that's what it was. Having General Dynamics as your host meant that resources were limitless and "site toys" were plentiful. In addition to new armored models fresh off the assembly line, the Land Systems facility also maintained a small museum of working tanks from the history of U.S. mechanized warfare. As long as he could hive away his foreboding, he was about to have a lot of fun with the M1A1 tank.

Bennett's plan for Sterling Heights used a standard approach to stagecraft that remains part of every presidential campaign. The tank ride would be "show-and-tell" on the dirt-covered proving grounds, a hands-on demonstration for the governor. The ride would then be followed by a speech in an adjacent area to defense workers in which Dukakis could reflect on the ride and tie it into his broader national defense policies.

Both the tank and the workers were props for different scenes in the same movie. Think of them as the "action" scene and the "courtroom" scene, both helping to advance the story. In whatever sequence Bennett directed the scenes—visual before speech or speech before visual—they would be reassembled by TV news editors, along with commentary by on-site correspondents, to create evening news packages seen by millions.

Bennett scouted what the image would look like from the edge of the proving grounds, where the reporters would stand and photographers would cover the event, but he also needed to experience how the ride would affect its passenger. From my own experience, the test drive is a prime perk of advance work. It might call for a few nights aboard an aircraft carrier, walking through the Kremlin or the Vatican off-hours, touring the Imperial Palace in Tokyo, hanging out in Barbra Streisand's house in Los Angeles or taking laps at the Charlotte Motor Speedway—all of them among my stops on the road as an advance man.

On a pre-advance trip to the Philippines in 1994 to scout sites for a visit by President Clinton, my colleagues and I borrowed a helicopter from the fleet of President Fidel Ramos to fly from Manila to the island of Corregidor. Once on the island, we explored the caves and tunnels from which General Jonathan Wainwright commanded his surviving forces from the U.S. defense against the Japanese occupation in World War II. Wainwright used the caves as a hideout before he was forced to surrender and the Bataan Death March began. It was a powerful and unforgettable place and story. Clinton never got to see the caves during his brief stop on Corregidor, but we did.

In Bennett's case, his test drive meant putting the 60-ton, 1,500-horsepower monster through its paces at the tank's cruising speed of 45 miles per hour. In his journal, Bennett recalled how he and press advance man Neal Flieger put the pedal to the metal. "I wanted to brief Dukakis on what it would be like; Neal wanted to check the shots from the risers; both of us wanted to ride in the damn tank," he wrote. "We did, and boy was it fun."[19]

Bennett rode where Dukakis would ride, in the tank commander's position, his torso protruding from the turret. "We all wore helmets with built-in radios, since the engine noise made unaided conversation impossible," he wrote.[20] He made mental notes about how dangerous the ride felt at top speed, and how gravitational forces pushed him hard against the turret's steel wall during full-speed turns. The ear-piercing noise of the turbine engines operating at full power and the danger of the tank cruising over the dirt course at high speed convinced Bennett that the visual couldn't realistically or safely happen without the candidate wearing a helmet. That helmet, it would turn out, became the focal point of the whole show.

As with other pivotal moments in history, had the chain of command allowed dissent to flow upward to the top echelon of the campaign, political history might have taken a new tangent. The die was cast for the Michigan trip before Bennett relayed his on-site intelligence to campaign HQ, but it didn't have to play out the way it did. Mindy Lubber might have been on the receiving end of Bennett's warnings, but she doesn't recall it setting off alarm bells. "If something was a big enough concern, it came to me, and I took it to others. I don't remember this being a big enough issue that it came to me. It was a fairly normal event and part of a typical road show," she said.[21]

Besides, with Sasso back in the saddle and the upcoming series of presidential debates, a ten-minute ride in a tank didn't seem to portend disaster in the making.

The operation would move forward.

THE TROUBLESHOOTER

THE DÉMARCHE

As Matt Bennett began to wargame how Murphy's Law could play havoc with his event, he reasoned that the two most likely sources of friction would come from his enterprising hosts at General Dynamics or nitpicking emissaries, dispatched by his minders in Boston, treading on his site. He began to erect defenses against both.

In 1988, as a novice advance man, I was usually among the last to leave the site the night before an event. After the stagehands and sound people left to throw back a few beers before grabbing some shut-eye for an early morning call time, the only people left were often a janitor and me. One reason I hung around was to ensure there weren't any changes made after I left.

If the next day's event was billed as a "picture of the day"—the image most likely to lead the evening news—a mysterious figure might appear in the hours before we put a site to bed. He would sit in an empty seat a dozen rows back to take the measure of the place. His name was Bob Bosch. He didn't usually talk to a newbie advance man like me, reserving his analysis for trip leads or headquarters. If Bob didn't like what he saw, the direction was sent down to upend the plan, even at the last minute. Bosch had that kind of power.

In Bill Clinton's 1992 campaign, that role fell to Steve "Rabbi" Rabinowitz. More genial and approachable than Bosch, Rabbi was a tough critic but a great teacher. He told you in clear but friendly terms why your site sucked. Rabbi knew how movement in front of the lens translated to media reporting behind it. He had seen this drama play out a thousand times before and developed a keen aesthetic for campaign imagery. He liked a "clean" shot, nothing behind the candidate except a backdrop that helped to tell the story.

When Bill Clinton won the presidency, Rabbi became the White House director of production for presidential events. He had a reserved seat on Air Force One, counseling advance people to carry out his vision and ushering the press pool into position to get the best shot when the president arrived at a site. Rabbi sometimes tried to tweak an event on the spot, as he did one rainy day in Denver on August 12, 1993.

Pope John Paul II was making his fifth visit to the United States, a quick stop in Colorado to celebrate World Youth Day with 500,000 Catholics in the park at Cherry Creek Reservoir. Prior to that, the pope's schedule called for a mass at Mile High Stadium preceded by a welcome from President Clinton on the tarmac of Stapleton Airport. Air Force One made up the backdrop along with the pope's Alitalia 747, contrasting liveries that represented two stems of global power and authority. President Clinton, with a tough first six months in the White House behind him, welcomed the chance to bask briefly in John Paul II's glow.

From his perch on the fringe of the event, Rabbi saw an extra papal photographer sticking to John Paul II like Velcro and mucking up the shot. It was a distraction to viewers back home watching the event live on television and a violation of the coverage plan carefully negotiated between the White House and the Vatican. Seeing the snafu playing out before his eyes, Rabbi bellowed into his walkie-talkie repeatedly to the advance team to "get the guy out of the shot" and started to approach the scene to fix it himself.

Just then, a man approached Rabbi from behind and said, "He's with me," inferring with Ben Kenobi–like calm that he was part of the official papal delegation and that his supplemental photographer ruining the tableau was not to be trifled with.

"I don't give a shit," Rabbi replied, his impatience with the interloper boiling over. He spun around and went nose-to-nose with the mysterious figure. "Who the hell are you?" Rabbi demanded to know.

Rabbi, the consummate event troubleshooter, had just invited trouble upon himself. It turned out that the man was a monsignor at the Vatican's offices in Washington, for all practical purposes an advance man for the pope. The issue didn't die on the tarmac. When Rabbi returned home from Denver, he found himself on the receiving end of a complaint from the State Department's protocol office, which also made its way to Mark Gearan, a former altar boy and then the director of communications at the White House, soon to be promoted to deputy chief of staff.

Rumors of a "Papal Démarche" aimed at Rabbi made its way through the West Wing. Some said the man was the Vatican's secretary of state, others said there was a physical altercation. Neither was verified. Months later, in the spring of 1994, *Esquire* magazine even reported that the pope himself had sent a handwritten letter to President Clinton to protest the incident, but such a letter, if it exists, hasn't yet emerged from the presidential archives. In any case, Rabbi, who had become a fixture on the new Clinton staff throughout the first half of 1993, took the incident as a cue that he was ready for private sector work. He would leave the White House several months later.

As much as Steve was my mentor, teaching me the linkage between choreography and press coverage, his planned departure was my big break. When I heard that a search was underway for his successor, I walked into Gearan's office and offered my credentials to make the jump from scheduler to director of production. Mark admired the big crowd events I had produced during the campaign and also took some pleasure in my eccentricities on the road. He liked to tell how I traveled with a Radio Shack answering machine to plug into hotel phone outlets to create my own mobile office in the field, among other tricks of the trade, but he warned me that my 1992 exploits alone wouldn't get me the job. He outlined a list of other White House staffers I would have to convince about my capabilities. After an in intense two-week lobbying campaign targeting West Wing decision makers, I won Rabbi's role of the senior event troubleshooter.

A few things might explain why I was chosen. In the 1992 campaign, I had a reputation as a site guy able to balance the candidate's needs with those of the press. As Clinton scheduler in 1993, I used the White House as a canvas for events that became widely disseminated images, using the eighteen acres at 1600 Pennsylvania Avenue as my own Hollywood sound stage.

The coverage earned me some fans, but also some chagrin from the White House Usher's Office, which guarded the Executive Mansion for the living museum that it is. Working on this beautiful set, I followed instincts honed by watching Reagan, as well as Rabbi's teaching how a lens craves action over stasis. Using the president and his visitors as my actors, I could orchestrate a daily drama in the White House's scenic venues: the

Rose Garden, the South Lawn, the State Floor, the East Room, the State Dining Room and other locales. I stopped short of installing Astroturf on the parquet floor of the East Room to welcome the Super Bowl champs, as Rabbi had done with the Dallas Cowboys in 1993.

As the new director of production, I was now tasked with offering up an assembly line of creative imagery to feed eager lenses in the media. I started my new job in September 1993 confident but inexperienced, with role models in Bosch, Rabinowitz and Jack Weeks, who was Dukakis's trip director in 1988. Each had skills I needed to emulate but styles that I wanted to avoid. I didn't always succeed in both respects, but I strived to be a troubleshooter who could get the job done without ruffling feathers.

TWEAKING THE PLAN

Mythology around the September 13 Dukakis trip is that *he went to a tank factory,* but this wasn't true. Weeks earlier, the Bush campaign had wanted to send its candidate to the actual factory where the M1A1 was assembled, at the government's Detroit Arsenal in Warren, Michigan. They were rebuffed by the Pentagon because political events are forbidden on government-owned premises. The Sterling Heights facility, however, was owned by General Dynamics as an outdoor showroom for its wares. It had enough acreage to put its tanks through their paces and was managed with Pentagon-specified standards for secrecy and security, but it was not where the tanks were actually built. This military-industrial loophole allowed Bennett to plan Dukakis's visit and ride.

The key prop for the visit, the M1A1 tank, also needed a loophole to make the ride legally viable. As a valuable piece of U.S. Army property, the tank selected for the ride had to be officially decommissioned, temporarily, to allow the political event to happen.

Boston had ordered Bennett to get Dukakis in the tank—much easier said than done. Campaign policy advisors and speechwriters can have vivid imaginations around a conference table, but it always takes an advance person to carry them out or become the scapegoat when plans veer off script. In my time in campaigns and at the White House, I had experience wearing both hats—the dreamer at the conference table and the implementer on the road. Dreaming is less complicated than implementing.

Even a novice advance person would not unconditionally trust a scenario sketched out by the hosts at General Dynamics. Bennett and Flieger knew Dukakis could not simply arrive at the facility and hop into the tank for a test drive. They had to block out and rehearse Dukakis's every step on Game Day, from the moment he emerged from his limousine to the moment he returned to it for the ride back to the airport.

Bennett didn't want to risk Dukakis climbing into the tank in full view of the cameras. The candidate might look silly pulling on his grey coveralls over his wingtips or, worse, slip as he tried to take his place in the massive machine. Luckily, Land Systems had a hangar-sized garage in which the awkward Game Day choreography of mounting and dismounting the tank could take place behind closed doors.

The phrase "Game Day," a staple of the advance lexicon, conjures comparisons to the NFL, with the advance team taking on roles similar to the coaching staff. Each coach had an assignment: Holtzman, with his legal training, managed the local politics; Flieger, with his experience in the House Radio-TV Gallery, put the press plan in place; and Bennett, as the site lead, choreographed the show. He would have to befriend his hosts, negotiate the routes with the Secret Service and know every move of the visit inside and out.

In such assignments, freedom of movement is essential for the advance team. Years later, in 1994, Bennett would serve as lead advance for President Clinton's overnight visit to the aircraft carrier USS *George Washington* positioned off the coast of Normandy to observe the fiftieth anniversary of the D-Day landings. When I arrived with Clinton on the deck of the *George Washington,* it was clear that Bennett, with every detail of the visit at his fingertips, had enjoyed the run of the ship during its long cruise to the English Channel.

Just as he did later aboard the aircraft carrier, Bennett tried to make himself at home at General Dynamics, but it required close partnership with Don Gilleland, the PR chief for Land Systems. The relationship didn't begin smoothly. "It took us about a half-hour to get in the damn door, having to get signed-in, checked-out and photographed," Bennett wrote, but his credentials still required that he be escorted at all times. "One of the first orders of business was getting that changed."[1] The team's new IDs provided unfettered access.

As Gilleland toured Bennett through the facility, the advance man noted that eight M1A1s were on hand, in addition to a well-preserved collection of predecessor models. All of them, Bennett felt, could combine for a stunning backdrop for Dukakis's speech. The more hardware that was available, the more the man standing in front of the machines looked like a credible commander in chief—or so the campaign hoped.

Gilleland told his guest that more equipment could be easily requisitioned. As accommodating as Gilleland was trying to be, Bennett had misgivings about his hosts. Most of the General Dynamics personnel, he reasoned, were Republicans, and a potential "ratfucking," when infiltrators from the other side sabotage an event, wasn't out of the question. As the days ticked down to Game Day, the advance team was in a tough spot, not completely at ease in their surroundings but driven by Boston to score a visual touchdown.

TOUGH CROWD

The main elements of the visit—though not all of the details—had already been sketched out during the early September planning meetings for defense week. As Boston envisioned it, the governor would fly to Detroit from his morning speech at the Council on Foreign Relations in Chicago, motorcade to Sterling Heights, take his tank ride and give another, more locally directed set of remarks on defense policy to a crowd at the facility. The hope was for as large a crowd as possible, made up of both white-collar General Dynamics management, who designed and sold the tanks, and blue-collar assembly-line labor from the United Auto Workers (UAW) union, who built the tanks piece by piece.

All of the visual elements of the day, from the Chicago speech to the Sterling Heights tank ride and remarks that followed, would be cobbled together by editors and producers for that night's news packages. The voice-over narration for the story would come courtesy of Sam Donaldson for ABC, Chris Wallace for NBC and Bruce Morton for CBS. Each would tell the story in his own way, but the images, and the way a viewer's brain processed them, would be roughly the same, appealing to Reagan Democrats in Macomb County and across the nation.

At most venues it is easy enough fill rows of seats and choral risers for a candidate's human backdrop. In a general election season, everyone wants a ticket to the Big Show. Problems arise, however, when you introduce non-credentialed audience members—outsiders—into private facilities that require security clearances. "We were told that under no circumstances could we bring in people (other than staff, press and security) that did not have GD clearance," Bennett wrote.[2] General Dynamics would provide the site for the speech, but they wouldn't cancel an assembly-line shift to conjure a crowd of on-the-clock employees whose jobs were underwritten by taxpayers' money.

A PR chief like Don Gilleland earns his salary by dodging snafus that may land on the front page. General Dynamics couldn't afford the headline "Taxpayer-Subsidized Salaries Fill Seats at Dukakis Campaign Event." Gilleland and his bosses were happy, however, to swing the doors open for buses of unchecked reporters to watch the M1A1 move across a mock battlefield at full speed. Gilleland knew the marketing value of putting military hardware into action from his days as a Pentagon advisor to the entertainment industry for TV shows like the 1980s drama *Call to Glory* on ABC. "We came at [the event] from different perspectives: we at General Dynamics saw great news media exposure for our tank. The Dukakis team saw an opportunity to make him look strong on defense. Ours was a product focus; theirs was a political focus," he remembered.[3]

To get past their crowd problem, the advance team brokered a compromise. They would bring in off-duty second- and third-shift UAW workers from another General Dynamics plant to fill the seats. Getting union workers to sacrifice their time off was a tall order, but Bennett paid a visit to the local UAW office to genuflect before the union boss, Perry Johnson. The pilgrimage resulted in Johnson's assurance that a sufficient showing of bodies, with proper security clearances, would arrive at the appointed hour to make the site look full.

PLAYING PATTON

Advance people lose a lot of sleep over political accoutrements. At night in his hotel room, replaying moments from his dress rehearsals, Bennett slumbered into a nightmare about attire, specifically the helmet. Any clothing or prop used in a shot needs to fit naturally into the scene and, critically, avoid making the principal look like an idiot.

Orchestrating President Clinton's trip to the demilitarized zone between the Koreas in July 1993, advance man Redmond Walsh equipped the commander in chief with an olive drab bomber jacket and a matching green ball cap with the initials "USFK" for United States Forces Korea. The president's motorcade drove forty miles through the rain from Seoul to Camp Bonifas, switching to twelve Humvees for the final leg to Observation Post Ouelette, where he and General Gary Luck could gaze at the enemy from behind sandbags. To complete the scene, Walsh made sure that Clinton had a pair of binoculars through which he could spy North Korean border guards spying back on him. The only problem was that Clinton neglected to remove the lens caps from the binoculars when the time came for the photo op, an omission that photographers caught on film and wired back to the United States.

Later that year in Seattle, where I was troubleshooting a speech site at the first Asia-Pacific Economic Cooperation Summit, I developed a liking for the blown glass creations of famed Tacoma artist Dale Chihuly. Chihuly was exhibiting his work in the Four Seasons hotel where Clinton would give his speech, and I asked to borrow four of the artist's pieces for our site in the hotel's Spanish Ballroom to lend a more colorful backdrop. We wanted visuals matching the Pacific Northwest theme of the summit, and I wanted to avoid another boring "blue drape" affair. As the speech started, I went to the back of the room for a wide view. It looked terrible, as if Clinton had assumed the central role in Botticelli's *Birth of Venus.* When I got back to the White House and saw that my psychedelic tableau filled the front page of the *Washington Times,* the full magnitude of my failure was on display for my colleagues in the West Wing. I thought I might lose my coveted new job within weeks of getting it.

The way to avoid such disasters is to walk in the candidate's shoes, over and over, to examine every angle of how an event will appear. The walk-throughs—or ride-throughs, in Matt Bennett's case—offer clues about how the event will be perceived by an audience. Replaying his test ride, Bennett knew the danger of riding in the turret at full speed. Using geometry, he measured the angles from which the press corps would view the demonstration, gaming out how it would look on the front page.

In the dress rehearsal, Bennett donned the same coveralls and helmet that his boss would wear in a few days, with his upper torso protruding from the commander's side of the turret. As he manipulated controls to rotate the turret and looked down the barrel of its 125-millimeter cannon, a General Dynamics driver steered the tank from its forward compartment. The tank's turbine engine muffled all conversation. Under deafening noise, the occupants secured the straps on their helmets, as Dukakis would do days later.

The helmet served two purposes. The first was for safety—almost anything is less hazardous than standing up in a tank with your skull exposed, executing S-turns and U-turns at forty-five miles per hour. The second was for communications—it was otherwise impossible for the riders to hear one another over the rumble of the Abrams's engines. "The reason we suggested Dukakis wear the helmet is because there's nothing soft in the tank. If he bumped his head in the tank, it would really hurt," Gilleland said.[4]

Without the headphones built into the helmet, Bennett could hear nothing as the tank rumbled along at full speed. Bennett knew that Dukakis, who abhorred photo ops without a purpose, would want to hear what was happening and ask questions. The candidate was also a rule-follower by temperament. As Nick Mitropoulos, the governor's ever-present body man during the 1988 campaign said, "Dukakis would never go anywhere without wearing his seat belt."[5]

As Bennett rehearsed his ride, he concluded that it was bumpy, noisy, sooty and uncomfortable, fun for a twenty-three-year-old advance man, but harrowing for a fifty-four-year-old governor with a million other things on his mind. Bennett didn't want to deliver a damaged candidate back to the campaign. Mindful of the campaign's standing prohibitions against headwear, he started his shakedown test believing that his candidate should avoid wearing the helmet for the image it might convey, but ended it convinced that the ride would be hazardous without one.

As Bennett caromed down the test track, Flieger, watching from the press area, felt his stomach churn too. The tank was huge, twenty-six feet long from front to back, twelve feet wide and eight feet high from track to turret, putting the rider's head a dozen feet in the air. This geometry had a parallel effect on the press: to keep their cameras on an even level with the candidate, reporters would have to be positioned three feet higher than usual on a makeshift platform, a wobbly perch from which to watch the action.

During the test run, Flieger could barely see Bennett protruding from the turret. "It looked like a guy sticking his head out of a house," he recalled. He tried to explain to his press desk in Boston that the picture would be tough to capture. "Boston was picturing Patton in the movie. That tank was probably a third the size of the Abrams," Flieger told me.[6]

In fact, the tank that General George S. Patton commanded as his Third Army drove toward Berlin was the M4 Sherman, nineteen feet long, eight and a half feet wide and nine feet high, making it seven feet shorter, four feet narrower and a hair taller than the M1A1. The M4 was like a wedding cake, much better proportioned to a man's torso sticking out the top. Patton's warhorse was also half the weight of the M1A1. Dukakis, small in stature, would seem smaller still in the giant M1A1 compared to the mythologized imagery of Patton in his M4, alighting from the tank with leather riding boots over his jodhpurs and a pair of pearl-handled revolvers strapped to his waist.

Dukakis was no George C. Scott. *Patton,* which won seven Oscars in 1971, was shot mostly in Spain using a revolutionary process called Dimension 150, invented for the gargantuan curved screens in majestic theaters. Shots of the actor came not from a press riser, but from director Franklin Schaffner's perfectly positioned cameras over many takes to ensure film editors could knit the movie together for maximum drama. Jerry Goldsmith's majestic musical score was another element impossible to re-create in Sterling Heights.

Bennett and Flieger were like the director, Schaffner, and the cinematographer, Fred Koenekamp, but every other member of the crew that day worked for someone else. While an advance team tries to control every element on set, the outcome of how it is ultimately pictured and reported is out of their hands. When the film leaves a site, an advance person can only cross their fingers that the scene will be favorably presented to the public.

SKY PIG AIRBORNE

Saturday, September 10, began a busy weekend in Boston and the gambit of a week on the road to establish, once and for all, the governor's bona fides on national defense. While advance teams were laying the groundwork for the road show, reporting in on daily calls to their scheduling desks, the Dukakis political and policy shops were shoring up endorsements and writing the speeches that the governor would deliver on the stump. John Sasso had only been back on board for a few days, but there was new excitement at headquarters on Chauncy Street, the result of both efforts by the campaign to open its tent to centrist Democrats and a series of stumbles for Vice President Bush.

That evening, the campaign named a dozen national campaign co-chairs drawn from those in high offices in federal and state government. The heavyweight list included, among others, Governor Mario Cuomo of New York, who had spent much of the campaign on the sidelines; Representative Norman Mineta of California; and Senators Bill Bradley of New Jersey, John Glenn of Ohio and Sam Nunn of Georgia.

Several co-chairs, led by Nunn and Les Aspin, chairmen, respectively, of the Senate and House Armed Services Committees, dined with Dukakis that night and joined him for a two-hour meeting on Sunday to finalize the message for national defense week. Nunn and Aspin were Pentagon hawks, often standing behind President Reagan when he rolled out foreign policy initiatives. Now, the Dukakis staff needed their endorsement to drive voter engagement in the South and Midwest, even if they didn't see eye to eye with the governor on every program.

At a news conference following the foreign policy parlay, during which details of the week ahead were released to the media, Dukakis charged that Reagan had created "the biggest procurement scandal in history and then searched for scapegoats, not solutions." The Pentagon was an easy target. In June 1986, Reagan's Blue Ribbon Commission on Defense Management, known as the "Packard Commission," famously uncovered overspending on items such as a $600 toilet seat and a $7,000 coffee pot. Standing shoulder to shoulder with the hawks, Dukakis said, "What you see here is an example of the way we're going to make national security policy beginning in January 1989, with a president and a Congress that will work together."[7]

Of the Pentagon, Aspin said, "There has not been management. We have not made improvements commensurate to the money that has been spent." Nunn weighed in too, saying of the Reagan administration: "You can't have a defense strategy based on a cash register." The rhetoric was steering toward Tuesday's visual of Dukakis in the tank, and backing from the hawks more than paid for the cost of their visit to Boston.[8]

Meanwhile, the Bush campaign was facing unexpected problems. Four advisors, Lee Atwater, Charlie Black, Paul Manafort and Roger Stone, were deflecting questions about an $800,000 lobbying contract that their old firm had with Prime Minister Lynden Pindling of the Bahamas to advance Bahamian interests via a "back-channel relationship" with the state department and congressional leaders. In his news conference, Dukakis said Bush had "to answer some serious questions" about the 1985 contract.[9]

On that same Sunday, another longtime Bush ally, Fred Malek, who had managed the GOP Convention in New Orleans, was forced to resign his post as deputy chairman of the Republican National Committee. His departure came following revelations of additional details of how he had participated in the counting of "Jewish-sounding names" at the Bureau of Labor Statistics when he served in the Nixon administration.[10]

Malek's departure came a week after Jerome Brentar, a Cleveland travel agent, also resigned from Bush's campaign for his support of John Demjanjuk, an Ohio auto worker facing extradition to Israel for trial as a Nazi war criminal.[11] The *Washington Jewish Week* inferred that Brentar was a Holocaust denier and that other members of Bush's coalition had ties to anti-Semitic groups. Bush fanned the stories by misspeaking on the campaign trail. "I hope I stand for anti-bigotry, anti-Semitism, anti-racism," he said. "That is what drives me. It's one of the things that I feel very strongly about."[12]

With Dukakis building bridges with the pro-defense wing of his party and Bush on the defensive, the week ahead was set up perfectly for the fall offensive.

As Sunday evening gave way to Monday morning, an aging Boeing 737 leased from Presidential Airways sat on the tarmac of Logan International Airport ready to take the Dukakis entourage south, then west. Nicknamed "Sky Pig" by television crews who made their home on the aircraft for long months of campaigning, its frequent flyers complained that the plane dripped water from the ceiling, had no stove for heating food and couldn't fly coast-to-coast without stopping for gas. But the thrifty Dukakis seemed to love the cozy 100-seat plane—"We've been on this plane for a long time," he said[13]—and it would continue to be his home for the remaining two months of the campaign.

On the Sky Pig manifest that morning was the governor, Nick Mitropoulos, trip director Jack Weeks, press secretary Dayton Duncan, Duncan's deputy Joe Lockhart and foreign policy advisors Madeleine Albright and Jim Steinberg, among others. As the 737 gained altitude—reporters sometimes said, "Up, pig, up!" on ascent—it began the short 300-mile flight to Philadelphia to begin national defense week.

TURBULENCE ON TOUR

The first stop on Monday started the tour off well. The venue for the governor's speech was Carpenters' Hall, a building steeped in history in the Old City neighborhood of Philadelphia. Befitting the building's stature, the Philadelphia advance team arranged for an honor guard of six uniformed national guardsmen to march onto stage in front of a large American flag to form a soldierly backdrop for the first national defense speech.

The guardsmen folded their hands behind their backs in the "at ease" position, but there was nothing at ease in the rhetoric that Dukakis aimed at Reagan and his anointed successor. The speech focused on fighting terrorism and drug trafficking and derided Vice President Bush for lax approaches to both. A small audience of about 200 people, a number easily vetted by the advance team, filled the seats in the hall. With good lighting, cameras can make 200 people look like 400 in cutaway shots, and a good advance person will position themselves out of camera range to initiate rounds of applause to register an audible endorsement picked up by reporters covering the event at the back of the room.

"Does this man," Governor Dukakis said, referring to the vice president, "a man who would encourage the president of the United States to undermine American interests and prestige by selling arms to Iran, have the judgment and the steadiness required in the Oval Office?" Using an easy target in Bush's running mate, Dukakis questioned whether Dan Quayle would be up to the challenge of leading the nation's anti-narcotics program. "I want a real war against drugs," Dukakis said, echoing a familiar refrain. "His answer to drug kingpins like Noriega is J. Danforth Quayle."[14] Pennsylvania had twenty-five winner-take-all electoral votes in 1988, and this stop in Philadelphia was designed to secure them.

Sky Pig then flew on to Cincinnati for the second leg of the tour. Ohio, with its twenty-three electoral votes, was another must-win state, and Cincinnati was in the heart of the more conservative counties. Dukakis's motorcade brought him to a General Electric engine plant, home to 19,000 workers, the largest employer in the area, where its personnel built the F110 engine for the F-16 fighter and the F101 engine for the B-1 bomber.

Ohio senator John Glenn, who had been part of the weekend meetings in Boston, was selected to introduce the governor in front of the GE workers. The Ohio advance team erected Dukakis's stage in front of a gleaming engine destined for the Air Force's KC-135 tanker. For a candidate espousing a "Conventional Defense Initiative," it was a safe choice of hardware compared to other engines manufactured at the plant that powered aircraft armed with nuclear weapons.

Glenn's presence at Dukakis's side was rich in political symbolism. He was a bona fide American hero, a combat veteran of World War II and the Korean War, a "Right Stuff" test pilot, and the first American to orbit the Earth aboard *Friendship 7* in 1962. If Glenn and Dukakis could steer these southwestern Ohio workers to vector away from Bush, one of the strongest ramparts of Republican support in the battleground states might be vulnerable.

The Ohio crowd of 2,000 people greeting Glenn and Dukakis, many times the size of the audience in Philadelphia, proved less hospitable than trip planners had anticipated. Dukakis had to shout over hecklers as he promised to maintain a strong defense. Murphy's Law was at work.

"Bush, Bush, Bush," many chanted from the crowd, with others booing loudly.

Some plant workers, separated from reporters covering the speech by a thin rope line, offered quotes to feed the stories. Employee Rob Burgess told the Associated Press, "Up until just a few months ago, he [Dukakis] was against the Stealth Bomber. The engine for it is made right here in this plant. I'm surprised he came out here."[15] Crowd quotes like that were the bane of a press advance person's existence.

The headline of the AP story read, "Pro-Bush Hecklers Drown Out Dukakis in a Sea of Boos." The headline of another story, by George Condon of the Copley News Service, said, "Dukakis Booed—Cincinnati Defense Workers Hoot at Democrat Nominee." The headline of Carl Leubsdorf's article for the *Dallas Morning News* read, "Dukakis' Pledge of 'Strong Defense' Gets Mixed Reception." The *Chicago Tribune,* the hometown paper where Dukakis would head next on his tour, carried the headline "Defense Workers Jeer Dukakis."[16]

After a hopeful start in Philadelphia, the wheels of national defense week were starting to come off in Cincinnati, and it was still Day One.

Joe Lockhart, who joined the Dukakis staff after the convention as deputy press secretary and would later serve as Bill Clinton's White House press secretary, told me, "I don't know if it was poorly advanced or if it was just bad luck, but the event didn't go off as planned."[17] The event was too large and the environment too hostile for the team to control. Ordinarily, an advance team can create audience separation from the press by using bike rack barricades or deploying burly squads of union muscle to surround protestors and quash dissent. The setup of the GE plant speech didn't lend itself to any of those standard tricks.

Lockhart watched the Ohio event descend into chaos and started ruminating on what might come next. The campaign couldn't afford another blown play. "One of the things I did before I went to sleep every night was to call the press advance people for the next day," he told me. "Most of the time, it was just, 'That sounds great,' and every once in a while it was 'That sounds crazy.' And there would be a discussion."[18]

The discussion between Lockhart and his press advance man, Flieger, two stops away in Michigan, wasn't reassuring. "Neal was incredibly competent in everything he did, including press advance," Lockhart remembered. "He said he thought the event would come off okay and the issue he had was he thought the helmet with his name on it had the potential to look pretty stupid. We, between the two of us, said, 'Okay, do what you have to do. Just make sure that whatever he does, he does not put the helmet on.'"[19]

Lockhart had no idea of the difficulties in having his simple in-struction carried out. Over the next twenty-four hours, the question of whether the helmet should sit on the candidate's head, or not, would be debated over and over.

But that was only one minor detail vexing Lockhart. As he went on with his tasks, he read news clips from Cincinnati as they spooled from fax machines provided by the local advance team. It was ugly. The lead paragraph of Condon's story, emblematic of other coverage, unnerved the traveling entourage, reverberating back to Boston. "Democratic presiden-tial nominee Michael S. Dukakis's carefully planned effort to portray himself as strong on defense ran into trouble yesterday," Condon wrote, "as hundreds of skeptical workers booed and jeered him in the nation's largest defense plant."[20]

In the days before the Internet, Lockhart, along with staff in the Dukakis and Bush headquarters, scanned "The Hotline"—a precursor to ABC's "The Note" and Mike Allen's POLITICO "Playbook"—to gauge the tone of stories. Both campaigns could read the negative stories that fed the country's newspapers. You didn't need live TV coverage of the tour for staffers on both sides of the political divide to realize the tour had hit a snag in Cincinnati.

Coming amid their own week of negative coverage, the press ac-counts from the GE engine plant offered succor to the strategists at the Bush campaign. If a few howlers could upend Dukakis in Cincinnati, similar insurgents might do the same, or worse, in Sterling Heights. With two days to go on defense week and the press turning sour, a contingency plan was needed urgently.

The traveling staff on Sky Pig put their heads together. They would have to answer to both Dukakis and the chiefs in Boston if there was another setback. "There was a quick huddle after the event where we said, 'We've got to get this back on track. We can't have two days in a row of this,'" Lockhart told me. They knew they had a good advance team in Sterling Heights, but Lockhart had heard the concerns from Flieger, usu-ally a cool customer, about the tank ride and the set-up for the speech. "The decision was to dispatch Jack Weeks, to have him leave the plane and fly directly to Michigan, bypassing Chicago, to make sure the event came off okay," Lockhart remembered.[21]

Jack Weeks, the campaign's trip director and chief troubleshooter, left Cincinnati immediately. He arrived in Sterling Heights just in time for Game Day.

GAME DAY

THE SWEEP

On the evening of September 12, 1988, Matt Bennett followed the same drill of most every site person, Democrat or Republican, in the few remaining hours before Game Day.

Often the last to leave a site before it's put to bed, a site guy obliges the "second supervisor" of the U.S. Secret Service who sweeps in at the last minute with one last walk-through to scrub for holes in the security plan. When that's done, only a night watchman is left behind to stand guard before the local cops arrive, along with the bomb-sniffing dogs, in the pre-dawn hours. They're soon joined by a squad of Secret Service "post-standers" arriving from far-flung field offices to monitor all of the points of entry of an event site. If the site exposes the candidate outdoors, a team of counter-sniper marksmen—"the CS guys"—take up spots on the roof to encamp with their binoculars and long rifles.

I would sometimes stand in disbelief at the overwhelming display of firepower. But always, the haunting shadows of Bobby Kennedy and George Wallace, gunned down at event sites within four years of each other (RFK at the Ambassador Hotel in Los Angeles and Governor Wallace at the Laurel Shopping Center in Maryland), reminded me that a preventative deployment of force is a necessary fixture of modern campaigning. A few of the foiled plots have been reported, but there are surely many more that remain undisclosed. The reality of attacks—like that which killed Yitzhak Rabin or left Gabby Giffords severely wounded—has done more than anything else to strip the spectacle of massive outdoor rallies from presidential campaign schedules. When they do happen, they are highly fortified.

By being first at the site in the early morning, I could be there to work through any required last-minute tweaks. These first hours create the most strain for an advance person to keep the plan together. The rest of the day might be chaotic and the ultimate outcome anyone's guess—a mix of how the speech goes down, how the crowd behaves, and how the press evaluates the moment. At dawn, though, it's just you, a few stray cops and an urn of coffee to keep everybody from grousing about the early call time. There would be an hour or so before the room was emptied to allow the "EOD dogs"—canine experts at explosive ordnance detection—to do their morning "sweep." When they've sniffed every cranny, curtain and chair, the site becomes sanitized, and anyone else entering has to pass through metal detectors and submit to a search of personal belongings. With that, Game Day is on.

For Matt Bennett, this Game Day would be different. The Dukakis trip director, Jack Weeks, was arriving many hours before his candidate. This left Bennett terrified.

THE TRIP DIRECTOR

If serving as a White House press secretary is the ultimate achievement for a political press aide, rising to the level of trip director represents the equivalent stature for an advance person. Achieving that stature means that you've not only demonstrated your fluency with advance work over several campaigns but also, equally important, that you've developed a personal rapport with the candidate and the traveling staff to the point that your judgment is considered peerless on how shit goes down on the road. You've earned the respect of the corps of advance people on a campaign because you've stood in their shoes countless times, but you also have the faith of the traveling entourage that you know how all of the logistics of the road show work, so they don't have to.

Trip directors trade the advance person's airline tickets and rental car vouchers for a permanent seat on the candidate's plane, but it's rarely a relaxed ride. The plane is always headed *somewhere* and the next stop could be a disaster. While the rest of the traveling staff attend to their jobs, such as polishing speech drafts and briefing the press pool in the back of the fuselage, the trip director stays singularly focused on moving the entourage from Point A to Point B, whispering in the candidate's ear about what's coming next and keeping the stray staff member or guest from getting lost in the shuffle along the way.

The candidate propelling forward, robot-like, from city to city, might have a queasy feeling about walking into an event, especially one with tricky choreography. An impending forty-five-mile-per-hour ride in an M1A1 Abrams Main Battle Tank qualifies on that score. But instead of turning for the exit or reaching for the Pepto-Bismol, you look to your trip director for a knowing nod of reassurance that quells the nausea. That nod means that the trip director has examined the schedule from every angle, thought through all of the potential problems and blessed the plan. On September 13, 1988, Michael Dukakis would be looking for that same nod from trip director Jack Weeks.

Except Weeks wasn't there. On the legs from Cincinnati to Chicago to Sterling Heights, the Dukakis campaign was shorn of its shepherd as Weeks streaked to the tank site to avoid a reprise of the calamity at the GE plant and a second-day catastrophe. Severing the candidate from his trip director is no small matter, even for one day. Trip directors know their candidate best, his likes and dislikes, and have a trained eye for trouble: a bad photo about to be taken, a reporter who gets too close or a supporter who never leaves the candidate's side, known in the business as a "clutch." The bet was that Weeks's skills would be better put to work in Sterling Heights than to have him on guard as the entourage made its way from Ohio to Illinois to Michigan.

A trip director overseeing Game Day at a site is no small matter for the advance team, either. In such cases, the team surrenders control. No advance person easily welcomes a last-minute visit by an emissary from "the Plane," something I've experienced from both sides as both visitor and visited. While some trip directors from the Clinton days, like Wendy Smith and Andrew Friendly, employed a lighter touch with their inspections, Weeks brought a heavy hand. In his journal, Matt Bennett recalled the prospect of Weeks's imminent arrival. "This did not fill my heart with joy, for I knew that Jack would be on my ass the entire morning (I was arriving at 5:00 a.m. to begin setting the site). As it turns out, I was right."[1]

When Jack Weeks conducted a walk-through, it was like Henry Ford taking a white glove to his assembly line. "I was happy that he was there, even though Jack was terrifying," Bennett told me. "I was scared of him. All the advance people were. He was an incredibly daunting figure on the campaign. He seemed like an all-powerful figure."[2]

To put this in some perspective, Weeks is the younger brother of Kevin Weeks, who, for years, was the right-hand man of James "Whitey" Bulger, the Boston mobster convicted in 2013 on multiple counts of racketeering, money laundering, extortion, weapons charges and involvement in at least eleven murders. While Jack and Kevin shared a South Boston upbringing, their paths diverged early on. Jack, blue-eyed and tightly coiled, followed the straight and narrow, becoming a Golden Gloves boxer like his father and made his way to Harvard on a scholarship.

"I was a kid from the projects of Southie who happened to go to Harvard," Weeks told me, but he never lost his street savvy.[3] He was an expert field organizer, a master of "the ground game" able to count supporters and get them to the polls on Election Day, among the most valued skills in politics. As an advance man, Weeks's special talent, drawn from his days in the ring, was to treat candidates like prize fighters. He played the corner man, bucking up his contenders, keeping them loose, stitching them up after a bad round and getting them back in the ring to fight another day.

Weeks was supposed to be a member of Harvard's Class of '75, but Vietnam got in the way. He was drafted during his freshman year and served as a military policeman guarding nuclear missile sites. When his hitch ended, he returned home to Boston, graduating from Harvard in 1979 and heading straight into politics. Before John Sasso tapped Weeks as Dukakis's trip director, he had already logged service on four prior presidential drives, including those of Ted Kennedy, Jimmy Carter, Gary Hart and Walter Mondale.

I first met Weeks at the Dukakis advance school at the Sheraton Tara Hotel in Framingham, Massachusetts, in the summer of 1988. I was twenty-three, he was thirty-six, and I can still remember feeling his presence for the first time as I retreated into a fold in a function-room partition when he strode past me, lest I accidently bump him. Once he was in front of the room, sharing his war stories, Weeks was captivating, bestowing on the school's pupils an advance man's life's lessons that remain with me to this day.

What few of us understood in 1988 was that, for all his bravado, Weeks was, at the time, a single dad trying to raise his two sons, one of whom was severely disabled (he has seven kids now). Back then, like so many in politics, the life Weeks chose brought sacrifice, and traveling full time with Dukakis made him ache to be with his boys. Despite this, his reputation preceded him as a resolute and creative advance man who, while brooking no bullshit, was relied on to watch the candidate's back at all times.

When Dukakis walked into the Omni to accept his party's nomination at the 1988 convention, it should have been a long-sought triumph for Weeks, but he fought back melancholy as it happened. "When everyone was on the stage and Dukakis was giving his speech, I looked around—and this was the most personal moment for me—I recognized I was a divorced father of two. My children weren't there. I was there alone and I felt a real lack of anyone with me that I loved," Weeks told me years later.[4]

Like the rest of the longtime Dukakis hands, Weeks returned from Atlanta and endured the August slowdown. He saw an opportunity forfeited while Atwater and crew mercilessly attacked his boss. But he also knew that Dukakis's nature was to keep his day job as governor and moonlight as a candidate. Weeks was ready in September when the road show returned to full speed but was also skeptical about the turn the campaign took with the arrival of the foreign policy hawks trying to morph Dukakis into one of them.

"I don't want to say what they did was wrong. Everyone operates on the last war," Weeks told me. "But there was a time when you go, 'Someone's not getting it,' and it wasn't just Mike Dukakis."[5] With the booing in Cincinnati and defense week headed into dangerous territory, Weeks saddled up for Sterling Heights to head off another ambush.

HUMAN CHESS

Before Weeks arrived, Bennett was conscious of the litany of issues threatening the event. The first was the awkward moment of having a five-foot-eight civilian transfer from the back seat of a limo to the turret of a tank high off the ground. Any number of things could go wrong. It could be a slippery climb. Photographs of an anguished grimace during ascent or a protruding posterior as he reached the turret could tell a bad story in itself. These were images unbecoming a national candidate in a business suit.

Bennett devised a series of human chess moves to leave the governor dressed, briefed and positioned atop the tank before he could be spotted. Dukakis would arrive at Land Systems and be ushered to a closed-door meeting of company management and labor leaders. This bought time for the press to disembark their buses, under Neal Flieger's escort, to positions on the riser overlooking the proving grounds. Their view, prior to the action, was a sealed hangar door, behind which the tank sat parked, awaiting its VIP passenger.

Meanwhile, after the private meeting, Dukakis would move to a screened-off area to put on gray protective coveralls over his business suit and wing tips. The outfit made him look like a Maytag repairman but for the yellow nylon rescue straps sewn onto the shoulders that provided handgrips for rescuers if a rider needed to be extracted in an emergency. After putting on the coveralls, Dukakis would be briefed on the ride by Gordon England, his official escort during the visit to Land Systems. Then Bennett—and other members of the traveling staff—would have a final chance to whisper wisdom into the candidate's ear. The last piece of behind-the-scenes choreography was the ascent to the turret.

"The bay doors would open, and they would come zooming out to face the awestruck press corps," Bennett wrote in his journal. "The tank would do several circles around the field, showing off General Dy's remarkable killing machine, and then they'd head back in. He would walk out to the stage, be introduced by a pack of pols (Senator Levin, Governor Blanchard, Congressman Hertel and Congressman Bonior all got into the act), give his 'tough on defense' speech, and we would triumphantly depart."[6] That was Bennett's hopeful plan, anyway.

Bennett thought he had it all figured out, but rumors were swirling that Pentagon officials, at the direction of the White House, were trying to scuttle the political ride on a government-owned tank. Had they succeeded, it would have required a last-minute detour to a local high school classroom instead of a national defense proving ground. In retrospect, that might have been a godsend. "There was much panic in Michigan and Boston when we heard of the Defense Department's inquiry into our event, but calls were made to Sam Nunn and Jim Wright, and the problem went away," Bennett wrote.[7]

A second problem was liability. Campaigns, like companies, need insurance for everything they do. Using a weapon of modern warfare as a political prop brought unique complications. It was one thing for an insurance carrier to issue a certificate to cover the slips and falls that typically accompany campaign rallies, quite another to mitigate the potential calamity of a seventy-ton tank ferrying a fifty-four-year-old governor. "General Dy did not want to be responsible if the tank ran over a reporter or tossed out our candidate," Bennett wrote.[8] This, too, was a task for Holtzman, the lawyer who worked as intermediary between

General Dynamics and Boston and helped to broker a risk-management solution.

With the tricky choreography handled and unconventional insurance coverage in place, the final problem to troubleshoot on Game Day was the "helmet issue"—and Bennett and Holtzman needed Jack Weeks to weigh in.

On the morning of September 13, "Jack came sweeping into the site, and took over absolutely, as only he can," Bennett wrote in his journal. "The GD people stopped talking to me and went to Jack for everything. He looked at my ideas for the stage and changed everything around," he added.[9] While the Game Day tinkering seemed to Bennett like a full rewrite of his script, he saw the value of having someone with four presidential campaigns and fourteen more years of experience to help call the shots.

Working with Bennett and Flieger, Weeks directed them to hone the site. They adjusted the press risers and hung a massive American flag as a cutaway visual for the speech. Weeks determined, reasonably, that no artificial lighting was needed for the post-ride speech, saving campaign funds for other uses. He even selected the entrance music for the governor as he made his way to the stage, sending a volunteer out to a local record store to buy the soundtrack for *Patton,* a theatrical detail that made it into the post-event coverage.[10] The pulsating drums and soaring trumpets of Jerry Goldsmith's score would be played after the tank ride and right before Dukakis arrived at the adjacent speech site to offer his remarks, an apt musical accompaniment to the campaign's crafted story.

STATE OF GRACE

An eyewitness to Game Day preparations was *Newsweek* photographer Arthur Grace, who was doing a behind-the-scenes portrait project of all of the candidates who were running for president that year, both Republican and Democrat. Grace enjoyed special access at their events to make black-and-white shots using a Rolleiflex Two and a Quarter camera that revealed the stagecraft behind the political spectacle. As it was the fourth presidential campaign he had covered, he knew his subject well. A trade-off for Grace's special access—a reason campaigns trusted him—was that all but one of his images each week would remain unpublished until after election day. Grace's 1989 book, *Choose Me: Portraits of a Presidential Race,* remains a unique document of the angles and moments that most campaigns strive to keep under wraps.[11]

As soon as he heard about the planned tank ride earlier that day, he thought it might provide an "interesting" picture, and not necessarily a good one for the candidate. A Massachusetts native and friend of John Sasso, and someone who wasn't on the same kind of daily news assignment as the other photojournalists covering Sterling Heights, Grace had a soft spot for Dukakis. He sensed, as photographers often can, that the event was headed for disaster. "Before we got there, I got on the press bus PA system and I told everybody, 'Look, I guarantee you that this is going to be the picture of the campaign,'" Grace told me. "'I advise everybody to put in a new cassette in your video cameras, and photographers to put a fresh roll of film in, because this is going to be it.'"[12]

After alerting his colleagues on the press bus, purely on the description of the event, Grace's concern grew exponentially when he arrived at Land Systems and eyed the enormous M1A1s that Bennett had put on display. He thought Dukakis was going to look ridiculous. "If they posed him with the tank in the background it would be okay," Grace told me. "But him sitting atop that tank? He'd look like a peanut. It was not the image they were looking for."[13]

Grace then did something unusual in his profession. In light of his friendship with Sasso and Susan Estrich, he tried to warn the campaign. In 1988, long before cell phones became a standard tool of politics, he hunted down a campaign staffer—he can't recall today who it was—and demanded to be put on the phone with Dukakis headquarters. "You better call Boston and change it," he remembers saying.

"Get 'em on the phone. Get 'em on the phone. I've got to talk to somebody there," Grace recalls telling anyone from the campaign who would listen.

A short while later, Grace found himself on a hardline telephone with an official at Chauncy Street. He asked first for Sasso or Estrich. "As a friend, I wanted to give them a heads-up to avoid what I thought was going to be a visual implosion," Grace said. Neither Sasso nor Estrich were available, but Grace remembers talking to "the top person there at the time," though who exactly it was remains unclear.

According to Grace, the official on the other end of the line listened and heard him out when he said, "You can't let him go on this tank. It's going to be the worst thing he ever did. Change the schedule. Do whatever you have to do, but change it."

Grace was asked to hold the line, which he did for a few minutes, as he recalls now more than a quarter century later. The official came back on the line and tried to reassure the photographer saying, "It's going to be okay."

Grace wouldn't accept being mollified and pressed his case. "No, it's not," he said. "The tank is huge and he is tiny!" He was asked to hold a second time, this time with a longer interval before the campaign official returned.

"No," came the second reply. "It's going to be okay. We're going to do this."

After Grace warned a final time that the ride would be a huge mistake, the phone call ended. "These people were fools," Grace remembered. "They didn't want to listen and they made a big, big mistake."[14]

Matt Bennett can't recall a *Newsweek* photographer roaming his site in the pre-event hours frantically waving a red caution flag but concedes that events could have unfolded as Arthur Grace describes. It was the fog of campaign war, and Bennett was too busy putting out other last-minute fires with Jack Weeks looking over his shoulder. He had no time, or authority, to broker a distress call back to Boston from a concerned photographer. For Bennett, that ship had sailed days ago. Boston had told him what they told Grace: the event was a go.

THE HELMET ISSUE

"To be fair, Jack did help a lot," Bennett wrote in his journal. "His biggest contribution, for me, at least, was his judgment call on the helmet problem."[15] The helmet issue was the subject of several of Bennett's calls to Boston and also the sticking point on Neal Flieger's call to Joe Lockhart while the entourage was in Cincinnati. They had worked through all of the other problems, but when the advance men tried to see around the corner and imagine the worst that might come from the visit to Land Systems, it was the image of the olive green steel orb on the candidate's head that kept giving them fits.

Bennett, Holtzman, Flieger and Weeks gathered around the massive tank as it sat idle in the hangar and the team outlined their concerns to the trip director. They offered the practical two-pronged rationale for wearing the helmet—safety and communications—and stressed that wearing it for a full-speed run was a rule General Dynamics wanted to enforce. This ran counter to Rule 1 about candidates wearing hats in public, a legacy provision in advance manuals resulting from the archive of bad pictures that odd headwear has contributed over the years.

Decades later, Weeks is adamant that he never gave the thumbs-up to the helmet. As he remembers it, he ordered trip lead Paul Holtzman to model both the General Dynamics coveralls and the tank helmet for his review. Advance people endure many humiliations in their line of work, and posing in the candidate's costume for the trip director is one of them. "Paul puts on the coveralls and I say, 'That's fine, Paul.' And he says he's got this helmet. And I say, 'Put the helmet on.' I say, 'There's a mirror. Go look at the mirror.' He looks at the mirror. I say, 'You look like a goofy fuck.' No helmet."[16]

This exchange, if accurate, is a pivotal moment in the history of Dukakis and the tank. Another person who could corroborate it has never spoken publicly about it. Over the course of three years working on this book, I made repeated attempts, through phone calls and emails, to talk with Paul Holtzman, now an attorney in Boston. Perhaps knowing that he holds the key to one of the great remaining mysteries of campaign screw-ups, he never returned my many messages.

Matt Bennett stands by his memory of the outcome of the Game Day conversation, and it tracks with a "have your cake and eat it too" strategy that advance people sometimes employ while crossing their fingers and hoping for the best. In his journal, Bennett noted that the team agreed that Dukakis "would wear the helmet for the fast pass through the proving grounds and doff his headgear for a slow, picture-taking pass."[17] The team's expectation—or hope—was that the riser full of photographers would be satisfied with more of a posed picture of Dukakis and England in the turret, without their helmets, moving past them slowly, and would go into "protective mode" as the tank picked up speed and zoomed away from them. The thinking was that the long-distance shots would be mostly unusable anyway, with the riders' faces shrouded under their helmets as they put the tank through its full-speed paces at the opposite end of the proving ground.

As a result of this compromise, the governor would have his high-octane ride and get to experience the full maneuverability and capabilities of the tank. He could hear the narration of Gordon England, his General Dynamics escort, and could remain safe in the process. And the press, which the team thought would want to have pictures of a clearly visible Dukakis, would have shots that catered to them too.

However the decision went down, the time for discussion was over. Dukakis's morning speech to the Chicago Council on Foreign Relations was about to conclude, and the governor's motorcade would soon convey him and his entourage back to Sky Pig for a quick flight to Sterling Heights. Game Day's opening whistle was about to blow.

The motorcade arrived at its appointed hour. While Flieger escorted the press corps to their position overlooking the field, Bennett wrote that "Paul and I took the apprehensive governor of Massachusetts" to his meeting with company officials and the labor representatives, followed by the requisite stop at the changing room to slip on their coveralls.[18] A photo from Gordon England's private collection shows him and the governor walking down a hallway toward the hangar, with both of them in their tank jumpsuits, the governor looking straight ahead, determined to get it over with but, from his expression, not overjoyed with his surroundings.

In *Choose Me,* ABC News correspondent James Wooten provided commentary that "there were moments in his campaign, both before and after he became his party's nominee, when Dukakis seemed utterly bored by the whole affair, as though there were other items that required his dispassionate attention, something else that interested him more."[19] Judging by Gordon England's photo, this was such a moment. Like Barack Obama, who harbors palpable disdain for manufactured campaign stagecraft, Dukakis didn't want to play his part in the drama. But while Obama has the charisma to make such dismissive nonchalance a selling point, it only made Dukakis look like he'd rather be in Brookline.

More than a quarter century later, Bennett's journal reads like an executioner's lament, the final paces of a guard marching his prisoner toward doom. More than a third of the current U.S. population hadn't been born when Mike Dukakis ran for president, but in most circles outside Massachusetts, he is remembered for little else beyond the ten minutes that were next to unfold under Matt Bennett's watch.

Dukakis arrived in the hangar, which by this point had been cleared of all nonessential personnel. While Bennett had thought that getting into the eight-foot-high tank would be awkward, that maneuver turned out to be easy. Dukakis, as if he had just graduated from army basic training, as he had done three decades earlier, hopped right in. All of Bennett's scrupulous efforts to shield Dukakis from the press during this potentially embarrassing moment proved to be unnecessary.

The looming issue was still the helmet. "I remember this distinctly," Madeleine Albright, another eyewitness in the hangar, told me. "The people in the factory gave him the helmet. They told him to wear it, and he hesitated, but they told him, 'You have to wear this, because this is where the audio equipment is inside. You can hear what the instructions are.' This is standard operating procedure. Everybody knows you don't wear hats during campaigns, for any number of reasons, but this was an instruction from the people that manufactured the tank."[20]

Albright was also skilled at seeing around corners, and she could tell what was coming next. "Everybody, the minute that he put it on, knew that this was not the best of all possible worlds," she told me. "But the bottom line is that people understood that he was following the instructions of the manufacturers of the tank. I certainly understood that he wanted to hear the instructions. I think it would have been weirder, frankly, for him to say, 'Oh my God, I'm in the middle of a campaign and I'm not going to put this on.'"[21] It was too late for that. He had passed the point of no return.

This particular helmet had a distinguishing feature. The basic version includes a curved steel plate that fits snugly over the skull and bulbous earmuffs with speakers inside that wrap around the middle of the head. A thick chinstrap, concealing a chunk of the lower face, holds the whole apparatus in position. The model given to the governor, however, had a white sticker about an inch and a half high and seven inches across with MIKE DUKAKIS stenciled on it in plain black letters. The labeled helmet framing the rider's bushy eyebrows, and the red tie and blue button-down shirt he wore beneath his jumpsuit, conspired to give the candidate his most damaging comparison of all: to Snoopy, Charles M. Schulz's comic creation, in hot pursuit of the Red Baron.

Joe Lockhart remembers what Dukakis told him after the ride. "His explanation afterwards was—and this is quintessential Mike Dukakis, completely understandable, for everybody else, this was a photo op—he wanted to understand how the tank worked," Lockhart told me. "So he put it on."[22]

In the end, there was no alternative after the final warnings were issued and ignored. The helmet invoked the Snoopy comparisons and the stenciled MIKE DUKAKIS across the brow made the governor look even more silly.

Just like in a football game, where the quarterback changes a play at the last second when his team approaches the line of scrimmage, could a last-minute "audible" have been called to keep the governor out of his helmet and coveralls? Could Bennett have erected a reviewing stand befitting a distinguished visitor and handed the candidate a pair of binoculars to watch the big tank pass in military review? In hindsight, sure, but it would have taken brass to defy Boston's best-laid plans.

Nick Mitropoulos remembers the action unfolding as Weeks describes it, with the "audible" called by an unidentified quarterback at some point during the ride, not before. "I think someone inside that tank told Dukakis to put the helmet on," Mitropoulos remembered. "That's why I always thought Weeks got a bad rap on this because, if not a Secret Service guy, someone from General Dynamics said 'Put it on.'"[23]

This chronology differs crucially from the memories of Matt Bennett and Gordon England. Exactly what was said to the governor in the hangar about the helmet, and in what sequence, could serve as a remake of *Rashomon,* the 1950 Akira Kurosawa film in which different characters provide alternative versions of a murder. Only Mike Dukakis might provide more clarity to the sequence of events, but he has declined multiple opportunities—perhaps in deference to the many people involved—to offer his own version of the story.

As Barack Obama reminded his audience in 2013, you wear a helmet at your peril, as Calvin Coolidge did when he was presented with, and wore, a native headdress given to him by Sitting Bull's nephew in 1927. Coolidge welcomed the moment, but friends thought it unbecoming. "I don't know why you object," Coolidge said. "The people have given me these costumes to put on. Why shouldn't I have my picture taken with it on to please them?"

The compromise solution was flawed from the start. The belief that photographers would keep their fingers off their shutters and refrain from doing the job for which they are hired until the campaign said "Go" was folly. The only way to ensure that a picture is not taken, as President Obama and his communications staff have learned from experience, is to not allow the unwanted moment to occur in public view.

THE RIDE FROM HELL

An aluminum gangway, similar to a wheeled ladder that helps fighter pilots ascend to their cockpits on the flight deck of an aircraft carrier, was rolled into position by General Dynamics personnel. "I climbed up on the tank to help the governor in and showed him where to hold on," Bennett wrote, "and he was soon joined by Gordon England and a female Secret Service Agent."[24]

The agent was Carol Marks, who later became the Special Agent in Charge of the Paris Field Office of the Secret Service. She was selected because she was the smallest agent in the Dukakis detail who could squeeze easily inside the tank. With the exception of a golf cart on a guarded course, at least one agent always accompanies the protectee in any type of motorized transportation beyond the White House grounds or the presidential retreat at Camp David. During my time in the White House, when we brought Bill Clinton to Charlotte, North Carolina, he drove his '65 Ford Mustang around the track of the Charlotte Motor Speedway with his Secret Service detail leader, Dave Carpenter, riding shotgun.[25]

With the riders in their respective positions—the tank driver and Agent Marks below, and England and Dukakis topside with their torsos sticking out of the turret—the massive hangar doors opened and the M1A1's 1,500-horsepower turbine engine roared to life. The tank edged forward slowly, but within a few seconds was in full view of the local and national press corps, along with other dignitaries invited to watch.

The event began according to the script with its Game Day adaptations. A recipe with last-minute ingredients poured in, and a bunch of cooks in the political kitchen, could not emerge from the stove untainted. The decommissioned tank eased out of the hangar with its topside riders, Dukakis and England, not wearing helmets.

In this last minute of calm, Dukakis was seen with his hands on the turret's machine gun as England, his host, pointed out the different triggers, knobs and dials that filled the commander's cockpit. If this showroom moment was all that would happen on the ride—a hands-on photo op for the candidate and a picture for the press—everyone might have gone home happy. But the ride was just beginning. In *Choose Me,* a photo by Arthur Grace shows Dukakis in this first minute. While the image might strike some as unpresidential, he was pictured in the best possible light, relaxed and smiling, and without a helmet. It was an image few ever saw after the ride got underway.[26]

After the first slow pass in parallel view of the press riser, the helmet-free photo op, the tank turned and headed to a far end of the field. Once there, it executed another turn, this time pointing directly toward the news cameras. Whether this maneuver happened as choreographed in advance, or as the result of an impromptu change in routing, is unknown. The tank then did something that ran counter to the careful planning of the advance team. It began to move at high speed directly back toward the press riser.

Jack Weeks remembers that he was shocked when, after the first pass, the tank headed away from the press riser and the event veered off script. "The tank went out on a big field," Weeks recalled. "It goes left, it goes past the press riser, it goes up to the far corner and it stops. My reaction is, 'Holy shit, the tank ran out of gas.' The headline running through my head is, 'Dukakis Campaign Runs out of Gas.' That's what's going through my mind. I don't know if you've ever seen an M1A1 tank move, but it moves very quickly. All of a sudden, it kicks up into speed, it comes running by, and he's got the helmet on."[27]

This is where Jack Weeks feels his deepest regret as an advance man. He had spent his political career positioning himself between his candidate and disaster, a human shield against humiliation. But for the shield to work, he had to stay within arm's length of Dukakis. This was his job as a prizefighter's corner man. He could stop the fight as long as he could stand in front of the oncoming punch and take the hit himself. Instead, he was a quarter mile away from a tank propelling forward at forty-five miles per hour, zigging and zagging, the turret twisting left and right, rendering the inexperienced rider nauseous. Watching it all from afar, he was powerless to interrupt history as it was unfolding.

The tank could only fit four people—the candidate, the escort, the agent, and the driver. Weeks couldn't drive a tank, so he was the odd man out. In Weeks's view, something in the real-time execution of the event went terribly wrong. "If anyone asks me what the screw-up was," he told me, "it was not having an advance person with him to protect him from what they did."[28] Weeks might have redirected the tank from heading back toward the press risers.

Through a camera's viewfinder, the tank became larger and larger as it approached the onlookers. Closer and closer it got, with the features of the governor's face coming into sharp focus. If it stayed on its current vector, it would plow straight through the press riser and take a hundred reporters along with it for a wild ride onto the streets of Sterling Heights. The helmeted governor, half of his torso protruding through the turret, is seen in this series of images with his white teeth fully visible, pointing toward the press that sat, at that moment, like sitting ducks. The M1A1's 120-millimeter smoothbore cannon was closing in on them fast, the leading edge of its barrel now just a few feet away.

For the photographers that day, and Vice President Bush's ad team weeks later, this was the "money shot," the close-up in crisp focus when the tank came near enough to the lenses to clearly see Dukakis's smiling face beneath the helmet bearing his name.

For the candidate, a fifty-four-year-old man, it was the equivalent of a roller coaster ride being videotaped by scores of reporters. The forward and reverse thrust was very real, as was the high-speed rightward and left-ward yaw of the turret. No grownup looks good in GoPro videos chaperoning their kids on the Coney Island Cyclone, and not many grownups feel good doing it, either. From Arthur Grace's vantage point, the governor looked unwell, as if on the final few turns of the Cyclone.

As the tank approached the press riser, the turret spun left at the last second, nearly decapitating reporters on the front row with its cannon. "The governor, who was controlling the turret, almost wiped 'em all out when, as he put it, he had Sam Donaldson in his sights," Bennett wrote in his journal.[29] The Abrams then sped away, taking its passenger with it, jolting his internal organs with abrupt ninety-degree turns. Like the Cyclone terminating its circuit on the wooden trusses high above Brooklyn, the ride was over.

The tank returned through the hangar doors from which it had departed only minutes before. The aluminum gangway was rolled back into position to allow Dukakis to disembark. Arthur Grace remembers Dukakis needing assistance to find his footing to make his way down the ladder. "He had some ill effects from his ride, shall we say. The fact was that he was not in great shape when the tank pulled in," Grace told me.[30]

Bennett, on hand at the bottom of the stairs, did what all advance men do at the end of a public event: he greeted that governor and helped him shed his protective clothing. "He didn't yet know of the humiliations to come when he arrived back in the shop to dismount. As he was climbing out of the tank, we all told him that he'd looked great (and we really thought that), and he was pumped up for his speech when he hit the rope line," Bennett wrote, his assessment of Dukakis's post-ride condition conflicting with that of Grace.[31]

What happened next—the speech to management and workers—had been the focus of intense planning during Bennett's advance assignment. Now it was a historical footnote. With close to a thousand people in front of him, the candidate echoed the themes from his speech in Chicago earlier that day, this time with an array of vintage tanks behind him, an American flag billowing to his right and a small step beneath his feet to elevate his stature. As planned, the *Patton* theme accompanied Dukakis's descent from the stage.

Photo op and speech. It was the same routine he had followed several times a day throughout the year, going back to the early months of his campaign. The difference that day was that the photographers had already couriered their film to bureaus to wire back to New York. Reporters already had pages of notes of color, and the TV producers had ten minutes of must-watch video to accompany their stories. They were all hard at work on deadline with their bosses on the East Coast watching the clock.

After the speech, Bennett escorted Dukakis back to his limo for the short ride back to the airport, the ritual before the governor's flight to Washington for the final leg of national defense week. For the staffers, it remained to be seen whether the story would have "legs." Joe Lockhart was hearing from producers that the visuals would allow them to report on the event with Reagan-like gusto. In spite of all of the Game Day hand-wringing, maybe the event would be remembered as a home run after all.

SIX

A STORY WITH LEGS

THE ROCKS OF NORMANDY

A looming anxiety any advance person takes into Game Day is that their event will backfire, imploding in front of the candidate and staff. A deeper dread is that it will spawn a negative story in the next day's paper, an image mocked around the water cooler. But the greatest fear of all is that it will "grow legs," metastasizing from one day of coverage to second-day stories, followed by chronic examinations in columns, polls, daytime talk radio, prime-time cable, late-night comedy and, worst of all, paid negative ads from opponents spanning days or weeks. This was the torment that kept advance people like me up at night in the 1980s, 1990s and 2000s. With the spread of social media in the 2010s, the legs on stories mutate at warp speed, and the nightmares become ever more terrifying.

In June 1994, as the White House director of production, I had the task of planning elements of President Clinton's trip to Normandy to honor the fiftieth anniversary of the D-Day landings. While Cornelius Ryan had published *The Longest Day* in 1959 and Stephen Ambrose came out with *Band of Brothers* in 1992, it was still years before Tom Brokaw and Steven Spielberg would immortalize the soldiers who freed the world through works like *The Greatest Generation* and *Saving Private Ryan*.

What little I knew of D-Day I learned through watching coverage of Ronald Reagan's speeches in high school. I would have to become a D-Day expert quickly, but it was the kind of assignment I savored, a mix of history, emotion and pageantry, and one that commanded blanket media coverage. It was a humbling and rare honor to disembark a U.S. government plane that brought our White House team to Normandy earlier in the year for the first of two site survey trips to plan the president's visit.

Phil Rivers, superintendent of the American Cemetery at Colleville-sur-Mer, where 9,387 headstones marked the graves of the fallen, served as our tour guide and teacher. His encyclopedic knowledge of the place and reverence for its hallowed grounds were readily absorbed by this pupil. On my trips to Normandy, and in my many questions lobbed at Phil, I scouted every potential venue for the president to visit. Back in Washington, with a box of videotapes accessed from the National Archives, I studied all of the raw news footage and government documentary video of how Reagan commemorated the fortieth anniversary in 1984.

That Reagan trip was a masterstroke of image and message, starting with a walk through stoic rows of white headstones and culminating with his speech, written by Peggy Noonan, to the "Boys of Pointe du Hoc." The speech, delivered under gray English Channel overcast, was an homage to the Second Ranger Battalion under the command of Lieutenant Colonel James E. Rudder, which had scaled the 100-foot cliffs above Utah Beach early on the morning of June 6, 1944. Noonan's words about the attack on the German casements were indelible coming from Reagan, and his delivery on that misty morning above the coast of France was pitch-perfect. But it was the visual of the president perched on a windblown promontory, the simple granite pylon behind him as he saluted the aging veterans arrayed before him, that made the moment unforgettable.[1]

When Clinton's turn came to honor the same heroes, the challenge was bigger for a president with a conflicted relationship with the military going back to his 1969 letter to Colonel Eugene Holmes, the ROTC head at the University of Arkansas. In that letter, Clinton thanked Holmes for "saving me from the draft."[2] As president, Clinton embraced his role as commander in chief but struggled to escape the shadow of that quote.

While Don Baer was working back in Washington to craft the message Clinton would share with the World War II veterans (he called his generation "the children of your sacrifice"), I was diagramming Normandy locations to match the sentiment. At the Colleville-sur-Mer cemetery, overlooking Omaha Beach, Clinton and his wife, Hillary, would walk through headstones, as the Reagans did, but to document a more intimate angle of the moment, they would be photographed using remote-controlled cameras placed discreetly among the rows of crosses. This was the kind of collaboration that defined the mutual dependence of advance people and the photojournalists who covered the White House. We wanted to tell a story, and they wanted a captivating picture taken from a unique perspective that would get their work on the front page. We were happy to oblige.

But we couldn't just mimic the Reagan playbook. We needed a new play. One thing Reagan didn't do was walk on Omaha Beach. No president had done that. To get there on foot from the cemetery required a long walk, good stamina and flexibility from the Secret Service, who brought to Normandy trepidation about exposing a president to sniper fire in a place renowned for it. We came up with a plan for a solemn walk a quarter mile or so to the beach, with Clinton accompanied by three D-Day veterans and the army's chief chaplain, Matthew Zimmerman, to offer a prayer for the fallen at the water's edge. Twenty-one Navy warships were positioned offshore in salute formation.

Back home, I identified three veterans, Joe Dawson, Robert Slaughter and Medal of Honor recipient Walter Ehlers, who planned to return to Normandy and would take the walk with Clinton to the spot where so many comrades, including Ehlers's own brother, had fallen on D-Day. Reading Ehlers's Medal of Honor citation was chilling. On June 9–10, among other acts of "conspicuous gallantry and intrepidity" near Goville, Sergeant Ehlers crawled forward "under withering machine gun fire" and put the gun crew "out of action," later diverting hostile fire onto himself.[3] He was a handsome young man in 1944. Fifty years later, the one-time security guard at Disneyland was soft-spoken and humble.

I spoke to family members of each of the veterans to learn their stories firsthand. Combining their backgrounds with Polaroids I shot on my survey trips, I laid out the movement in storyboard form and used the pages to brief the White House staff back in Washington. The frame of Clinton, Dawson, Slaughter and Ehlers on Omaha Beach, backed by the USS *George Washington* off in the distance, if we could pull it off, would match speechwriter Don Baer's message of "We are the children of your sacrifice."

On the date of the fiftieth anniversary, June 6, 1994, it was all going according to script. After delivering his speech in front of Donald De Lue's monumental twenty-two-foot-high sculpture titled *The Spirit of American Youth Rising from the Waves,* Clinton and his procession gathered at the top of the bluff overlooking the beach and began their journey. I was positioned ahead of the walking party on the beach, along with a pool of reporters and photographers, and the Secret Service agent overseeing security for the movement, ready to record the moment.

While the walkers were halfway through their descent, our agent received an instruction through his earpiece. The Secret Service counter-sniper teams positioned at a vantage point to cover the walk didn't want the president to get beyond their range near the surf. They asked me to mark a spot seventy-five feet or so onto the sand and tell Clinton he should go no further. My problem was that I had nothing on hand to define a visual marker. Looking around, I saw a ribbon of large stones at the high-water mark of the tide that separated the sand and the dune grass that covered the long slope to the cemetery. Racing against time, I hauled about a dozen of the stones onto the beach and piled them into a small pyramid to mark the boundary. When the president arrived, I whispered into his ear about the Secret Service request and pointed out the pile of stones that constituted my marker. He nodded in compliance with the direction.

The press pool was with me as I worked. Their eyes were on the president and his party, their ears attuned to any words they could make out. In her pool report, Karen Ball of the *New York Daily News* heard Joe Dawson describe to Clinton the scene fifty years earlier. "This was all chaos of dead men and wounded," he told him, the president asking a slew of questions in response, amazed by the lack of cover on the expansive beach.[4]

The pool and I watched as the men made their way solemnly to the beach. The picture came off as planned, with Chaplain Zimmerman leading Clinton and his companions in prayer. Accepting that we were in the middle of a global news event, it was a scene that was as genuine and poignant as it could be in these circumstances. With tight security around the perimeter, there was almost no one else on Omaha Beach except for the principals and the press pool, which stood a respectful distance away to record the moment for posterity.

Then something intervened that upended the best-laid plans. Unbeknownst to me, a senior White House aide had cut a side deal for an exclusive *Newsweek* photo op to be shot by famed photographer Eddie Adams. Adams had earned the Pulitzer Prize for his famous 1968 image of General Nguyen Ngoc Loan executing a Viet Cong prisoner on a Saigon street. Adams's quick reflexes allowed him to make that image but, fumbling with his lenses, he wasn't as fast in 1994 as he had been in '68. As Clinton waited, standing at the edge of the beach, he looked at me with an uncomfortable expression of, "What am I supposed to do now?" As Ball noted in her pool report, the image of a solitary president standing on Omaha Beach with warships off in the distance "looked like a made-for-TV shot," but that particular framing was never supposed to happen.[5]

Clinton was at the end of a week-long trip to honor the turning point of World War II. We had traveled from Italy to England and now to France, a journey overflowing with emotion at every stop and with very little sleep for the president and his traveling party. At each point on the schedule, at the Sicily-Rome American Cemetery in Nettuno, the Maddingly American Cemetery in Cambridge, and now at Colleville-sur-Mer, Clinton was confronted by endless rows of white crosses. Overwhelmed by the sacrifice that the crosses represented, anyone might have the image of the grave markers seared into their subconscious. "I'm about out of words," he would say a few minutes later. "I've never experienced anything like it."[6]

At the end of his journey, as he waited for Adams to take pictures, the president knelt at the small pyramid of stones that I had placed minutes earlier at the request of the Secret Service. I watched, stunned, as he rearranged them into the form of a cross, standing back a few feet when he had finished in a final moment of silence. It wasn't part of the plan, but the cameras kept rolling, as they needed to, with the president out in public.

That moment, like the one with Dawson, Slaughter and Ehlers, was wired back to photo bureaus. European news outlets played the image up big, and footage from the beach filled evening news packages. I hoped the shot might convey Clinton's reverence for the vets but worried that, without his companions by his side, the power of the scene might be lost. While the day yielded many stories underscoring the president's homage to the veterans and helped to better inform a new generation about D-Day, it didn't take long for an alternative version of events to creep into the American subconscious.

By the time I landed back in the States, Rush Limbaugh was already hard at work, on the air day after day using Omaha Beach as an example of Clinton's phoniness. The drumbeat fomented fury among those on the far right who hadn't yet found a reason to despise the man in the Oval Office. They had one now. They might have had substantive disagreements with Clinton for decades, but their anger over an image at Normandy still lingers.

The mockery wasn't limited to Limbaugh. In her June 19 article in the *New York Times,* columnist Maureen Dowd weighed in with "Beached," her account of weather-related logistical missteps that stranded many of the traveling press. Her piece ended with the scene on the beach. "The tableau was appealing: the young President enjoying the company of the aging heroes," she wrote. "But suddenly the President's aides began tugging the veterans away, mid-conversation, so that Clinton could walk off at sunset down the beach in his dress shoes and have a preplanned meditative moment, with the bluffs on one side and the sea dotted with warships on the other."[7]

Dowd, among the stranded reporters waiting for a fogged-in military helicopter, wasn't an eyewitness to that scene, but she wrote about it with a "you are there" sense of drama just the same. In addition to Karen Ball's pool report and footage from the filing center, she referenced the account of one photographer to conclude the moment had been "preplanned," which fit her narrative but simply wasn't true. More than Limbaugh's on-air tirades, Dowd's writing in the *Times* legitimized the myth, spawning more stories, like the late Michael Kelly's 12,000-word opus on "The President's Past" that appeared in the *Times* at the end of July of that year, ending on the same scene ("staged as carefully as a small movie," Kelly wrote) and making roughly the same point.[8]

We helped to give the story its legs. The president had to go to Normandy, as Reagan did ten years earlier. He had to say the right things, as Reagan did, and had to do it in a way that helped reporters tell the story. Check, check, check. But he went one step too far on the beach. The story got legs because we went off script to satisfy security needs and placate Eddie Adams and *Newsweek*. I pushed my stagecraft to the limit into risky territory, the mix of an emotionally raw moment, a pile of stones and a president with too much time on his hands. I unknowingly provided a prop to the president, one that he seized on. Clinton tried to express his grief in a deeply personal way, and it backfired miserably.

SCRAMBLE IN THE FILING CENTER

Just like in Normandy, the scene at the Dukakis filing center in Sterling Heights six years earlier was one of pictures and images moving on wires and bouncing off satellites, and a story sprouting legs. The legs would get progressively longer in the ensuing weeks and, fairly or not, contribute to Michael Dukakis's political obituary.

The final page of Matt Bennett's six-page narrative on advancing Dukakis and the tank has nothing to do with actual advance work. Eager for instant feedback, he monitored how the event was being analyzed by the most important judge: the media. They were indeed the judge, and often jury, of how political events "played" and also, two decades before the arrival of social media, the only conduit through which Americans would have the slightest inkling of what happened at General Dynamics Land Systems.

The global media gathering at campaign events in the weeks counting down to an election are a big, diverse, competitive group. Among those signing up for transportation on planes and buses, and for phone lines and electrical power at event sites, are print reporters, TV and radio correspondents, producers, cameramen, sound technicians and photographers. They see events in different ways, through different prisms, catering to different audiences, seeking different angles to make their coverage unique. And they're in a rush. They might have an hour to work before the buses pull out.

"Setting up the file," the makeshift traveling newsroom, falls to the press advance person. To ease the logistics of moving from an event to a workspace, the grandly named "filing center" is located near the site, often in a vinyl tent sparsely furnished with banquet tables, chairs and phone lines. There is nothing grand about it, but it is the reporter's temporary home. To keep the press corps—numb from repeated takeoffs and landings each day—further anesthetized in this nomadic existence, the advance team furnishes the filing center with a hot buffet meal, larded with pasta and trays of desserts. Campaigns do not lend themselves to healthy lifestyles. A complex accounting system managed by the campaign ensures that media organizations using the jet and ground transportation, workspace, technology and food are billed back their proportional share of the costs.

While advance people like Bennett do their work, harried reporters scribble their observations in notebooks while other reporters, anchored to their computers, course their fingers frantically over their keyboards, racing against deadline to turn a moment on the campaign trail into a narrative story. Cameramen and photographers shoot the action on videotape or film (and now digital media cards). The video gets edited onsite into stand-alone "packages," or the footage is transmitted raw and unedited via satellite to network bureaus for inclusion in other stories. The still pictures, back then, were couriered as film rolls to a processing darkroom and wired to newspapers around the country.

Collectively, a vast multimedia archive is created in the filing center from a single event that unfolds over the course of just a few minutes. Such was the case with Dukakis and the tank, and Bennett wanted to watch the process unfold with his own eyes.

"The ladies and gentlemen of the press were laughing so hard when they saw the helmet-clad governor that an NBC crewman almost fell under the tread of the passing tank. They did not, as we naively hoped, use the more flattering footage of the helmet-less Duke, opting instead for the infamous Snoopy pictures," Bennett wrote in his journal.[9]

Joe Lockhart remembers it differently. "The interesting thing for me was that the Dukakis advance operation didn't have a visual flair. It was just, sort of, 'Put a microphone up and have him talk.' The television people were frustrated that they never got a good picture of Dukakis after eight years of Reagan. They would tell me, 'This is not hard.' So, we do this event, and at least two, maybe three of the main TV producers came up to me afterwards and said, 'This is the best event you guys have put on since you've been doing this campaign. You finally figured it out. Do more of this.'"[10]

"Do more of this" worked for Reagan, who leaned into his role. It didn't work for Dukakis, who looked during his ride like he wanted to pull the lever on the M1A1's ejector seat, if it had one.

Lockhart wouldn't accept the "do more of this" reassurance as the verdict on what he just saw and waited for the first "wire report" to confirm the success. Wire reports, written by correspondents for the AP, Reuters or in those days UPI, would appear in newspapers that didn't have manpower or budget to send their own reporter on the bus. The stories, usually written sparely, without flair or flourish, would get an edit in "the bureau," adding in detail gathered from around the campaign for extra context. The story then moved onward "over the wire" to news organizations subscribing to the feed.

As Bennett wandered over to the filing center to take stock of his work, those stories were in the final stages of composition. Jim Irwin of the AP was one of the first to file a story with a Sterling Heights dateline. "Michael Dukakis donned a helmet and coveralls Tuesday to take a spin in a tank," began Irwin's lead paragraph, "then emerged to declare his support for beefed-up conventional spending." For color, Irwin added in the second paragraph, "A smoke screen of oil fumes trailed from the tank during its 10-minute jaunt at speeds approaching 40 mph."[11] Color, as it's known, from events like this settles deep within the consciousness of news consumers and takes on a life of its own.

Senator Carl Levin, one of the speakers at the 1,000-person speech following the tank ride, added more color for Irwin's dispatch. Addressing the crowd at Land Systems, he said, "Today we witnessed the best tank driver of all the candidates for president."[12]

Irwin also quoted Dukakis directly. "We need a new president," Dukakis said, "who will invest our dollars in the fiber and muscle of our national defense," with the candidate adding, "I am going to make our conventional military one of our top priorities. We are not going to squander billions on weapons that don't work."[13]

Working nearby Irwin were veteran reporters of the major national newspapers. If wire pieces just give the facts, big-time reporters weave in analysis, perceptions and atmospherics. In 1988, decades before these scribes would shoulder the added burden of blogging, tweeting and creating multimedia content for their news "platforms," they were on the hook for only one story per day of 1,000 words or so, which they transmitted via dial-up modems to meet a late-afternoon filing deadline. Their pieces filed, these reporters could get back on the bus to the airport or hotel for a few drinks in the bar and an overnight stay. Bob Drogin of the *Los Angeles Times* and Bernard Weinraub of the *New York Times* were among the big-time boys on the bus that day in Sterling Heights.

Drogin was a keen observer of Dukakis's self-assuredness on policy matters and discomfort with political stagecraft. Under the headline "Dukakis Calls for Use of Economic Leverage on Soviets" and featuring a photo of Dukakis in the gunner's hatch of the M1A1, he filed a 1,274-word story for the September 14 edition, fairly long even by 1988 standards.[14] When Drogin filed a piece months later analyzing why Dukakis lost, he wrote that "the tank fiasco . . . helps explain how and why a nominee who seemed unbeatable in July lost the election to George Bush by a wide margin on Tuesday."[15]

That assessment of Dukakis's fatal flaws was just beginning to germinate while Drogin raced to finish Wednesday's article. Before getting to the tank visuals, he referenced the morning speech in Chicago, saying that "Dukakis stressed that the United States can take advantage of serious Soviet economic problems and new Soviet leadership to press for reductions in Warsaw Pact forces in Europe, to end nuclear proliferation, to reduce domestic terrorism, to bring respect for human rights and to ease repression in Eastern Europe."[16]

It was all good, so far. The substance on defense week was getting through. If you're a campaign staffer in Boston perusing the clips from Sterling Heights, you like what you're reading from Drogin's lede. But Drogin then turned his attention to the tank.

> To provide a fitting TV backdrop, Dukakis later donned a jumpsuit and roared around a grassy field in an M1A1 Abrams battle tank. Perched in the gunner's hatch, he grinned under a huge helmet, his hands on a 7.62-millimeter machine gun.
>
> With a General Dynamics technician at the controls, the 63-ton tank suddenly lurched into high speed and aimed toward a line of reporters. It cornered at the last second, spraying a cloud of dirt, but the giant 120-millimeter cannon barrel swung low as it turned and nearly decapitated a cluster of TV cameramen.
>
> Back in his suit, and on a flag-draped stage flanked by six more tanks, Dukakis appeared pleased by his mock assault on the national press. "What did you think?" he asked. "Did I look like I belonged up there?" Delighted aides played the theme from the film *Patton* when the rally ended.[17]

That's called *color*. When there's too much of it, substance gets buried, and that's what happened on September 13. Among Drogin's readership in the Los Angeles media market, Johnny Carson's writers at their Burbank studios were taking note of the words and looking at that front-page picture as they prepared that evening's monologue.

Bernard Weinraub, Drogin's competitor who was covering the campaign for the *New York Times,* dispensed with substance altogether for the story that he was writing for the *Times*'s readers on the other coast. Contrasting with Drogin's 1,274 words, Weinraub filed a far shorter piece that amounted to 274 words oozing sarcasm.

"Forget John Wayne and Clint Eastwood. Forget Rambo. Meet Macho Mike Dukakis," read Weinraub's lead paragraph. "At least that's what his image makers are struggling to convey," Weinraub continued, adding, "Mr. Dukakis spent an inordinate amount of time showing he wasn't one of those pasty, buttoned-up Cambridge types, soft on defense, the kind of fellow George Bush rails against." Further down, Weinraub wrote, "The Democratic candidate grinned like Sly Stallone. The tank sped, invasion-style, but slowed as the driver pointed the 120-millimeter cannon's turret conspicuously toward reporters in the stand. Those in the first row ducked beneath the gun."[18]

In the penultimate paragraph of his brief dispatch, Weinraub, referring to the governor's "new make-my-day style," quoted him murmuring "Rat-a-tat." Weinraub added, "No one fell. Then the band played the theme song from the film *Patton,* lest anyone forget that Macho Mike had come and gone."[19] With Weinraub as the chronicler of Sterling Heights, Carson didn't need his staff of comedy writers to polish the humor contained within.

THE PACKAGE

It would be unseemly for Matt Bennett to peer over Drogin's or Weinraub's shoulders as they pecked away on deadline at their early generation laptops. There's an unwritten rule about filing centers. Reporters work out in the open at banquet tables, but the presumption is that they're working privately in their newsrooms. Bennett would have to wait until the next day to read what they had written. But since the TV footage came with sound, he could readily eavesdrop on what the TV correspondents were seeing on their monitors, "tracking" into their microphones and saying to their producers, either in person or through a squawk box. He could also watch and listen to how they recorded their "stand-ups" into camera. This chatter might have given Bennett a sense of how the event was really going down.

Compared with the reporting of the elite newspapers on the West and East Coast, how the event played on TV, in the 1988 campaign cycle, would have an outsized impact on how the electorate judged the candidate. While the top-rated prime time show on NBC averaged 23 million viewers that season, the nightly network news shows still captured a fair share of that audience. In 1988, the combined average evening news viewership on NBC, ABC and CBS was over 40 million people.[20] On any given night in 1988, Tom Brokaw's *NBC Nightly News,* which included about twenty-three minutes of recorded "packages" and seven minutes of ads, was watched in about 10 percent of the nation's roughly 90 million households.

After the event concluded, NBC's Chris Wallace took his place in front of one of the M1A1s to record his stand-up. It was nine sentences that, when edited together with footage from the tank ride and other video from the campaign trail that day, would comprise exactly two minutes of NBC airtime, including Brokaw's "toss" to Wallace.

Watching a nearly thirty-year-old newscast, complete with ads, is like stepping into a time machine to see an America unencumbered as it is today by marketing pitches for controlling maladies like bladder control and erectile dysfunction. In Brokaw's September 13, 1988, edition of *Nightly News,* a full five minutes were devoted to reporting on the campaign. The political segments followed a cheery ad featuring a flirtatious couple touting Kellogg's new product, the Nutri-Grain Biscuit.[21]

As the Nutri-Grain spot ends, Brokaw returns to screen, looking like the young man of our memory, in blue suit and yellow tie, the "Decision 88" graphic over his left shoulder. He tells his audience about mounting problems plaguing the Bush campaign, mentioning the resignations of his staff members over the anti-Semitism issue, with the photo of Bush in the graphic, against a blue backdrop, looking a little beleaguered.

Shifting in his chair, Brokaw segues to Dukakis as the image over the anchor's shoulder switches to a smiling Governor Dukakis against a more vibrant red backdrop, as if the producers were judging through their photo selection and graphic treatment which candidate had a better day. "For his part, Michael Dukakis took the gloves off today and took on Bush and his running mate, Dan Quayle," Brokaw said, setting up the toss to his colleague in the field. "NBC's Chris Wallace is traveling with the Dukakis campaign tonight."

As the package starts, Wallace is heard but not seen. As footage plays of the tank approaching the press riser, Wallace says, "Don't call Michael Dukakis soft on defense. Today he rolled across the plains of Michigan like George Patton on his way to Berlin." Establishing in the initial frames that Dukakis was in the turret, the footage shifts to the long-shot of the Abrams maneuvering at full speed, the candidate indiscernible. "Continuing his blitz on national security issues," Wallace says (the word *blitz* evoking, of course, World War II imagery), "Dukakis rode on an M1 tank, one of the few weapons he wants to spend more on than the White House does."

Only watching the next frames over and over, many years later, could I more fully appreciate that the man in the tank seemed to be holding on for dear life. Had it been me, I would have been grateful for the helmet that was protecting my head. The grainy video shows Dukakis clutching the tank's machine gun with his right hand, and with his left hand a steel railing at the lip of the turret hatch. Barely visible, to Dukakis's right, is the helmet of Gordon England, the governor's official escort from General Dynamics. This is the last image that viewers of *Nightly News* saw of Michael Dukakis in the tank.

But the package wasn't over. Not by a long shot. The next bit of imagery and sound would come from the speech after the ride. Still off camera, Wallace tells viewers, "And talking to the people who make the tank, he fired a round at George Bush." Introducing that thought is the cutaway shot from the post-ride speech, the camera shooting over the governor's left shoulder to the crowd beyond. Adding to the composition, beyond the crowd, is the massive American flag that Bennett and Weeks had draped over the General Dynamics hangar that morning. Seeing your cutaway used so prominently and effectively in a network news package elicits high-fives from advance people, the visual reinforcing a perception that large crowds are listening attentively and approvingly to every word that the candidate says.

Dukakis is heard for the first time in the next frames, the "head-on" shot of the speech, which again shows Bennett's mastery of advance. The tight shot needs to tell a visual story, and this one does. From the camera recording the speech from a platform behind the crowd, the machine gun of an M1A1 is trained directly at the lens, buttressing a rhetorical question issued by the candidate. Dukakis asks his audience, "If you can't stand up to the Ayatollah, and if you can't say no to Noriega, what are you going to do at the other side of the table with Mikhail Gorbachev?"

With this shot lobbed at the Republicans, the action now shifts, to lend drama to the package, to a scene that Wallace couldn't witness, an event from that same day when the vice presidential nominee, Dan Quayle, appeared in Indiana. The event is far less polished than Dukakis's, with an establishing shot of Quayle and his wife, Marilyn, being introduced to a small audience in the corner of a low-ceilinged, crowded room. "The Republicans are trying to stop this image-toughening," Wallace reported. "Today Dan Quayle ridiculed Dukakis's foreign policy credentials." With characteristic sheepishness, the Indiana senator sounds almost embarrassed as he stands before a bank of microphones to deliver a canned attack line. "The governor of Massachusetts," Quayle pauses for emphasis, "he lost his top naval advisor last week. The rubber duck drowned in his bathtub."

It's a weak line, but the Quayle setup allows Wallace and his editors to switch the action back to Chicago and the day's first event, Dukakis's speech before the Chicago Council on Foreign Relations. The sequence begins with an establishing shot of the room in the Chicago hotel. Wallace, off camera, says, "The governor views Quayle as one of his best attack points in going after Bush." Wallace's voice-over, steering a viewer sympathetically toward Dukakis, is notable given the correspondent's long career that followed 1988 as an anchor and Sunday-morning talkshow host for Fox News Channel.

With the action still in Chicago, the shot shifts from the wide shot to the close-in, head-on shot, allowing Dukakis another rhetorical question, this time issued with a backdrop of carefully placed American flags. Referring to Bush, Dukakis says, "My friends, if he truly believes that J. Danforth Quayle is qualified to be one heartbeat away from the presidency, how can we trust his judgment?"

The video shows Dukakis's head moving rhythmically left and right, another telltale sign of obsessive advance work. The hints are confirmed in the next frames, a cutaway shot revealing that Dukakis is using a teleprompter, commonplace today but rare in 1988, indicative of a major policy address. As the camera pans the room, Wallace says, "Beyond the one-liners, Dukakis laid out his views on relations with the Soviets." To emphasize the gravity of those "views," the editors include close-ups of well-dressed men and women watching intently in the front row. "His goals for arms control and ending regional conflicts sounded much like administration policy," Wallace's voice reminds us, "but Dukakis emphasized using Western economic clout to pressure Gorbachev." The nodding heads of the front-row audience members affirm the speaker's message.

In Wallace's report, Dukakis gets one more head-on sound bite, and one more rhetorical question, to punctuate Wallace's script. "He [Gorbachev] wants expanded economic contact with the West," Dukakis says. "He wants to join the international economic institutions. What is he prepared to do in return?" It's a taunt to Vice President Bush. To give the package the drama it needs, the onus is on the NBC editors to scour incoming campaign videotape from around the country that day to find a suitable rebuttal from the vice president.

What's available is a clip of Bush at a Missouri airport tarmac, local politicians flanking him on either side. Behind him are the steps of Air Force Two, guarded by military personnel. While Quayle might not have been ready for prime time in his brief clip in the NBC package, the trappings of power and symbols of incumbency frame the Republican standard bearer. Wallace says, "Later, speaking in Missouri farm country, the vice president suggested that Dukakis might oppose selling American wheat to the Soviets." With that brief lead-in, Bush gets his one counterpoint in the two-minute piece. "I will not use food as a foreign policy weapon," Bush says. "I will never go back to this grain embargo."

All that is left, before tossing back to Brokaw, is Wallace's on-camera "stand-up." It is the few seconds of airtime in which a viewer can note that the NBC correspondent slogged along with Dukakis on the trip to Sterling Heights instead of watching the action remotely from the Washington bureau. Correspondents will travel the world, logging thousands of miles, and rarely see a candidate (or president) in person, but if they can do their stand-up against an identifiable geographic marker of the event of the day, it allows the vivid imagination of the viewer to relate to how dogged the day's reporting assignment might have been.

Not to miss the opportunity, Wallace delivers his stand-up in front of Matt Bennett's formidable fleet of M1A1 tanks. "Dukakis did not offer any bold initiatives today," Wallace offered, with the olive-colored steel of one of the tanks behind him. "In fact, he said little that hasn't been said by Ronald Reagan. But for a candidate who's trying to show he's in the mainstream on foreign policy, that may not be so bad. Chris Wallace, NBC News, with the Dukakis campaign in Michigan."

That's how two minutes of news—a combination of video footage, camera angles, sound bites and narration—introduced more than 10 million people to Dukakis and the tank. A similar package, with his trademark bluster, came from Sam Donaldson for ABC's *World News Tonight.* Bruce Morton, of the *CBS Evening News,* filed a more modest report. But all three networks couldn't ignore the color. From the three packages, roughly 40 million viewers in all ended the evening of September 13 with images in their heads of Dukakis screaming across a dirt field in a machine known as Whispering Death.

Most of those who watched the news that night might have filed the pictures away somewhere in the back of their heads, mixed with advertising come-ons for Nutri-Grain Biscuits. Some might have thought, before they read follow-on stories, that Dukakis looked Reaganesque, as the TV producers suggested to Joe Lockhart. Some might have instantly concluded that he looked like an idiot. For one attentive viewer, Sig Rogich, watching the reports from his apartment in Washington, D.C., the two-minute package hatched a kernel of an idea. He grabbed a yellow legal pad and began to jot notes.

TANK YOU VERY MUCH

THE GIFT

In 1988, there was no YouTube to help stories sprout legs. For most households, there was no method of on-demand video retrieval of any kind, unless you count the small fraction of VCR owners swapping early VHS or Betamax cassettes with their neighbors. These viewers, however, were more likely consumers of illicit fare rather than videotapers of Dan Rather, Peter Jennings or Tom Brokaw. Without a method of redistributing TV news footage, it meant that news events, however noteworthy or embarrassing, often vanished forever after their first airing into the archive vaults of the TV networks. They would reappear only rarely, trotted out from time to time for a highlight reel or a documentary months or years after the fact.

The premise of something catastrophic caught on tape and spreading coast-to-coast as a viral contagion was still far in the future. The raw footage that helped to end the political career of George Allen in 2006, with his "Macaca" comment, or Mitt Romney in 2012, with the surreptitiously recorded "47 percent" video, likely wouldn't have sprouted legs in 1988 when video was on the air one day and in the vault the next. Those homicides by video started with a leak before penetrating the mainstream media vortex. For anything to break through in 1988 and "get legs," it would need an accelerant.

That thought might have reassured Mindy Lubber, Dukakis's campaign scheduler, as Chris Wallace's package aired on TV screens at headquarters in Boston. While Joe Lockhart was getting attaboys from network producers, the staff back home could ingest the news objectively, outside the candidate's sanitized bubble. Lubber said that she and her colleagues knew "instantaneously" that the tank event had backfired.[1]

"The second we saw that picture on the six o'clock news, we had pains in our stomach," Lubber said. "It didn't work. The picture is everything. Regardless of anything that came out of the governor's mouth, we saw the picture, which was Mike Dukakis with his head sticking up in that goofy hat."[2] The hope was that the mishap would fade after one news cycle, but that depended on the images remaining contained.

While Lubber had her instant reaction, so too did her GOP opponents. At Bush-Quayle headquarters in Washington, the rapid realization was that the campaign had received, in the words of deputy campaign manager and future RNC chairman Rich Bond, "a huge gift."[3] The gift would unwrap slowly. News of the tank ride made its way east from Michigan at the speed of a newspaper delivery truck. Bond remembers it wasn't until the next morning, at his usual 7 a.m. meeting with campaign manager Lee Atwater, research director Jim Pinkerton and others, that the magnitude of the gift began to come into focus.

"I think either I saw a still photo or video of it and—I don't know who cracked the joke at that point—but I remember somebody said, 'My God, he looks like Alfred E. Neuman,'" Bond told me. "Atwater and I, and Pinkerton, all about the same age, grew up as kids reading *Mad* magazine. And we just, literally, convulsed with laughter because it completely undercut, visually, any credibility Dukakis had as commander in chief. He looked ridiculous. You could tell he was a fish out of water, that he was very uncomfortable. It didn't take Roger Ailes and his team long to seize on that as metaphor of how ill-suited Michael Dukakis would have been as commander in chief."[4]

Campaigns have traditionally had two pipes through which they can broadcast a message, positive or negative, to voters. One is "free media" (now sometimes called "earned media"), where you get news organizations to spread the word. It doesn't cost anything (thus "free"), other than working the phones to reporters or spinning away over drinks in hotel bars, usually on a reporter's expense account. The other way is "paid media," where you produce an ad and pay a radio station or TV network or affiliate to run it during regular programming. Today, there's a third pipe, called "owned media," where you produce your own persuasive video content and host it on websites or blogs, distributing it further through social networks like Instagram, Facebook, YouTube and Twitter.

It would take almost five weeks for the paid-media exploitation of the tank visual to launch, but the Bush campaign's free-media machinery mobilized immediately. David Demarest, Bush's communications director, had a team of aides sitting outside his office who spent each morning combing through news clips to develop what they called the "Line of the Day." This single page of talking points was routinely run past campaign chairman James Baker and Lee Atwater for approval and then blast-faxed from a bank of ten fax machines to trusted recipients around the country. The faxing went first to surrogates on the East Coast, then to the central time zones, and finally to the West Coast. Each recipient of the Line of the Day was then instructed to fax the talking points to ten more surrogates, creating a pyramid process of early Twitter-like efficiency. The Line of the Day that seized on the Dukakis event at Sterling Heights quickly spooled its way onto thermal paper and into the output trays of a thousand fax machines.

The surreptitious onslaught still makes Demarest chuckle. "We actually had great fun with the tank," he told me. "For about three days, I think, we highlighted the tank issue in our Line of the Day, all replete with 'tank you very much,' 'no tanks,' and little plays on words like that." Demarest, who now serves as vice president for public affairs at Stanford University, added, "From where we sat, however the tank ride was calculated to portray the governor, it didn't come across that way, and it gave us an opportunity for caricature."[5]

In the September 14 edition of the Line of the Day, the morning after the tank ride, a passage from Demarest's team read, "Look for Michael Dukakis to parrot the views of conservative Senator Sam Nunn, who gave him a 'tutorial' in foreign affairs last Sunday afternoon. The American people deserve better than a crash course in international relations seven weeks before the election."[6] In the September 15 edition, the team had Sterling Heights in their sights. "Sitting in a tank does not make America stand tall," the talking points read as they snaked their way around the country electronically.[7]

Aboard Air Force Two, disciplined candidate that he was, Vice President Bush apparently got the memo. His rhetoric in the days that followed aligned perfectly with the message his headquarters was putting out. He was scheduled to visit the Flag City Festival in Findlay, Ohio, on Friday, September 16, where he would hold his first Q&A session with reporters since two weeks prior. Findlay, forty miles south of Toledo, had started to market itself as "Flag City" in the 1960s and proudly lays claim to that nickname still. For candidates wrapping themselves rhetorically in the Stars and Stripes, there's no better pulpit from which to preach. Whatever reticence Bush harbored about engaging with the press after the recent negative spate of stories about his campaign receded in Findlay, surrounded as he was by kids waving miniature flags and fortified with Demarest's talking points about the tank.

The cameras crowded around Bush as he spoke with a phalanx of Boy Scouts and Girl Scouts arrayed behind the vice president. "Now he rides around in a tank. He jumps out of the tank, takes off the helmet and comes on with different positions," Bush said. Accusing Dukakis of a "thirty-day conversion" on defense issues, he added, "He's now trying to say that the man who has opposed every new weapon system somehow belongs in a tank gunner's helmet. It's time to take another message to Michael and it's very straightforward: you cannot fool the Soviet leadership by knocking America's defenses for ten years and then riding around in a tank for ten minutes." For emphasis, echoing a line direct from Demarest's team, Bush added, "The tank did not fit."[8]

As Bush was knocking Dukakis, his image-makers crafted a powerfully pastoral scene to trump the optics Dukakis offered in Michigan. They created helmet-free, flag-infused, front-page visuals underpinning Bush's critique of his opponent. The Boy Scouts, Girl Scouts and Campfire Girls then joined the vice president to hoist a jumbo-sized American flag at the first day of the Findlay festival. "The flag is back," he said at the event, the photographers clicking away. "Today, America is flag city and we can never let that change again."[9]

By the end of the week, the Bush counterpunch, transmitted quickly around the nation through wire stories, opened the door for longer news accounts and campaign commentators to weigh in. The stories began to flow in one direction, anti-Dukakis, buttressed by a week of contrasting visuals: of one candidate in a tank and the other wrapped in flags.

On Saturday, September 17, next to a photo of Bush at the flag festival, Christine Chinlund of the *Boston Globe* observed, "Sprinkled throughout the day's patriotic message were accusations that Dukakis—Bush now calls him 'Stealth Man'—is trying to fool the American people and the Soviet government into thinking that he now supports a strong defense."[10] The Bush message team couldn't have benefited more from Chinlund's story in Dukakis's hometown paper if they'd written it themselves. This was free media at its best, hitting a candidate in his own backyard, complete with hagiographic images.

On Sunday, September 18, the *State-Journal Register* of Springfield, Illinois, offered an editorial with the headline "SOLDIER DUKAKIS CASTS A FALSE MILITARY IMAGE." With six weeks until Election Day, these editorials in battleground states had a persuasive effect on voters just tuning into the campaign. The *State-Journal Register* editorial began, "Little did we know that, behind the façade of a onetime Harvard professor and liberal governor of Massachusetts, there lurked a hidden hawk, a revanchist Rambo eager to defend America's global interests with military might." The editorialists, seizing on the "Rambo" comparison, had probably read the short Bernard Weinraub piece in the *Times* that first attached the Sylvester Stallone character to Dukakis's tank ride. The editorial went on, "Fearful of being pinned down in a politically vulnerable position by George Bush's withering soft-on-defense barrage, the Democratic presidential nominee has dropped to his knees and enacted a battlefield conversion for network film crews."[11]

Never mind that Bush was also courting network film crews for free media with his flag-draped photo ops. The *State-Journal Register* editorial writers honed in on the very same word—*conversion*—found in Bush's Findlay talking points. "Under such desperate circumstances, even the most hypocritical, opportunistic flip-flops on key issues are performed without a trace of shame," the editorial concluded.[12]

On Monday, September 19, Rowland Evans and Robert Novak weighed in with their influential syndicated column, concluding that the Dukakis campaign had erred in devoting the prior week's schedule to national defense issues. "To Bush strategists," Evans and Novak wrote, "Dukakis was playing on their turf." The duo noted that the tank ride "eclipsed on the evening news" the substantive address that Dukakis delivered in Chicago earlier in the day. "It was an unforgettable image that everybody seemed to have seen," they observed, drilling the tank further into the national subconscious. "Howls of laughter echoed through Bush headquarters in Washington," they wrote, as if they just got off the phone with Rich Bond, "where ridicule was prepared for the candidate's speech Friday. Democratic insiders could only shake their heads in dismay."[13]

By Tuesday, September 20, one week after the tank ride, and one week after Jim Irwin of the Associated Press filed his first dispatch from the filing center in Sterling Heights, another AP story confirmed that the tank ride created collateral damage on a national scale for the Dukakis campaign. "Poll Indicates Dukakis Lost Ground with Tank Ride," the headline read. The national poll of 1,002 registered voters was conducted between Friday, September 16, when Bush visited Findlay, and Sunday, September 18, after a weekend of campaign coverage in which local papers, editorial writers and pundits each took their turn creating new content from a different angle on the action at Land Systems.

Of the respondents in the poll, conducted by nonpartisan firm KRC Research, "25 percent said they were less likely to vote for Dukakis based on what they had seen or heard about the tank ride," the AP story said.[14] What voters had *seen* and *heard* was by now roundly negative. The story's legs were getting longer. In another story, KRC pollster Gerry Chervinsky said, "Even Johnny Carson made jokes about the ride. The poll is just proof of what everyone has been saying" about an event taking on a life of its own.[15]

Not that the tank ride was a total turn-off for Dukakis fans. Seven percent of respondents said it made them more likely to vote for the Democratic nominee, while 60 percent said the event hadn't hit their radar or had no effect on their opinion. It might be a silver lining.

It was a slim hope at best. In the fight for a marginal edge in battleground states like Illinois, home to that blistering *State-Journal Register* editorial in the Sunday paper, every vote counts. Extrapolating the national sample in the KRC poll onto a big, diverse, Rust Belt state like Illinois, the results are meaningful.

Illinois has been held by the Democratic nominee in every national election since 1988—Clinton twice, Gore and Kerry once each, and Obama twice again. The state has proven its Democratic mettle over and over and was ripe for a Dukakis win. And yet, of the 4,559,120 votes cast in the state on Election Day in 1988, Bush won by 94,999 votes, or about two percentage points. If 32 percent of voters, according to the poll, had their views shaped one way or another by the tank ride, four out of five of them became less likely to vote for the Democrat as a result. Applied to Illinois, with its twenty-four electoral votes up for grabs, the state became a much steeper uphill climb for Dukakis one week after he rode in the M1A1.

On Wednesday, September 21, Lois Romano, a veteran Style Section reporter for the *Washington Post,* published a 2,347-word profile of Christopher Edley, the Dukakis campaign's issues director, that couldn't escape the tank's gravitational pull. "Even last week," Romano wrote, "after he had spent what seemed like a lifetime helping to polish Dukakis' speeches on Soviet relations and defense, Edley found it hard to swallow when the evening news featured Dukakis riding in a tank."

"I guess the visual was too good," Edley told Romano. "It's disappointing. The network stories mentioned the fact that Dukakis had given an important speech on Soviet relations but said almost nothing about his policies. . . . From my point of view, instead of commenting on a tank ride for 45 seconds, they could have put five bullets on the screen that talked about the future of U.S.-Soviet relations."[16] If Edley's ire was aroused by Chris Wallace's package (which, if anything, portrayed Dukakis more positively than Bush that day), he had only his own campaign to blame.

In the final days of the general election, in an interview conducted in Kansas City, Missouri, on October 27, Dan Rather of CBS asked Dukakis, "Governor, who put that helmet on you and who put you in that army tank?" The candidate wouldn't answer, even though Rather put the question to him twice. Finally, Dukakis said, "Michael Dukakis put me in."[17] Eight days after the tank ride, as the chatter surrounding it had skewed decidedly negative, the legs of the story were long and getting longer. And yet no one would have predicted that the worst was still to come, that the ride from hell would eventually achieve its notorious stature as the worst political event in history.

THE TANK AD

Campaigns don't turn on one event, the thinking goes. From the moment Dukakis rode in the tank on September 13, there were still seven weeks until Election Day, plenty of time for a reenergized candidate to take the gloves off and fight back. A few days of negative chatter could be absorbed and forgotten, but Dukakis also needed the snafu in Sterling Heights to die a quiet death. It couldn't, by any circumstances, evolve into a groundbreaking TV ad from his opponent that used actual news footage to congeal the doubts, reflected in polls, that Dukakis didn't have what it takes.

While a stack of articles were born from the tank ride in September and October—accompanied, from time to time, by a still photo of Dukakis in the M1A1—the video began to disappear. No doubt a blow had been dealt, but memories could lapse and wounds could heal if an aggressive Dukakis emerged on the road. That was my thinking, anyway, as I headed out on the campaign trail as an advance man after the contentious October 13 debate in which Dukakis whiffed at Bernard Shaw's curveball question from the moderator about the death penalty.

I had been working for the Democratic National Committee finance team up to that point, helping the party finance chairman collect the big checks from donors that drove the DNC's get-out-the-vote apparatus. While it made for a great job on the cocktail party circuit, a life on the road was where my heart was since my stint working for Senator Paul Simon's campaign early on in the cycle. Now it was my turn to start spending some of the money that I had spent the last four months collecting.

As advance people, producing events in hamlets in the battleground states, we were living in a bubble, like Dukakis himself, cocooned within our assignments, unaware of the machinations in Boston and Washington. Those of us operating in small cells around the country had seen the headlines. We were mindful of the lessons of Sterling Heights (Dukakis never wore another hat, as far as I know), but two decades before YouTube, we assumed that footage of the tank ride was in the rearview mirror. As long as we did our jobs and built big crowds, those of us on the road were conditioned to believe a comeback was still possible.

As our advance teams hit their stride, producing increasingly effective rallies in major media markets, two Madison Avenue ad men for Bush-Quayle had already been at work for weeks secretly hatching a thirty-second spot in an editing suite that would undo all of our progress.

On the night of the tank ride, Sig Rogich, director of advertising for Bush-Quayle, was in his rented Washington, D.C., apartment, preparing to attend an evening political event. Rogich, a creative genius from Las Vegas making his way among the Eastern Establishment Republicans that surrounded Vice President Bush, was a little out of his element. Washington wasn't his town, but he committed to live there to see the campaign through. He was watching ABC's *World News Tonight* out of the corner of his eye when Sam Donaldson's package from Sterling Heights filled his screen. Watching the video, the spark of an idea instantly filled his head. Later that night, he took out a pen and yellow pad and began to sketch out a campaign ad that would eventually become "Tank Ride."

Rogich, who had served on Ronald Reagan's "Tuesday Team" that hatched the patriotic "Morning in America" spots for the 1984 reelection, had been lured away once again from his lucrative ad agency to create ads for Vice President Bush. Rogich, in turn, recruited Jim Weller, another 1984 veteran, and they began working together on the team led by Roger Ailes, the Bush-Quayle media guru.

Rogich and Weller wanted to re-create the magic that propelled Reagan to reelection over Walter Mondale. They hoped to burnish their legacy with more "Morning in America" type spots again portraying America as "the city on the hill." They began with uplifting spots featuring images of Bush and his legion of grandkids gamboling over his Kennebunkport compound, with a tender-voiced narrator and calming music to match the visuals. But they could go negative too. Just as they had brainstormed the famous "Bear" ad in 1984, suggesting Reagan was better prepared than Mondale to counter the Soviet menace, they created "Revolving Door" in 1988, the dark, portentous spot in which the narrator reminds viewers gravely that Dukakis's "revolving door prison policy gave furloughs to first-degree murderers not eligible for parole."[18]

The morning after Rogich's late-night scribbling, he shared his notes with Weller, and together they wrote the first draft of the script for their new ad. But the script was just words. In the visual medium of television, image was what counted, and there was only one visual needed for the spot percolating on the scribbled pages of Rogich and Weller.

After getting Ailes's script approval, they needed footage from Sterling Heights, easier said than done before the days of campaign trackers. Broadcast networks had the video, but none would sell it for political purposes. "We found an eleven-second snippet from an independent guy," Rogich told me, "and we bought it. If you look at the commercial closely, it's just looped. We used it over and over as we filled out the spot. And then we froze the frame at the end."[19] In all, the ad featured seven video cuts, one of them repeated and one reversed, totaling eleven seconds of footage stretched to fill the thirty-second spot. The magnified freeze frame at the end was the "money shot" from Sterling Heights, the helmeted Dukakis smiling, his finger pointing to the camera, frozen for eternity.

Rogich and Weller's script, and the independently acquired eleven seconds of tape, then required multiple rounds of editing to turn it into an ad. When one cut was finished, it would go into testing with focus-group audiences to ensure it didn't cross a line that the ad men might have been too distracted by their work to notice. The actual video of the tank ride had no soundtrack. It needed dramatic sound. To create an audio track for the spot, Rogich and Weller added artificial noises sounding like squeaky grinding gears to mimic tank treads. They then mixed these new additions with canned engine noise to re-create an enhanced sensation of watching the tank ride up close.

As initial cuts of the ad were screened and tested, Roger Ailes decreed that additional "supers," or scrolling text, be superimposed over the director's cut. The supers contained a litany of charges against Dukakis, making the ad effective even without sound.[20] Rich Bond, the deputy campaign manager for Bush-Quayle, told me that "Ailes was always very good at saying, to really test the impact of an ad, watch the ad with the sound off."[21] The supers might have strained the artistic vision of the ad and Sig Rogich's Madison Avenue sensibilities, but they twisted into Dukakis like a knife.

In much smaller white lettering, appearing for only two seconds of airtime, is the tiny disclaimer, "Paid for by Bush-Quayle '88," a vague, almost hidden reminder that we're watching a political attack ad instead of the evening news.

The final element of the spot was the narrator's deep baritone voice reading Rogich and Weller's script. For a different ad, the same narrator might have adjusted his octave and inflection to wax on about George Bush's love of family and country. Not this time. In the spot that came to be known as "Tank Ride," his tone is businesslike, approximating an objective correspondent like that of NBC's Chris Wallace:

> Michael Dukakis has opposed virtually every defense system we develop.
>
>   He opposed new aircraft carriers.
>
>   He opposed antisatellite weapons.
>
>   He opposed four missile systems, including the Pershing Two missile deployment.
>
>   Dukakis opposed the Stealth bomber and a ground emergency warning system against nuclear attack.
>
>   He even criticized our rescue mission to Grenada and our strike on Libya.
>
>   Now he wants to be our commander in chief?
>
>   America can't afford that risk.[22]

"Tank Ride," written, approved, edited, tested and finished, by Rogich's estimation, over two and a half weeks, sat in limbo after the ad team completed their work. Would it run or not? It was quite possible that one of history's most memorable political ads might never air. That final salvo—*America can't afford that risk*—cut deep into Dukakis's negatives, and the charges in the rest of the script, if true, were similarly damning. But maybe it was too much. Maybe it wasn't needed. There were variables that could alter the dynamic of the race in the coming days. Depending on current polling, the ad might be needed sooner, later, or not at all.

Almost five weeks had passed since the tank ride, and still no ad appeared on air. "We were in Seattle, Jim Weller and I," Sig Rogich told me. "We had done the spot and were comfortably ahead in the polls, according to our tracking. I questioned whether we should use the Dukakis commercial. I called [campaign chairman] Jim Baker and said, 'I'm just not sure we need it, and wouldn't it be better to close the campaign out on a real positive note?'" Even the man who first scribbled the script for the ad on a yellow legal pad was having second thoughts.

But not James A. Baker III. As Rogich told me, "Baker said, 'We took a vote, and you lost.'"[23]

The guns were loaded on Tuesday, October 18. It was a full campaign day for both candidates. With three weeks to go until Election Day, every minute and every media market counted. Governor Dukakis devoted himself completely to Michigan that day, aiming to lure back those Reagan Democrats who deserted Jimmy Carter and Walter Mondale and secure the twenty precious "winner-take-all" electoral votes that came with them. He held rallies in Kalamazoo, Saginaw and—with a sunset speech set against the backdrop of the MacLouth Steel Products Corporation—Trenton, Michigan. Years later, MacLouth would go bankrupt, leaving the hulking remains of the plant to rot away. But on October 18, it stood tall as a setting for the diminutive candidate trying to regain his stride.

For his part, Vice President Bush headed to Westminster College in Fulton, Missouri, again seizing a Reaganesque backdrop. Westminster was the spot where, in 1946, former British prime minister Winston Churchill, a hero of World War II, visited the United States to deliver his famous speech in which he coined the phrase "the Iron Curtain." The Cold War may have been playing out its final stanza in 1988, but it could still be milked for Republican stagecraft. Bush used the speech to warn, referring to Dukakis, that "it would be far too simple, even dangerous, to conclude that Soviet foreign policy is driven exclusively by economic weakness." He added that the Soviets are "also restrained by our strength, our ability to deter aggression, the unity of the democracies."[24] Bush won the day in rhetorical points, but he would win the night with advertising dollars.

That evening, after the network newscasts featured another round of packages from the campaign trail—Dukakis in Michigan, Bush in Missouri—voters might have thought they could unwind with the national pastime. The Los Angeles Dodgers traveled north for Game 3 of the 1988 World Series against the Oakland A's. The Dodgers had won the first two games of the series, but Oakland came back in Game 3, winning 2–1 on a Mark McGwire home run that secured the victory for A's pitcher Rick Honeycutt.

During the game, politics intervened between innings when, after long weeks of prep, the Rogich-Weller ad debuted on network television. The tank footage had rarely been seen for five weeks. Now, as NBC announcers Vin Scully and Joe Garagiola took a break in the action, the roughly 34 million World Series viewers watched Dukakis roll once more, this time with the damning narration. A *New York Times* story about the series noted that NBC was charging as much as $275,000 for a 30-second spot,[25] a substantial investment by the Bush campaign to bring the Sterling Heights event back to life. It would pay off handsomely. While the A's would win Game 3, they would lose the series. And in between innings, when "Tank Ride" finally premiered before all of those attentive eyeballs, Bush would win over millions of viewers, and maybe the presidency too.

The next day, with Dukakis trying to build on his late-campaign momentum, his staff at Boston headquarters fought back against what they perceived as a viciously disingenuous spot. "The Bush people don't mind using innuendo instead of fact," said David D'Alessandro, the head of Dukakis's ad team, in a *Boston Globe* story about the spot. "They don't allow facts to get in the way of an ad." Dukakis spokeswoman Lorraine Voles told the *Globe,* "It's just irresponsible. It's so misleading. Some of the information is flat-out distortion. We've seen this time and time again. These things have been pointed out to them. This is not an unconscious thing on their part."[26]

Voles proffered a litany of inaccuracies in the ad. She denied Dukakis had opposed the Grenada and Libya missions. She said he supported the Trident 2 missile system and the new Stealth bomber, two components of America's nuclear triad. She pushed the reporter to explain to readers that Dukakis did, in fact, support strong nuclear and conventional deterrence. But one woman's voice in campaign headquarters was no match for a paid media juggernaut. The *Washington Post* reported that the Bush campaign had saved half of its $30 million ad budget, in which "Tank Ride" would have a starring role, for the last three weeks of the campaign.[27] No effort by Lorraine Voles, no matter how heroic, could defend against that kind of advertising firepower.

A LIFE OF ITS OWN

In an age before YouTube opened the spigot on smartphones replaying any video at any hour of the day, Rogich's ad seared the tank in the minds of voters. It was like watching Chris Wallace's package on endless loop, but replacing the correspondent's effort to provide an objective voice-over with a one-sided closing argument to a jury of millions of people. In a piece in the *Washington Post,* Lloyd Grove wrote, "Before [the tank] was a commercial, it was news. And before it was news, it was a campaign visual." Grove described what the viewer was seeing as "the collision, and perceptual fusion, of advertising and news."[28]

Grove got big names to opine in his piece, including Roger Ailes, the man who green-lit the tank ad. "The television commercial is the art form, but television news always reflects it because television has a bias for action and pictures," Ailes told him.

Republican media consultant Robert Goodman put a finer point on it. "What is completely similar is that both advertising and television news are very controlling. They don't let you decide for yourself what to think. They tell you how to feel. The network news is theatrically produced to provide that feeling."

Giving Democrats a voice in the article, David Axelrod, who would become Barack Obama's media advisor, told Grove, "One of the things you strive for in putting together an informational or negative spot is to replicate the style of the news. It adds credibility, because you can deliver it in such a way that it appears factual."

Brian Healy of CBS added, "In the 1970s, when we looked at commercials and advertising techniques, and the pacing of popular TV programs, we saw the American mind was capable of handling a lot of different camera angles, quick shots and short bites, because Americans had seen commercials all their lives. So we have borrowed from the advertising techniques of commercial filmmaking to put our spots together."[29]

It took only eleven seconds of video for Sig Rogich and Jim Weller to contort, flip, loop and freeze the news so it looked like cinema. All that was missing was a new narration of the story, which they supplied in the form of a tightly written script.

Governor Dukakis has long said that his mistake in 1988 was a failure to punch back when attacked, but the truth is that he did try to punch back against the tank ad—and failed. On Friday, October 21, three days after Rogich and Weller's spot hit the airwaves, the Boston team aired a response featuring, surprisingly, the tank ad itself.

The one-minute spot, twice the length of the ad it took to task, opens on a TV showing two seconds of the M1A1 motoring toward the camera. Rogich's artificial tank noise is heard and the frames stay on screen just long enough to establish it is a replay of the tank ad. But just as the voice of the Bush narrator is about to begin, a hand emerges and shuts the TV off, like an authoritarian parent governing the viewing habits of a child. The camera pulls back to reveal that the parent is Governor Dukakis himself, in a blue shirt and burgundy tie. With his right hand draped over the monitor, his left fist wedged into his hip and looking right into the lens, the governor begins his response.

"I'm fed up with it," he says. "Never seen anything like it in my twenty-five years of public life: George Bush's negative TV ads. Full of lies and he knows it. I'm on the record for the very weapons systems his ads say I'm against. I want to build a strong defense. I'm sure he wants to build a strong defense. So this isn't about defense issues. It's about dragging the truth into the gutter, and I'm not going to let them do it." The script goes on for another 117 words, with Dukakis making the kind of rational and, for an ad, long-winded argument you might expect from him. Then the screen fades to black.[30]

Michael Dukakis is today, by all accounts, content as a professor of political science at Northeastern University in Boston. He and his wife, Kitty, have eight grandchildren. If he muses on the catastrophe of September 13, 1988, he keeps his thoughts largely to himself.

"Should I have been in the tank?" he told *U.S. News and World Report*. "Probably not, in retrospect. But these days when people ask me, 'Did you get here in a tank?' I always respond by saying, 'No, and I've never thrown up all over the Japanese prime minister'"—a jab at Bush, who did that in early 1992. "But, you know, things happen."[31]

Matt Bennett kept a souvenir from Sterling Heights: the gray General Dynamics coveralls that Dukakis wore during the tank ride. For years he put them on for Halloween. He once called the Smithsonian and left a message offering the suit to the Museum of American History, but no one ever called him back. According to sources I talked to, the helmet made its way back to Boston and eventually landed in the possession of John Sasso, an ironic souvenir of a failed campaign offensive and a political comeback that never came to be.

Bennett never forgot the lessons of Sterling Heights. He applied them religiously when he became Vice President Al Gore's trip director—the role Jack Weeks had played in the Dukakis race. As he told me, "If an advance person said to me, 'This is going to be bad,' I spend serious time thinking about that because I've been that guy."[32]

The many unsolved mysteries of the Sterling Heights tank ride gnawed at me for decades as I studied the art and science of advance work. People like Matt Bennett, Jack Weeks, Joe Lockhart, Madeleine Albright, Arthur Grace and Gordon England told me all they could remember about the scene just before the tank departed the hangar. It left a few critical gaps, especially what was percolating in the mind of the candidate, like *Should I take this ride, or not?* Only two people held their silence. One was Paul Holtzman, the lead advance man on the Sterling Heights team. The other was Michael Dukakis.

To give him the last word, I wrote Dukakis a note, mentioning my work for him in 1988, our shared alma mater and even the fact that he and my mother were high school classmates. "I know this is not your favorite topic," I wrote, "but I hope you would allow me to talk with you about it and get your unique perspective a quarter century later."

He wrote back the next day:

> *Josh:*
>
> *I am very grateful for all you did in 1988, and I don't want to sound uncooperative, but I think the tank thing has run its course. I didn't lose the election because of it any more than Romney lost his election because of "America the Beautiful." I lost the election because I made a decision not to respond to the Bush attack campaign, and in retrospect it was a pretty dumb decision.*
>
> *Mike Dukakis*[33]

After receiving his first response, I peppered Dukakis on several occasions by email with specific questions about September 13, even offering to come see him in Brookline to talk about it. While he was always cordial, he wouldn't reopen the wound. He wouldn't—or didn't want to—acknowledge that stagecraft matters, that it is the common denominator of television news coverage and photo journalism. These moments and images, in turn, feed polls, pundits, columns, editorials, late-night comedy and, finally, word of mouth among voters (today magnified exponentially through social networks). Knowing this, a candidate who wants to win needs to do so with style in addition to substance. It's something Mike Dukakis never wanted to accept.

Even today, the last word is not written. The story's legs inch ever longer. Every presidential campaign after 1988 had at least one key moment in which the candidate, through their own actions or those of their staff, found themselves in a Dukakis-and-the-tank-like mess. These moments shared a common thread of accentuating something about the candidate's character that, fairly or not, was stewing just below the public consciousness but needed an image to focus the press's and public's enduring conversation.

Chances are it has happened within the last twenty-four hours. Search your Twitter feed right now for the phrase "Dukakis tank" and up will pop a string of references posted within the previous news cycle to someone in the public eye doing something ill-considered. When an event from nearly thirty years ago is at the top of someone's mind somewhere, that's the definition of a story with legs. Every day, another person on another stage is "getting tanked."

The trophy president: *President Obama teaches "Politics 101"—"You don't put stuff on your head if you're president"—to the Navy football team during their White House visit to collect the Commander in Chief's Trophy. April 12, 2013. (AP Photo/Susan Walsh)*

The advance man, then and now: *Matt Bennett, with Bill Clinton's trip director, Wendy Smith, in Lansing, Michigan, in 1992 and in Washington, D.C., in 2015. (Photos/Collections of Josh King and Matt Bennett)*

Sitting pretty: *Arthur Grace's photograph in his 1989 book,* Choose Me. *A rarely seen photo depicts Dukakis on the M1A1 as his advance team wanted the day in Sterling Heights to play out—a commanding (helmetless) leader. September 13, 1988. (Photo/Arthur Grace)*

The money shot: *Going off script, the tank commander approaches the press riser, teeth bared, the M1A1's machine gun trained on the media, "Mike Dukakis" stenciled across his helmet. September 13, 1988. (AP Photo/Michael E. Samojeden)*

Before: *Dukakis and Gordon England of General Dynamics in jump suits designed for extraction in case of emergency, surrounded by the campaign entourage en route to their tank ride. September 13, 1988. (Photo/Collection of Gordon England)*

After: *Dukakis descends a portable ladder from the M1A1's turret inside the hangar at General Dynamics Land Systems at the conclusion of his high-speed tank ride. September 13, 1988. (Photo/ Arthur Grace)*

Paying for groceries: *President George H. W. Bush with an apple, a quart of milk, and light bulbs at the NCR point-of-sale exhibit at the National Grocers' Association annual convention in Orlando, Florida. February 4, 1992. (AP Photo/Barry Thumma)*

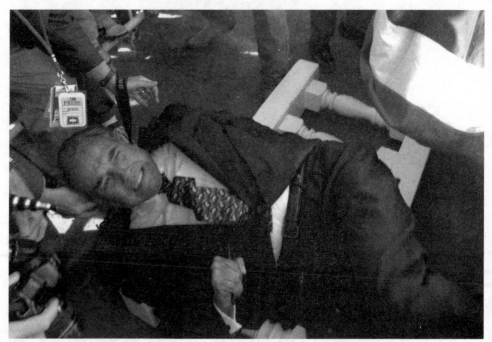

Taking the plunge: *Senator Robert Dole grimaces as his head is cradled in the hands of AFP photographer David Ake after falling from the stage in Chico, California. Ake didn't get the shot; Rick Wilking did. September 18, 1996. (Reuters Photo/Rick Wilking)*

Summer cruise: *Vice President Al Gore and New Hampshire governor Jeanne Shaheen paddle down the Connecticut River on July 22, 1999. A dam's floodgates were opened upstream to raise the river's water level. July 22, 1999. (AP Photo/Toby Talbot)*

The green screen: *Senator John McCain speaks before a new green backdrop in Kenner, Louisiana, on June 3, 2008. The Colbert Report converted the video into a chroma-key composite that allowed viewers to insert new, creative backdrops. (AP Photo/Bill Haber)*

Tacking: *Senator John Kerry windsurfs off Nantucket on August 30, 2004. Grainy video of the sojourn became the backdrop for "Windsurfing," a political ad from the Bush-Cheney campaign. (AP Photo/Laura Rauch)*

Vanilla walls: *Two weeks into President Obama's first term, official photographer Pete Souza snapped his boss on the phone in his private study off the Oval Office. The shot was included in Souza's "First 100 Days" Flickr album. February 3, 2009. (White House Photo/Pete Souza)*

Obama and the batsman: *It wasn't the "Field of Dreams" moment I envisioned, but cricket legend Brian Lara still taught President Obama a thing or two about keeping his eye on the ball at the Marriott in Port of Spain, Trinidad. April 19, 2009. (White House Photo/Pete Souza)*

The Beer Summit: *President Obama, Harvard professor Henry Louis Gates Jr. and Cambridge police sergeant James Crowley bury the hatchet over a brew in the White House Rose Garden. July 30, 2009. (White House Photo/Pete Souza)*

Oval briefing: *The author with President Clinton, Chief of Staff Leon Panetta, and Housing Secretary Henry Cisneros before an event in the White House Rose Garden. June 6, 1996. (White House Photo/Bob McNeeley)*

Fly on the wall: *The author, far left, with pool photographers shooting through the glass of the Oval Office as President Clinton worked on a speech. November 17, 1993. (White House Photo/Bob McNeeley)*

Best laid plans: *The author, far right, with French and American officials inspecting scale models for the 50th Anniversary of D-Day in Normandy, France. March 9, 1994. (White House Photo/Bob McNeeley)*

Flying high: *The author with advance mentor and Hollywood producer Mort Engelberg in the staff conference room aboard Air Force One. April 9, 1995. (White House Photo/ Bob McNeeley)*

Last day in office: *The author and President Clinton, with the crowd behind them in Room 450 of the Eisenhower Executive Office Building, in a pose that Clinton would regularly strike at rallies at the author's request. December 9, 1997. (White House Photo/Bob McNeeley)*

PART TWO

GETTING TANKED, 1992–2012

HISTORY REPEATS ITSELF

Or Does It?

WHAT ARE THE OPTICS ON THIS?

The Roosevelt Room in the West Wing of the White House, located just steps from the Oval Office, serves as an all-purpose meeting space for staffers. Prior to big events in the final stages of planning, with the portrait of Teddy Roosevelt by Tade Styka watching from above the fireplace, those of us on staff would convene meetings to walk through the logistics of upcoming domestic or international forays. The dialogue had a familiar pattern. I could almost set my watch to when one senior advisor or another, troubled by something he or she just heard, would hush the others around the mahogany conference table and ask, "What are the optics on this?"

If you've ever worked in politics, you've probably found yourself in a similar conference room, strategizing over the "optics" of a campaign event. Chances are that you, or someone beside you, has cautioned about the perils of your candidate looking like the next "Dukakis in the tank." When the most seasoned political pro, a thoughtful master of the issues, declares, "It's not about the optics," it's probably about the optics.

The conversation has traversed that course in every presidential or midterm election cycle since 1988. As much as the strategic "wise men" (and women) hew toward "substance," the common denominator in politics is what people see, and how they react to what they've seen. Whatever you call it—the image, visual or picture—that is what participants in these meetings obsess over, just as Teddy Roosevelt fussed over how photographers saw him in his Brooks Brothers tailored uniform leading his soldiers up San Juan Hill.[1] Belying the cautions throughout the history of American politics, in each of the elections since Dukakis's ride, someone, somewhere, gets tanked.

In politics, in the face of obvious disaster, history repeats itself. Even before my firsthand experience with the advance men and women in 1988, I curated a sense of which visuals worked and which ones didn't. This particular set of skills involves seeing a public moment framed in multiple dimensions and from multiple perspectives.

For starters, you have to put yourself in the candidate's shoes, seeing a crowd the way he or she sees it. You also have to visualize how everything will look from the wings, standing with the staff, praying that calamity won't strike. From another angle, you have to be a voter in the crowd, taking it all in like a fan at a ballgame. At still another vantage point, you have to be on the press riser with the reporters, sharing their jaundiced view of it all. You also have to be back in the newsroom, thinking like an editor with a business sense of how it will "drive clicks" or look in tomorrow's paper. You have to be in the voter's home, watching the nightly news package on a sofa and rendering an opinion on how the scene moves you. Finally, you have to be at the water cooler in the office the next day, sharing a laugh over the candidate's miscue as filtered through a late-night comedy show or tipping your hat to his bravura performance.

When you can see politics from each of these angles, and see it a few days *before* the event is scheduled to take place, you have the makings of a solid advance man.

THE MAKINGS OF AN ADVANCE MAN

I don't know exactly when I started seeing politics across these dimensions. Though I have hazy memories of Richard Nixon residing in the White House, I have only vague recollections, as a seven-year-old, of news reports about George McGovern, Nixon's 1972 opponent. I hold more vivid impressions of Election Night, 1976, amplified by a photograph of eleven-year-old me in pajamas—the PJs hidden by a blue blazer—accessorized by one of my dad's neckties. I am seated at a bedsheet-draped aluminum typing table temporarily positioned in the vestibule of my parents' dining room.

Behind me, affixed to the wallpaper by tacky adhesive that displeased my mother, a six-foot-wide, homemade U.S. map fashioned from tracing paper provided a theatrical backdrop. A black rotary phone, connected to nothing, detritus from a household swap to touch-tone from a few years back, sat on the table within arm's reach. I wanted the phone to be "hotline" red, but I had to take what I could get. A Radio Shack earphone, flesh-colored wires coiled like a strand of DNA, was jammed into my ear. It actually had a purpose: it was connected to a portable radio with a feature allowing it to tune into VHF broadcast channels, in my case WBZ-TV-4, then Boston's NBC affiliate.

Connected like this to network TV audio, I was plugged in to the Election Night "Decision '76" coverage team of John Chancellor and David Brinkley reporting from Rockefeller Center. My audience of two, mom and dad, watched rapt as I regurgitated Chancellor's commentary that was flowing into my ear, giving my parents real-time results from across the country. My updates, like the networks', tracked the closing of polling places from east to west in the continental United States. Cutouts of the states, in blue and red, were ready for me to tape onto their respective positions on my map—my version of NBC's "Big Board"—when Chancellor broke in with the network's call. I had spent several days making the state cutouts. California was easy. Michigan was fun. Maryland was a bitch.

Above the map was a tally board that I would amend through the night with stenciled numbers on three-by-five-inch index cards recording electoral votes for Jimmy Carter and Walter Mondale and their opponents, Gerald Ford and Bob Dole. They weren't as visible as network chyrons, but my stenciled cards recorded the final results: 297 for Carter and 240 for Ford. My blue cutouts filled in the western states and red filled in most of the east, including a sweep of Texas and the South, visual reinforcement for my reporting that it was Carter's night, a pleasing result for a pediatrician and his social-worker wife. In one home in Waban, Massachusetts, at least, my coverage beat Cronkite in the ratings.

Never losing the excitement of that night, I went to work twelve years later, fresh out of college, on the 1988 presidential campaign. While I was a Reagan fan for most of the 1980s, a real-life version of Michael J. Fox's Alex P. Keaton character on NBC's *Family Ties,* my disillusionment over the Iran-Contra scandal initiated a political conversion somewhere between my junior and senior year. Heading to Washington after receiving my degree, I thought my own conversion would be mirrored around the country, with the outcome of the '88 election differing from the 1984 and 1980 campaigns. What did I know?

I followed politics enough to know that Reagan had the Democrats' number when he led the ticket. But Reagan had ridden in his last rodeo. His campaign-trail magic, so perfectly tuned to the early 1980s, was term limited. His anointed successor, George Herbert Walker Bush, didn't seem to have the right stuff. Like many Americans being reintroduced to Bush as a presidential candidate for the first time in nearly eight years, I was amused by *Newsweek*'s October 19, 1987, cover photo of the vice president in his yellow rain slicker. It featured Bush behind the wheel of his cigarette boat off Kennebunkport, with the ironically derisive headline "George Bush Battles the 'Wimp Factor.'"[2] The image looked stout enough—the storied navy aviator ready for another voyage into battle—but the jumbo-sized white words superimposed on the picture twisted a viewer's perception.

Indeed, the vice president's son, the future president George W. Bush, fumed over the photo and berated the article's author, Margaret Warner, about the magazine's layout. "I was red hot," the younger Bush wrote in his memoir, *Decision Points*. "I got Margaret on the phone. I . . . told her that I thought it was part of a political ambush. She muttered something about her editors being responsible for the cover. I did not mutter. I railed about editors and hung up. From then on, I was suspicious of political journalists and their unseen editors."[3]

If it was an ambush by *Newsweek*'s editors, I was caught in it too. From my superficial vantage point just a few months out of college, looking at that picture and thinking about that headline, I thought this guy could be taken.

Just before I graduated, the Democrats lost their front-runner, Gary Hart, to scandal. In 1984, unschooled in early season political field tactics where activist support and organization can trump image, I had picked Hart to win. Back then, like many others, I was visually captivated by Hart when, wearing Levis, a plaid shirt and red suspenders, he scored a bull's-eye in an axe-throwing competition at the annual Woodman Conclave in Berlin, New Hampshire. Hart politely declined an offer to compete in the log-sawing and pole-climbing competitions but eagerly took a full-length double-bit ax in hand and flung it at a three-foot target twenty yards away. As Jeff Greenfield wrote in *Then Everything Changed*, "the footage made every weekend newscast, and became the image in every piece all that week in the run-up to the primary."[4]

I hadn't seen optics like that since looking at pictures by presidential photographer Michael Evans of Reagan clearing brush with a chainsaw at his Santa Barbara ranch. With his lumberjack routine and Rocky Mountain mystique, Hart seemed to do Reagan one better and was ready to draw a generational contrast with Walter Mondale, and Bush, too, in the general election.

But Hart was gone, the victim of his own brazen dare to the media to put a tail on him, his reputation permanently tarred by a smoking-gun photo with bare-legged Donna Rice on his lap in Bimini. The photo, which Rice acquaintance Dana Weems provided to the *Miami Herald*, was eventually made public after Hart suspended his campaign.[5]

Rumors were one thing, but the Bahamian shot of the smiling Rice in a white cotton sweater reclining on the senator, he wearing a tee shirt bearing the silkscreened logo of the *Monkey Business*, the eighty-three-foot yacht on which Rice and Hart sailed, sealed his fate for history. Like the goofy black-on-white label on Dukakis's tank helmet four years later, the words "Monkey Business" branded across Hart's chest were right out of Nathaniel Hawthorne. Had the ship been called something innocuously maritime, the awfulness of the Weems snapshot might not have constituted political suicide. But "Monkey Business" on Hart's shirt captioned the image better than any newspaper photo editor could hope to.

Hart wasn't the only candidate who had a decent shot to turn back Bush. With Dick Gephardt, Michael Dukakis, Bruce Babbitt, Al Gore and Joe Biden, and others who flirted with candidacy, including Mario Cuomo, Bill Clinton and Chuck Robb, there was enough Kennedy-esque timber among the 1984 class of candidates to outgun the incumbent vice president, the guy *Newsweek* labeled a wimp.

Even with Hart gone, I sensed that newsmagazines would eat up images of another true-eyed axe thrower. Governor Babbitt had some of that outdoorsy ruggedness, manifested by photos of him biking across Iowa and hiking in the White Mountains of New Hampshire. But even that level of fleecy athleticism probably wasn't required to beat the tennis-playing Bush. As *Newsweek*'s cover hinted, Bush's patrician air smelled like mildew to a certain segment of the electorate. If that wasn't enough, the stain of scandal tattooed on him by the Iran-Contra affair seemed enough to sink his candidacy. But again, what did I know?

With Bush tarred by a leading newsmagazine as something less than the presidency required, with its additional constitutionally bestowed title of commander in chief, I didn't imagine 1988 would hand a three-peat to the GOP. Whoever the Democratic nominee ended up being, I plotted my route to the White House coursing through New Hampshire. I knew the state top to bottom from a lifetime of skiing there. I could get from Point A to Point B, thus passing my first test as an advance man. Following a brief detour in Washington after graduation, I arrived in Manchester in the summer of 1987, my possessions stuffed into a used Volkswagen Jetta, and made my first home in the Granite State in a ramshackle apartment on the east side of town.

SANTAYANA'S MAXIM

I wasn't a standout student at Swarthmore, an academically intense institution where my freshman classmates already had courses in political philosophy under their belts when they showed up for orientation. Instead of Hobbes and Locke, my guiding lights were Chancellor and Brinkley. If I did brave a philosophy class, I'm sure I never studied the Spanish naturalist George Santayana, who wrote in his 1905 treatise *Reason in Common Sense*, "Those who cannot remember the past are condemned to repeat it."[6]

Santayana's maxim is readily applied to political and military conflicts. The origins of World War I have been compared to Russia's 2014 annexation of Crimea. The CIA's use of waterboarding to extract information from Al Qaeda suspects after 9/11 has drawn many analogies, including the 1902 use of the "water cure" by U.S. troops in the Philippines against the *insurrectos* during the Spanish-American War.[7] So much about the Age of Optics, it seems, comes with a precedent.

Santayana references veer from the serious to the comic. Presidential debates are fertile territory for cautionary tales of repetition. In the modern era, Ronald Reagan humbled Jimmy Carter in his October 28, 1980, debate with his "There you go again" line.[8] He did it again four years later, on October 21, 1984, in his second debate against Walter Mondale. Responding to a question from Henry Trewhitt of the *Baltimore Sun,* he said, "I am not going to exploit, for political purposes, my opponent's youth and inexperience."[9] Scrupulous coaching of Mondale should have prepared him for an attempt by Reagan at a comic put-down.

One of the strategists who coached the seventy-two-year-old Reagan to victory that year might have been a surprise to some. According to an account by veteran Republican operative Roger Stone, Stone hand-carried a long memo to Reagan from former president Richard Nixon urging humor to upend the age issue in the debate. "Don't try to hide from the age thing," Nixon wrote, according to Stone, "make a joke about it." Reagan did just that. "Everybody roared," Stone remembered, "and that was the end of Mondale."[10]

Entering the 1988 campaign, my handicapping of the race drew on memories of those two debate moments and how the candidates comported themselves in public. In 1980, Carter appeared dour, bearing the burden of the fifty-two American hostages held captive in Iran. Without having to shoulder that responsibility, Reagan, coming off two terms as California governor, appeared upbeat in public. In 1984, history repeated itself again. Walter Mondale, the inheritor of Carter's legacy, carried his predecessor's dour demeanor with him onto the public stage. Compare that to Reagan in 1981, who cracked jokes upon entering the George Washington University Medical Center after surviving an assassination attempt, appearing unflappable in even the direst of circumstances.[11]

Could it be that, in 1988, the Republicans could play the western optimism card again and win once more? If George H. W. Bush, born in Massachusetts and raised in Greenwich, Connecticut, was the man holding that hand of cards as a Texas transplant, it didn't seem likely. Not likely unless, as fate would have it, his opponent turned out to be Michael Stanley Dukakis.

One of Carter's defining moments came on July 15, 1979, the "Crisis of Confidence" speech, remembered today as the Malaise Speech even though that word—*malaise*—wasn't actually used in Carter's text but was found in an outline for his remarks in a memo from pollster Patrick Caddell.[12] Carter, returning from a presidential trip to Japan, had planned to spend a few days of downtime in Hawaii on the return leg; instead, he canceled his vacation to head to Camp David to work on his remarks. The speech's confessional tone, and the messy cabinet shakeup that followed, gave Carter a momentary uplift, but critics soon pounced on it. The fallout was never forgotten.

Similarly, on June 19, 1984, at his speech at the Democratic National Convention in San Francisco to accept his party's nomination, Vice President Mondale told the delegates, and the millions of voters watching at home, that "Mr. Reagan will raise taxes, and so will I. He won't tell you. I just did."[13] I watched his speech again recently. Many of his words were poetic, but the tinny, Minnesota-accented timbre of his voice didn't match the gravity of his pronouncement. Mondale's strong, no-nonsense message might have landed in viewers' ears differently if it was delivered more authoritatively. Responding to the delegates' frenzied "We want Fritz" interrupting chants, Mondale smiled, looking almost puckish just after delivering his most remembered line. In her book *Packaging the Presidency*, Kathleen Hall Jamieson observed that "where the focus of the Democratic fall campaign should have been on whether Reagan was being truthful in saying he would not raise taxes, the Democrats instead permitted the Republicans to identify Mondale as a gleeful taxer."[14] Like the Malaise Speech, Mondale's honesty backfired in performance with his body language.

I should have seen it all coming four years later. The possibilities seemed so different at the Omni in Atlanta, where I watched Dukakis accept the nomination with his rousing entry into the arena and the flattering lighting, booming sound and up-tempo cadence he used for his remarks. As much as advance people try to cast their candidate in a positive light, the professional production techniques of a convention speech are hard to replicate, day in and day out, on the campaign trail. Dukakis never rose again to the theatrical heights he put on display in the operatic production in Atlanta.

Four months after Atlanta, I left Logan Airport on Election Day 1988, a member of the defeated campaign, thinking back on the September 13 tank ride. I had to believe that future campaigns, Democrat or Republican, would never again make the same mistake of self-inflicting a wound in the Age of Optics that an opponent could so effectively exploit. Like me, future campaigns weren't reading George Santayana, at least not closely enough.

OVEREXPOSED

Beneath the superficial wound of an optical misstep, deeper injuries come from creating an image of someone you're not. Unless you're Donald Trump, the corollary of this, equally dangerous, is to expose your hidden flaws. Voters crave genuine authenticity, which always reveals your warts. But most warts can, or should, be concealed with self-discipline, at least long enough to serve in office and then retire from daily scrutiny.

The Dukakis team wanted to create, in their candidate, the image of a strong commander in chief, but that simply wasn't in his DNA. He was many things—an honest man and a competent executive, to name two—but not a tank commander who could fill the helmet of George S. Patton. Many members of my class of political operatives, Democrat and Republican, who came of age in 1988 haunted, as I was, by Dukakis's plight, would move on to run winning national campaigns and serve in the nation's high offices. But many, too, would repeat the mistakes of history. In ensuing campaigns, the march of technology and the changing business model of the news business would only magnify their missteps and create immediate consequences for the candidates.

Eighteen years after Dukakis's tank ride, Republican senator George Allen was running for reelection in Virginia against Democratic challenger Jim Webb. Webb was a graduate of the U.S. Naval Academy, a Vietnam veteran and the secretary of the navy under Ronald Reagan. With this long resume, Webb packaged himself as a conservative Democrat vying for a traditionally Republican seat that was skewing toward the middle by changing demographics in the Northern Virginia suburbs. In these circumstances, compounded by growing disenchantment with President George W. Bush, the seat would be tough for the conservative Allen, the son of former Washington Redskins coach George Allen, to hold.

On August 11, 2006, Senator Allen's campaign caravan brought him to an outdoor rally in the town of Breaks, near the Kentucky border. As had become common by 2006, Allen was followed by a "tracker," a person with a video camera whose primary mission was simply to record the candidate's speeches to unearth misstatements or other fodder for "oppo," or opposition research. Though it's almost redundant now when many people who show up at an event post their own smartphone footage of rallies on Facebook, tracking was a great job for kids just starting out in politics in 2006. Like so many other changes in politics, tracking was a role that didn't exist when I started working for Senator Paul Simon in 1987.

The job of tracker in the pre-iPhone age was simple. You would check the published campaign schedules for "open press" rallies held by the opposing candidate. After parking your car at the event site, you would set up your tripod and camera in some unwanted, off-center position on the press riser that the rest of the photojournalists weren't fighting for. All you had to do was train your lens toward the stage and press the "record" button. By plugging your camera's audio input into the "mult box" on the press riser, you were afforded a crisp, clean sound feed piped in from the podium. It was that easy.

As you listen to the same campaign stump speech over and over, you might become numb to what's being said. But you challenge yourself with a few simple questions as the candidate launches into rhetorical autopilot. Is the candidate saying anything on the stump that might be slightly off script? Could it be construed as out of character, unnecessarily hostile, an exaggeration or, as a negative ad might put it, a lie?

When the candidate points directly at you and says into his handheld microphone something that might be taken as a racial slur, it's a good idea to note that down for your bosses back in campaign headquarters. Then get them the tape as quickly as possible.

This actually happened at the Allen rally in Breaks, Virginia. The tracker's name was S. R. Sidarth, an Indian American born and raised in Fairfax County and employed to tote around a video camera for the Webb campaign. In the course of Senator Allen's remarks, perhaps exasperated at having been followed from event to event by someone who didn't look, at first glance, like a registered Virginia voter, Allen diverted from his standard stump speech, pointed to Sidarth and twice referred to him as *Macaca,* which was not Sidarth's name.

"This fellow here over here," Allen said, wagging his index finger at Sidarth, "with the yellow shirt, Macaca, or whatever his name is. He's with my opponent. Let's give a welcome to Macaca, here. Welcome to America and the real world of Virginia."[15] Though he didn't know it, Allen was, in fact, welcoming Sidarth to his home state.

At the time, few if any regular watchers of midterm stump speeches had any idea what the term "macaca" meant, and it will probably always be a point of debate. Explanations were offered that "macaca," or "makaka," is Portuguese for a female monkey. Other discussions of the term's roots suggested that, in the Belgian Congo, colonial whites called Africans *macaques,* or tree-dwellers.[16] In any case, the comment didn't sit well with the increasingly Democratic suburbs up north. As the days ticked away to Election Day, Allen's lead in the polls eroded. When all of the votes were counted, Jim Webb won the election by 9,329 votes, or four-tenths of one percentage point.

Eight years later, Montana senator John Walsh followed a different path to ignominy, but suffered a similar fate. Walsh brought to office prestigious military credentials, like Jim Webb, that might help him hold the seat Max Baucus occupied for thirty-five years. Capping off a distinguished thirty-three-year career in the Montana National Guard, Walsh had been appointed as adjutant general in 2008, resigning in 2012 to run for lieutenant governor, an office he held until his appointment to the Senate.

While pursuing a master's degree in strategic studies at the Army War College in 2007, Walsh wrote his fourteen-page thesis—"The Case for Democracy as a Long Term National Strategy"—that included long unattributed sections, often word-for-word, from an essay authored by the Carnegie Endowment for International Peace. The revelations exploded in a July 23, 2014, article in the *New York Times* by Jonathan Martin under the headline, "Senator's Thesis Turns Out to Be Remix of Others' Works, Uncited."[17] The telltale fingerprints of well-researched oppo could be detected between the lines of Martin's story.

The next day, on MSNBC's *Hardball,* Chris Matthews piled on Martin's *Times* piece, saying, "In politics, words matter, especially when you steal them from someone else, and then get caught red handed."[18]

To recover, the playbook called for Walsh to sit down with a national reporter in a business-like setting, look into the camera, and apologize. But the day after losing Chris Matthews's confidence, he tried to "walk back" the problem in a brief interview with Chris Moody of Yahoo News on a tree-lined street in Bozeman wearing a black vest over a short-sleeve white golf shirt, "I admit I made a mistake," he told Moody. "I've made mistakes before in life and will probably, unfortunately, make mistakes again, and you have to, you know, pick yourself up, dust yourself off and move forward."[19] Instead of taking his medicine, Walsh hedged, winding up as roadkill on the Bozeman thoroughfare. He announced on August 7, about two weeks after the Martin story appeared, that he would not seek reelection.

Walsh had been undone by a different kind of oppo than what S. R. Sidarth gathered on George Allen. No tracker was needed to unearth the fatal flaw. The evidence was delivered from a desktop. Mark McLaughlin, a researcher for the National Republican Senatorial Committee, had spotted suspicious passages in Walsh's writing. Rob Collins, the executive director of the NRSC, told an audience that McLaughlin, his researcher, "just put it through a translator that checks for plagiarism and the entire last five pages turned bright red. So he said: 'Boy, we got something here.'"[20]

From YouTube in 2006 to Mark McLaughlin's plagiarism translator in 2014, the landmines facing potential candidates have become ever more lethal. Thinking about Allen and Walsh, I kept having flashbacks to my time in New Hampshire in 1988, when the Dukakis campaign edited together, and leaked to the press, an attack video against Delaware senator Joe Biden. Biden, it appeared, had taken passages of a stump speech by British Labour leader Neal Kinnock and made them his own. This oppo work, decades later, could have been done far more efficiently by uploading the comparison reel onto YouTube and pointing selected reporters to the link.

FEEDING THE NARRATIVE

In the run-up to 2016, video of potential candidates has already been extensively catalogued for future comparison reels and negative spots. New Jersey governor Chris Christie's one-hour, forty-eight-minute "Bridge-Gate" news conference[21] on January 9, 2014, following his firing of aide Bridget Kelley, could, with editing, have provided content for a battery of negative spots if Christie had found his way onto the ticket. And if that didn't work, unfair as it may be to ridicule a candidate's personal appearance, images of him in a too-tight softball uniform at Yankee Stadium could have been construed, in a rough-and-tumble general election matchup, to make voters wonder if Christie was fit to be president.

Similarly, former secretary of state Hillary Clinton tried, with the June 2014 publication of her memoir *Hard Choices,* to set the stage for her second presidential run. Instead, in those formative months of the campaign, she gave critics early ammo to highlight the personal wealth that she and her husband amassed after he left office. Launching her book tour with an interview with ABC's Diane Sawyer, she said, "You have no reason to remember, but we came out of the White House not only dead broke but in debt. We had no money when we got there, and we struggled to piece together the resources for mortgages for houses, for Chelsea's education. It was not easy. Bill has worked really hard. And it's been amazing to me. He's worked very hard."[22] Coverage of the Clintons, both positive and negative, represents a quantifiable revenue source for news organizations when the traffic that these stories drive is calculated. The revenue only increases when the stories cast the family in a more scandalous light. The dollars started flowing again when *Hard Choices* hit the bookshelves.

Within days of the Sawyer interview, Secretary Clinton made the not-so-hard choice to walk back her comment. "I regret it. It was inartful," she told Fusion TV's Jorge Ramos. "It was accurate. But, we are so successful and we are so blessed by the success we've had. And my husband has worked incredibly hard."[23] The walk-back fueled another round of stories.

Secretary Clinton was in a tough spot. Her book deal with Simon & Schuster brought its own economic windfall and, with it, a catalyst for additional paid speaking appearances. But Simon & Schuster also needed to recoup its investment, and publicity tours both drive book sales and keep the author in the spotlight. There was little chance that Secretary Clinton would have emerged from the series of interviews without bruises to show for it.

Christie and Clinton play hardball in the Age of Optics and know the stakes well. When the governor steps before a hundred cameras trained on him, or when the secretary sits down for a televised chat with Diane Sawyer, there is money to be made on both sides of the camera. The principals and their staffs understand that the pluses of public speaking outweigh the minuses of remaining mute. Similarly, editors know that scandal stories get more readers, and support more ads, than those about health care or climate change. Christie lived to fight another day, even when his critics declared him a dead man walking. And Clinton's path to her party's nomination, burnished by her time as America's top diplomat, has endured past those early stumbles on her way.

Every day that politicians pursue a reckoning with history, they struggle with repeating history's mistakes. Scenes like the ones I experienced in the Roosevelt Room replay like clockwork. There's always someone to caution about the lessons of Dukakis and the tank. Every four years, new cautionary tales of public missteps, and the way they're characterized by the press, live on in infamy.

If you don't believe me, ask George H. W. Bush, Bob Dole, Al Gore, George W. Bush, Howard Dean, John Kerry, John McCain and Mitt Romney. Each man could see a clear path to his party's nomination when he decided to throw his hat into the ring, but each of them also had to know that the media would have their antennae up for moments that would feed the evolving narrative about them.

In 1992, "Bush and the Supermarket Scanner," the story of a simple presidential trip to Orlando, Florida, gone awry, picked up where "The Wimp Factor" left off and hurt his reelection prospects. Anything Bush did that hinted he was out of touch with ordinary Americans might be seized on by the media to advance that storyline.

In 1996, the indelible image of Dole's perilous fall from a stage in Chico, California, the moment captured painfully on film, augmented voters' impressions that he might be too old to be president. Dole, a World War II veteran, had waited patiently for his turn to be the nominee—too long, in the minds of many who chronicled his career.

In 2000, Gore tried to reintroduce himself to New Hampshire voters by canoeing down the Connecticut River, but instead reinvigorated a narrative among the press about his authenticity. Gore had no idea that the planning by his scheduling office and advance team for that event had taken a risky turn, but it didn't stop reporters from using it as prime example of who they thought Gore really was.

In 2003, the second President Bush announced what appeared to be the end of combat hostilities in Iraq, but his backdrop of "Mission Accomplished" on the USS *Abraham Lincoln* came to symbolize the pitfalls of U.S. foreign policy after 9/11. The White House tried to craft a story to explain the sign away, but even Bush would later admit it was a mistake.

In 2004, "The Dean Scream" in Iowa, which was, more than anything, the result of a faulty sound system, put an exclamation point on the end of the former Vermont governor's White House ambitions. To those in the room, the speech hit the right notes, but on television, the sound piped into the cameras made him seem unhinged.

Later that year, Democratic nominee Kerry went windsurfing off the coast of Nantucket against the advice of aides, providing imagery, like Dukakis did with the tank, for the most memorable negative ad of that campaign. Unbeknownst to Kerry, he was walking right into a Republican trap when he pulled on his board shorts.

In 2008, McCain traveled to New Orleans to reboot his brand for the general election against Barack Obama. Instead, he created a comparison that showed how badly he was outgunned. A split screen of two simultaneous events, one featuring McCain that evening in New Orleans, the other featuring Obama in Minnesota, demonstrated through live television that only one candidate was ready for prime time.

In 2012, Romney serenaded a Florida audience with his rendition of "America the Beautiful." But Romney's song, like Dukakis's tank and Kerry's windsurfer, provided a prop to help his opponent define him. Another Massachusetts politician would bite the dust at the hands of a blistering TV ad featuring his own appearance in public.

These eight memorable moments, like the unforgettable one in 1988, did not singularly destroy the political prospects of the protagonists, but they added incendiary fuel to the fire. The candidate's preferred positioning was upended, due to his own or his staff's error. These events wouldn't have happened had the candidate or politician remained cloistered, curled up with a good book. The problems wouldn't have been amplified without mistakes in strategy, tactics or execution. But each of these snippets of visual history feature a unique mix of a self-inflicted wound caught on video, exploited by opponents, and magnified by the media that willingly, sometimes carelessly, often enthusiastically, fanned the flames.

History repeated itself eight times over, with each incident telling a slightly different story, at a slightly different angle, about getting tanked in the Age of Optics. Many observers know parts of the story about a few of the moments, but few know the details about all of them, or what happened behind the scenes.

1992: BUSH AND THE SUPERMARKET SCANNER

(Or, How a Courteous Gesture Cemented the President's Elitist Label)

FLYING INTO A STORM

The first time I flew on Air Force One, in early 1993, on a leg from Andrews Air Force Base to Boston's Logan Airport, I discovered upon bounding up the rear retractable staircase one of the reasons why George H. W. Bush enjoyed his turn at the presidency and would lament losing it. The plane is awesome, and he was the first president to fly in its modern incarnation. The modified Boeing 747-400, a "VC-25A" in its military designation, is an airborne West Wing, with an expansive conference room where we could pass the time airborne doing what we'd done in the Roosevelt Room: obsess over the optics of events about to unfold.

There are two identical Air Force Ones (one with tail number 28000, the other with 29000), each with spacious living quarters for the First Family and an office for the president among its four thousand square feet of floor space. The aircraft's military crew serves a hearty menu curated to match the mood of the traveling staff. Once, after a wintry slog through Eastern Europe that brought us from France to Russia to Ukraine to Belarus, the galley staff greeted us with hot towels, cheeseburgers, French fries and beer to remind the weary sojourners that, after a quick stop in

Geneva, we were headed back home. Fully fed, we could enjoy an untroubled sleep on the long flight back across the Atlantic.

Big, beautiful aircraft need to be flown to keep their crews trained and their costs rationalized. With such airborne opulence at their disposal (the planes replaced the narrow-bodied 707s that served every president from Kennedy to Reagan), presidents take to the air with ease, destined for stops around the country, or the world, generally at least once a week.

They need to. A reality of the modern presidency is that making news requires getting out of town. The institution of the presidency, which includes the office holder and his staff—as well as the press corps—is always in search of fresh venues and backdrops to convey action and drama. Just as the president fields thousands of invitations to speak at one convention or another, news organizations want to realize a return on investment for stationing their seasoned correspondents at the White House. That return is clear when they're on the road filing newsworthy stories rather than parked in the briefing room during quiet days when the president is only holding closed-door meetings. To feed everyone's appetite for fresh imagery and color, daily action is required in front of the lens. Air Force One, and the chartered press plane that usually follows it from Andrews, leads them to the selected stage set for the day.

The president flying from Washington to Florida for a single speech, for example, with a bulky retinue of Air Force staff, Secret Service agents, staff and press in tow, is routine. Occasionally, a newspaper would print a story quantifying the total cost of such trips, often underestimating it. In response to a Freedom of Information Act Request, the Air Mobility Command disclosed in 2015 that the cost per flying hour (or "CPFH" as the Air Force calls it) for Air Force One is $206,337, which includes the cost of "fuel, flight consumables, aircraft overhaul, depot level repairables, and engine overhaul."[1]

What this doesn't include are the cost of those cheeseburgers (passengers, including the First Family, are billed for their food and beverages) or the gargantuan bill of ferrying armored limousines and helicopters to distant locales to support the president's point-to-point movements. When you add up the total tab for sending the president on a round trip visit to Alaska with a few in-state sightseeing stops—as President Obama did in the summer of 2015—the numbers add up fast. You can't fault Alaskans for inviting their leader to visit, or the president for accepting the invite. The vast expense of moving the president safely is generally understood on all sides as the cost of maintaining the institution of the presidency.

In 1992, President George H. W. Bush knew he needed to be on the road as a matter of political survival. With economic challenges closing in on him in Washington on February 4, 1992, he likely welcomed the chance to board Marine One for the ten-minute flight to Andrews and then spend a few hours aloft en route to Orlando in his airborne office. His destination was the annual convention of the National Grocers Association, where he would give a speech on the economy and have a fateful encounter with new innovations in retail point-of-sale technology. Little did the president know, as his plane began its decent over Central Florida, that history would repeat itself so soon, with Bush and the supermarket scanner becoming the Republican equivalent of Dukakis and the tank.

There were similarities, and there were differences.

Both the Dukakis and Bush episodes were fleeting ticks on the political clock, "visuals" of just a few minutes to underscore a substantive speech of greater length that followed at the same stop on the itinerary. Both were examples of two men exhibiting a polite gesture as a visiting dignitary, demonstrating curiosity about an object on display by one's host. And both events will likely be included in each man's obituary, inflection points in their impressions left on the public. At one moment, some said, Dukakis showed himself ill suited to the role of commander in chief. At the other moment, the sense from the news coverage was that Bush was out of touch, an elitist incapable of connecting with the common man.

But in other ways, the two events couldn't be more different. Dukakis's team obsessed over the tank ride, the visual itself a calculated effort to rebrand the candidate. For the Bush team, orchestrating an "official" (as opposed to political) trip to Florida in early 1992 was a routine exercise to buttress his economic plan. He would give a speech, but as an honored guest he was also expected to take "an exhibit tour," a brief diversion tacked onto the schedule to mollify a host. While the logistics of the Grocers Association tour weren't obsessed over, as Matt Bennett had done with the tank, it had the benefit of providing a visual to bolster Bush's message that private industry was doing its part to drive the economic recovery.

Another difference was that, although there were chuckles about the tank ride on Game Day, the impact of Dukakis's gaffe was slower to metastasize, the result of an opponent creating an incendiary paid TV spot that reignited negative perceptions about the candidate weeks after the fact. The impact of Bush's run-in with retail technology was almost immediate, the result of a *New York Times* reporter, Andrew Rosenthal, writing a story for the next day's paper from the cocoon of the White House filing center. Rosenthal's story, the headline that went with it and its page-one placement used the event as a metaphor to broaden the overarching narrative that emerged with *Newsweek*'s "Wimp Factor" cover from 1987.

Using a few tidbits of color provided by a print pool reporter who witnessed the exhibit tour, in addition to a video replay of the tour provided by pooled television footage, Rosenthal authored his damning 862-word story about the Orlando stop. The impact of the story was heightened by the chuckle-inducing word choice of a headline writer back in New York, who decided the reporter's copy merited an eye-catching title, and editors, who thought the story deserved to be on page one, thereby magnifying its significance to readers. "Bush Encounters the Supermarket, Amazed," ran the headline in the *Times*'s bold serif typeface. For those who picked up the front page of the February 5 edition to scan the day's top stories, Rosenthal's story began thusly:

> As President Bush travels the country in search of re-election, he seems unable to escape a central problem: This career politician, who has lived the cloistered life of a top Washington bureaucrat for decades, is having trouble presenting himself to the electorate as a man in touch with middle-class life.
>
> Today, for instance, he emerged from 11 years in Washington's choicest executive mansions to confront the modern supermarket.[2]

The biggest difference between the contrasting 1988 and 1992 events is that the Dukakis episode, seen in hindsight a quarter century later, seemed to capture a number of authentic weaknesses in the candidate and his campaign. The Bush scanner "scandal," on the other hand, while perpetuated in campaign journalism and lore even to this day, got the man wrong, though it might have taken a lot of us a long time to figure that out. As recently as February 2015, Rachel Maddow trotted the Bush video out again on her MSNBC show to illustrate an example of "a super rich guy who didn't know the fundamental basics of peasant life."[3] And Maddow is but one example. A limited Lexis-Nexis search of "Bush" and "supermarket scanner," from 1992 to today, offers up 353 separate citations.

THE COURAGE TO SERVE

In early 1992, I was getting back into politics after a three-year hiatus. I had been living in the Caribbean since 1989, helping to launch a cellular phone service, and was planning to attend business school the following September.

With a few months to kill before I needed to show up for b-school orientation, I went to New Hampshire to advance Nebraska senator Bob Kerrey, the Medal of Honor recipient who lost a leg in Vietnam and was running for president. To build affinity with Granite State voters, the Kerrey campaign asked me to set up a day of skiing for the senator at Gunstock, a favorite mountain of in-state residents. I set up a pool of reporters and photographers to shadow Kerrey on the mountain. The pool rode on a snowcat grooming tractor while Kerrey spent the frigid morning on skis. The image of a guy schussing down a public ski hill on a prosthetic leg was intended to establish a visual contrast to President Bush, the incumbent, who had a preference for fishing off the secluded rocky shores of nearby Kennebunkport, Maine. Bush's pose on the back of his boat was more sedentary than Kerrey's atop his skis, the president's boat protected from unwanted approach by a flotilla of Secret Service and Coast Guard vessels.

Lifestyle contrasts such as these were impossible for an average voter's mind to completely filter out, notwithstanding the decades of service that George H. W. Bush rendered to his nation. Many people who voted against Bush in 1992, denying him reelection and inaugurating the Clinton era in American presidential politics, may have a reference point of when they reconsidered that decision.

Some may have reevaluated Bush after the first, second, third or fourth of his voluntary skydiving forays, commemorating his seventy-fifth, eightieth, eighty-fifth and ninetieth birthdays, the most recent one coming on June 12, 2014, when he tweeted, "It's a wonderful day in Maine—in fact, nice enough for a parachute jump."[4] The jumps, and the photos that accompanied them, provided documentary evidence that the intestinal fortitude of the elder statesman had not deserted him, even if he had been deserted by the ability to use his legs at the time of his last freefall.

As wire images reminded readers at each five-year interval, Bush's later jumps as a senior citizen contrasted with his nightmarish one as a strapping young navy pilot on September 2, 1944. It was then that the twenty-year-old lieutenant junior grade, one year out of Philips Academy, flew his TBM Avenger off the USS *San Jacinto* in search of a Japanese target on the Pacific island of Chichijima. Bush's plane was downed by Japanese antiaircraft guns during the bombing raid, bringing an ignominious end to his fifty-eighth combat mission during World War II. Bush was plucked out of the sea by the submarine USS *Finback* and was eventually awarded the Distinguished Flying Cross.[5]

Only grainy film footage documented Bush's rescue by the *Finback*, though it endured through the decades as a staple of his political marketing efforts. I remember reading a long *New York* magazine cover story on Bush by the late Michael Kramer for the January 21, 1980, issue titled "George Bush: A Republican for All Factions." The cover photo featured a realistic painting by Frank Morris of Bush in a trench coat, the artist hinting back, perhaps, to Bush's days as CIA director. Morris lionized Bush in a heroic pose, looking more like a covert operative on a street corner in Prague than a patrician shielded from the Cold War struggle. The suave image might even have persuaded Upper West Side Democrats, the typical subscribers to the magazine, to form a positive impression. Inside the issue, Kramer described the dire action in the water surrounding the *Finback*, noting, "The enemy sent a patrol boat to get him, but an American submarine got there first. What's more—get this—there's a film of the rescue, courtesy of a crew member of the U.S.S. *Finback*. Hell, even John Kennedy had to wait till Hollywood created *PT-109*, a film of *his* war exploits."[6]

Decades later, weekend television producers, hungry for feel-good stories on slow summer news days, zealously covered each Bush parachute jump as a former president. The middle-of-the-broadcast packages, imbued with Bush's self-deprecating humor, allowed his detractors to reassess their views of the hardy old man, thanks to the up-close visuals of his recreational airborne activities. On his last jump, from 6,000 feet over Kennebunkport in 2014, Bush fell gently to Earth while harnessed to Sergeant 1st Class Mike Elliott, a retired member of the Army's Golden Knights parachute team. Hundreds had gathered to see him land. "He has a lot of courage. We need more like him," said seventy-nine-year-old David Morris of Melrose, Massachusetts, in a news account at the time.[7]

TRAVELING COMPANIONS

If not the parachuting, then perhaps it was the high-minded, hatchet-burying charitable work that brought forth a career reassessment of the

forty-first president. On December 26, 2004, as most people had tuned
out global news for the holiday season, a 9.1-magnitude earthquake was
recorded in the Indian Ocean off the west coast of Sumatra, Indonesia.
The quake created a tsunami that swept across low-lying areas of fourteen
surrounding countries, killing an estimated 240,000 people and leaving
1.7 million people homeless.

The countries most affected by the tsunami were Indonesia, Sri
Lanka, India and Thailand. Often, the visuals associated with response
efforts to such natural disasters include U.S. military aircraft being
offloaded with supplies along with evening news video reports of volunteer drives back home. In the days following, fresh reports will show
a United Nations secretary general, flanked by his entourage, walking
amid the ruins.

This time, however, two former U.S. presidents, George H. W. Bush
and Bill Clinton, avowed former adversaries, disembarked from their
blue-and-white government aircraft as partners. Providing an intergenerational angle for the story, news accounts were quick to point out that
the airplane was supplied by one of their children, President George W.
Bush. In a letter to his friend Hugh Sidey, *Time* magazine's legendary
columnist, Bush Senior wrote that Clinton would always wait at the top
of the aircraft stairs for his slower companion so they could exit the plane
together. "I thought I knew him," Bush wrote, "but until this trip I did
not really know him."[8]

Clinton could have ambled right off the plane, but that would have
defeated a key purpose of making the joint trip in the first place: the
image. If Bush knew Clinton better, if he was more aware of the visual
tactics that Clinton used to beat him in 1992, he would have sensed more
fully the shared stakes each man had in appearing side by side on the
aircraft stairs after the tsunami. The two presidents were there to bring
aid and comfort to the stricken, but they were also there to galvanize a
global response through carefully staged optics. Bush's successor knew
the distinct power conferred on those who exit a plane—positioned at an
upward angle before the lenses—bearing the insignia of the United States
of America. In Clinton he should trust.

Clinton used many visual tricks out of habit. At events during his
campaigns and throughout his presidency, he had a trademark move of
biting his lip before answering a question, visualizing the act of emoting.
He might then reference the questioner by name when answering with
empathetic phrases like, "I feel your pain." At their three-way debate with

Ross Perot at the University of Richmond in 1992, Bush, too, paused before answering a question, but only to check his watch, an act caught on camera by AP photographer Ron Edmonds that was immediately seized on as betraying a lack of caring.[9]

Years later, with the political hatchet buried, those money shots on the Asia trip were the pictures instantly beamed around the world by agency photographers assembled on airport tarmacs. They knew their assignment. They were there to give newspaper editors their first image of the stop, a picture of presidential bonhomie fit for the front page.

Bush's and Clinton's first four-country trip, and the trips that followed to bring relief to those affected by Hurricane Katrina later that year, were a perfect marriage of politics, publicity and philanthropy. Through their efforts, and airtime donated by the networks for public service announcements featuring the ex-presidents side by side, hundreds of millions of dollars were raised. Taking nothing away from their shared altruism, the very visible philanthropic campaign also made Bush relevant again for a generation that remembered little from his time in office that ended twelve years earlier.

Bush's first trip to Asia with Clinton inaugurated their new, positive profile as a buddy act of former rivals. In a photo by Gerald Herbert of the AP, Bush and Clinton are seen in shirtsleeves, surrounded by children in Weligama, Sri Lanka. In Herbert's frame, Clinton is reading the kids a book while Bush looks on. "The children danced, sang and drew pictures of their experiences," the accompanying AP story said, quoting Clinton, "There was a lot of emotional damage here that's not visible to the eye. We don't want them to be suffering from this five or 10 years from now."[10] Bush never gave the best quotes, but with his sidekick Clinton doing the talking and the photographers clicking away, he didn't need to. President Bush became beloved again just for being there.

THE PERFECT STORM

I started reassessing Bush, the man I worked against in 1988, three years after the tank ride, in October 1991, long before most of the revisionism began. While I was moving from Miami to Boston to work on the 1992 campaign, the ruinous nor'easter depicted in Sebastian Junger's *The Perfect Storm* crashed ashore in Kennebunkport. Sea levels rose much higher than the first floor of the president's beloved shoreline compound, Walker's Point, where Bush's family had "summered" for eighty-nine years at the time of the storm. When the waves retreated, they had laid waste to the main floor at Walker's Point and carried out to sea a flotsam of treasured possessions and memorabilia belonging to the Bush family.

Michael Wines wrote a piece for the *New York Times* on November 3, 1991, that resonated with me at the time. "A shaken President Bush and his wife, Barbara, led reporters through their devastated vacation house today," the story began. An image taken during the tour showed a forlorn president, in gray slacks, beige ball cap and work gloves, climbing over the detritus of his household goods. The picture, with furniture upended and wallpaper peeling away, was devastating to look at, no different than images of any American whose life was upended by disaster. In that moment, for me, Bush became one of us, as resolute as any other citizen to get up from nature's sucker punch and climb back into the ring. In his story, Wines quoted Bush as saying, "Unfortunately, the sea won this round. We'll see how we go in the next one."[11]

After the Perfect Storm hit Walker's Point and Bush reacted to it with sadness and strength, the guy was okay by me. I found myself inoculated against the temptation to quickly and easily label him elitist when the *Times* had its way with the supermarket scanner story.

Walker's Point, in the decades since, has become a familiar backdrop for how we now perceive the ex-president. In 2013, he shaved his head at the compound in solidarity with a two-year-old boy named Patrick, the son of an agent on his Secret Service detail who was suffering from leukemia. Genuine, heartfelt gestures such as these, along with more superficial ones like wearing brightly hued socks, are among the things, in addition to parachute jumping, that a wheelchair-bound man can do to earn new fans even in his octogenarian years.

The photo of the bald man and bald boy went viral. Bush and his wife, Barbara, had lost a daughter, Robin, to leukemia, making the act deeply personal for the couple. The act was also a paean to the Secret Service agents who guarded them day and night, from the time he first ran for president to the present. "A lot of the agents shaved their head," Bush told his granddaughter, Jenna, a contributing correspondent for NBC's *Today* show. "I said, 'Well why not me?' It was the right thing to do."[12]

So many of the images of President Bush, from being plucked from the Pacific Ocean as a twenty-year-old to jumping out of a plane as a ninety-year-old, belie the long misunderstood video footage from Orlando that formed the perception of him as hopelessly out of touch.

THE SCANNER

The political reality that George H. W. Bush faced in early January 1992 was a world away from the one he faced a year earlier, when Operation Desert Storm led to the high-water mark of his approval ratings. The economy slumped, erasing any sense of invincibility. The defeat of Saddam Hussein's Republican Guard was history, replaced by a war to improve financial fortunes back home. The misfortune facing many Americans proved an Achilles' heel for the president, one that was exploited by his critics like James Carville, Bill Clinton's top advisor, who pounded away at his colleagues to keep their eyes on the prize and repeat the mantra over and over: "It's the economy, stupid."[13]

When President Bush, in Tokyo on January 8 for a visit with Japanese prime minister Kiichi Miyazawa, fell ill at a banquet in his honor and vomited in the prime minister's lap, fainting momentarily, political invincibility gave way to human mortality. "I remember breaking out into a cold sweat, water just pouring off of me, and the next thing I knew, literally, I was on the floor," Bush dictated to his diary.[14] Bush's dinner was being covered by a late-night press pool, which set up a camera in the back of the banquet hall at Akasaka Palace. Not expecting any real news to happen during the course of the meal, the footage was shot at a long distance, the camera zooming in hastily to capture the moment out of focus. The footage nevertheless led the morning news shows, and a freeze frame of the president, overcome by nausea, filled the newspapers.

If it wasn't the sushi, Bush may have gotten sick from reading his news clips. As Adam Clymer wrote before the trip to Tokyo in the *New York Times* on January 3, "In contrast to the scene a year ago, when most lawmakers were here early expecting to confront the grave issue of war in the Persian Gulf, few are in town now, and the choices they face seem harder to grasp. The Democrats, who control the schedule, see the struggling economy and the unraveling health care system as issues on which they have a natural advantage over the Republicans."[15] Returning from Japan, Bush needed to turn his fortunes around.

By tradition every January, following Article II, Section 3 of the Constitution, the president may give "to the Congress Information of the State of the Union, and recommend to their Consideration such Measures as he shall judge necessary and expedient."[16] On January 28, 1992, facing reelection later that year, President Bush addressed Congress, outlining a nine-point plan for economic recovery from the recession of the early 1990s.

Bush, like Reagan before him and Clinton after him, then embarked a series of domestic trips to "sell the message" to sympathetic audiences. At his daily briefing to the press corps on Monday, February 3, Press Secretary Marlin Fitzwater outlined the week ahead. "We go to Orlando, Florida, tomorrow," Fitzwater said, "to address the National Grocers Association. The president will talk about the economic plan and the State of the Union message. On Thursday we go to Cleveland, Ohio. The president will address the Greater Growth Association of Cleveland and will announce his health-care plan."[17]

It's no surprise that Florida and Ohio were Bush's immediate stops after the State of the Union speech to advocate for his agenda. Though cast as "official travel"—meaning that taxpayers, not a political committee, bore the cost of the trip—those two states would be integral to the president's reelection. Just showing up, even in an official capacity, would land Bush on the front page of the *Orlando Sentinel*, the *Cleveland Plain Dealer* and on the three local newscasts of the network affiliates in those key media markets. Even as Fitzwater spoke, a White House advance team was on the ground in Orlando and Cleveland, laying groundwork for the appearances, preparing motorcades and working with hosts to smooth any rough edges.

Grocers gathering in Orlando were a reliably friendly audience. With 5,000 of them flying in for several days of plenary sessions, major industry vendors were also attracted to sponsor the show, erecting demonstration booths in the exhibit hall of the Orange County Convention and Civic Center to display their latest wares. One exhibitor was NCR, the iconic name in cash registers, which was displaying a new scanner that could both weigh produce and read the striped Universal Product Codes, or UPCs, even if they were ripped and jumbled.[18] Bob Graham, an NCR representative, stood by as the president approached on his pre-speech tour to put the new machine through its paces.

As Fitzwater tells the story in his book, *Call the Briefing!*, the demo almost didn't happen. "Our advance team had some new people who thought it would be a great picture to have the president appear with a life-size statue of Daisy the Cow that was part of a milk exhibit. Always afraid of pictures that might hold the president up to ridicule, I grabbed the lead advance man and screamed at him to get the president away from the phony cow. Unfortunately, he guided the presidential party across the aisle to the National Cash Register company's checkout scanner exhibit."[19]

Steering a president from one exhibit to another in a convention hall is no easy trick. The Secret Service creates a phalanx around their protectee, inside of which are allowed only aides with identifying "hard pins," or guests whose backgrounds have been vetted and wear "soft pins" with colors and codes affording limited access at a specific site.

Even with these restrictions, the secure "bubble," as it's known, can seem like a swarm. Add to this the need to provide press coverage of the president's public movements, and you have a circus in the making. Press pools are supposed to be the antidote to circus-like scrums at political events, but they bring problems of their own.

POOL DUTY

The routine of "mounting a pool" of reporters and photojournalists from among the press corps became standard practice after the assassination of John F. Kennedy, when Abraham Zapruder's film captured the only known documentary footage of the president's murder. In the decades since, various incarnations of "the pool" have emerged, matching different types of presidential events and movements. Among the pool configurations, there's an "in-town" pool for visits around Washington, a "travel pool" for trips out of town, and a "tight pool" for specific events with limited space for bodies and equipment.

The alphabetical rotation for pool assignments is managed by the White House Correspondents Association but facilitated by the White House press office, the arrangement bringing with it a series of conflicts and complexities regarding media independence. Simply put, the press couldn't secure close-in proximity to the president without cooperation and support from the White House. In its current form, the travel pool includes, among others, a TV crew and correspondent, wire reporters from the AP, Reuters and Bloomberg, photographers from the AP, Reuters and Agence France Presse (AFP), and a print reporter from among the newspapers that maintain a permanent White House correspondent.

On Tuesday, February 4, Gregg McDonald of the *Houston Chronicle* drew the assignment of print reporter for the travel pool that accompanied President Bush to the supermarket technology exhibit. This meant that McDonald would be assisted by the White House advance staff to be as close as possible to the president throughout the day. In exchange for this intimate access, in addition to doing his own reporting for the *Chronicle,* McDonald served as the "eyes and ears" of his fellow print colleagues who had to remain back at the filing center due to space limitations. To share observations with his colleagues sitting behind banquet tables and staring at their laptops, McDonald would write a pool report, or dictate it to a White House press aide, who would then make photocopies (the White House press office traveled with its own heavy mimeograph machine back in those days) and pass them out to those reporters or producers working away on their stories.

I've always been fascinated by the unique nature and special power of pool reports, and I keep an almost complete set of them from the Clinton years in a large bookcase in my study. While reporters have to follow a certain style for copy destined for publication, they can be less restrained, more colorful—and often very funny—if they think they're only writing for their peers, impressing them with their wit and wisdom. The color has dimmed over the years as pool reports have been distributed electronically and could fall into anyone's hands, making the writer accountable for any bias or mistake therein, but in the days of the first President Bush and President Clinton, they were a hoot to read.

If a White House advance person maneuvered the pool reporter within earshot and eyesight of an emotional moment, it could augment the impact of a story. When this duty fell to me, I always tried to ease "the pooler" into position to eavesdrop on a scene or feed as much color as I could to whoever had the duty, knowing that anything that made it into a pool report would be distributed to all of the influential correspondents on a trip with the validating imprimatur of one of their own.

I remember being dispatched on an overnight flight from California to Greeleyville, South Carolina, in June 1996 to help stage a last-minute speech in a cornfield abutting a church in the small town. In sweltering heat, President Clinton would promise more federal help to investigate a recent rash of arson in places of worship with predominantly African American congregations. Creating the speech site in the cornfield was a *Field of Dreams* moment in itself, and all credentialed media could cover it. Correspondents like Bill Neikirk of the *Chicago Tribune* wrote up the story of 1,000 people gathered on the hot South Carolina day to hear Clinton, the consoler in chief, compare "the church and its congregation to Shadrach, Meshach and Abednego, biblical characters who survived the fiery furnace. 'They can burn the building down, but they can't burn the faith out,'" Clinton said to the assembled crowd in the cornfield.[20]

In such stories, the visual carries broad emotional weight in addition to the reporter's copy. In Greeleyville, only the pool would enter the newly rebuilt Mt. Zion AME Church to see and hear the president kneeling in prayer with local ministers. The space was too small, and the moment too somber, to allow a larger gaggle into the pews. Accompanying Neikirk's article was an AP photo from the pool photographer showing Clinton, flanked by Bishop John Adams and Reverend Terrance Mackey, their heads bowed. This was not the kind of image that Clinton's opponent that year, Bob Dole, could match.

CZAR FITZWATER

Gregg McDonald didn't carry the weight of similar responsibility when he followed President Bush around the exhibits at the National Grocers Association, but the impact of his two-paragraph pool report would be far greater than the one reporting Clinton's prayer in Greeleyville. With McDonald watching, Bush politely asked his host, Bob Graham, if this was "the newest scanner."

"Of course," Graham answered, "this looks like a typical scanner you'd see in a grocery store," but then he went on to describe its unique new features, including the ability to weigh produce and read mangled UPC codes.[21]

"Isn't that something," Bush reportedly said,[22] a comment that spurred a host of interpretations. In McDonald's pool report, he noted that the president had "a look of wonder" on his face. That was it. It could have been real wonder. It could have been polite wonder. The pool report didn't elaborate. But the look of wonder, as reported by Gregg McDonald, is what associated Bush with a supermarket scanner for eternity (apart from his pool report, notably, McDonald made no mention of the incident in his own story filed for the *Chronicle* from Orlando).

Back in the filing center, with McDonald's pool report for color and the video footage from the pool as a reference, Andrew Rosenthal wrote his story for the *Times*.

It's hard to overstate the power of a front-page *New York Times* story in the early months of the 1992 campaign. The narratives that the *Times* promoted in February might remain through November, especially if augmented by other memorable visuals, like Bush looking at his watch during the October 15 debate in Richmond. There was no cable TV news besides CNN, and only Carson, Letterman and *Saturday Night Live* to amuse late-night TV audiences. If the *Times* used its front page to engage in mockery, it would become part of the national dialogue.

Fitzwater saw the problem and sprang into action. "It was one of those stories," he wrote, "where the truth never catches up with the lie. No other reporter at the event wrote the story this way. Reporters started arguing about what actually happened. I urged all reporters to go view the pool videotapes of the episode. Then we contacted NCR and asked them to give interviews to reporters about what actually happened."[23]

Retelling the story in *Call the Briefing!*, Fitzwater aimed his ire at Rosenthal, the son of A. M. Rosenthal, the former executive editor of the *Times.* He charged that the reporter "spoke openly of his dislike of Reagan and Bush" and pointed to the difficulty the son had in living up to his father's reputation, noting the competition he thought Rosenthal was facing against the *Times*'s other White House correspondent, Maureen Dowd.[24] Fitzwater made other accusations, too, unrelated to Rosenthal's reporting.

In an email, I asked Rosenthal, now the editorial page editor of the *Times,* to help me better understand his coverage of the scanner from the long view of history. He refused to revisit the story again. "This is a subject about which I long ago got tired," he wrote back.[25] He wanted me to know, however, that he had, indeed, looked closely at the video footage of the tour while writing his story in the filing center, as did two other editors of the *Times* at a later time.

Indeed, long before the *Times*'s public editor reviewed such controversial stories from an independent perch, the newspaper published a follow-on piece a week later, by reporter Joel Brinkley, based on further forensic analysis of the videotape. The White House, Brinkley noted, had stepped up complaints that "Mr. Bush has been mistreated by the newspaper reports, editorial cartoons and satirical comments by columnists and commentators who said the encounter bolstered the argument that the President was out of touch with ordinary life." Brinkley added that once the story became fodder for late-night comedians, among others, "White House aides began vigorously arguing that the whole episode had been cruelly misinterpreted."[26]

Ultimately, "Round Two" of the *Times* coverage of the scanner incident offered a verdict buttressing Rosenthal's original story, concluding the president "seemed unfamiliar with even basic scanner technology."

As if to rub salt in the complainant's wound, Brinkley reminded readers that by complaining about the coverage, "the White House has kept alive a story that would otherwise have died down after one or two days."[27] Writing about the incident in the *American Spectator* just after the campaign ended, Brit Hume, then the chief White House correspondent for ABC News, noted that "stories about rich and powerful people and their alleged insensitivity to everybody else" is "one of the oldest forms of journalistic demagoguery." Rosenthal's *Times* article, and its placement, Hume charged, "spectacularly illustrated" the problem.[28]

Nearly a quarter century after it happened, wounds on both sides seem to remain open. Regarding the slew of personal accusations that Fitzwater lobbed at the reporter in his book, Rosenthal wrote to me, "Please be aware that most of what he said about me, especially my personal life and views about other journalists was entirely made up."[29]

For his part, President Bush became a critic of Rosenthal as well, but within the confines of intimate correspondence. Famous for his typewritten notes to staffers, the president sent his press secretary a screed on the morning that the story ran.

> To: Czar Fitzwater
> Re: Overnights
>
> Once again my ire turns to Rosenthal. The NCR people were explaining brand new technology to me. Not simple checkout technology. Please tell that little "____" that I am tired of his editorializing every day his 'news ???@#$$%> & coverage.
>
> Feeling better now—forget it, but what a terrible little guy he is turning out to be. What is it about him?
>
> Thanks for Listening, GB[30]

Later, the president received a letter from Arthur Ochs Sulzberger, then the chairman and CEO of the *Times*. It read, in part:

> There was no question that Andrew Rosenthal's article on the supermarket electronic checkout system was "just a teeny-weeny bit naughty." Little did any of us expect that the story would be picked up by others, including some not too subtle political cartoonists.
>
> The purpose of the story was to have a little bit of fun, and if we had too much at the expense of the President, I apologize.[31]

After the fact, and after the damage had been done to the president's reputation, Sulzberger could apologize for his newspaper being "just a teeny-weeny bit naughty."

In the days following, White House efforts to debunk "scanner-gate" were moderately successful. On February 11, the AP ran a 434-word story, "White House Has Media Rescanning the Scanner Caper," which included a reexamination of the pool video with a quote from NCR's Bob Graham saying that "the whole thing is ludicrous. What he was amazed by was the ability of the scanner to take that torn label and reassemble it."[32]

On his "Osgood File" segment for CBS Radio, Charles Osgood accepted the verdict of the video evidence and Fitzwater's vehement protestations. "Fair is fair," Osgood said, "and especially since I joined the herd last week and took the occasion to pontificate about how unfortunate it is that we isolate our presidents so much," he told his audience that what the scanner does is "really something."[33]

In truth, it matters little whether George H. W. Bush was amazed by a supermarket scanner, only that the president's perilous political position at the time was undercut by a prominently placed story and headline about something extraordinarily mundane. *Time* magazine's Michael Duffy, another pool member, labeled the incident "completely insignificant as a news event," noting that "If anything, he was bored."[34]

With a triumphant war in the rearview mirror, an economy hitting the skids, and a State of the Union revival plan to sell, Bush just wanted to get through the day in Orlando and the next event on his schedule, his speech before the grocers. Like the dutiful, polite son of Prescott and Dorothy Walker Bush that he was, the president was doing what he was trained to do his entire life: be respectful of others. He wasn't taking the proactive step of climbing aboard an M1A1 tank to try to be someone he wasn't. In fact, he was being exactly who he was. History had not repeated itself, but the result was the same.

The ephemeral pushback that Fitzwater offered could only go so far. History quickly claimed back the scanner episode as evidence of a George H. W. Bush that many critics wanted to see. In a piece called "So Long, Poppy" for the November 1992 issue of *Playboy,* Robert Scheer offered an interim coda on the Bush political legacy, the negative tone of which prevailed until the revisionism of the following decade. "Fact is," Sheer wrote, "he doesn't care. This guy was bred into a noblesse oblige so cushioned by privilege that he assumes the rest of us are similarly buffeted from the rude economic shocks of this world. No, it's not cute that he didn't know what a supermarket scanner was. It's a damned serious omission in his education about how the rest of us live."[35]

As Brit Hume wrote for the *American Spectator,* "It may be the only time on record where anybody got an exclusive story out of a pool report. Such is the *Times*'s influence, however, that the story became part of the legend of a President who just didn't know how things were out there in the real world."[36]

In the decades since George H. W. Bush spent a few minutes innocently walking through the exhibit hall at the Orange County Convention and Civic Center, every election cycle unfolds featuring video segments and stories about famous political gaffes, both national and local. Invariably, the fateful minute that Bob Graham showed the president NCR's new scanner makes a cameo, sometimes in silent footage shot by the pool, sometimes in the still photo captured by the AP's Barry Thumma. Commentators always seem to have a field day with it, sounding smart, cautioning about candidates seeming out of touch. As the finishing touches are put on these pieces, most are oblivious to the facts about how the most influential national newspaper was comfortable that day being "just a teeny-weeny bit naughty."

In Thumma's image, we see Bush as we remember him, hair neatly parted, wire-rimmed glasses hanging from his nose, one hand in the pocket of his pinstripe suit, the other stretching to press one of the register's buttons. His body leans awkwardly into the moment, a reminder that playing to the visual wasn't in his blood, as it was for his predecessor, Ronald Reagan, or his successor, Bill Clinton. In the foreground of the frame sits a carton of milk, a light bulb and an apple, items ready for checkout, props for this political tour. They are the same staples that, in future years, George and Barbara Bush might have bought in Kennebunkport, using a supermarket scanner and thanking the store clerk politely as they finished their provisioning for Walker's Point.

1996: DOLE'S PRECIPITOUS FALL

*(Or, How a War Hero Bending
over a Balustrade Became
Too Old to Be President)*

TABLE STAKES

Political visuals work best when they make a candidate look *presidential*, adding to a perception that the job fits the man, or woman. They're most catastrophic when they feed a negative perception—true or not—among the segment of voters you most need to persuade. The most sought-after segment in a presidential campaign is the moderate middle 15 percent of the voting population that swing elections. After all, the largest voting bloc has no affiliation at all. According to Pew's 2013 data, 32 percent of registered voters are Democrats, 24 percent are Republicans and 38 percent classify themselves as Independent.

Presidential election strategy is straightforward: hold on to your base and fight like hell for the middle. But thanks to the wisdom of the Founders, presidents are chosen not by popular vote but by 270 electors representing, together, all of the states. A national election, then, is really fifty smaller contests, with the outcome of many of them preordained by each state's glacially changing political makeup. In reality only a few states—the *battleground* states—are in play each election, where the fight for the middle more resembles hand-to-hand combat.

Setting aside other ingredients needed to win an election—carving out appealing stands on issues, producing creative ads and identifying supporters and getting them to the polls—national elections between the conventions and Election Day in the Age of Optics, at least through 2012, quickly devolve into a daily beauty contest of dueling events created by advance teams.

The metaphor of the beauty contest cannot be underestimated. Since 1992, with the exception of Bush v. Gore in 2000 and Bush v. Kerry in 2004 where the finalists were of roughly equal age and physical stature, the younger, more energetic, more seemingly adroit candidate has claimed the White House. As crass as that may be, the presidential candidate is an actor on stage, and the better trained and equipped he or she is to perform in a daily theatrical show—often with multiple matinees—the easier it is to win.

Each day from dawn to midnight, the candidate flies from city to city and strides, like Miss Kansas, across the catwalk in a swimsuit, often to be admired, sometimes to be heckled, in full view of the cameras. The political candidate, like the beauty contestant, is careful to be poised and well-spoken, dreading a verbal miscue or physical stumble revealing a blemish that balloons into disaster.

KENT GRAY ON SITE

On September 18, 1996, Bob Dole was Mr. Kansas, many years past his prime swimsuit days, if ever he had them. What Dole did have, in abundance, was political gravitas from his decades of public life and his heroic service in World War II. Those attributes left him with little margin for error, pitted against a younger, more agile incumbent in Bill Clinton, resurrected from his party's humiliating defeat in the 1994 midterms.

Dole's margin for error against Clinton evaporated further as he tumbled from a four-foot-high stage—the equivalent of the pageant catwalk—in Chico, California. The fall itself wasn't fatal. Candidates do stumble. But once he's pictured on newspaper front pages across the world as a man who stumbles *and* can't get up, the resulting metaphor quickly becomes part of *the narrative* and easily lends itself to political obituary writers.

You don't want to be the site advance man when this happens. Kent Gray, then twenty-six and the product of a politically connected Springfield, Illinois, family, was that guy.

Gray, whose father was a longtime aide for Illinois governor Jim Thompson, had been involved in local politics and done advance work since he was sixteen, learning from mentors who taught him the ropes. He had worked at learning the craft in his home state until, as a College Republican at Loyola, he was tapped to go out on the road for the first time. Gray, now a lawyer with a practice in Springfield, still carves out time to do advance work, but his fateful trip to Chico still haunts him, now nearly twenty years later.

In 1996, Tim Unes, a Dole advance veteran, assigned Gray to manage motorcades at the GOP Convention in San Diego. Gray was good at computers, too, so Unes found other uses for his talents. "He said, 'Okay, you've got a job,'" Gray told me. That's how advance careers begin, having the right skills in the right place at the right time, with a suitcase packed and a political godfather to give you your first shot. When the convention ended, Gray returned to Springfield, but he was soon called to pack his bags again. "Can you take the next two and a half to three months off for the campaign?" he was asked. The campaign bought him a one-way ticket.[1]

That first one-way ticket led to others, bringing Gray ultimately to Chico, California, to a Dole team that included Vin Demarco leading press, Ray Joyner Jr. on site and Ray Martinez—the same guy who first introduced me to advance when, as Nancy Reagan's advance director in 1987, he gave me a tour of the White House—as the team lead. They settled on the baseball field near the Chico Elks Lodge for their event, estimating by its dimensions that a daytime Dole rally could accommodate 7,000 people.

THE ROAD TO CHICO

In the hours before his caravan got to Chico, Dole's day began like most in the heat of a presidential campaign. The odd thing about the schedule that day—at a time when every day on the road was precious—was that California was not considered a battleground state that year. Changing demographics and Clinton's dogged courtship of its voters during his first term had put it out of reach for a Republican. Spending time and money there, unless it was part of a broader national message, was a peculiar choice for the GOP nominee in the middle of September.

While a candidate's plane might touch down in non-battleground states for a can't-do-it-anywhere-else photo op (like in the shadow of

Mount Rushmore) or to feed perceptions that all states are in play, the aircraft usually vectors between states like Florida, Ohio, Nevada and Colorado, where the election will be won or lost. In those states, half of the middle 15 percent are inclined to like you, but they can turn on you if you screw up in public; the other half of that 15 percent are inclined to dislike you but can be won over by your authenticity, humor or if the opponent does something so dumb that they surrender the support leaning their way.

In 1988, Michael Dukakis was trying to win Michigan, but the campaign tactic of putting him in a tank backfired and fueled perceptions that he was trying to be someone he wasn't. In 1992, George H. W. Bush was stopping in Florida to sell his economic recovery plan, but the overblown media coverage of his routine visit to the NCR scanner display in Orlando reinforced a brewing belief that he was an elitist and out of touch.

In 1995, during the run-up to his candidacy, Bob Dole was fighting a sentiment that he was too old to be president. He tried to shrug off stories like Ceci Connolly's for the *Washington Post,* "Age Question Growing Old for Bob Dole," in which she quoted opinion shapers like Rep. Charlie Bass of New Hampshire, who said, "Lamar Alexander made a . . . comment about how he can walk across the state, something Bob Dole couldn't do."[2] Dole's spokesmen were quick with rebuttals against ageism with doctors' analyses professing to the senator's good health. The problem was that even pushing back against the age narrative gave it credibility, adding fuel for still more stories.

Dole traveled to California on September 18 to attend a fundraiser, make a speech decrying the glorification of drugs by the entertainment industry and appear at the late-afternoon rally in Chico. On a warm afternoon on the field of dreams that Kent Gray created, the early moments of the rally would show that, while Dole was no Miss Kansas, the war hero and Washington insider could, on occasion, attract the same kinds of crowds and enthusiasm as Clinton and neutralize his generational appeal.

But in Chico the beauty contest took an ugly turn. Unlike the Dukakis and Bush calamities, where outside forces exposed the candidates' weaknesses, the fault for Dole's sideways tumble from the stage into a scrum of photographers rested squarely on the shoulders of the advance team. A white balustrade on Dole's stage created a nostalgic tableau until it suddenly gave way and angled forward, bringing Dole down behind it.

The crowd gasped, wondering where the candidate had gone. "The story that came out immediately was the railing broke loose . . . but obviously it was a prop," Gray told me. "It wasn't ever screwed down and it wasn't meant to be screwed down. It was just one of those freak accidents where somebody moves too close to the front of the stage and they fall off the front."[3] Down Dole went, like a WWE pro wrestler thrown through the ropes to the hard concrete floor below.

When I would wake up in a cold sweat, thinking about how advance mistakes can affect the outcome of an election, my nightmare was always the photo of Dole, then age seventy-three, lying on his back in Chico, as helpless as a turtle flipped on his shell. I see him in those insomniac moments like millions saw him that day, immobile and confined in a coffin of photographers, unable to right himself on his own and grimacing in pain no doubt exacerbated by his lingering war wound. That image, shot by Rick Wilking of Reuters while David Ake, a photographer for the Agence France-Presse, cradled Dole's head in his hands, filled the September 19 front pages of newspapers across the country and around the world.

I've watched the video a hundred times. Dole is down and up in twelve seconds. But within that fraction of a minute, Wilking captured a shot for the ages. That's why still photography can often be more devastating than video. The newspaper only has space for one image, the one that conveys the most dramatic moment of the story. You don't see what the camera saw before and after, and there is never a second take.

The fall happened so fast that Kent Gray didn't even see it. This was the part of the rally that should be on autopilot. "Nobody thought it was a big deal to put what essentially were twenty-four-inch-tall fake balustrades on the front of the stage in front of the podium," Gray told me. "It would almost be like someone tripping over the fern next to the podium on either side." A representative of the staging company that Gray hired to help build his site mentioned off-handedly that she had some "little fencing things that are weighted on the bottom" that could "kind of dress up the stage." It was the worst advice Gray ever received doing advance work.[4]

MY ROAD TO 1996

Patiently waiting his turn for the GOP nomination, it was finally granted to Dole in 1996. He faced an opponent, Clinton, badly weakened by first-term missteps. But as a candidate, Dole's wartime infirmity limited his options on the campaign trail. Ronald Reagan clearing brush in Santa Barbara, Gary Hart throwing an axe in New Hampshire and Bill Clinton's early ability to embrace and emote with voters were outside his physical repertoire. Those retail politicking skills alone, however, wouldn't decide this election. Electoral math still held hope for a Republican who could survive the convention-to-Election Day beauty contest without incident.

I didn't know Kent Gray at the time of Dole's fall in Chico, but as soon as I saw the photo on the front page of the newspaper, I knew how he felt. As the director of Senator Paul Simon's advance team in New Hampshire eight years earlier, I too had watched my candidate—and his family—plummet live on television as a Primary Night stage collapsed beneath their feet. From then on, I would do jumping jacks on a stage in the early morning hours of Game Day to administer a pre-event stress test.

Faulty staging was only one of many lessons I learned in my years as an advance man leading up to the challenge of helping Bill Clinton get reelected. My advance education, begun in 1987, was still in its formative period in the early days of 1992.

Long before George H. W. Bush's political renaissance as an ex-president, his blind spot for the power of visuals, especially around natural disasters, was plain to see when Hurricane Andrew swept across Florida in 1992. Both Clinton and Bush made trips to the state in the storm's aftermath, but Clinton—then the Arkansas governor with no cleanup duties—had the upper hand. Bush had to answer for federal crisis management in the face of the disaster and also had to show empathy in front of the lens when consoling the Floridian victims. He didn't rise to the moment.

Ironically, thirteen years later, George W. Bush, the president's son, would face the same challenge with Hurricane Katrina. Caught flat-footed by the storm, Bush skipped an on-site inspection of the affected areas, opting instead to make a flyover in Air Force One, inviting ridicule along for the ride. An airborne vantage point might aid assessment of the storm's damage. It would also spare local law enforcement from providing Bush security on the ground when they had a million other issues to deal with. But taking to the skies sealed the president off from those who were suffering. Adding to his problems, his "attaboy" to FEMA director Michael Brown—"Brownie, you're doin' a heckuva job"—won the award for off-key political sound bites for 2005.[5]

While 2005 was bad, 1992 was much worse, politically, for the Bush family. From his vomiting in Tokyo to the scanner incident in Orlando to the plodding response to Hurricane Andrew, optics got the best of the forty-first president. The blame for economic hardship hitting voters across the country eventually arrived at the steps of Bush's White House.

Bush's continued political struggles opened the door to my political opportunity. The scene in South Florida made me rethink spending the next two years of my life at business school. I could double down on working for Governor Clinton and hope to find a job in Washington when he won. Who needed b-school? From the moment that Andrew hit Miami until President-elect Clinton walked onto the stage in Little Rock on November 3, I had an education in the business of politics like nothing I could have imagined.

While I had done some work for Clinton before the Democratic Convention came to New York, it was only after the convention that I elevated my advance work to a new level. I was dispatched to Weirton, West Virginia, to produce a stop on the first Clinton-Gore bus tour, followed up by stops in Lansing, Michigan; Waco, Texas; Oakland, California; Des Moines, Iowa; Wilmington, Delaware; Hartford, Connecticut; and the scene in Ocala, Florida, that I recounted earlier.

A kid from the comfortable Northeastern suburbs will understandably experience a continued awakening when dispatched to a struggling steel town like Weirton. When I got there, the townsfolk were quick to tell stories of the time Jack Kennedy came through for a town hall on May 1, 1960, and gave us photos of that event as our guide. It was that fresh in their memory, and they had rarely welcomed a presidential candidate since. Naturally, when we set up our stage for Clinton and Gore when their bus pulled into town, it was positioned, by popular demand, on the exact spot from which Kennedy spoke.

Later in 1992, with the election one day away, I was building a site at the Brendan Byrne Arena in East Rutherford, New Jersey. The stage was much more expansive than the humble platform in Weirton. To fill it, I called the Manhattan theater where *Les Miserables* was in its Broadway run and offered its cast a chance to perform live at a final rally. They jumped at the casting call. Before a packed arena, the company belted out their rendition of "One Day More" while thousands of audience members waved placards saying the same thing. The message on the front page of the *Newark Star-Ledger* the next day was clear: the curtain would soon fall on the twelve-year-run of Reagan and Bush.

Like many advance colleagues, I drove my overloaded Jetta to Washington, full of hope for employment but with dubious prospects. I took any advance work that came my way, including a road race that President Clinton and Vice President Gore ran in Washington, D.C. To create a flattering picture of the event, I used the trick I deployed with Bob Kerrey on the ski slopes a year earlier, putting the pool on a flatbed truck (rather than a snowcat) to watch the runners advance toward the lens. It was like viewing the lead pack of the Boston Marathon, except that the front-runners in Boston aren't surrounded by Secret Service agents.

A few weeks into the new term, I produced the rollout of the administration's new high-tech initiative in Silicon Valley, again employing event production techniques seldom seen during the preceding dozen years of White House stagecraft. On the way back from California, I received a page from one of the president's longtime aides, Stephanie Streett, asking to meet with me to discuss my becoming one of the president's schedulers. My gamble to postpone business school paid off with a job in the White House.

The scheduling job, which I started in February, led, by October, to the job of a lifetime: director of production for presidential events. As the president's "visuals guy," I traveled the world, orchestrating events in the White House and on the road, sometimes seven days a week. While I wasn't naive about the problems that plagued Bill Clinton during his first two years in office, I sidestepped them by staying focused on my job.

As ugly as things got in the tabloids with palace intrigue stories like Travelgate, Whitewater, Vince Foster's suicide, "Don't Ask, Don't Tell," and the failed health-care initiative, the institution of the presidency had to keep moving forward. The president still had to put on his suit each day and perform his duties, wherever those duties took him. That meant trips across Europe, Asia and the Middle East, with me either a few stops ahead, putting the details in place, or aboard Air Force One, working to orchestrate the road show at each stop.

After a year of globetrotting, the president's travel narrowed to domestic trips in the weeks before the 1994 midterm elections. Air Force One touched down in all the key battleground states to try to preserve the Democratic majorities in the House and Senate, but nothing that year could quell the Republican tide. The GOP picked up fifty-four House seats and nine Senate seats, ushering in the era of Newt Gingrich as House Speaker and returning Bob Dole to the post of Majority Leader, a post he last held eight years earlier in 1987.

DOLE'S ROAD TO 1996

Bob Dole, the senator from Russell, Kansas, first elected to the U.S. House in 1960 at age thirty-seven, joined Gerald Ford as his running mate in 1976 and launched his own bid for president in 1980. Against Ronald Reagan's juggernaut, he never really got up to bat. After receiving only 597 votes in the New Hampshire Primary, he withdrew from the race and returned to the Senate to wait out the Reagan years for his next turn at the plate.

That turn came in 1988, which started with promise when he beat then–vice president Bush in the Iowa Caucus, only to lose to Bush in the ensuing New Hampshire Primary. Super Tuesday delivered a southern sweep for the vice president, convincing the Kansan that he would again have to head for the dugout. Presuming that Vice President Bush would prevail in the race to succeed Reagan and win reelection, it meant that Dole would not have another shot at the presidency until 1996, when he would be seventy-three years old. He had waited long enough.

Dole, like President Bush before him, was a decorated World War II veteran, but Dole bore the scars of war more visibly than his longtime rival. On April 14, 1945, six months after Bush was plucked from the Pacific by the USS *Finback,* Second Lieutenant Dole was a platoon commander in Italy with the 10th Mountain Division, leading an assault on Mount Belvedere in the Apennine Mountains. The battle, amid a haze of German machine-gun fire and mortars, was a killing field for young American men, with 13,000 engaged in the fight and 1,000 never coming home.

Dole was struck by a grenade fragment that tore into his right shoulder, crushed a piece of his spine and left him lying in a gully. He barely avoided death on foreign soil, only to spend three difficult years in army hospitals where he overcame paralysis during his convalescence. He earned two Purple Hearts and a Bronze Star for his gallantry and returned to civilian life, miraculously able to walk again. A permanent effect of Dole's wounds was an inability to use his right arm to do more than clutch a pen, which he would do as a visual cue to well-wishers to avoid shaking his hand. His ailment didn't inhibit his electability in Kansas, but it limited his versatility as a glad-handing campaigner, baby kisser and nimble actor in all manner of photo ops. The images of Dole in public had a sameness about them that masked his constant pain.

I watched Dole as an eleven-year-old during the 1976 campaign and, unaware of the depth of his sacrifice, thought he looked and sounded angry and bitter. Such is the impression a boy forms, watching a man who rarely smiles—the uncle, perhaps, who suffered a stroke years back and you can't understand why he seldom changes facial expression at family gatherings.

I wasn't alone in labeling Dole, though his reputation in the media came more from his political tactics than his physical bearing. Reporters liberally applied the term "hatchet man" to Dole in many stories they wrote. "'Hatchet Man' Image Must Stay Buried: Dole Walks Fine Line in Attacking Bush," blared a headline for a 1988 *Los Angeles Times* article by Michael Wines. It was typical of the genre of Dole profile pieces, the body copy detailing a bill of particulars of Dole's caustic broadsides over the years against his opponents. Wines used terms like "mean-spirited" to describe a man who said of Vice President Bush, on different occasions, that he "had an indoor job, no heavy lifting" at the White House and "not many of us started at the top and stayed there."[6] Articles like that— and there were many—create an indelible mark on the minds of voters, making it an uphill climb to boost a candidate's "likeability" ratings in polls. Not many people envision their president as a hatchet man, though twenty years later, in 2016, Donald Trump might prove the exception.

When I got to the White House in 1993, it appeared to impressionable young aides like me that Dole actually deserved the hatchet-man label. He seemed unwilling, even at the urging of wise men like Robert Strauss over dinner with the new president at Duke Ziebert's on July 1, 1993, to give Bill Clinton a break with his first-year legislative agenda.[7]

In 1996, I watched Dole again at the GOP Convention in San Diego, curious about why the operatives running the event designed such an austere, low-rise stage to crown their nominee. It was a missed chance, I thought, to put on a rousing show and bury the hatchet-man image. By contrast, our lofty convention dais at the United Center in Chicago, put into action after a triumphant whistle-stop train tour originating in Huntington, West Virginia, and touching six states on our way to Illinois, was a towering edifice. At his acceptance speech on August 15, Dole, hearkening back to a simpler age of country roads and war heroes, said, "Let me be the bridge to a time of tranquility, faith, and confidence in action."

BUILDING AMERICA'S BRIDGE

Dole's message played into our hands. The bridge metaphor was powerful alright, but with a new millennium near, it needed to span forward, not back. In the West Wing, President Clinton was guided on his 1996 come-back by the triumvirate of consultant Dick Morris, pollster Mark Penn and communications director Don Baer, my boss at the time. Through polling, focus groups and mall tests, Morris, Penn and Baer settled on a theme for the campaign—"Building a Bridge to the 21st Century"—underpinned by forward-looking phrases like "Protecting American Values" and "Strengthening American Families." The research-tested nuggets were positive but vague aphorisms that scored well with swing voters—"soccer moms," as they were dubbed that year. Thanks to our advance teams, the verbiage also looked great on TV and in photos, easily digest-ible messages that we connected visually with the president through stra-tegically placed signage at his events.

Every day, as we planned presidential campaign stops, I would take direction from Baer to construct made-for-the-camera stage sets in cit-ies across America that rammed our theme home. Before camera phones allowed advance people to send pictures of prospective event sites back to the White House, I would use graph paper to sketch out an elevation drawing of every scene, imagining how the cameras would frame a tight shot days before an event. Even if the evening news only used a few sec-onds of the president's speech in their packages, they invariably focused on our sets that said "Building America's Bridge" or a similar construct. The message, a direct rebuttal to Dole's nostalgic, backward-looking re-frain, was getting through.

A sense of momentum was getting through, too, judging by the turn-out for our events. Reporters would ask us for a crowd count, and we'd pass on inflated numbers that partisans said came from the local police. In truth, without an aerial photograph to section the crowd in countable grids, estimating audience size in those days was mostly guesswork. Even so, reporters dutifully scribbled the numbers in their notebooks and in-serted them into their stories.

Crowd building is an advance art unto itself, enhanced significantly to-day by social media. But in 1996, crowds were still raised the old-fashioned way, by leafleting bus stops and parking lots, phone-banking, producing crude radio spots, arranging promotional appearances by major and minor celebrities, and even using cash to coax senior citizens out of their homes to fill four square feet of space in a high school gym. The real heroes of an advance team were the "crowd guys" who could lead an army of volunteers fueled by pizza to blanket a town with paper and get the locals to brave sheets of rain and blistering sun to fill the event spaces we picked.

We picked large venues, such as the Red Rocks amphitheater outside of Denver, and filled them with 10,000 people stocked with young activists. In Tempe, Arizona, we stretched the metaphor further, choreographing Clinton's entrance by having him cross a pedestrian bridge, over the crowd, to our big gathering outside. To the bridge we affixed massive letters spelling out "Building a Bridge to the 21st Century" that were plainly visible to the scores of photojournalists covering the president's stop. Pictures from that event didn't need to show Clinton up close: the crowd, and the words we plastered to the bridge, effectively told our story.

Implicit in this stagecraft—having the president stride confidently across a bridge accompanied by college students—was that, echoing Congressman Charlie Bass's comment in New Hampshire a year earlier, Clinton could pull off this stunt, Dole couldn't. Stretching the metaphor further, Clinton was young, Dole was old.

Youth wasn't always a positive. At the start of Clinton's term, he was criticized for having a senior staff dominated by those in their thirties. With a deep respect for the military, who made up much of the permanent staff of the White House, I was dismayed by the arrogance of one fellow aide rumored to have said to General Barry McCaffrey, then an assistant to the chairman of the Joint Chiefs of Staff, "I don't talk to people in uniform." Missteps like that, along with the firing of the travel office staff and the president's infamous Air Force One haircut by coiffeur Christof on the apron at Los Angeles International Airport— however overblown the coverage of that was—fed the criticisms of a staff too adolescent for the roles they were given. At the 1993 Gridiron Dinner, Dole joked, "There are a lot of complaints around town, Mister President, about the youthfulness of the White House staff. Personally, I don't have a problem with that. After all, Chelsea's got to have someone to play with."[8]

In the long run, Dole's age put him in the weaker position, and he was unwilling to market himself aggressively as a member of the Greatest Generation, a term yet to be popularized. In a *New York Times* profile in 1995, Dole demurred about talking more about his past. "That's hard for me to do," he said. "I don't know if it's generational. You don't want to get up and talk about yourself, how tough it was, how you had all these problems in the hospital. You can be too self-serving in this business. There's a balance . . . I still haven't found."[9]

Dole, who in addition to his war wounds had also been treated for prostate cancer, tried to use humor to rebut the chatter about his age.

He would point to a Senate colleague, ninety-two-year-old Strom Thurmond, as a measure of comparison. "Some think I'm too young," he said. "I've been willing to put Strom Thurmond on the ticket for balance."[10] The humor did little to detour the Bridge to the 21st Century. Dole would have to find another wedge to make a generational argument that his temperament was better suited to the Oval Office than Bill Clinton and his army of young aides. When all else fails, blame Quentin Tarantino.

THE CAMPAIGN FALL

September 18, 1996, put Dole's awkward outreach to a younger generation on full display. While Dole was flying to California, I was headed to Seattle to connect with a Clinton bus tour through college towns in Washington and Oregon, a trip designed to connect the president with the region's youth. The planned stops for the buses turned out massive crowds at train depots and demonstrated, for the press corps that filled a small fleet of buses of their own, Pacific Northwesterners' embrace of the Democratic ticket in a region synonymous with the ABC series *Twin Peaks*.

Meanwhile, at Chaminade, a Catholic prep school in the San Fernando Valley, Dole had Hollywood—which turned out shows like *Twin Peaks* and movies like *Pulp Fiction*—in his sights. In his speech, he pointed to Clinton's admission to casual marijuana use as "moral confusion" and fingered both *Pulp Fiction* and *Trainspotting* for supposedly glamorizing heroin. The speech might have elicited cheers at Chaminade, but it flopped with a broader audience of Californians.

Dole's spokesman, Nelson Warfield, later admitted Dole had never seen the films he criticized. Moreover, he proffered a clunky new slogan for his audience—"Just Don't Do It"—that was a mash-up of two older phrases, Nancy Reagan's anti-drug slogan of the 1980s ("Just Say No") and Nike's tagline for athletic daring ("Just Do It"). Convinced that he was onto something with "Just Don't Do It," he awkwardly led the high schoolers in the refrain, over and over, like a scratched vinyl record.[11]

"As president," Dole said at Chaminade, "I will encourage the movie, television and music industries to embrace a no-use, zero-tolerance message in the products they market to America's youth."[12] It landed like a glancing blow to the state's economic engine whose capital, Hollywood, stood just twenty-three miles away.

Quentin Tarantino, the director of *Pulp Fiction*, met Dole's weak jab with a swift counterpunch. "How can a leader condemn works of art he hasn't seen?" Tarantino said. "At best it's pandering and puppeteering and makes Dole look like the bore at a party mouthing opinions loudly about issues he knows nothing about."[13]

Aping Nike's popular ad campaign, Dole probably didn't intend to offend, but the global leader in exercise gear was next with its rejoinder. "We're a sports and fitness company," said spokesman Jim Small, "and we're uncomfortable about being brought into the political arena."[14] If Dole was vying to win the Michael Jordan Primary, he shot an air ball at Chaminade. While Nelson Warfield continued to fend off attacks by Tarantino and others, the Dole campaign caravan moved on to Chico, in Northern California, where Kent Gray's advance team had constructed a classic outdoor rally.

Video seen from two angles suggests that Chico had all the makings of a Clinton-style hoedown. Hundreds of helium-filled balloons bulged against thin restraining netting, ready to fill the blue skies above. A well-appointed brass band was playing refrains of "This Land Is Your Land" as the candidate made his way across a crowded stage bedecked with a red carpet, festooned with patriotic bunting and the old-school white balustrade right out of *The Adventures of Tom Sawyer*. The crowd, larger than the Dole events I had monitored in recent weeks, included many attendees holding aloft handmade signs with phrases like "Chico loves Dole" for the cameras to shoot and log as "B-roll." From the healthy-sized audience and the celebratory midday images just before the speaking program got underway, it was possible to consider that, maybe, the campaign day in California wasn't a lost cause after all.

Dole darted from the back of the stage toward the balustrade determined to press some flesh prior to his speech. His gait accelerated in forward momentum that would have qualified him to march across Clinton's pedestrian bridge in Tempe, Arizona. Like a sprinter thrusting out his chest to shave milliseconds off his time as he crossed the finish line, Dole's left thigh made light contact with the railing. The senator had to trust that the balustrade would anchor his weight as he leaned over it to shake the hand of an eight-year-old child standing below. It didn't.

Instead, a three-foot section of the decoration gave way, plummeting four feet to the ground, the senator coming down on top of it. From the camera's position at the back of the rally site, Dole was missing in action for twelve seconds. When the candidate disappeared from view, his

Secret Service detail converged, as their training dictates, and lifted him onto his feet. He quickly raised his left fist aloft to signal that he was in one piece, and pumped the air twice more for emphasis. Making his way along the buffer zone between stage and crowd, he completed a dozen more left-handed handshakes before waving and climbing the stairs back to the stage from whence he fell.

A bystander was heard to ask Dole if he was hurt. "Nah," came the reply. "I've got to reshine my shoes." Once he regained his composure, Dole tried to make light of the snafu. "You can always say I've fallen for Chico," he said. Another quip came from the candidate's mouth that was widely quoted: "I think I've just earned my third Purple Heart going over the rail."[15] A man who suffered far worse in his life, he knew instinctively that humor offered his best chance of reassuring his audience.

In fact, Dole was lightly wounded by the fall. His spokesman, Nelson Warfield, already on defense for the remarks at Chaminade and another gaffe that day in which Dole mistook the Los Angeles Dodgers for the Brooklyn Dodgers, said his boss poked himself in his left eye during his fall, leaving it bloodied. "He might have broken a blood vessel," Warfield said, "But he feels great." To preempt further commentary, Warfield added, "This should put to rest the age question once and for all. If Bob Dole can take a tumble like that and hop right back up on his feet and deliver a great speech, he's strong enough to be president and go a couple of rounds with Mike Tyson too."[16]

While Dole's fall fell on Kent Gray's watch, the advance man initially had no idea that he went down. The team had constructed a holding tent behind the dugout of the Elks Lodge baseball field where Dole readied to make his entrance. Gray, doing what site leads often do as master of the event, performed the role of "Voice of God," the announcer who grandly invokes a baritone to introduce the candidate on stage.

"It's all burned in my mind," Gray told me. "We're standing there and [Dole] points at the microphone clearly saying 'Is it on?' So I checked the switch and I'm like, 'No, it's not on.' He's like, 'Well, Kent, what are you going to say today?' 'Well, Senator, I thought I'd do something along the lines of ladies and gentleman, the next President of the United States, Bob Dole.' He was like, 'I like it. I like it.'"[17]

After Gray made his announcement, Dole walked out into the California daylight for his fateful encounter with the balustrade. His principal duties done, Gray stayed behind. Waiting for "This Land Is Your Land" to die down and the introductory remarks to get underway, press advance lead Ray Joyner approached Gray with a grave sense of alarm.

"I'm so sorry. I'm so sorry," Gray remembers Joyner saying.

"What's wrong?" Gray replied. For a site advance person, it could be any of a dozen snafus. The balloons were released early. A protester interrupted the speech. Someone fainted a few rows back. It could be anything.

"He fell off the stage," Joyner reported.

"What do you mean he fell off the stage?" Gray asked in disbelief.[18]

Later, on his campaign plane, Dole was eager to inspect what photographers saw during the chilling twelve seconds of his ordeal. "I'm feeling fine, but I want to see your little slideshow," he said. The photographers obliged and showed him the images on their laptop computers. "Yikes," he said as the scene replayed before him of his Secret Service agents helping him to his feet. "My hair stayed all right—enough hair spray," he volunteered to the press cohort.[19]

The incident was too much for reporters to ignore. Scores of stories appeared about the fall, many of which connected it to the candidate's age. Almost twenty years later, any survey of exactly where the painful plummet was pictured will be incomplete, though many stories retrieved in databases noted that the photo appeared on the front page. As the *Los Angeles Times* reported, "The incident did, however, provide the sort of television moment that campaigns try to avoid—a visual metaphor for a presidential bid that has stumbled."[20]

"I think we all kind of knew that we'd really screwed something up and that we needed to try and make amends for it," Gray told me.[21]

WHEELS UP

For the advance team, as Gray recalled, "It was a tough wheels-up"— the moment when the candidate's plane takes off, usually a time for pounding back a few beers and swapping war stories before getting a follow-on assignment. Instead, Gray and his team confronted their responsibility and did something noble. They resigned on the spot. "The four of us stood at the bottom of the air stairs and asked to speak to Sheila Burke (one of Dole's traveling aides)," Gray told me. "We all tendered our resignations at the bottom of the air stairs." Burke heard the team out, nodded, and went back up on the plane as the stairs retracted into the fuselage. Dole's aircraft, the *Citizen Ship,* departed Chico a few minutes later.

For a short time, Gray and his team believed their presidential advance careers were finished. They joined their Secret Service counterparts at a local pub "to figure out what in the world had gone on that day." Only the lead advance, Ray Martinez, had a mobile phone to communicate back to the campaign, but each of the team members had been issued SkyPagers, which could receive short alphanumeric text messages. "About halfway through our dinner at Sierra Nevada Brewery," Gray recalled, "we all start getting sky pages that say 'resignation not accepted, Delta E ticket waiting for you all at the airport, see you at the next stop.'"

The team would stay together, in large part, for a series of follow-on advance assignments. Gray remained a member of the Dole advance team until the last day of the campaign. One of their next stops was an agricultural show in Amana, Iowa, where they built a red-and-white barn as a backdrop in harmony with the locale. With their creative juices still flowing, they again proposed something novel to their scheduling desks at headquarters. "I think we actually pitched a plan to have Senator Dole ride in on a John Deere combine and we went over and over and over again how we could make it safe. In the end, headquarters said, 'Maybe not for Team Chico this time.'"[22]

The effects of Team Chico's stage disaster continued to reverberate after Dole left California. The following day, in Las Vegas, Tom Raum of the AP filed a story that noted, "Age is considered such a potent issue in the presidential race that Dole and his aides worked overtime to show he was all right after Wednesday's tumble."[23]

Dole's medical report, detailing a bruised ankle and a scratched eye but nothing major, came from Dr. Rudy Manthei, an ophthalmologist called to the scene by the campaign. The upbeat diagnosis was reinforced by Sheila Burke, Dole's chief of staff, who was a fixture on the campaign plane and also a registered nurse.

While they worked to contain the damage, Warfield and Burke couldn't contain the headlines that coursed around the world. "Dole Jokes about Fall; Says He Was Trying to Do the Macarena," read one AP story.[24] "Dole's Campaign Takes a Tumble," intoned *The Australian.*[25] In Britain, the *Daily Mirror* weighed in with "It's Dole Over Now; Fall Dashes Poll Hopes; Bob Dole in Election Campaign Stage Fall." The *Mirror*'s article said what U.S. newspapers were too polite to say: "It was a fatal blow to Dole's claim that he's fit to take over from 50-year-old rival President Bill Clinton, who is photographed jogging every day. And it's certain to cost him millions of votes when he's already trailing in the polls."[26]

The days that followed brought more comparisons to presidents and candidates playing out their worst moments in public. Jimmy Carter's fainting spell during a road race near Camp David was noted in some articles, as was Dan Quayle's misspelling of "potato," George Bush's illness in Japan and, of course, Michael Dukakis's ride in the tank.

In a *Los Angeles Times* story—"Dole's Tumble Sends His Aids Spinning: GOP Team Scrambles to Keep the Candidate's Fall in Chico from Becoming an Enduring Image of His Campaign"—Maria L. La Ganga and John Broder sought out political scientist Marc Ross to analyze the fall in the context of the age issue. "The dilemma for candidates for high office," Ross said, "is that when they engage in actions that confirm existing images, those are much more likely to stick. Dole has done some things that fit with his obvious weaknesses, like what happened Wednesday." Rutgers University political scientist Ross Baker was more direct. "It was like Jerry Ford falling down the steps of his plane; it just confirmed all the preconceptions we had—Ford is a bumbler, Dole is old."[27]

THROUGH THE VIEWFINDER

The most intimate shots of campaign events come from the buffer zone that the Secret Service mandates between the stage and the public gathered to watch the event. The only ones allowed inside the buffer are the agents, a few traveling staff members, and a small pool of photographers who have been pre-identified by the campaign and pre-screened by the Service. They're usually the most experienced, battle-tested photographers working the event. They crouch down low with their eyes through the viewfinder, ready to capture any moment that evokes the prevailing news of the day.

The image that Ross Baker referred to in the *Los Angeles Times* piece, the image seen by almost all who would cast a vote in the election six weeks later, could only have been shot from the buffer. Rick Wilking, the Reuters photographer who captured the image, was a renowned photojournalist with whom I logged tens of thousands of miles traveling with President Clinton. While he could photograph beautiful campaign panoramas, this shot showed the tightest possible focus. It was a frame of Dole's grimacing expression, his head cradled in the hands of another photographer, his suit coat still buttoned and his tie scrunched up. It's not the kind of image an advance man ever imagines while drawing up a diagram of an event site. That was how Bob Dole was pictured that day.

The picture was one of eight frames that Wilking said he shot over the course of twenty seconds. They were "the biggest pictures of my life," he admitted. "I went into instinctive mode. I took pictures that I didn't know I had until I looked at them later."[28]

David Ake, the photographer in whose hands Dole's head was cradled, would miss the story that day. As a human being, he had little choice in the matter. He dropped his camera to stop the candidate's skull from crashing into the ground.

Seconds earlier, Ake had been in the buffer zone, his eye peering through the viewfinder at a candidate reaching over to shake a hand. It was a nice moment, Ake thought, with an angle that only pool photographers get when they can literally look up the nose of their subject. But that shot would get no space in the papers on September 18. "I called my boss that night and told him we weren't going to get much play tomorrow," he told the *New York Times*.[29] Instead, Ake got a letter of thanks from Dole.

If there were recriminations against Kent Gray and Team Chico, their names were never publicly disclosed. Lloyd Grove of the *Washington Post* got one unnamed Dole official to say that the advance person on point had been told "very clearly that nothing like this can ever happen again. But we're not going to have a ritual bloodletting over it."[30]

Michael Deaver, the man whose work during the Reagan years inspired me in the first place, was less charitable in his comments to Grove. "If I had anything to do with it, he wouldn't be doing advance any more. I'd reassign him. He ought to be taking care of the baggage for the media."[31]

Most of Grove's article, however, was not about advance work, but about metaphor and its effects on a seventy-three-year old candidate. The fall was a metaphor for age. "It was a harrowing series of images," the article began, "reprinted yesterday in newspapers all over the country and repeated relentlessly through countless television news cycles." Grove got numerous Republican wise men, like Alex Castellanos and Tony Blankley, to weigh in that the candidate's resilience and humor might have won the day, but Deaver was unvarnished in calling it like he saw it: "Of course it's negative," Deaver said, "because it's a picture you don't want."[32]

In 1996, Dole couldn't escape the metaphor, or the math: there was a twenty-three-year age difference between him and his opponent. On October 26, 2016, Hillary Clinton will turn sixty-nine years old, twenty-four years older than Marco Rubio, a possible opponent, another wide age gap. Secretary Clinton has many skills as an effective campaigner on the stump, and her chances for besting a younger rival may be more closely identified with Ronald Reagan when he ran in 1980 than Bob Dole in 1996. Just in case, her advance teams have learned from Kent Gray's experience to secure the decorative elements of their sites. Out of an abundance of caution, she would be well advised to stay away from the lip of the stage.

2000: GORE FLOATS INTO "FLOODGATE"

(Or, How a Dam Release Turned an Environmentalist into a Hypocrite)

THE SHAKEDOWN SUMMER

In the middle months of 1999, Vice President Al Gore, then fifty-three, expected to be elected president in a year and a half. Had he won, he would have been fifty-four shortly after his inauguration, the average age at accession, exactly, of the forty-four men who have served in that office. While he fell in middle of this pack, age-wise, his resume put him near the peak of American politicians. His seven years of service as vice president following his eight years in the Senate and twelve in the House of Representatives certainly should have signaled to him—and others—a sense that his life's work in politics was reaching an apex.

But a cloud hung over Gore. He was endeavoring to succeed a scandal-shrouded boss while that boss's wife, Hillary Rodham Clinton, was herself emerging from her husband's shadow to run for the Senate from New York. Making matters worse, Gore's staff and consultants were enmeshed in rivalry, giving him conflicting advice.[1] While a recipe for success on the campaign trail is to project the image of "the happy warrior," a confluence of factors left him in an unhappy spot from which to debut an eighteen-month drama.

There was also the *thing* about Gore: a perception—cross-examined and reconsidered only *after* he left office—that he was prone to exaggeration or, as Lou Dobbs put it on CNN, "delusions of grandeur."[2] The real *thing* about Gore, this many years later, might be that the D.C. press corps didn't much like him. Could they be blamed for that? In the way he comported himself on the stage or in on-the-record interviews, he wasn't a natural. Unlike Clinton, he didn't easily warm to strangers.

Gore was also emerging into his own amid a sea change in the TV news business. Long the sole twenty-four-hour cable news channel, CNN was joined by MSNBC on July 15, 1996, and Fox News Channel followed later that year on October 6. The three networks competed intensely, putting up prime-time programming that was built on parsing and amplifying the newspaper and magazine reporting of the day.

The cable networks had plenty to parse and amplify from a casual comment Gore offered up during a late-night 1997 conversation with Rick Berke of the *New York Times* and Karen Tumulty of *Time* aboard Air Force Two. These kinds of chats often comprise a bonding strategy for presidential candidates to forge closer ties to the reporters on their beat. Instead, the chat session spawned the urban legend that Gore boasted of being the model for the Oliver Barrett IV character in Erich Segal's *Love Story*. Closer examination of a range of reporting shows that he never made that claim.[3]

And then there was the "Internet" fiasco. An interview of Gore by CNN's Wolf Blitzer in 1999 was misconstrued from Capitol Hill to green rooms all around Washington implying that the wonky vice president claimed he had "invented" the Internet. A closer watch of that interview shows that he didn't say that either.[4]

Finally, there was Love Canal. At an event in 1999 in New Hampshire, Gore told students that, while researching a mysterious illness affecting a girl from his home state, he "found a little place in upstate New York called Love Canal." He *did* say that, but when you read the quote in context, it's called *conversation,* as in "I found a little restaurant in Greenwich Village"—it doesn't mean you *discovered* it.[5]

Further deconstruction of Gore's choice of words in his pre-campaign positioning is folly. Eric Boehlert in *Rolling Stone* and Evgenia Peretz in *Vanity Fair,* among others, did a thorough autopsy of those moments years ago.[6] Anyone searching for a classic origin story of how "narratives" of public figures are formed should study the source materials, follow-on stories and the revisionist analysis of Gore's so-called lies.

The upshot is that the late 1990s "exaggerations" of Al Gore say more about the media and our pop culture than they do about the man. It was simpler, cheaper and easier to serve up superficial, reprocessed mockery about an individual than dive deep into issues like foreign policy and climate change.

Reporters like Boehlert and Peretz, or one-time insiders like me, can wag our fingers against popular mythology all we want. It matters little to a defeated politician. The die was cast on Al Gore in 1999 when, to drive chatter, eyeballs and votes, the influencing class of the Age of Optics decreed certain "truths" about Gore, if they are repeated over and over, to be self-evident.

Water-cooler chatter of the strain that infected Gore is bred by what leads the news the night before, how the late-night comics twist it for laughs and where it pops out from the paper as you sip your coffee on the commuter train. Attitudes formed in the evening during cable news prime time harden overnight, glazed by the heat from the picture on the front page and the first twenty minutes of the network morning shows. The process is magnified in a media town like New York, where tabloids like the *Post* and *Daily News* scream from every street corner. The "wood" from those papers informs columnists and comedy writers about what material might kill in a monologue or in 750 words along the edge of a page of newsprint.

A photo, and the story behind it, can drive punchlines for a week or more. At the worst possible time in his political career, when he had to redefine his character and cleanse himself from a year of scandal that started steps from his West Wing office, Gore's team made an unforced error in the execution and aftermath of a photo op. It was seized on instantly by the media and his enemies, adding to the ingrained, if unfair, perception of the candidate as hypocrite.

In July 1999, the Gore presidential "road show" went through its shakedown summer. This was a time to clear the cobwebs from seven years as the presidential understudy and get into fighting trim against New Jersey senator Bill Bradley, a political icon who proved to be more of a warm-up bout than a title card fight.

In the early months, some events on the vice president's schedule were political in nature, paid for from his campaign coffers. Some events were official in nature, with Gore performing vice presidential duties as a representative of the federal government, but still seen by the news-consuming public through the prism of a man seeking even higher office.

As the pace of campaigning picked up, reporters like Katharine Seelye of the *New York Times* and Ceci Connolly of the *Washington Post* took on the Gore beat full time, competing for every scoop, the words in their stories periodically freshening the unflattering episodes of the Gore mythology.[7] Through their reporting, and that of other news organizations, every abnormal tic, imprecise phrase and awkward image mattered. Such warmed-over gruel was easier for readers to digest than substance. While the traveling press doesn't like to admit it, the road show is more like a concert tour than an exercise in civic discourse, and the reporters are the jaded rock critics. Their job is to uncover evidence, preferably visual, that the band on its summer tour doesn't have its shit together.

As my old friend Mike Feldman, an ex-advance man who served that summer as Gore's senior advisor and his traveling chief of staff, told me, "The fact of the matter is that 'the road show,' however you define it, at that point in time and still to this day, is still a series of productions. Everything is designed to try to convey some sort of message about the administration's agenda, and also about the priorities of the man who might be potentially running for president."[8]

CRISIS MANAGER

Feldman was no rookie on the road show. A veteran of the 1992 campaign like me, we bonded during a 1993 trip to Silicon Valley to lay the groundwork for Clinton and Gore to unveil their new high-tech initiative at the headquarters of Silicon Graphics, then a leading maker of high-powered workstations for design and special effects firms. The hundreds of engineers who worked at SGI, and their CEO, Ed McCracken, were focused on where the new team in the White House would take U.S. technology policy. McCracken opened the company's doors wide to us, and we graciously accepted his hospitality.

On site selection visits like our trip to Northern California, a tape measure makes the first calculation of how many people can cram into a location. Wearing a producer's hat, you pinpoint where lights, cameras and staging will go. Importantly, you also need a human barometer to gauge how generous a host will be to underwrite the myriad costs of your event. Working in the White House is fundamentally different from campaigns, where you can use donors' funds to produce any kind of extravaganza.

Silicon Graphics offered the best mix of people, products and open space—and an open wallet, thanks to Ed McCracken—to host a great event. While Feldman worked the politics of bringing the president and vice president to Northern California, I focused on transforming the Silicon Graphics cafeteria into a Town Hall venue, linked to the rest of its campus by remote video hookups. With some spare time on site, I sat down with Silicon Graphics visual engineers to produce a special effects–driven video for the event intro that used SGI's then-revolutionary technology to morph Clinton's image in a long line of great presidents, from Washington to Jefferson to Lincoln to FDR and JFK. Next stop, Mount Rushmore.

This event wouldn't have been tried in the Reagan years. Had I pulled that stunt of morphing Clinton's image from a line of great predecessors in the run-up to the 2000 campaign, or more surely today, I would have ignited a small scandal and been run out of town. But back then, there was no YouTube, and only the Silicon Graphics team and I had a copy of the video.

On Game Day, the film brought down the house and even got the press laughing before the event settled into a geekfest with Clinton and Gore hatching their new ideas against a backdrop of computer monitors feeding a constant image of the Presidential Seal. While a supermarket scanner had "amazed" President Bush, Clinton and Gore seemed at home amid the advanced wizardry of Silicon Graphics. The setting created a high-tech composition for evening-news packages and still photos for the next day's papers. It didn't hurt that the new policies resonated with the sympathetic audience of super-smart engineers, adding to the favorable television coverage.

Six years later, with Clinton in near-retirement and Gore in the spotlight, an advance man's prescription to highlight the vice president's priorities was to get out of Washington and away from his boss's shadow. The destination: a picturesque spot in an early primary state in which to remind voters through imagery of your sterling environmental credentials, for example. You might prefer to sit around a table and lecture for hours on the topic, but you've got to scale the communication to an electorate with better things to do on a beautiful July day. One picture, and the few seconds it takes to absorb it, is the most attention you might hope to expect.

Another dividend of the precise outdoor visual is the power to awaken local activists from an eight-year slumber to support your cause. Done well, they would see the next morning a large, four-color shot covering the top half of the *Concord Monitor*. The picture would feature the splendor of the New Hampshire backcountry with a casually attired candidate placed artfully in the middle of a gently flowing river. Any outdoorsy Granite Stater gazing on such an image would feel a sense of kinship with the candidate, or so the thinking went. *That guy*, they would conclude, *shares my values*.

But an advance-man-turned-advisor like Feldman knew from experience that it was precisely these moments that could turn hellish in a hurry, especially with a hyper-competitive press corps in tow. "It is, in a sense, a transaction," Feldman told me, "where you have something you want from the event, the media has something that they want from the event, and those things are not always aligned."[9] The somethings of which Feldman spoke were badly misaligned when Gore traveled to New Hampshire on July 22, 1999.

EARTH DAY

Seven years before that trip to New Hampshire, in 1992, President George H. W. Bush had mocked Gore as "Ozone Man" in one of Bush's flailing broadsides against a ticket that was faster, fresher and more polished than he and Dan Quayle.[10] The president, facing two opponents, Bill Clinton and Ross Perot, found himself on the losing side of the environmental issue, among others, and was denied a second term in office.

While Gore was in office as Bill Clinton's wingman for the seven years that followed, he tried—but couldn't always mollify—each constituent for whom the environment was a ballot-box issue. Though the Clinton years left some green voters disappointed, Gore had worked hard to maintain his conservationist cred, often taking the lead on choreographed White House events designed with a "green" patina.

Since 1970, thanks to the vision of Senator Gaylord Nelson of Wisconsin, Earth Day had been celebrated each year on April 22. During the Clinton-Gore years, that day afforded us a chance to bring the president and vice president outside together somewhere for a back-to-nature image.

On April 22, 1996, our White House scheduling office sent the pair, looking like park ranger trainees, on a mission to the C&O Canal National Historic Park in Montgomery County, Maryland. Their job was to roll up their sleeves and haul away a mess of logs and branches from a

paralyzing winter blizzard that closed off 6.4 miles of the 184-mile tow-
path. With Clinton in khakis and Gore in jeans, and both wearing tan
leather work gloves, they were seen smiling and straining to toss a massive, rotten stump away from a pile of debris. The wire image ended up
on the front page of many newspapers.

Beyond scenes casting him as a boy scout, Gore nurtured his conservationist cred by returning to writing. In 1994, he penned a fresh introduction for the thirtieth-anniversary edition of Rachel Carson's *Silent Spring,*
the landmark book that helped launch the U.S. environmental movement
in 1964. This followed earlier turns as an author, including 1992's *Earth
in the Balance,* which staked his claim to his trademark issue.[11]

Now, approaching the 2000 campaign, the environment might
again serve Gore's political purposes. His likely opponent, Texas governor George W. Bush, the son of Gore's 1992 opponent, appeared to have
environmental liabilities from his record that could be exploited. Bush
had signed widely criticized legislation as governor that established a voluntary program for Texas industrial plants to reduce air pollution. The
law was roundly derided by Democrats for allowing in-state corporations
to skirt environmental responsibility.

There were substantive contrasts between the two men on this and
many other issues, but the coming 2000 campaign was already being
reduced by the media to a simple story of the studious, colorless fellow
(Gore) against the kid who made friends easily but focused blithely on his
schoolwork (Bush). The caricature was unfair to both men, but the narrative was easy to follow, the characters played to type and the resulting
news product kept viewers' attention.

As Gore's advance team deployed to New Hampshire to orchestrate
the latest chapter of the environmental play—Gore announcing a federal
grant to cleanse toxins from a river and canoeing down that very river—
they walked into an accidental trap. They missed the warning signs that
in planning a photo op, no gesture, no matter how small, can help sink a
campaign. By most measures, artificially raising the river's water level to
buoy a downstream paddle is no small gesture.

"An event that backfired, creating a potential embarrassment,"
Mike Feldman told me, remembering the incident many years later, "is
more interesting to the media than the message you're trying to deliver.
I approached every day with the question: what could go wrong?" But
Feldman was no longer the advance man scouting the way. Seven years

removed from that role, he could only implore young colleagues to serve as his early warning radar.

That job began with the advance team. "There are so many moving parts, so much travel, and sometimes three, four or five markets a day, with dozens of events in the course of a week"—what Feldman summed up as "the precariousness of the road."

In listening to conference calls about upcoming stops, Feldman could only run through his mental checklists. "What hand grenade is going to go off today? What mine are we going to step on? What are the things that are going to potentially trip us up?" Feldman repeatedly asked himself those questions and hoped Gore's advance teams were doing the same.[12]

Not sufficiently enough, as it turned out. When a minor photo op—a four-mile canoe trip down the Connecticut River near Cornish, New Hampshire—becomes a scandal in itself, there's deeper trouble ahead. Welcome to "Floodgate."

DOWNSTREAM FROM WILDER DAM

The summer of 1999 was marked by drought conditions in the Northeast United States. The National Oceanic and Atmospheric Administration issued warnings of "record and near-record short-term precipitation deficits occurring on a local and regional scale." Down on the farm, it resulted in agricultural losses and drought emergencies in several states, costing eastern growers as much as $1.1 billion in lost income.[13]

Also, in July, just as the campaigns on both sides were eager to get their road show operations underway, politics took a temporary backseat to national tragedy. A small airplane, a Piper Saratoga, piloted by John F. Kennedy Jr. and carrying his wife, Carolyn Bessette, and his sister-in-law, Lauren Bessette, crashed into the Atlantic Ocean on July 16 off the coast of Martha's Vineyard, Massachusetts. The occupants perished, sending the country into a week of national shock and then mourning for the loss of an icon of a bygone era. On every medium were melancholy reminders of decades of heartbreak befalling the Kennedy family.

Visual retrospectives rushed into production in TV newsrooms showed the image of the boy who, in Alan Stanley Tretick's famous October 1963 photo for *Look* magazine, peered through the secret door of the Resolute Desk while his father worked away in the Oval Office. Jackie

Kennedy didn't like her children being photographed for political purposes, but she was out of the country when Tretick got that frame.[14]

In a stark contrast to that final endearing moment preserved on film between father and son, viewers were riveted to live coverage of the search for the bodies of JFK Jr. and the Bessette sisters. The victims were finally pulled from the ocean floor by Navy divers on Wednesday, July 21. They were cremated that evening at the Mayflower Cemetery crematorium in Duxbury, closing a final chapter of America's Camelot.

Meanwhile, 175 miles away in Cornish, New Hampshire, a Gore advance team was balancing both the drought conditions and the somber national mood as they put the finishing touches on a signature Gore event. Along the banks of the Connecticut River, they were preparing for the vice president to tout a federal grant that would provide $819,000 for projects to restore the waterway, which had become so polluted that by the 1950s inspectors taking water samples from the river took to wearing gas masks to accomplish their task. The river had been a haven for settlers during colonial times and a busy thoroughfare for commerce in the following centuries, leading to its degradation. During the Clinton years, it was one of fourteen waterways designated as an American Heritage River, making it eligible for federal funds to assist in their cleanup.[15]

On July 22, the day after Kennedy was cremated, the Gore advance team had arranged a speaking opportunity to announce the Heritage Rivers designation, an event tailor-made for a natural backdrop. Gore, at a microphone erected near the riverbank, said, "Environmental protection and economic growth are not opposing forces, but go hand in hand." With the flowing water behind him, Gore added, "To me, these are more than public policy issues, they are moral issues. We have to make the twenty-first century the time we right the environmental wrongs of the past."[16] Cameras dutifully recorded the remarks and reporters scribbled in their notebooks, but the main event was still to come.

To give photographers a newsworthy visual to buttress Gore's message, the vice president would embark, via canoe, on a leisurely paddle four miles down the river. In conference calls with the advance team, Gore's assistant press secretary, Nathan Naylor, pressed them to arrange a vantage point that allowed lenses to capture the full panorama of the idyllic scene. No problem, they told Naylor. On site scouting visits, they had found a dry sandbar in the middle of the river that provided a perfect angle to film approaching watercraft. On Game Day, Naylor would escort the pool to that spot to await their prized catch.[17]

According to the plan, New Hampshire governor Jeanne Shaheen would paddle in the bow of the canoe, with the vice president navigating the red craft from the stern. The forecast called for good weather, and the canoers would be suitably decked out in khaki pants and golf shirts and properly fitted with life preservers to make the trip. The image was a no-brainer. The only nagging worry for the advance team, one they thought they'd put to rest days before, was *would there be enough water?*

Water flow on the river near Cornish was regulated by the Wilder Dam, built in 1950, located several miles upstream. The dam, owned by Pacific Gas and Electric, "impounded" the river for forty-five miles upstream, creating a reservoir that drove turbines providing forty-two megawatts of hydroelectric power to nearby cities and towns. In the summer months, especially these parched summer months of 1999, the utility released millions of gallons of water at timed intervals during the day to meet peak power demand in nearby communities. When the water was released from the dam, the level of the river would rise commensurately, by as much as a foot in the dry months. A calculated bonus from the artificially rising tide meant that a canoe could float down the river without the risk of running aground.

Daily massive releases of water weren't just normal, they were necessary. But for the advance team planning Gore's canoe trip, a water release was also expedient, if it could be well-timed. A rise in the water level of eight to ten inches would ensure that the canoe carrying Gore and Shaheen would cruise above any embarrassing obstacle during its four-mile journey, a logistical detail that commanded attention on daily trip calls.

In addition to Nathan Naylor, another Gore aide monitoring the calls for the July 22 trip was my old friend Matt Bennett, now Gore's trip director. Bennett had held that role since 1997, logging hundreds of thousands of air miles with the VP on trips around the world. His wife, Sue, was expecting their first child, and the road show would soon end for Bennett, the duties of trip directing a new candidate and fatherhood of a newborn baby being both similar yet fundamentally incompatible. As trip director, Bennett oversaw the staff on Gore's plane and tried to keep the entourage on schedule, all while staying abreast of the planning process for upcoming trips and preparation for diaper-changing.

"At some point," Bennett told me, the VP's scheduling office "became concerned because the local contact said, 'Look it's summer, and that time of day, at this time of year, the river is low. And it's a dam-controlled river and we might not even be able to canoe on it. The water is released every day, but the timing doesn't work very well. If you guys were here three hours later, it would be fine. But the river's going to be low and that could be a problem.'"[18] It's not a problem, however, if you control the levers for the floodgate.

The Gore advance team and the Secret Service were working with Sharon Francis, executive director of the Connecticut River Joint Commissions, on planning for the trip. The Joint Commissions' statutory mission is to preserve and protect the resources of the Connecticut River Valley and guide its growth and development. Having the vice president fly up from Washington to showcase their work and bestow $819,000 in federal money for river-related projects, including $100,000 for the commission itself, meant that Francis had a hefty stake in making sure everything came off without a hitch. "As hosts for our vice president on the Connecticut River, we felt a responsibility for his safety and that of the governor and the river's other guests," Francis said later.[19]

The issue of safety and water level never reached the vice president before the trip, according to Bennett, but it was a hot topic of conversation on daily trip calls. "As is typical with these kinds of scheduling things, we just said, 'All right, let's see if there's any way of sorting that out so that we don't hit bottom on the river,'" Bennett told me.[20]

On the morning of July 22, as Air Force Two descended toward the Lebanon Municipal Airport in New Hampshire, Bennett, Feldman, Naylor and Chris Lehane, Gore's press secretary, reviewed their schedules one last time for the vice president's trip to New Hampshire. The day would have two planned stops, the environmental remarks and canoe trip near Cornish, and a picnic in the Seacoast area of the state later in the afternoon. By the time the foursome arrived with the vice president at the Seacoast, they would have to reckon with an inconvenient truth: the Connecticut River Joint Commissions had requested that the river be raised through a dam release to smooth Vice President Gore's ride downstream.

TIN MAN IN A BOAT

At the time Gore flew to New Hampshire, Bill Clinton's taint from scandal was beginning to fade. On February 12, following his impeachment trial, the Senate acquitted him on perjury charges, 55 to 45. The Dow Jones Industrial Average eclipsed 10,000 for the first time on March 29 and, on April 20, Clinton again rose to the role as consoler in chief after teenagers Eric Harris and Dylan Klebold killed twelve students and one teacher at Columbine High School. Even with this turn in perceptions regarding Clinton's job approval, there was persistent coverage of a deepening divide between the president and vice president who had so amicably shared the stage that Feldman and I set up at Silicon Graphics six years earlier.

A month before the canoe trip, on June 16, Gore formally launched his candidacy before 8,000 supporters in his hometown of Carthage, Tennessee. "If you entrust me with the presidency," he told the crowd, "I will marshal its authority, its resources and its moral leadership to fight for America's families." Moral leadership wasn't a term he used lightly. "With your help," he added, "I will take my own values of faith and family to the presidency to build an America that is not only better off but better."[21] Reference to "values of faith and family" was thinly veiled code quickly deciphered by the press.

While Gore had stood by his boss throughout the impeachment, in an interview on ABC News's *20/20* to preview his campaign launch, Gore said that what Clinton had done "was inexcusable, and particularly as a father, I felt that it was terribly wrong, obviously." Quizzed on his feelings when Clinton wagged his finger at the cameras in the Roosevelt Room of the White House and declared, "I did not have sexual relations with that woman, Ms. Lewinsky," Gore added, "I didn't like that moment at all."[22] That was how Gore managed his message in the summer of 1999, trying to cast himself as his own man.

Things did not start well with "the Maureen Dowd primary." The *New York Times* columnist had her antenna finely tuned for anecdotes that allowed her to tweak Gore, and while she was also tough on George W. Bush, it came off in print in a more big sisterly sort of way. In an October 9, 1999, column under the headline, "Here Comes the Son," she described Gore as "stiff" and wrote, "W. is loose because his father never expected him to be President." She also included this suggestive exchange with the Texas governor:

> "'You're so much more mature now,' I remarked to the Texas Governor.
> 'So are you,' he replied saucily."[23]

Dowd didn't write that way about Gore. Before any votes are cast, pundits track a dashboard of varied indicators—the amount of money raised, the favor of party elders, fawning from columnists—as pre-primary

"primaries." Dowd, who had covered President George H. W. Bush as
White House correspondent was, in the view of some, a primary unto
herself. Getting on Dowd's good side, or at least minimizing her ridicule,
can be a leading indicator of how early donors, activists, and coastal opinion shapers will flock to your candidacy. In her June 16, 1999, column
reacting to the dueling announcements of candidacy by Gore and Bush,
Dowd began, "Al Gore is the Tin Man: immobile, rusting, decent, badly
in need of that oil can."[24]

Amid paragraphs describing Bush as the scarecrow in her *Wizard of
Oz* meme, ascribing to him a string of adjectives including "charming,
limber, cocky, fidgety" and noting his campaign accessories of mono-
grammed ostrich cowboy boots and oversized belt buckles, she added
that "Al Gore is so feminized and diversified and ecologically correct, he's
practically lactating."[25]

The image of the vice president lactating was particularly damning,
and her dismissal of Gore's environmental record as "ecologically correct" was equally dismissive. By any measure, Gore was a genuine environmentalist, spending much of his free time with his family pursuing
activities that were far more in tune with nature than most men his age.
Bush might go mountain biking to burn off steam, but Gore preferred
the canoe.

I had already helped to produce some made-for-camera "back to nature" moments for Bill Clinton by the time the 1996 campaign geared
up, including a whitewater trip on the Snake River near Jackson Hole,
Wyoming, during the summer of 1995. It lasted less than two hours, in
contrast to the week-long, no-press paddle down the Colorado River that
Gore enjoyed with his family that same summer. Clinton was an environmental tourist, with the press in tow. Gore was the real deal, and the
privacy he demanded was authentic.

In New Hampshire, on the Connecticut River instead of the Colorado, it was different. Despite being an official event to do government
business, it was plainly obvious that this was the very media market where
Gore would face his first big test as a candidate against Senator Bradley
in that state's Democratic Primary six months hence. The Office of the
Vice President reached out to the Connecticut River Joint Commissions
to help organize the downriver trip, but even when you're playing with
water, it's still easy to get burned.

Rather than risk their candidate running aground, the decision was
made to move up the timing of the dam's daily water release. This assured

that the canoe ride would go smoothly, but the planners didn't fully game out a scenario of the water release itself becoming a story. "A host wants to be helpful," Mike Feldman told me, "and somebody along the way didn't process the fact that it could potentially be embarrassing. We were out of the event before I heard anything about it or before I knew there was an issue."[26]

After the vice president's remarks announcing the government grant, the Gore flotilla embarked, including canoes and boats filled with security and staff. Feldman and Bennett were in their own canoe, out of the cameras' sightlines.

Naylor, who skipped the remarks to pre-position the press pool on the sandbar, stood aghast on the riverbank: his sandbar, the carefully chosen vantage point for image-making, was submerged under inches of water. "I could tell right away that the throw was way too far. Few had long lenses and the stills were starting to grumble," Naylor told me. A "throw" is advance-speak for distance, and "long lenses" is the photojournalists' jargon for heavy zoom lenses that can easily capture the quirks of facial expression at a distance of fifty yards. "I asked our advance man, 'What gives with the sandbar?'" he said. "It was here yesterday," came the reply.[27] Not wanting to miss the shot, Naylor forged MacArthur-like into the river, telling his poolers to roll up their pants and follow him to take up positions on the sunken berm.

Print reporters traveling under Naylor's escort mingled with onlookers on the riverbank. Bill Sammon, a correspondent for the *Washington Times*, was among those who rolled up their cuffs, but he returned to dry land to acquaint himself with John Kassel, director of the Vermont Department of Natural Resources. As the barefooted reporter chatted with Kassel, the Vermont official didn't immediately process that he was talking with a newsman, or that his casual observations of the scene playing out on the river in front of them were being noted for the record.

SAMMON ON THE RIVER

The first story emerged from the river trip just as the Gore campaign might have scripted it themselves. "Gore Says Environmental Concerns and Economic Progress Go Together," ran a headline from an article by Ann S. Kim for the Associated Press.[28] The just-the-facts piece would find its way into many newspapers, connecting Gore with the nearly $1 million earmarked for river cleanup. The press staff of a campaign loves wire stories like Kim's because the pieces weave themselves into small markets where the local papers can't afford to send reporters to cover national campaign events in person.

In the *Dallas Morning News,* George W. Bush's hometown paper, the story was even better. "Gore Seeks Edge in Campaign with Environment Issue; He Says Protections, Growth Linked," read the headline. Gore couldn't hope to win Texas, but it was good to needle Bush in his geographic power base. Susan Feeney, the *Morning News* correspondent, echoed Kim's story with 800 words reinforcing Gore's message. In her story, Feeney quoted Tom "Smitty" Smith, the director of the Texas office of Public Citizen, a consumer watchdog group, who said, "Basically, Governor Bush has a horrible environmental record."[29] A few more stories like this and the canoe trip might be a home run.

A third story followed in sync with the prior two. Sandra Sobieraj, an AP reporter who covered Clinton and Gore closely, favorably contrasted Gore's positions against those of Bush. Sobieraj included a comment from spokesman Chris Lehane that any campaign would covet: "In 2000, the American people will have a stark choice," Lehane said, "between the vice president and whoever the Republican presidential candidate may be when it comes to the environment." Always quick to launch a missile at his opponents when reporters craved a quotable quip, Lehane added, "Republicans seem to believe it's more important to protect the polluters."[30]

But while Kim, Feeney and Sobieraj were doing their reporting, Bill Sammon remained busy talking with John Kassel. Those few minutes of conversation—a reporter listening intently to the unguarded musings of a man with an official state position—spawned a series of stories by Sammon and a legion of follow-on coverage from mainstream news outlets that would dominate campaign news in the week to come. A headline from the story, authored by Sammon and Laura Vanderham, screamed, "New Hampshire Opts to Float Gore's Boat; 4 Billion Gallons Released for Photo Outing."[31]

The lead paragraph of Sammon's *Washington Times* story went in an entirely new direction than those of the AP and the *Dallas Morning News.* "Nearly 4 billion gallons of water were unleashed from a massive dam yesterday," Sammon and Vanderham wrote, "to raise the level of the Connecticut River in Cornish, N.H., so that Vice President Al Gore's canoe would not get stuck during an environmental photo opportunity."

The toughest commentary for the piece came from Kassel, who told Sammon, "They won't release the water for the fish when we ask them to, but somehow they find themselves able to release it for a politician." Sammon noted that Kassel "groused" as he "clambered up the riverbank after the four-mile canoe trip." Giving the reporter a tip that would inform a total of four stories by Sammon, and scores more by other reporters and additional commentary from TV and radio outlets, he said, "The only reason they did this was to make sure the vice president's canoe didn't get stuck."[32]

With a tip like that, Sammon knew we was onto something beyond a routine photo op. He began making calls. Reflecting on the action along the riverbank that day, Nathan Naylor told me, "I've often wondered if I didn't march the cameras into the current would Bill have been so interested in the story?"[33]

In the course of his reporting, Sammon found Cleve Kapala, director of government affairs for Pacific Gas and Electric, owner of the Wilder Dam, who said that his company was asked several days earlier by the Connecticut River Joint Commissions to release water earlier than planned to add downstream depth to the river at the appointed time. "The river was pretty dry and no one wanted the canoes to be dragging on the bottom," Kapala told Sammon. "Vice President Gore's people were concerned that we not raise the level too high, either, because they didn't want it to be dangerous."[34]

Far more than the stories by Kim, Feeney and Sobieraj, Sammon's piece infused dramatic elements into the fluid scene on the river and the steps taken at the dam to create it. "The water was less than 8 inches deep in many spots at 6 a.m. yesterday, when Dennis Goodwin of PG&E pushed a few buttons at his control panel at Wilder Dam, unleashing 180,000 gallons per second," Sammon wrote. "The dam is 10 miles upstream from the point where Mr. Gore's canoe was to enter the water, and Mr. Goodwin wanted to have a good three hours for his unusual task."[35]

Sammon's use of Kassel as a source allowed him to connect the dots that the water had been boosted by eight to ten inches on the stretch of river over which Gore paddled. "There are people on the phone right now telling them to shut it off," Kassel told the reporter. On the other end of the phone, Sammon noted, "Mr. Goodwin confirmed that, as soon as Mr. Gore disembarked the canoe, the dam's floodgates were closed."[36]

Reading Sammon's story, the picture he paints of Dennis Goodwin sealing the floodgates as Gore disembarks sounds like standard Secret Service protocol for watching a president go "wheels-up" following a visit. In that scenario, the advance team stays in place and the counter-assault team follows Air Force One until the plane's wheels leave the ground. The thinking behind that is that if the plane for any unknown reason doesn't take off, the agents are back on guard. There was no real imperative for Goodwin to keep the floodgates open ten miles upstream while Gore was ending his canoe trip, but *just in case* the vice president decided to extend his journey, the water level would remain high.

To cap things off on the first of four *Washington Times* stories, the enterprising reporters unearthed an earlier *Rocky Mountain News* item from 1996 in which the Denver Water Board opened the gates of the Chatfield Reservoir in Colorado to unleash 92 million gallons of water into the South Platte River "to make a robust background for Mr. Gore's visit to the area,"[37] as the story read. Sammon noted that state officials in office at the time, along with Vice President Gore, had issued statements "deploring" the misuse of state resources. There was no connection between the two events, but there was an implication of a pattern of hypocrisy of an environmentalist politician manipulating the environment to leave no stone jutting out above the water that might mar the imagery.

Speaking years later, Feldman respects the role of reporters to call out mistakes. "I'm not big on placing blame on our press corps for digging in around issues like this," he told me. "If you run for president, you have to be prepared to deal with diligent reporting."[38] In the same breath, he points out that the guy at the top doesn't vet the details of each event. That was the reality Gore faced just weeks after announcing his candidacy. He had to stomach writers like Maureen Dowd imagining him lactating, and then get up the next day with a smile on his face as the central character in events that he parachuted into. The questions he encountered when he landed weren't from reporters seeking his views on the environment, but rather the next installment of the story of Gore the hypocrite.

"You're beginning to make your first impressions as a potential candidate in your own right, you're a high-profile person, you cannot possibly be responsible for everything that happens at every level of a negotiation leading up to an event like that," Feldman told me, "and yet you're the guy that's being skewered."[39]

With Sammon's story hitting the newsstands the next day, the mainstream media followed along with the current of maritime metaphor. "Special Dam Release to Keep Gore's Canoe Afloat," read a headline from the Associated Press.[40] "Controversy Muddies Gore Float Trip," added the *Atlanta Journal and Constitution*.[41] "Gore Takes Aw-Shucks Tour (and Hits a Bump)," was the banner in the *New York Times*.[42] "Gore's N.H. Canoe Trip Leaves Questions in Wake," the *Boston Globe* headlined. "The photos of Vice President Al Gore and New Hampshire Governor Jeanne Shaheen canoeing down the sparkling Connecticut River Thursday were scenic and beautiful," wrote Jill Zuckman for the *Globe* in her lead paragraph. "Yesterday, however, Gore aides spent the day trying to drown out questions about who asked the local power company to release 4 billion gallons of dammed water to lift the river level—as well as the canoes," she added.[43]

Lehane pushed back against the stories throughout the afternoon while Gore attended the Seacoast picnic. He tried to reason with the *Globe*'s Zuckman and the *Times*'s Melinda Henneberger but made little headway. He briefed the vice president about the brewing stories while he tried to gather more facts. "When it was brought to our attention, we specifically asked them not to do anything out of the ordinary," Lehane said in Henneberger's story. "They raised the river and it has no impact on the environment. It's not our screw-up and nothing bad happened," Lehane added.[44]

In the days that followed, Republicans seized on Sammon's reporting of the 4-billion-gallon water release, which they equated to a more eye-popping 180,000 gallons per second when the floodgates were opened. The Republican national chairman, Jim Nicholson, put a price tag on the release at $1.7 million, citing water use rates provided by the Pennichuk Water Works, which serves the region. "So much for the environmentalist vice president," Nicholson was quoted as saying.[45]

Locally, New Hampshire State GOP chairman Steve Duprey weighed in too, asserting that the value of the release constituted an "in-kind" corporate campaign contribution by Pacific Gas and Electric, later filing a complaint with the Federal Election Commission to question its legality. "The vice president says one thing on the environment and does another," he told reporters.[46]

Doug Hattaway, a Gore spokesman, shot back. "Duprey's up a creek without a paddle. He should be ashamed of wasting taxpayers' money on a frivolous complaint that he knows is totally invalid."[47] But the volley extended the life of the story, which is exactly what the Republicans wanted. The spin and counterspin hearkened back to the effort, a dozen years earlier, by Lee Atwater and his Republican cohort to define Michael Dukakis over Willie Horton, the Pledge of Allegiance and President

Reagan's musing that the Massachusetts governor may be "an invalid." The more noise that was created by the to and fro, and the more days the arguments spanned, the more stories were written.

On Saturday, July 24, Sammon, who had introduced the controversy with his first dispatch and earned his newspaper widespread credit for original reporting, filed his second story for the *Washington Times*. The new piece claimed that the vice president was told immediately after his river trip about the water release, despite having said that he didn't know about it until reading Sammon's initial story.

"I told the vice president about it as we walked to the stage," said Sharon Francis of the Connecticut River Joint Commissions in the new *Washington Times* piece. "He kind of laughed and said, 'I'm very familiar with fluctuating water levels. We've got that in Tennessee, too.'"[48] Lehane, after gathering more details on the conversation between Francis and Gore, explained to Sammon that his boss was simply acknowledging, having grown up along a river, how dams work.

The water released from Wilder Dam to elevate Gore's trip was probably no more or no less than on other summer days. The adjusted timing, one story pointed out, was similar to accommodations for other canoe trips, such as one by the Boy Scouts.[49]

Despite the efforts to clarify facts, the pushback was drowned out by the casual observations of crusty New Hampshire voters who reacted negatively to the growing flood of news accounts. The river-inspired metaphors continued through the weekend and into the next week. Dan Balz, among the most admired political writers inside the Beltway, wrote about the incident as "4 Billion Gallons for a Photo Op,"[50] giving it mainstream credibility. *Newsweek,* jumping into the river story, termed it the "photo op from hell."[51]

The hyperbole, and the torrent of stories, editorials and late-night jokes that continued for a week after the canoe trip, added to the narrative of a calculating public official who might be something different than the environmentalist he professed to be.

A week after the canoe trip, the RNC issued a news release quoting Chairman Nicolson saying, "I want to thank the Gore press office for their work in keeping the story of Gore's hypocrisy flowing. While some have accused the vice president of being shallow, I think his staff has shown remarkable buoyancy and depth."[52]

Bill Sammon wrote his third story about the canoe trip on Monday, August 2, correcting himself by noting "revised" data from Pacific Gas and Electric that reduced the amount of excess water released to 500 million gallons, down from the 4 billion gallons he originally reported, the outsized figure that spawned follow-on articles by a broad array of national media outlets. Still, he wrote, "The constant revisions and backpedaling by both PGE officials and Democratic defenders of Mr. Gore have served to prolong what some Republicans initially expected would be a one- or two-day story about an embarrassing political misstep. Eleven days after the canoe trip went bust, GOP operatives are still gleefully lampooning the vice president in the same way they accused him of having claimed to invent the Internet."[53]

The damage was done. A Fox News/Opinion Dynamics poll of 905 registered voters brought bad news. The poll, taken after the canoe trip, contained results that 44 percent believed "Gore is not the strong environmentalist he claims to be" while only 29 percent said that his environmental credentials remain intact.[54]

Sammon's final story, on August 6, would detail the New Hampshire State Republican Party's FEC complaint asking the commission to investigate whether Gore had accepted an illegal campaign contribution to float his canoe.

Eli Attie, a Gore speechwriter with whom I worked during the Clinton years, later told *Vanity Fair,* "The reality is very few reporters covering the 2000 campaign had much interest in what really motivated Gore and the way he spent most of his time as vice president: the complexities of government and policy, and not just the raw calculus of the campaign trail." Offering a different perspective on the same article, Carter Eskew, Gore's strategist and a founder, along with Feldman, of the Glover Park Group, took some responsibility for not forging a better relationship with reporters. "We basically treated the press with a whip and a chair," he told *Vanity Fair,* "and made no real effort to schmooze at all."[55]

Matt Bennett, who rode in a canoe with Feldman in the flotilla, falls in line with Eskew. "The way that it manifested itself the most was Gore's incredible hyper-caution around the reporters who traveled with us," Bennett told me. "Gore's view, which we all shared, was that there was a purely adversarial relationship." One tactic in creating harmony with reporters—private chats on the campaign plane—was off limits. "Gore would not come back on the plane to talk to them because they would refuse to allow him to talk off the record, which is what the reporters who followed Governor Bush would allow," Bennett told me. "And so he would never let his guard down and it was very difficult to get a nice story like this written because they just seemed to be out for his blood all the time. And this was a perfect example."[56]

Feldman looks back on the failed canoe trip as inconsequential in a campaign that would go on for eighteen more months and ultimately be decided by 537 votes out of 100 million cast. Instead, Feldman saw it as a lesson that helped Gore develop thicker skin for the hard road ahead. To point to any single thing and say that it was decisive in the outcome of the election, he told me, is "enough to drive anybody crazy."

"It wasn't a clear path" for Gore, Feldman told me. "He had to carve out a path to be able to get people to hear him and listen to his message. It is one of the things that you have to endure and have to overcome to be elected president in the modern era. Every day is a series of these challenges, and there's something elegant about it."[57]

Elegant or not, the lessons Al Gore learned in 1999 would be put to use ultimately as a private citizen. He would have the rest of his life—watching America enter a new century, brave the wounds of 9/11 and the wars that followed, and reach the depths of an economic crisis—to think about what he learned on his last campaign. The Connecticut River canoe trip might not have been decisive for Gore, as Feldman said, but it was instructive—for every candidate who followed in his wake.

 **TWELVE**

2004: BUSH, DEAN AND KERRY

*(Or, the Sign, the Scream
and the Windsurfer)*

THE HIGH-WATER MARK

The Age of Optics, inaugurated with Dukakis's tank ride in 1988, reached its zenith during a sixteen-month stretch in 2003 and 2004, and has been in slow decline since.

Facebook was founded in 2004, YouTube in 2005 and Twitter in 2006. It would take a few years for each social medium to become rooted in political discourse, but their rise was matched by a commensurate decline of newspapers and packaged TV news. Networks still aired segments and newspapers still ran photos, but their impact became diluted. A 2012 Pew Research Center study revealed that among those under thirty, "as many saw news on a social networking site the previous day (33%) as saw any television news (34%), with just 13% having read a newspaper either in print or digital form."[1]

As Twitter feeds now grow stale by the hour, so too does the staying power of any single image that once remained in popular consciousness for days. The role of the advance man, once a type of movie producer entrusted to create and communicate a dramatic story from a day in the life of a campaign road show, is now becoming—with some notable exceptions—more of a functionary executing the orders of headquarters or the White House.

That was still far from the case during the presidential campaign cycle of 2004, the first to seriously harness the political power of the Internet beyond fundraising. It was an effective organizing tool, as Howard Dean proved, but also a burgeoning reporting medium, from TV networks posting content to the web to advance people emailing images of proposed event sites back to headquarters.

For George W. Bush, too, the 2004 campaign was taking shape as a referendum on his brand of swaggering leadership that he relied on during his rise to power on the thinnest of margins in 2000 and his early prosecution of the wars in Iraq and Afghanistan. If he won in 2004, his critics, current and future, could not deny that his vision for the country was reaffirmed by American voters, a test his father failed in 1992.

The dominating backdrop during 2003 and 2004 was "GWOT"— the Global War on Terror. The pivot from domestic to military stagecraft happened in one moment at the Booker Elementary School in Sarasota, Florida, when Bush, two-thirds through his first year in office, was reading a book to schoolchildren to promote his "No Child Left Behind" legislation, which he had framed as the early trademark of his presidency.

The date was September 11, 2001. Midway through the ordinary stop, Chief of Staff Andrew Card whispered to the president that America was under attack. That blurry video of Card and Bush, and the presidential grimace that followed, brought the Age of Optics into a new era as Air Force One embarked for unplanned stops at Barksdale Air Force Base in Louisiana and Offutt Air Force Base in Nebraska before finally returning to Washington, a city transformed over the course of hours from a peacetime to wartime footing.

A few days later in New York City, on September 14, President Bush climbed atop the rubble of Ground Zero with a bullhorn in his hand and retired 69-year-old firefighter Bob Beckwith by his side. Beckwith, who had mounted the rubble to test its firmness for the president at the request of White House adviser Karl Rove, wanted to climb down when Bush climbed up, but the president told him to stand fast.

In his book *Bush at War*, Bob Woodward reported that advisor Karen Hughes was "absolutely beaming. This was an amazing moment, she thought—eloquent, simple, the perfect backdrop, a moment for the news magazine covers, the communications hall of fame, and history."[2] Just as Hughes suspected, the picture filled front pages and served as the iconic image on the cover of a special issue of *Time* under the headline "One

Nation, Indivisible," with the familiar red letters of TIME becoming, for this one issue, red, white, blue and black.[3]

With the coming 2004 campaign as a backdrop, Bush argued with characteristic single-mindedness that America needed to follow GWOT to its end. Former Vermont governor Howard Dean, another 2004 candidate, said the country should get out of the war. And Massachusetts senator John Kerry, who would eventually win the Democratic nomination, flip-flopped on the topic of a supplemental appropriation for military operations—a proxy for the war itself—with his answer in a town hall with veterans at Marshall University on March 16, 2004. Strutting the stage, clutching a handheld microphone in his fist, he said, famously, "I actually did vote for the 87 billion dollars, before I voted against it."[4]

Kerry's quote consumed five seconds but haunted him throughout the campaign. Governor Dean, for all of his passionate opposition to the war, is more remembered for the "Dean Scream" in West Des Moines, Iowa, on January 19, 2004. And the verdict on the military policies of President Bush, who spent eight years in office, might be boiled down to two words affixed by an advance team to the bridge of the USS *Abraham Lincoln* during Bush's onboard speech on May 1, 2003: "Mission Accomplished."

Bush's visit to an aircraft carrier. Dean's scream. Kerry's town hall—the basis for a devastating Bush-Cheney TV ad featuring the senator windsurfing off of Nantucket. Each event was created and amplified by fateful actions and decisions of staff, and each marks a stain on the politician's legacy, examples of how production design, event management and image strategy can define a leader's place in the memory of the American public. Together, the three events represent the high-water mark of the Age of Optics, three of the most extraordinary specimens of the intersection of advance work and message, and they all happened within one year of each other.

MARSHAL MOMENTS

During the Clinton years, one of my duties was to help produce images that accentuated the president's role as commander in chief. As a kid growing up, drawn magnetically to landmarks, museums and ephemera of military history, these were some of my most memorable moments as a member of the White House staff. I could look at a setup for an event that involved the armed forces and draw a parallel to past images of presidents in wartime.

For me, Clinton going to snowbound Fort Drum, New York, to visit the 10th Mountain Division was like Washington's 1777 winter at Valley Forge. His stop in Baumholder, Germany, to meet Brigadier General William Nash and his officers about to deploy to Bosnia was akin to Lincoln's visit to George McClellan's encampment with the Army of the Potomac near Sharpsburg in 1862. And a trip to McDonnell-Douglas to take delivery for the Air Force of a new C-17 transport plane in Long Beach, California, was like FDR's 1943 trip to Camp Carson, near Colorado Springs, to watch the Arsenal of Democracy in action.

Whenever we would plan a military-related event, I would consult my archive of imagery for inspiration—oil paintings of the winter at Valley Forge, wet plate collodions by Mathew Brady and Alexander Gardner of Lincoln with his officers, and photos of FDR, usually in his car, inspecting military materiel as it rolled off the assembly line.

Still latched to my advance man's tool satchel—filled with a tape measure, rifle scope for checking "the tight shot," chalk for marking out the stage, duct tape for any of a thousand uses—are commemorative luggage tags issued by the State Department for each overseas military-themed trip, starting with Normandy on June 6, 1994, to celebrate the 50th anniversary of D-Day, the day that ended with Clinton's cross on Omaha Beach.

The luggage tags span the globe. Later that year, on October 28, we flew by helicopter from Kuwait City to visit soldiers of the 24th Mechanized Infantry Division on station at Camp Doha in the Kuwaiti desert. In 1995, on March 31, Air Force One took us to Haiti, where President Clinton addressed U.S. forces at Warrior Base in Port-au-Prince as Operation Uphold Democracy wound down. A year after that, a team of us embedded at Tuzla Air Base in Bosnia-Herzegovina for a week with the soldiers of the 1st Armored Division to lay out Clinton's stop to thank troops deployed in Operation Joint Endeavor. A few months later, on April 17, we were on the deck of the USS *Independence* at port in Yokosuka, Japan, lauding sailors for protecting U.S. interests off the coast of Taiwan. On one of my last trips for President Clinton, I was his lead advance for his visit to Ramstein Air Base in Germany on May 5, 1999, to review Operation Allied Force, the NATO-led air campaign flying sorties over the Federal Republic of Yugoslavia.

I was privileged to take part in each of these visits, and others with a military focus, and I learned much each time about the service and sacrifice of our men and women in uniform. But I also knew that, somehow, my years in the White House were spared by history from major combat that cost large numbers of American lives. The invasion of Iraq, originally known as Operation Iraqi Freedom, began on March 20, 2003, and didn't end officially until December 18, 2011, when the last U.S. troops in Iraq crossed the border into Kuwait, eight years and eight months later, with casualties amounting to nearly 4,500 U.S. troops killed and 33,000 wounded in action.

THE SIGN

On May 1, 2003, six weeks after Operation Iraqi Freedom began, President Bush traveled to San Diego aboard Air Force One and changed into a Navy fight suit, an abrupt departure from the business suit that defines the standard presidential uniform. It was the Mother of All Visuals, with the commander in chief properly outfitted for aerial combat. Cameras watched as the onetime Air National Guard pilot of F-102 Interceptors climbed into the cockpit of a Lockheed S-3 Viking, dubbed Navy One, and took off, heading west over the Pacific Ocean. The plane, with Commander Skip Lussier at the stick (except for a brief handover to President Bush, adding to the optics of the moment), flew thirty miles from shore onto the deck of the USS *Abraham Lincoln,* executing a perfect tailhook landing as live television coverage chronicled the event.

At home in Washington, I watched the events unfold with shock and awe.

Growing up in the 1980s, while some kids collected comic books, I collected *Time* magazines and still have hundreds of musty issues stored in my basement. I'll go downstairs from time to time and travel back thirty years through the pages that chronicle the end of the Cold War. In one issue is a small picture of a man observing a naval exercise, his back to the camera, saluting warships as they pass him in review with the words "Commander-in-Chief" embroidered on the back of a naval officer's ball cap. Seeing the man's hidden face was unnecessary to establish his identity. The words on the hat, and the ramrod-straight bearing of the man, signaled it was Ronald Reagan.

With Reagan as my inspiration, I would scour old images in *Time* during the 1990s to brainstorm ways in which Clinton could validate visually his appreciation of the military, a delicate dance given his draft history. Photos of Clinton walking with Marines across the South Lawn, or sitting with soldiers in a recon tent in Bosnia, were inspired by my archive of prior presidents. In my files is a memo I once wrote proposing that Clinton travel to the 1995 G-7 Summit in Nova Scotia by way of a U.S. attack submarine. This idea came from images of FDR and Winston Churchill meeting secretly aboard the cruiser USS *Augusta* in August 1941, anchored in Placentia Bay, Newfoundland, where they hammered out the Atlantic Charter defining Allied goals for the postwar world.

While Clinton and John Major, the British prime minister, weren't Roosevelt and Churchill, a submarine arrival would make for a grand entrance to the summit. It couldn't be a long trip, I reasoned, departing with fanfare from the Portsmouth Naval Shipyard for an overnight cruise through the waters of the Gulf of Maine to make landfall the next day in Halifax. The idea never left port. The concept was so farfetched, I never sent the memo. We arrived in Halifax via fixed-wing aircraft like every other world leader.

Eight years later on the *Lincoln,* I had to hand it to Scott Sforza, the guy who filled my job in the Bush White House, for pulling off a stunt we would never dare to attempt. The *Lincoln* and her crew were on their way home to Everett, Washington, after a ten-month deployment, the longest of any aircraft carrier since Vietnam. Their mission, by all rights, was accomplished, but that's not how the world read the two words hanging from the bridge, perfectly positioned above the president's head during his speech later that day.

"Mission Accomplished," in the months and years that followed, would become the most criticized political event since Dukakis and the tank. But, like the Dukakis disaster, attitudes about it would unfold at a snail's pace compared to the Age of Twitter, when opinions congeal in a matter of minutes.

Sforza flew to the *Lincoln* several days before the president arrived. For an advance person, there's little to match an assignment onboard a navy ship. As a government official overseeing the movements of the commander in chief onboard, an advance person is afforded senior officer status, assigned a stateroom and given full access to nonclassified areas of the ship. If you can sleep through the nonstop steam catapults and arresting hooks of the patrol sorties, it's a cruise unlike any other.[5]

For the Bush advance team, all of the plans were in place for the May 1 visit to the *Lincoln.* While the president soared across the skies toward the flight deck in the cockpit of his S-3 Viking, the remainder of the essential White House staff and press corps were transported aboard in sorties of Grumman C2-A Greyhounds,[6] a slow-moving airborne ferry with twin turboprops that can accommodate twenty-six strapped-in passengers per trip.

President Bush's speech was timed perfectly to hit "magic hour" in the Pacific Ocean, that ideal moment of day that Hollywood producer Mort Engleberg first taught me about, where the sun's afternoon rays bestow an amber glow on a face in front of the lens. This is when Mother Nature assumes the role of cinematographer and illuminates a normally pale-faced president with majesty, making him look like Peter O'Toole in *Lawrence of Arabia* and making Scott Sforza a modern-day David Lean. And magic hour on the West Coast—about 3:00 p.m.—was 6:00 pm on the East Coast, timed perfectly for maximum live viewership on cable and last-minute editing into network news packages that were already suffused with images of the tailhook landing.

In prime time that evening, while talking heads opined on cable, video from the carrier filled living rooms, overwhelming barbs from Bush's critics with clips of Navy One landing and "Hail to the Chief" playing as the president made his grand entrance for his speech. You could criticize Bush all you wanted, but the brain couldn't help but be glued to his determined stride from the *Lincoln*'s superstructure to his stage half a football field away. The "walk-out," as it is known, is intended to supply cable networks with sufficient exalted imagery to cover an anchorman's voiceover, and this extended walk-out on the *Lincoln* transformed that half-minute of news footage into a "Mr. America" pageant.

The president, after a costume change from his tailhook landing, now wore a blue suit, red tie and American flag lapel pin, his regular workday mufti. He stood behind his familiar Blue Goose lectern with the presidential seal affixed, the talons and olive branch of its bald eagle on proud display. The ship's crewmen in rainbow-colored jerseys—they're called "skittles"—were arrayed in the background in gauzy focus, occupying different heights in the scenic composition. Some skittles were positioned on the flight deck and others on the wings of F/A 18 Hornets of Strike Fighter Squadron 115, a visual reinforcement of the message that the nation's military stood behind its commander in chief.

Finally, above the president's head in bold white letters against a flowing U.S. flag motif, were those two triumphal words, "Mission Accomplished," in billboard scale. The sign, designed by Sforza and the advance team and produced by an outside vendor, was affixed to the bridge so that it would be clearly seen from all angles for news coverage. The sign stood out when lenses viewed it as a wide shot, when photographers working from the buffer zone right in front of the stage framed the president at close range and when TV cameras behind the crowd zoomed in for a tight shot to record Bush's words. From every angle, "Mission Accomplished" was the simple two-word message.

For an average viewer at home, proud of what U.S. forces had done in Iraq and invoking memories of 1986's *Top Gun,* it was hard to tamp down the testosterone. The sign worked well in the moment, but soon became a problem. The reality was that had the banner never been there, Bush (who never actually said the words "mission accomplished") would have gotten all of the benefit from the trip and far less blowback.

Maureen Dowd amplified the cinematic drama in her next column. "Out bounded the cocky, rule-breaking, daredevil flyboy, a man navigating the Highway to the Danger Zone, out along the edges where he was born to be, the further on the edge, the hotter the intensity," she wrote. "He flashed that famous all-American grin as he swaggered around the deck of the aircraft carrier in his olive flight suit, ejection harness between his legs, helmet tucked under his arm, awestruck crew crowding around. Maverick was back, cooler and hotter than ever, throttling to the max with joystick politics."[7]

A day after the landing, on May 2, I appeared on Brian Williams's MSNBC show along with Jay Carney, then a correspondent for *Time.* "It was billed as an address to the nation," Williams said as he introduced our segment. "Millions of Americans have only known those as sober speeches from the confines of the Oval Office. Nobody ever said it couldn't be done from a carrier deck. All it took was thinking outside the box, or outside the oval, in this case."[8] Turning to me, sitting on set, Williams asked if I thought the carrier landing and speech was a "Mr. Gorbachev-tear-down-this-wall" moment for Bush.

I wouldn't let myself go that far but was still in awe of the spectacle. "Any actor needs a great entrance, and there's never going to be a better entrance than that to any event," I told Williams. "It's a triumph of costume. Presidents really are only allowed to come out in public in a business suit or casual golf attire. This was their excuse to put him in an olive flight suit, with a parachute on." I didn't mention the Nova Scotia submarine idea.

Carney was equally impressed. "There's a lot of politicians who, even with the justification of a war behind them, had they done that, wouldn't have looked quite right when they got off that plane. Bush looked like a fifty-year-old fly boy." Offering the political calculus facing Bush with an election sixteen months away, he added: "A sitting president has a certain amount of leeway, as Josh knows, to use the trappings of office for political advantage, and the fact is Bush will spend close to $300 million next year trying to get reelected, and he will not make a better investment" than the carrier landing.[9]

What is the actual dollar value of the flattering *Top Gun*–style photos filling the front pages of newspapers while, on cable, the footage airs over and over, dwarfing the back-and-forth of the talking heads? In the Age of Optics, it's almost incalculable, as Carney added: "We all look at that and know this is a photo op, this is a political image, and yet we run it because photo editors see it, and they think it's too good not to run."[10]

Only in the weeks and months that followed did criticism of the *Lincoln* event get traction, far slower than if Twitter been around to galvanize negative opinion. When the criticism started in earnest, bloggers weighed in early, followed by the mainstream press. President Bush found himself on defense in news conferences,[11] as did spokesmen Ari Fleischer and Scott McClellan.[12] The sign itself became an assignment for journalists, challenging the White House line that the crew requested the banner and probing who actually hung it on the *Lincoln*.

No matter who birthed the idea, as a prop for national television, it was positioned perfectly for maximum visibility, and that expertise could only have come from the advance team. In *Time* in November 2003, former general Wes Clark said that Bush "blamed the sailors for something that his advance team staged," adding, "I guess the next thing we are going to hear is that the sailors told him to wear the flight suit and prance around on the aircraft carrier. This is a president who does not want to take accountability."[13]

Gradually, even administration officials conceded the mistake. When presidents prepare to make a major announcement, the text is "routed" for comments through senior advisors with a stake in the outcome. Defense Secretary Donald Rumsfeld, in a 2006 interview with Bob Woodward, said he was shown a draft of the speech while on a trip to Baghdad and removed references to "mission accomplished" in the text. "My God, it's too conclusive," Rumsfeld said, adding, "They fixed the speech, but not the sign."[14]

One aide who remained unrepentant was Scott Sforza, who had deployed to the *Lincoln* to oversee the complex production. After overseeing the hookup of satellite dishes and fiber optics on the ship to allow live transmission of the speech, he helped pinpoint where the sign would go on the carrier. "Much has been talked about that event," he told me, "and if you go back to what it was really all about, I think the one thing that people regret the most is people on the outside not understanding what really happened, and I think the press really mischaracterized the entire event. I say this because we personally met with those on the ship and the intent of the message that was put on the ship—Mission Accomplished—was really aimed at the families on the shore."[15]

Sforza may be correct to say the sign celebrated the *Lincoln's* crew, but the two words were positioned for broad public consumption without that context. By design, nothing in political advance is intended to happen by accident, especially when it comes to framing the tight shot. When you place a billboard dead center behind the president in a televised address, it serves as the administration's intended message for viewers around the world.

On the fifth anniversary of the speech in 2008, Jon Stewart opened *The Daily Show* by announcing, "The Bush White House has gained some perspective on that fateful day." He played a clip of Press Secretary Dana Perino at her briefing, saying, "President Bush is well aware that the banner should have been much more specific and said, 'Mission Accomplished For These Sailors Who Are On This Ship On Their Mission.'" Stewart then quipped, "Oh, and that the war should have been more carefully planned and probably shouldn't have been started." For visual punch, Stewart ended the segment with a doctored image of the sign using Perino's elongated message.[16] Awkward as Perino's phrasing was, it would have spared Bush unending broadsides from his critics.

All presidents approaching the end of their tenure sit obligingly for retrospective interviews and are asked if they have any regrets. As George W. Bush's retirement grew near in late 2008, he suggested that "Mission Accomplished" was one thing he'd take back, if take-backs were allowed in geopolitics. In a CNN interview, he conceded, "I regret saying some things I shouldn't have said, like 'dead or alive' or 'bring 'em on.' My wife reminded me, 'As president of the United States you better be careful what you say.' I was trying to convey a message, but I probably could have conveyed it more artfully," he conceded.

Later, talking about the *Lincoln,* he added, "They had a sign that said 'Mission Accomplished.' I regret that the sign was there. It was a sign aimed at the sailors on the ship; however, it conveyed a broader knowledge. To some it said, well, Bush thinks the war in Iraq is over, when I didn't think that. But nonetheless, it conveyed the wrong message, so there are things

I've regretted."[17] Had that two-word slogan not hung from the bridge of an aircraft carrier on May 1, 2003, George W. Bush would have had to come up with something else he regretted during his eight years in office.

THE SCREAM

On June 23, 2003, less than two months after President Bush landed aboard the *Abraham Lincoln,* Howard Dean, who had left office as governor of Vermont six months earlier, announced his candidacy for president. Coming from a small state with no natural fundraising base and harboring an unabashed liberal streak, he was the longest of long shots.

And yet, Dean became a hot commodity in a crowded Democratic field that included John Kerry, John Edwards, Joe Lieberman, Dick Gephardt and Wes Clark. He distinguished himself from this pack though prodigious fundraising, using the Internet to bring in $50 million, mostly in small donations. The money gave Dean "major candidate" status, and with it the ability to flood early voting states with staffers. But Dean also differed from his competitors by his unwavering opposition to the war in Iraq, which in June 2003, the "Mission Accomplished" snafu notwithstanding, was still widely popular.

Dean thought differently. "Every American president must and will take up arms in the defense of our nation. It is a solemn oath that cannot—and that will not—be compromised. But there is a fundamental difference between the defense of our nation and the doctrine of preemptive war espoused by this administration," Dean said in his announcement speech in Burlington. As he spoke, his sleeves were rolled up above the elbow in trademark fashion, with leafy Vermont trees in the backdrop behind one shoulder, a church steeple on the other. "The president's group of narrow-minded ideological advisors," he went on, "have embraced a form of unilateralism that is even more dangerous than isolationism."[18]

By autumn, Dean was the Democratic front-runner. His face filled the covers of magazines and his campaign used new online tools like Meetup.com to track supporters. On September 7, 2003, the *Boston Globe* released a poll showing Dean had opened up a twelve-point lead in New Hampshire over his nearest challenger, Massachusetts senator John Kerry, and was even drawing support from those who voted for John McCain in 2000.

Nine days before Christmas, Dean still held a big lead in national surveys. A CBS News poll taken between December 14 and December

16 showed him with 23 percent support among primary voters, trailed
by Wes Clark and Joe Lieberman, each with 10 percent. While the Iowa
Caucus, the first stop on the road to the nomination, was only a month
away, statewide tracking data showed Dean's support there had crested
around Thanksgiving.

Air was leaking from Dean's campaign where it mattered most. His
ads in Iowa failed to hit their mark. His message turned messianic, shed-
ding the allegiance of older voters without replacing their support with
younger ones. Ultimately, Dean's momentum was fleeting as he failed
to deliver 18- to 25-year-old delegates in Iowa energized by the Internet.
They would be crucial to victory but were AWOL at the caucuses. When
the votes were tallied, Kerry won with 37.6 percent, Edwards was second
with 31.8 percent and Dean was third with 18 percent. Staffers and supporters, shocked by the results, made their way to the Val Air Ballroom in
West Des Moines for what was supposed to be the victory party.

One of those staffers was Beau Willimon, then twenty-four years
old. Today, he's the toast of Hollywood and Washington—the executive
producer and showrunner of Netflix's hit series *House of Cards*. But Willimon began in politics like the rest of us, as a volunteer advance man.

As an undergraduate at Columbia, Willimon befriended a Democratic operative named Jay Carson, who got him involved working for
New York senator Charles Schumer, followed by work on Hillary Clinton's 2000 senate campaign and the presidential campaign of Bill Bradley. Ultimately, the visual arts major found himself doing advance work
for Dean in Iowa. After traveling all over the state helping to produce
Dean's events, Willimon's penultimate in-state assignment was as press
advance for the Dean victory party—assuming it would be a victory—at
the Val Air.[19]

Press advance and site advance share a close kinship. While the site
person focuses on producing the show on stage, the press advance person
obsesses on how that show can be most effectively and positively covered
by the media. If the site guy hasn't paid enough attention to sound amplification and distribution, lighting, staging for TV cameras and power,
cabling and food for the traveling press corps, the press guy rightfully
should be all over his ass.

It was Dean's last stand in his long Iowa crusade. The candidate was
losing his grip, as was his advance team, where you're only as good as your
last event. The breakdown happened at the worst possible time as plans
fell into place for the party at the Val Air.

Even in defeat, a victory party can result in a raucous reboot and the start of a second chance to turn the tide at the next state on the schedule. The event at the Val Air was no different, especially since so many of Dean's staffers and volunteers were temporary out-of-state transplants and would soon be heading to New Hampshire and the primaries and caucuses that followed. Win or lose, they wanted to revel in the moment which, for most, would mark the end of their character-building stay in Des Moines.

The Val Air was the right venue for such revelry. Built in 1939 by Tom Archer, a pioneer in the ballroom business, it has a capacity of 3,000 people and regularly books popular traveling music acts that fill the space. The rock-and-roll venue was fitting for Dean's finale, a generational contrast with the hotel function rooms leased by his competitors. The crowd builders had been hard at work, filling the place for Howard Dean's speech that would bring down the curtain on the caucuses. Joe Trippi, Dean's campaign manager, recalled in *Esquire* magazine that "We walked into the room and it's 3,000 people, and they're out-of-their-minds crazy, a euphoric celebration for Howard Dean. One of the biggest celebrations that I'd ever seen in my entire time in politics."

With 95 percent of the caucuses reporting, Dean took the stage. In the image from the head-on camera at the Val Air, a viewer at home had no way to fathom the enormity of the crowd positioned at the front and to either side of Dean's unremarkable framing on the main stage. There were no live cutaway shots to provide a reverse angle, as there might be at a highly produced pool event. There was no "jib camera" either, a cinematic crane sometimes used at special political gatherings to offer a sweeping shot from above the crowd that conveys exuberance among the audience. With many other candidates to cover that night, the press didn't have the time, resources or inclination to include those elements.

As the head-on pool camera zoomed in, it showed Dean standing before a choral riser of supporters, with Senator Tom Harkin, his ardent supporter and a legend in the state, behind him to his right. Above the supporters was a massive "Dean for America" sign, advertising his Internet address and toll-free number in a "step-and-repeat" pattern to elicit as many more contributions as he might muster, a tactic first employed by John McCain after the New Hampshire primary four years earlier. In the first few seconds of the speech, everything in Dean's cadence looked and sounded normal.

In print, Dean's speech is the kind of message that might resonate with a large throng of young people who need, above all, to be motivated to stick with the candidate, to pack up their cars and leave, immediately, for the next state on the political calendar.

Here is how the roughly 700-word speech began:

> I'm sure there are some disappointed people here. You know what? You know something? You know something? If you had told us one year ago that we were going to come in third in Iowa, we would have given anything for that.
>
> And you know something? You know something?
>
> Not only are we going to New Hampshire, we're going to South Carolina and Oklahoma and Arizona and North Dakota and New Mexico, and we're going to California and Texas and New York. And we're going to South Dakota and Oregon and Washington and Michigan. And then we're going to Washington, D.C., to take back the White House. Yeah![20]

The speech went on for another 575 words, but history will not likely note anything beyond its 108th word, which transcribers recorded as "yeah." In any of the news videos of the remarks, Dean's voice is all that's heard, with little or any crowd reaction. To those watching on their sofas, Dean's "yeah" comes off as the most guttural, choleric howl ever uttered by a major presidential candidate.

It was immediately dubbed "The Dean Scream." Late-night comedy writers had a field day. Channel surfing after 11:30 p.m. in the days after Iowa, viewers heard the following from the monologues:

> Jay Leno: "Did you see Dean's speech last night? Oh my God! Now I hear the cows in Iowa are afraid of getting Mad Dean Disease. It's always a bad sign when at the end of your speech, your aide is shooting you with a tranquilizer gun."

> David Letterman: "Here's what happened: the people of Iowa realized they didn't want a president with the personality of a hockey dad."

> Conan O'Brien: "Howard Dean came in a disappointing third place in Iowa. Afterwards Dean said, 'Iowa is behind me and now I look forward to screaming at voters in New Hampshire.'"[21]

Dean wouldn't last another month as a presidential candidate. After coming in second in the New Hampshire primary on January 27, he ended his campaign on February 18 after coming in a distant third in the Wisconsin primary.

But there's something interesting about the night at the Val Air that got little notice. In addition to the many versions of the head-on video of Dean's speech that still course through the Internet, including doctored ones that make his concession speech sound even more contorted, there is a YouTube video of that same night, taken from just offstage, that has been seen less than 3,000 times. It reveals a deafening crowd scene, wholly unlike the sound picked up by the single handheld mic Dean clutched in his fist.

The revelers chant, "Dean, Dean, Dean, Dean," over and over.

Dean comes onto stage like a rock star, grabs an American flag and waves it for the audience. They respond even louder. At this moment, he's not Dean. He's Bono.

Then the crowd quiets, and allows Dean to speak. He begins his first forty-seven words in a soft-spoken tone, rhetoric that sounds fine in both the network and the amateur video. It's only when he begins to rattle off the names of states—states these volunteers can't wait to get to—that the roar of the audience overwhelms the candidate on stage. As Dean is "screaming," he's actually just trying to hear himself speak over the deafening decibels.[22]

And yet, none of the anchors and their producers watching the drama unfold in their New York or Washington studios, the pundits cranking out their columns for the next day, or the viewers at home, got any of that. They just heard a deranged-sounding guy chortling at the top of his lungs. Suddenly, it seems very clear to all of them: thank God for John Kerry—this Dean guy should never get within a mile of the Oval Office.

Garrett Graff, Dean's deputy national press secretary, told *Esquire*, "It was the first genuine viral moment of video on the Internet, even before YouTube existed." The pool video of the Dean Scream was replayed 672 times in one news cycle and was immediately ranked among the worst gaffes of political speech of all time. At the core, though, the root of the Dean Scream was a failure of event production and advance work.

"Not to get too technical here," Beau Willimon told me, "but the advance team will use something called a 'mult box,' and the mult box is where all of the news organizations put their feeds into so that you can have one microphone."[23]

The benefits of the mult box (short for "multiple output box") is one of the first lessons taught at advance school. It looks like an aluminum briefcase, with the main audio line from the speaker's microphone fed into it. The wiring within the box splits the audio feed into a dozen out-puts. "The one microphone," Willimon told me, "prevents you from hav-ing that giant bouquet of microphones that you saw in the eighties and before. And what that one microphone also does is create a very localized radius of sound that it's picking up, meaning that anything more than a few feet away is on a much lower level."[24]

A political rally is not like one of Willimon's *House of Cards* epi-sodes, where the sound is mixed perfectly to capture the characters' lines and a natural-sounding level of background noise. Nor is it like a rock concert, where musicians have their sound balanced by large on-stage monitors so they don't sing too softly or over-project to the room. Political events, in contrast, are often last-minute productions lacking in professional sound engineering. No one on the Dean campaign, in-cluding Beau Willimon, anticipated the victory party sounding like it did at the Val Air.

All these years later, the Dean Scream still grates on Willimon, a theatrical perfectionist. The dependence on the mult box, he said, mini-mized the raucous energy at the Val Air, energy Dean tried to equalize with his elevated voice. "What is a little disingenuous about that," Wil-limon told me, "is that if the energy and volume of the event and the crowd is a big part of the overall picture, that's not going to be picked up by the mic."

At those noise levels, without adequate monitors on stage, anyone is going to scream. "So, out of context, of course, he looks a little un-hinged," Willimon added, "but if you were in that room, it didn't seem that way at all."

Beyond the thirty seconds of video ending in the scream, Willimon shared with me his memory of "the bigger issue," a narrative unfolding as the caucus approached. The view from those following the campaign, Willimon said, "was that 'here's a guy who might not be electable, who might be a little unhinged from time to time, and who wasn't prepared or have the gravitas to be president of the United States.' Now that's a big narrative," Willimon said. "The media doesn't construct those narratives. They're not that powerful. The best of journalists have a sense of what is bubbling forth among the people, and then they find the stories that will confirm or address that narrative."[25]

That's why tank rides, supermarket scanners, stage falls, canoe trips and screaming, as evanescent as those episodes are, can be so damaging. A conclusion hardens in the mind of the observer. Dukakis was unfit to be commander in chief. Dole was too old. Gore was a hypocrite. Dean was unhinged. None of those mental associations may have been fair, but they stuck when reinforced by the visual.

"Having spent many a long day side by side with the candidate, there are clips—audio, visual, photo stills, dozens of a day—which could be used out of context to tell a story that is not necessarily reflective of the event but is reflective of the bigger narrative," Willimon told me. "Most of the time, they dissolve into the mist because, out of context, they make no sense. But if it hadn't been the Dean Scream, it would have been something else."[26] In 108 words at the Val Air Ballroom, the story had a beginning, middle and end.

In the decade since the Dean Scream, a revisionist history has emerged among members of the media who are willing to own up to how the scene at the Val Air was trivialized for chuckles by television anchors. On his Slate podcast, Dave Weigel welcomed Dean as his guest, admitting, "I'm in the camp that always thought it was a bit insane the way we in the media covered that," adding, "You got completely manhandled by the press."

"I got manhandled by cable television," Dean replied. "Well, I guess the networks fell for it too. It is true that it was a big media screw-up, on purpose, because they couldn't resist the entertainment."[27] Even today, CNN.com still hosts video of the event under the headline "2004: The Scream That Doomed Howard Dean."[28] In fact, Dean was probably already doomed. The scream just made him a laughingstock for years to come.

Dean knew that, in politics, winning matters and losers become targets. "The big problem was that I was leading the polls and I was supposed to come in first in Iowa and, for the last three weeks in Iowa, I had been falling for a variety of reasons. And I came in third in Iowa. And you can ask Hillary Clinton what happens when you're supposed to come in first in Iowa and you don't," Dean told Weigel.[29]

Like the good advance man he was, Willimon grabbed his bags after wrapping up work at the Val Air and raced through Des Moines to his next assignment, Dean's airport departure for New Hampshire. At the airport, his role would be to establish the position on the tarmac from which cameras can record the farewell wave. As the charter plane flew toward Manchester, with Willimon in a rear seat, he and his colleagues were in a midnight news vacuum at 38,000 feet. They knew they had lost, and lost badly, but had no idea that the Scream would take on a life of its own.

Over the years, Dean has seemed to resign himself to the unique place in history that he created on stage at the Val Air, and can even find humor in it. Nine years later, stumping with Bill de Blasio during the New York mayor's race in 2013, he looked much as he did in 2004, aged very little, still sporting his country doctor persona with blue shirt, red tie and sleeves rolled up at the elbow.

With a handheld microphone in his right palm and the 6-foot-5 de Blasio towering above him, Dean told the crowd, "I realized as I was getting up here tonight and taking off my coat, that this shirt, which is kind of wrinkled, the reason it's wrinkled is that it's ten years old. This is the shirt that I was wearing when I gave the scream speech in Iowa." The New York crowed roared with laughter and applause.

Then, mimicking the same emphatic arm movements of his original scream speech, he said, with a devilish smile, "So we're going to Brooklyn, and then we're going to the Bronx, and then we're going to Staten Island, and then we're going to go to Manhattan, and all the way to Gracie Mansion. Yeaagghh!"[30]

THE WINDSURFER

Howard Dean's campaign had to die so that John Kerry's might live. A campaign that started disastrously with Mark Leibovich's *New York Times Magazine* profile of the senator, in which Kerry came off as the henpecked, fidgety second husband of Teresa Heinz, finally found its footing just in time to take advantage of Dean's implosion.

Kerry won 38 percent of Iowa's delegates at the January 19 caucuses, following it up with a win in the January 27 New Hampshire Primary and dominance over the field on Super Tuesday. A man whose long career of service built slowly toward a presidential nomination saw that dream realized on Thursday, July 29. On that night, on stage at the FleetCenter in Boston, standing beneath a massive electronic American flag and in front of 4,422 delegates and a nationwide audience, he snapped his right hand to his forehead, saluted the crowd and proclaimed, "I'm John Kerry, and I'm reporting for duty!"[31]

John Kerry had been reporting for duty, and earning notoriety for it, most of his adult life. It started with coverage he received after returning from Vietnam, where he earned three Purple Hearts and a Bronze Star. On April 23, 1971, after testifying against the war before a Senate committee, he tossed some of those ribbons near the front of the Capitol while other veterans did the same. In an account by the *Boston Globe*'s Tom Oliphant, Kerry said as he discarded his ribbons, "There is no violent reason for this; I'm doing this for peace and justice and to try to help this country wake up once and for all."[32]

Thirty-three years later, after vanquishing Dean and his other Democratic foes, Kerry had chosen North Carolina senator John Edwards, one of those opponents, as his running mate. The image of these two senators on stage together at the FleetCenter for their convention, both survivors of the primary fight, was symbolically captivating. The north/south pairing, with a Massachusetts-born standard bearer atop the ticket, was redolent of Kennedy and Johnson in 1960. Moreover, on high-definition TV, the youthful-looking duo (Kerry, then sixty-one, was physically fit and looked younger, and Edwards, at fifty-one, looked younger still), compared favorably to Bush and Dick Cheney and evoked comparisons to Clinton and Gore at Madison Square Garden in 1992. But the particular timing of Kerry's acceptance of the nomination in Boston, coming one night after the rousing keynote address of Illinois state senator Barack Obama, was problematic.

The seventeen-day spectacle of the Olympic Games, held every four years, always plays havoc with convention scheduling. The 2004 Games, held in Athens between August 13 and August 29, was no exception. With attention diverted to Olympic venues, it was hard to make news in political venues. President Bush, as the incumbent, could choose whether his convention would go first or second, and he decided to commence his on Monday, August 30, after the closing ceremonies in Athens. Kerry had to wait almost a full month after his convention, when Bush was formally nominated, to start spending the $74.62 million in federal funding allocated to the Democratic nominee.

Kerry's August lull drew a comparison to another campaign—1988—when Michael Dukakis, also of Massachusetts, left his convention in Atlanta for a vacation in the Berkshires, followed by an extended period tending to state business. Senator Kerry, one of the wealthiest men in Congress as a result of his 1995 marriage to Teresa Heinz, also took time off to enjoy the end of the Bay State summer, retreating to his Nantucket home for four days of R&R while the Republicans convened. It was in the waters off Brant Point, on the same Sunday that the Olympics ended in Athens, that Kerry rigged his high-performance NeilPryde sail to his windsurfer for a quick spin near his beachfront home.

The pool that was shadowing the Democratic nominee to watch his public movements hadn't been notified of the sojourn. A network correspondent and crew happened to be taping a segment in the area near Brant Point when they saw Secret Service agents, police and Coast Guard personnel—and Kerry, struggling with his windsurfer. The chance Kerry sighting created a conundrum for David Wade, Kerry's longtime spokesman. Rather than coming right out and saying that Kerry ditched his pool, Wade argued that the activity was not *technically* windsurfing but rather, as MSNBC's Becky Diamond reported, "setting up and testing his new sail in the waters close to his home." Moreover, the activity—however Wade described it—took place off a private beach, thus technically permissible under pool rules.[33]

The media covering Kerry on the island weren't buying it. In the MSNBC item, it noted, "He windsurfed past Brant Point and the lighthouse, and the pool has been mobilized before to cover him in that same area of the Nantucket Sound (which, the last time your Massachusetts pooler checked, was not a privately owned area)."

As Kerry headed to church that evening, reporters tossed questions his way about his unannounced foray into the water. Kerry demurred, saying, "I barely got out. I was testing my stuff." To quiet the pool's protests, he then invited them to watch him windsurf on his next outing.[34]

Kerry had been warned. A senior advisor, David Morehouse, was a veteran advance man from Pittsburgh and onetime boilermaker (he's now CEO of the Pittsburgh Penguins) with a genuine affinity for the common man. His early warning radar went off whenever Kerry did something that hinted at his net worth or, taken out of context, could be exploited by opponents. "Everything we did," he told me, "we thought of Dukakis."[35] Morehouse told Kerry that windsurfing wasn't a blue-collar worker's idea of weekend recreation. Kerry countered that, on Nantucket, the sport was a common pastime of plumbers and electricians. But Nantucket plumbers and electricians aren't representative of their landlocked rank-and-file union brotherhood, was the essence of Morehouse's rejoinder.

The images of Kerry windsurfing—in flower-patterned board shorts, white sun shirt and wraparound sunglasses—while the Republicans gathered in New York were quickly noticed by the late-night comics. In a monologue early in the following week, Jay Leno said Kerry is "at his home in Nantucket this week doing his favorite thing, windsurfing. I mean, even his hobby depends on which way the wind blows."[36] Piling on, David Letterman joked, "John Kerry, of course, yesterday went windsurfing because when you're in a statistical dead heat, it's time to kick back and relax."[37]

Stephen Robinson of London's *Daily Telegraph* panned the footage from across the Atlantic for his readers on the other side of the pond. "He allowed himself to be filmed windsurfing off Nantucket," Robinson wrote, "the playground for the wealthy elite of the eastern United States and exactly the sort of place that American politicians who might be seen as too liberal for national office should keep away from."[38] On CNN's *Crossfire,* conservative host Bob Novak piled on, too: "Two days ago, he was windsurfing in Nantucket, which is I guess how eastern rich guys have a good time."[39]

The comparisons of Kerry and Dukakis, two men from Massachusetts, were inevitable. They started in early summer with Kerry's slow response to attack ads by the Swift Boat Veterans for Truth. They spiked again in the wake of the windsurfing imagery. Under the headline, "Who Among Us Does Not Like Windsurfing?," the *New York Times*'s Kate Zernike wrote on September 5, "Like the helmeted Michael Dukakis peeking out of the tank, or the first George Bush bewildered at the grocery scanner, the photo of Mr. Kerry windsurfing played into the negative stereotype his opponents are trying to play up—in this case, that of the out-of-touch, elitist Massachusetts liberal."[40]

Even some Democratic politicians, like Congressman Charles Rangel, openly criticized the imagery. "I smell the same New England genius that I smelled in the Dukakis campaign in 1988."[41]

For those whose memories stretched back to the 1980s, the comparisons were stark. George W. Bush at his ranch in Crawford was like Reagan at his ranch in Santa Barbara. John Kerry vacationing in Nantucket echoed Dukakis in the Berkshires. On September 17, Maureen Dowd put the matter in perspective as only she can. "The White House," she opined, "has cleverly co-opted the imagery of Westerns, leaving Kerry to star in a far less successful movie genre: the Eastern." She went on: "In Westerns, the heroes are men of smoke-'em-out edicts and action, played out in gorges on their ranches; in Easterns, the heroes have windy, nuanced dialogue, delivered with a lockjaw in mansions on Beacon Hill and on windsurfing expeditions off Nantucket."[42]

As with Dukakis, had the media alone had its fun at Kerry's expense for a few cycles, the windsurfing outing might have been quickly forgotten. After the conventions, as observers trained their sights on the upcoming debates, the tacking off Brant Point would have faded from newscasts. But with a huge advertising budget to burn in just sixty-two days until Election Day, Bush advisors watched the same footage as viewers of Leno and Letterman and started their creative juices flowing. They imagined the metaphor of the sailor's tack, turning left and right into the wind, as the perfect assessment of their opponent.

Hunkered down in New York, Mark McKinnon, Bush's media advisor, welcomed the footage as a gift, just like the one given to Bush's father sixteen years earlier on September 13, 1988, when Sig Rogich first saw Dukakis and the tank in Sam Donaldson's package for ABC's *World News Tonight*. As Anne Kornblut wrote for the *Boston Globe*, "The image was simply too much for senior Bush strategists to resist." She quoted McKinnon, who said, "I thought it so perfectly conveyed the message."[43]

The message, McKinnon recalled, emerged from the town hall Kerry held with veterans at Marshall University in Huntington, West Virginia, on March 16, shortly before Super Tuesday. McKinnon had thought that Howard Dean would be a tougher challenger to Bush, but he saw at Huntington that Kerry "was the perfect opponent for us," he told me. "You always want your opponent's weaknesses to reflect your assets," McKinnon went on, "and Dean was a little unhinged, but he was strong. People saw him as tough and clear-minded about where he wanted to go. He had clear positions."[44]

Not so John Kerry, at least judging from one unfortunate line he uttered at Marshall. Surrounded by veterans as he took the stage, Kerry raised the topic of a supplemental appropriation in Congress for military operations in Iraq. How Senator Kerry voted on the appropriation was seen as an indicator of his views on the war itself. "I actually did vote for the 87 billion dollars," he said, famously, "before I voted against it." In his book *Courage and Consequence*, Bush advisor Karl Rove said, "It gave us the line that perfectly encapsulated who he was and the have-it-both-ways candidacy he was building." Like every other event that spring, it was captured by TV pool cameras. "In thirteen words, he had told Americans he was an unreliable, inconsistent weak flip-flopper unfit for the Oval Office," Rove wrote.[45]

Kerry had walked into a trap in Huntington. McKinnon told me of a call he received from Rove right before Kerry embarked on his West Virginia trip in which Rove told him, "We're going to bait the trap with some cheese." To set the bait, Rove asked McKinnon to quickly create a TV spot that would run in West Virginia that trumpeted Kerry's vote on the appropriation. "We said let's set him up to make sure he gets asked that question at the veterans' meeting. So we cut an ad, overnight, and sent it down to West Virginia and just bought everything (as in available TV commercial inventory) for the next twenty-four hours. When Kerry got there, everybody was talking about the ad," McKinnon told me. When the question was asked, and answered, McKinnon thought, "Holy carumba. I mean that, you know, this could be the campaign."[46]

The ammunition wasn't needed immediately. In fact, it would be better for Bush if the town hall statement could marinate during the spring and summer. It would take months for the words at Marshall to be matched with the visuals off Nantucket, the damning statement simmering on a back burner until added to the right footage to turn it into a toxic concoction of accusation and humor.

Like Rogich watching the tank, McKinnon watched the windsurfer with awe and elation. "As soon as we saw the footage, that ad made itself in thirty seconds because it was so obvious what we're going to do with it," McKinnon said.[47] Rogich had stretched eleven seconds of tank footage into a thirty-second spot by reversing it and augmenting it with artificial sound effects. McKinnon could do the same thing with a few seconds of windsurfing, artificially creating the act of a sailor tacking back and forth, or "flip-flopping" in political terms, by reversing the video footage over and over.

"Just immediately, we had the flip-flop idea," McKinnon told me, and "he looked ridiculous because he's in those purple board shorts. Not only knowing conceptually we were going to do the flipping ad, we also knew that he was going to look so out of touch because, you know, what's the demographic of windsurfers in America, there's maybe, I don't know, 5,000 of them?"[48] To turn the footage into an ad, using the same playbook of Sig Rogich and Roger Ailes in 1988, McKinnon turned to Sara Taylor, in the Bush political office, and Russ Schriefer, the Republican ad man based at Bush headquarters in Virginia, to cut a new spot for the president's campaign. The bruising tagline for the ad came quickly to Schriefer: "John Kerry, whichever way the wind blows."

After acquiring the windsurfing video, Schriefer went to his studio in Washington, D.C., with his video editor, Matthew Taylor, and got to work. It didn't need to look good to kill. "There's nothing particularly amazing about the production quality other than Kerry going back and forth and flipping the footage," Schriefer told me. The ad shows Kerry, tacking left and right nine times in the shadow of a ferry boat. As Schriefer remembers, "We added a little sound effect of the wind and then McKinnon came up with the brilliant idea of adding the 'Blue Danube' waltz theme behind it, which I think really made it."[49] The ad was finished in one afternoon.

The final script, pegged to Kerry's quote from his town hall, was narrated by Burt Pence, a well-known voice actor whose credits include serving as the "in show" voice for NBC's *Meet the Press*. Pence's LinkedIn page touts his specialty of "convincing television viewers, radio listeners and people online to buy what I'm selling." In his voice-over for Schriefer's script for "Windsurfing," Pence was selling hard:

> In which direction would John Kerry lead?
>
> Kerry voted for the Iraq war, opposed it, supported it, and now opposes it again.
>
> He bragged about voting for the $87 billion to support our troops before he voted against it.
>
> He voted for education reform and now opposes it.
>
> He claims he's against increasing Medicare premiums but voted five times to do so.
>
> John Kerry: whichever way the wind blows.[50]

With the West Virginia flip-flop, the Nantucket footage, Matthew Taylor's editing and Burt Pence's voice, Schriefer's ad had all the ingredients of a classic. But there was one more element that gave the spot its lethal effectiveness: the music.

Sometimes, consciously or not, music will evoke a subliminal message of its own. The "Blue Danube" waltz was composed by Johan Strauss II, an Austrian composer, in 1866. While it was a hit at the Paris World's Fair in 1867, it became part of the American subconscious through Stanley Kubrick's *2001: A Space Odyssey*, when it provided the soundtrack for the film's depiction of a space plane docking with a space station. Kerry's grandfather, Frederick Kerry, was born in Austria and lived in Mödling, a suburb of Vienna, until emigrating to the United States in 1905. The fact that Senator Kerry studied in Switzerland and spoke fluent French and German, conspired, along with Strauss's music, to cast him as "the European Candidate."[51]

"My recollection," Mark McKinnon told me, "is that I heard the 'Blue Danube' in my head the minute I saw it."[52] I asked Russ Schriefer if the score's European patina was a factor in its selection. "I guess so, yeah," Schriefer allowed. "It just fit. It was just genius. We had some other track and Mark put the 'Blue Danube' underneath. It just all fit."[53]

"Windsurfer" made its national television debut on Wednesday, September 22, a little more than three weeks after Senator Kerry made his foray off Brant Point. Mike McCurry, Kerry's senior advisor, immediately called on Bush's campaign to repudiate the spot, just as Lorraine Voles had done on Dukakis's behalf sixteen years earlier. And, like the Dukakis campaign, the Kerry campaign rushed a paid response onto the air calling "Windsurfer" a "juvenile and tasteless attack ad."[54]

In its coverage of the spot the next day, the *New York Post* called "Windsurfer" "amusing" and broke down some of the visual cues that McKinnon and Schreifer might not have imagined would get picked up, including the cost of Kerry's wrap-around sunglasses at $150. "The sail on Kerry's windsurfer goes for $850," the *Post* reported, "his swim trunks cost about $145; and his Swatch top costs at least $150."[55]

McKinnon told me that the Bush campaign "more than doubled" the normal paid rotation for "Windsurfer" than for any other ad that they aired. History was his guide and he knew he had a winner. "It was like a flashback to Dukakis," he told me. "When we saw that image of Kerry, it was the gift that just kept on giving. And we ran the hell out of that ad, way more than you would a normal ad, just to make sure we imprinted that image on everybody's mind. It was devastating."[56]

Since the dawn of the Age of Optics in 1988, most of the major off-script moments have come from candidates or politicians doing their job. The mistakes on the campaign trail have been committed in the course of a planned event, through faulty advance or staff work, the effects compounded by amplification, exaggeration and redistribution by the media. In the case of Dukakis—and now Kerry—the snafu was magnified well beyond the initial damage by an opponent's paid ad. The ad, in turn, was replayed over and over, at no additional cost, by the media, amplifying its impact even more.

Dukakis's Michigan tank ride was planned in intimate detail. George H. W. Bush was pilloried in Florida thanks to a misinterpreted pool report. Bob Dole fell from a poorly constructed stage in California. Al Gore's New Hampshire river trip was sunk by an ill-timed water release. George W. Bush's advance team was a tad too clever in their sign placement on an aircraft carrier in the Pacific Ocean. Howard Dean was undone by an inadequate sound system in Iowa.

But John Kerry? On a day off from his official duties in Nantucket, against the advice of his staff, he tarnished an image built over the span of his career by opting to go windsurfing in the wrong place at the wrong time. He didn't have to venture outside, where the press pool lay in wait to find and feed a story for air. He could have played it safe, sticking to a game of cards with friends and family inside his oceanfront home.

Kerry was no political rookie. He knew the traps and the ways to stay out of them. Don't make news was one. Allow the Republicans to have their days in the sun in New York was another. Keep your mouth shut was a third. Stay out of view was a fourth. Winning the White House might be worth avoiding all of the traps and a temporary sacrifice of freedom. But in the face of the risks that had undermined his predecessors, Kerry refused to wear a straitjacket.

It wasn't the last time he would make the mistake of believing that activities he considered private would not be exposed by his status as a public figure. Nor would it be the last time his representatives would deny, despite video evidence to the contrary, that it happened. In the summer of 2013, as secretary of state, he did it again, boarding his yacht, *Isabel,* on the same day that Egyptian president Mohammed Morsi was being removed from office. There's nothing wrong with checking out your boat while Egypt unravels, but what made it so curious, so Kerry-like, was the denial by State Department spokeswoman Jen Psaki that it happened, even in the face of video of the excursion broadcast by CBS News.[57]

To windsurf, or not to windsurf. To yacht, or not to yacht. That is the question. Searching for the answer—why—comes back again to Kerry's comment in front of veterans at Marshall University. "I actually did vote for the 87 billion dollars, before I voted against it." As Mark McKinnon made clear in thirty seconds set to the "Blue Danube" waltz, you can't have it both ways.

 **THIRTEEN**

2008: MCCAIN GOES GREEN

(Or, How Bad Branding Made
Mockery of a Maverick)

In the summer of 1999, at about the same time Al Gore canoed down the Connecticut River for his four-mile sojourn, I was given a copy of John McCain's book, *Faith of My Fathers,* written with his longtime aide Mark Salter. The book, an early entrant in the literary canon of pre-campaign manifesto, was one of the best of the genre. Before chronicling the harrowing incident where McCain's A4 Skyhawk was shot down over North Vietnam and his ensuing five and a half years of captivity in the Hanoi Hilton, the book told the story of three generations of a navy family.

The book begins with McCain's meditation on a photograph. It showed McCain's grandfather and father, John Sidney McCain Sr. and Jr., on the bridge of the USS *Proteus,* a submarine tender, in Tokyo Bay a few hours after the Second World War had ended. The snapshot of the officers in their service khakis showed two men, one at the end of his career, the other at the beginning. As McCain wrote, his grandfather and father "would never see each other again."[1]

The elder McCain, with a grimace on his face in the photo, had been forced to relinquish his command following damage to ships in Admiral William Halsey's Task Force 38 from a violent typhoon near Okinawa. He didn't want to attend the Japanese surrender on the deck of the USS

Missouri, but did so at Halsey's request. As soon as was practicable, he would leave Japan to return to the United States. He died four days later from a massive heart attack at his home in Coronado, California. His grandson, John III, was only nine years old at the time. The ignoble end to McCain Sr.'s career may have been the topic of the intimate conversation between father and son on the deck of the *Proteus,* but the story was never chronicled except in an oral history that McCain Jr. gave to the Naval Institute thirty years after the war. As McCain III wrote in *Faith of My Fathers,* "My father never mentioned it to me."[2]

I was struck by the candor throughout the book. The story of three generations of that family, culminating in McCain's account of his brutal tenure as a prisoner of war, stood in opposition to the manufactured imagery that I had helped to craft for most of the decade. A man who flew off the deck of the USS *Oriskany* and ejected when a missile hit his aircraft, nearly drowning in Trúc Bạch Lake, was an image as far as I could imagine from those in which my Clinton-era colleagues and I traded; stagecraft made possible through a dam release to raise the water level on a river, for example.

My wife, a Democrat like me, is from New Hampshire, and we spend a lot of time there on holidays. During the run-up to the 2000 New Hampshire Primary, we quietly rooted for McCain's maverick candidacy to keep things interesting. For me, *Faith of My Fathers* had a lot to do with it. Always feeling a little out of place with my own generation and how history spared us from military service in a time of war, I was drawn to the long naval legacy of the McCain family. As a political operative, more practically, I was also drawn to McCain's openness with the media, made famous by his "Straight Talk Express" campaign bus and his retail campaign style. It was a style of necessity, as I would discover, that manifested itself in 114 town hall meetings with voters in the Granite State.

McCain didn't have much choice about his campaign strategy. Short on money, facing a better financed and better-produced opponent, George W. Bush, he relied on earned media generated from hours of freewheeling conversation with reporters on the bus and a groundswell of support from veterans, cobbled together stop after stop, by patiently answering question after question at VFW halls throughout New Hampshire.

On the eve of his primary win in New Hampshire, local TV showed McCain in his element, a VFW hall in Franklin, with post commanders and ladies' auxiliary members arrayed behind him. He would beat Bush by nearly twenty points, arousing in moderate Democrats a hesitant belief that a McCain nomination would prompt a hard choice at the ballot box in the 2000 general election. As his New Hampshire campaign manager, Mike Dennehy, would later describe it, McCain's improbable victory was "a perfect storm that came together,"[3] a very different kind of storm than that which sank his grandfather's career.

McCain's advantage didn't last long. Bush won the South Carolina Primary on February 19, employing no-holds-barred tactics developed by native son Lee Atwater and his protégés. There were "push polls" in the state suggesting McCain fathered a black child out of wedlock[4]; rumors that McCain's wife, Cindy, had a drug problem; and murmurings that McCain himself was either a homosexual or mentally imbalanced, a "Manchurian Candidate" emerging from his captivity as a prisoner of war.[5]

The tactics worked. Bush never looked back. McCain managed a victory in his home state of Arizona and in Michigan on February 22 but lost to Bush in the next thirty-eight of forty-two contests, most of which were uncontested following McCain's withdrawal on March 9.

During Bush's years in the White House, McCain soldiered on in the Senate, rebuffing efforts by Ted Kennedy to encourage him to switch parties and refusing John Kerry's entreaties to join him on a unity ticket in 2004. In 2007, McCain, then seventy years old and eight years older than his "Straight Talk Express" days, decided to give the presidency another shot. Like Dole in 1996, it might be McCain's "turn" as a party elder to become the GOP standard bearer, but winning the White House as a septuagenarian was another matter.

For one thing, McCain was less agile on the stump than he was in 2000. Additionally, a Republican had held the White House for the last eight years, preparing to leave office with approval ratings hovering in the high twenties to low thirties, stacking the odds against him. As was the case in 1992, the country seemed ripe in 2000 for a new generational and ideological tack.

Even before McCain could grapple with his eventual Democratic opponent, who himself had risen to notoriety on a book about his father (Barack Obama's *Dreams from My Father* was published in 1995), he had to outlast competition within his own party. McCain's major opponents were skilled practitioners of stagecraft, including Mitt Romney, the handsome private equity pitchman turned governor; Mike Huckabee, an ordained minister turned governor; Fred Thompson, an actor turned senator; and Rudy Giuliani, a crusading prosecutor turned mayor turned

9/11 hero. Each would test his skills in the national political spotlight, and each would have his moment in the sun.

A final problem for McCain was keeping his own campaign shop intact. After announcing his candidacy in Portsmouth, New Hampshire, on April 27, 2007, he raised just $25 million in the first half of that year, well short of his goals. With only $3.2 million in the bank and $1.8 million in debt, longtime McCain aides John Weaver and Terry Nelson left the campaign, followed by the bulk of his press team, leaving Rick Davis in charge as campaign manager. If McCain was going to win the nomination, he'd have to do it the old-fashioned way, starting with carrying his own bags through airports to take commercial flights from state to state, and once again boarding the Straight Talk Express.

THE TERMINATOR'S MAN

Rick Davis steered the campaign through an agonizing but ultimately victorious primary season, then ceded day-to-day control to Steve Schmidt on July 2, 2008. Schmidt, who had run Arnold Schwarzenegger's successful 2006 reelection as governor of California, made Schwarzenegger look *presidential* through well-crafted events, taking full advantage of the trappings of incumbency and the candidate's infectious charisma as an actor and celebrity.

On October 21 in Trabuco Canyon, California, the governor arrived to campaign at a biker's rally on the saddle of his burgundy-colored, leather-appointed Indian motorcycle, sporting a bomber's jacket with the state seal on his left chest and the state flag on his right shoulder. These instantly identifiable symbols of power, gracing the chest and shoulder of the star of *The Last Action Hero,* made for an irresistible package in a state drawn to stardom. The image was like tailhooking onto an aircraft carrier but without the S-3 Viking and the Pacific Ocean below. As a candidate for governor of the ninth largest economy in the world, he looked every bit the part that Ronald Reagan played in 1984. After a succession of bland California governors, Schwarzenegger made campaigning fun again, with Schmidt pressing all the right buttons.

As John McCain readied to take on the marketing phenomenon that was Barack Obama in the summer of 2008, he needed every ounce of presidential stature that Schmidt could bestow upon him. "There are 125 days left until the American people will decide the next president," Schmidt told Dan Balz and Michael Shear of the *Washington Post.* "Senator McCain is the underdog in the race. We suspect he is behind nationally five to eight points but well within striking distance. I will help run an organization that exists for the purpose of delivering John McCain's message to the American people."[6]

McCain said Schmidt would oversee message, advertising, scheduling, advance work and the political operation, leaving only fundraising beyond his purview. Balz and Shear noted "the sloppy staging of events" among the litany of complaints about McCain's candidacy by GOP wise men before Schmidt took over. Along with Schmidt's elevation, the *Post* story pointed out that "the campaign has recruited Greg Jenkins, who oversaw advance work for the Bush White House, to take charge of the staging of McCain's events, which have been a sore point among some."[7]

KENNER IS MCCAIN COUNTRY

Louisiana, with its rivers, levees and special tax incentives put in place in 2002 to attract producers in the entertainment industry, has earned the nickname "Hollywood on the Bayou" for the many films and TV shows that shoot against the backdrop of its exotic locales.

One Louisiana backdrop that wasn't so exotic may have been the final straw for Rick Davis. The production took place on June 3, at the Pontchartrain Center in Kenner, Louisiana, near New Orleans, a few weeks before Schmidt formally assumed command of McCain's operation. McCain's highly promoted major speech that night in Kenner exposed strategic failings of scheduling, speechwriting, advance work, stage managing and event design and production—the critical elements of a successful general election road show. On that evening, these table stakes of political stagecraft blew up in John McCain's face.

The speech at the Pontchartrain Center, 3,169 words in length, taking twenty-two minutes to deliver, was billed as a moment to reset the McCain-Obama race. It started with a paean to Obama and Hillary Clinton for their long, hard contest. "Senator Obama has impressed many Americans with his eloquence and his spirited campaign," McCain said, and "Senator Clinton has earned great respect for her tenacity and courage."[8] But the setting was also used to distance McCain from another politician: George W. Bush. By staging the speech near New Orleans, it took as its symbolic backdrop Ground Zero of the most visible domestic failure of Bush's presidency: the federal government's response to Hurricane Katrina.

McCain's remarks had been heavily worked over. Excerpts had been released to the media ahead of show time, a message-framing tactic to feed interest in the speech and give reporters a head start on writing for

evening blogs and the next day's papers, and to give morning show producers enough time to frame their packages. To ensure McCain got every
word right, the campaign used a teleprompter to feed him line after line.
Senator Obama had used the teleprompter with great success leading up
to his nomination, allowing him to seem more measured and polished behind the podium; conversely, Senator Clinton, like her husband, typically
bypassed prompters in favor of a memorized stump speech.

A special new eight-by-eight-foot green "hard wall" backdrop was
created for the Kenner venue with the message "A Leader We Can Believe In" printed in a "step-and-repeat" pattern that no camera could miss
while zoomed in on the candidate. This was a trick we had introduced
to political stagecraft and perfected during the Clinton years. Few might
watch the full twenty-two minutes of McCain's address at the Pontchartrain Center, but connecting him visually with the phrase "A Leader We
Can Believe In" might be sufficient to ram the message home to voters
watching the news from the corner of their eye while on a treadmill or in
a barber's chair.

The McCain phrasing was designed to be captured in every picture
from Kenner. With its single star in the center and yellow rays emanating left and right to the fringe of the hard wall, the bold headline sat just
above the candidate's head as seen from the head-on TV camera. The
motif, with the star and rays resembling an admiral's epaulet, was repeated on a smaller scale across the hardwall in a checkerboard wallpaper
pattern, intermingled with the URL for the campaign's website. Adding
the URL, it was hoped, would elicit additional campaign donations if
voters liked what they saw.

There was another not-so-subtle contrast between the Republican's
message and that of his opponent. Obama's standard signage said "Change
We Can Believe In" but, just two years before, the top line on his resume
read Illinois state senator. Obama may well be promising *change*, but Mc-
Cain, who had been serving his country since graduating from the United
States Naval Academy in 1958, had been demonstrating the distinguishing word on the two signs—leadership—since before Obama was born.

UP IN ST. PAUL

The McCain campaign had put in place all of the elements of a solid
night of political production, but their first failure was one of strategic
scheduling.

That same evening, 1,200 miles away in St. Paul, Minnesota, history was about to be made. The Xcel Energy Center, which would welcome the GOP Convention later that year, was packed that night with Democrats, a crowd of 17,000 people, with an overflow audience of 15,000 watching on Jumbotrons outside. They were gathered, with typical Obama campaign precision, using social media (the registration page still resides online),[9] and would bear witness as he officially became the Democratic nominee for president, the first African American candidate to secure the support of enough delegates to do so.

The stage at Xcel was erected according to state-of-the-art presidential advance theory. A four-foot-high walkway conveyed Senator Obama and his wife, Michelle, to the main platform from a hidden position in the stadium's concourse. From the concourse, the walkway vectored on a forty-five-degree angle to the bunting-wrapped stage situated in the middle of the crowd. The effect created a striking visual of being surrounded by people on all sides. That raised walkway, which the Secret Service often vetoed for outdoor rallies due to security concerns, allowed for a minute or so of the Obamas to be seen, on national television, almost surfing atop a sea of exultant Minnesotans chanting "Yes, we can!"

When the entrance music quieted, and after Barack and Michelle circumnavigated his podium, exchanging a "fist bump" to celebrate the end of their sixteen-month journey, she would leave the frame. The cheers, though, stretched for minutes more, allowing cable anchors like CNN's John King to reflect on the moment's historic import. As that was happening, Obama took his place behind the podium, which was angled toward the press riser to keep his teleprompter panels out of the tight shot. Hundreds of people filled the frame behind the candidate, far enough in the distance to be seen in soft focus and not distract the viewer. Like everyone else in the camera's field of vision, those behind Obama waved American flags and his trademark "Change We Can Believe In" placards. That same message filled the stadium scoreboards and LED ribbons along the balconies, and was affixed to the front of the podium in crisp focus. Sixty feet away, TV cameras and still photographers couldn't miss it.

The *Minneapolis Star-Tribune* turned to a native son, U.S. Representative Keith Ellison, to put the night in perspective. "It's a huge thing," Ellison said. "Our country is a country that for 2-1/2 centuries had Africans as chattel slavery and a century after that had Jim Crow. America as a country keeps on getting better."[10] No matter how strong McCain's presentation was in Louisiana, it couldn't match the magnitude of what was going down in St. Paul. Against this overwhelming display of emotion and imagery, Minnesota's Republican governor Tim Pawlenty, himself a future presidential candidate, could only offer a mild rebuke in the same *Star-Tribune* story. Obama, Pawlenty said, was "a gifted orator and speaker, but being able to read a teleprompter is not preparation to be president."[11]

GREEN WITH ENVY

The second failure of McCain's event was one of design and production.

Obama had to wait several minutes for the cheers to die down at the Xcel Energy Center, aided by his extended walk-out and the pulsating soundtrack from the event's rock concert–style sound system. Meanwhile, at the Pontchartrain Center, McCain's ovation came and went in twelve seconds. Obama issued twenty-seven "thank-yous" over the course of a minute and a half to shush his crowd, interlaced with several "thank you, Minnesotas" and "thank you, St. Pauls"—his trademark nod to local intimacy—before he began his acknowledgments. By contrast, McCain stood over the shoulder of Louisiana governor Bobby Jindal as the governor issued his introduction of the candidate, gave Jindal a half hug, threw out five staccato "thank-yous" and moved deliberately into his text.

Once McCain started to speak, his prompter proved his antagonist rather than his tool. His torso, stiffened by injuries from ejecting over North Vietnam and the torture of his captors, limited his ability to use the machine to his advantage. As he read his words, he pivoted between three angles relative to the head-on camera. He would look forty-five degrees to the right, reading from one glass panel, then forty-five degrees to the left, to read from the other one, pausing occasionally in the ninety-degree pivot to utter a few words directly into the lens.

McCain's slavishness to the device, rather than using it to feed him a line to deliver with perceived authenticity—his opponent's distinguishing talent—was painful to watch. Those in the Kenner crowd seeking a real connection with McCain—the occasional ad lib that breaks up formality—were denied it by the artificial barrier of the prompter's glass panels. And on TV, McCain's pacing, gesticulation, volume and inflection remained metronomic, like a test of the Emergency Broadcast System.

The reviews were not good.

Marc Ambinder, writing for the *Atlantic,* noted that "the green background is very weird and very jarring. On this stage, theatrics matter."[12]

In his blog, *The Daily Dish,* Andrew Sullivan added, "From the re-branded green background to the silly attempt to capitalize on Democratic divisions to the Clintonian cooptation of an Obama meme—'a leader we can believe in'—McCain's opening gambit in the general election was, in my judgment, underwhelming." Sullivan focused his criticism less on the content of the message than on the stagecraft. "It was the delivery and the response that threw me off," he wrote. "To be blunt, McCain can be a pretty bad public speaker. He has a mild, relatively high-pitched voice and an uncomfortable way of smiling broadly and speaking softly as he makes tough attacks on his opponent."[13]

Predictably, the late-night comedy shows were next to weigh in. The next night, Stephen Colbert told his viewers on the *Colbert Report,* "There's no denying it, last night was truly historic. For the first time in the history of American politics, John McCain stayed up past 7 p.m. At McCain's rally, well over a dozen people electrified the atmosphere. . . . Now McCain may not be the best speaker, but he is working on it. Last night he took the bold step of enhancing his performance by speaking in front of a green screen, issuing a bold challenge to Americans to make him seem interesting."[14]

And then Colbert did something very Colbert-like, a bit that Johnny Carson, David Letterman or Jay Leno might never have tried during their heyday on late night. He used "green screen" technology to earn extended comedic mileage at McCain's expense.

A "green screen," television production slang for chroma key compositing, is used to remove the existing background from a person in a video and replace it with a different image. Put to use by late-night comics, the effects can be deadly. As Colbert said, "I don't want to bog you down with technical TV jargon, but basically Jesus made green a magical color—anything you film in front of it can become something else!"

Answering his own rhetorical challenge to make McCain "seem interesting," Colbert issued an aside to a member of his stage crew. "I will be first to pick up that gauntlet," Colbert said. "Jimmy, let's spice him up!"

As Colbert said this, McCain's green "A Leader We Can Believe In" backdrop was replaced by different video clips to provide a new distraction for the candidate's robotic remarks. First to appear over McCain's shoulders were a pride of prowling lions moving menacingly toward his head. The lions were followed by carnival dancers from Rio de Janeiro. The third clip featured Charlton Heston behind McCain in the famous chariot race from *Ben Hur*. A fourth showed a lunar lander descending onto alien tundra.

Colbert wasn't done. He followed up the clips with an invitation to his viewers. He called it "McCain's Green Screen Challenge" and asked his audience at home to download a segment of the speech that replaced the green "A Leader We Can Believe In" hard wall with a real "green screen." Colbert challenged the creative types watching him to take a step beyond lions, carnival dancers and *Ben Hur* to apply any theme of computer geek-driven inspiration that struck their fancy.[15]

Viewers jumped at the chance to "jazz up the old maverick," as Colbert said, pushing the comedic envelope beyond the host's tepid initial offerings toward the deeply bizarre. Days later, introducing the first selected entries, Colbert allowed that "McCain's rhetorical style could best be described as 'tired mayonnaise.'" To make him "interesting," viewer Michael Linback put McCain in a wild rave party. Next, Sarah McGarr inserted the senator in front of an oncoming fiery crash at a NASCAR race. Finally, Drew Hudson decolored the McCain footage and placed him, in black and white, next to a young Queen Elizabeth as she addressed her British subjects. Over the end of the footage, in the format of a political ad, Hudson superimposed the words: "John McCain—*He's that old.*"[16] It was a hilarious bit, fit Colbert's demographic perfectly and caught on, big time.

The "Make McCain Interesting" meme continued at regular intervals throughout the summer, the editing becoming ever more cinematic. John Knoll grafted McCain's head onto a guitar-playing torso that appeared to belong to Elvis Presley in a full pelvic tilt—"Just like Elvis, there is widespread belief that John McCain is still alive," Colbert announced after the clip ran. Next, Don Hegarty put McCain's head on the body of William Shatner as an agitated James T. Kirk, supported on either side by Leonard Nimoy's Mr. Spock and DeForest Kelley's Dr. McCoy—"McCain has boldly gone where no man has gone before," Colbert quipped, "chiefly due to an enlarged prostate." The last and best of this set of entries came from Wayne Simbro, who spliced McCain into Madonna's iconic "Vogue" video, originally directed by David Fincher in 1990, replacing Madonna with McCain amid the bare-chested Art Deco stylings of photographers George Hurrell and Horst P. Horst.[17]

Colbert's recurring green-screen segments were too good for Comedy Central to let go as laugh-inducing summer fare. Mercifully for McCain, the "last shot" of the challenge at the senator's expense aired on

September 2. In that final set of clips, screened right before the Republican Convention got under way, "Brian R." inserted McCain's head in the sand at the finish line of an iguana race, with reptiles inching toward a calamitous rendezvous with the candidate's eyes. "Ryan S." placed McCain's head onto that of a surfer from a mid-1960s beach party movie. Colbert chastised Ryan on air, reminding him that the challenge was "to make McCain interesting, not to make surfing boring."[18]

It is easy to dismiss such antics as visual catnip for college students staying up late and smoking weed, but at its core, it hit on something systemic underlying the 2008 race. Age hadn't been a factor since Clinton v. Dole in 1996, long before Jon Stewart and Stephen Colbert launched their shows on Comedy Central.

A generation that hadn't read *Faith of My Fathers* sought a leader relevant to them. McCain would be seventy-two upon taking office, Obama forty-seven, a gap of twenty-five years separating them. As Ezra Klein wrote in the *Los Angeles Times* two days before McCain's speech in Kenner, "The real significance of the age difference is not about health and mortality but about worldview, about ideology, about how the candidates understand the threats we face and the world we're in."[19]

Stewart's and Colbert's viewers were also voters. About 23 million young people turned out in 2008, 10 percent more than 2004 (itself a record), with young voters breaking for Obama over McCain by 68 percent to 30 percent. It was, according to CIRCLE, which tracks political engagement of young Americans, the highest share of the youth vote won by any candidate since exit polls began reporting results by age in 1976. And the dominating youth advantage for Obama was recorded not just on the coasts, but also in the battlegrounds. "[The youth vote] is turning states that [Obama] would've lost or barely won into more comfortable margins," said John Della Volpe of Harvard's Institute of Politics. "Not only are they voting in higher numbers, they're voting more Democratic."[20]

When Robert Draper of the *New York Times Magazine* dissected the innards of McCain's campaign in an 8,000-word analysis in the October 28, 2008, issue, just before Election Day, he called out the evening of June 3 as a dark night for both candidate and staff, with Steve Schmidt left to account. The green backdrop, Draper wrote, was "a poorly executed version of an idea Schmidt borrowed from the eco-friendly 2006 Schwarzenegger campaign." Draper added that "McCain was so frustrated by his own, at times, stumbling performance that he vowed never to deliver another teleprompter speech again."[21]

In another profile of Schmidt, Jim Rutenberg and Adam Nagourney of the *New York Times* cited aides looking back on June 3 "as probably the worst night" of the campaign. Against the sea of humanity greeting Obama in St. Paul, McCain could only respond with, as they wrote, "a lackluster speech in a half-empty hall, posed in front of a pea-green screen that became fodder for late-night comedy." In recounting the fiasco, the reporters added that Schmidt "could barely hide his fury in the coming days, as he announced—to anyone who would listen—that he would personally make certain the McCain campaign would never again embarrass Mr. McCain."

For emphasis, Rutenberg and Nagourney inserted a one-sentence paragraph to highlight a one-sentence quote from Schmidt: "Fun Steve is dead."[22]

For the rest of the campaign, while Obama continued to give flawless prompter-guided speeches in front of large crowds, conferring a sense of momentum of its own, McCain's best moments came in the smaller, quieter, less-structured setting of the "town hall." That format, in which the candidate shares a few opening comments and then answers any and all questions, helped McCain win in New Hampshire in 2000. But eight years later, against an exquisitely marketed and produced opponent, candor and openness paled in comparison to rock music, big crowds, waving placards and scrolling prompters.

THE WALL IN ST. PAUL

One of McCain's last chances to reverse the race came on September 4 with his speech to accept the nomination at the Republican Convention at the Xcel Energy Center in St. Paul. The crowning moment, to date, of his political career came twenty-four hours after the momentous appearance by forty-four-year old Alaska governor Sarah Palin, crowning her with the vice presidential nomination. If McCain and Palin could leave Minnesota with a "convention bounce," all of the indignities of the summer might be forgotten. Bizarrely, McCain's speech would invite a new wave of green-screen comparisons to his lamentable outing on June 3.

McCain's big moment at the Xcel Center was preceded, one week before, by Senator Obama's own nomination acceptance speech to a packed Invesco Field, home of the Denver Broncos. It was a bold, unconventional move to stage the historic event at an outdoor venue. The stadium's capacity was 84,000. By filling it, Obama's campaign would match the youthful audacity of the last time such a ploy was planned, in 1960, when

John F. Kennedy capped his party's nomination at the Los Angeles Memorial Coliseum, site of the 1932 and 1984 Olympic Games.

The Democrats easily filled Invesco on the night of August 28, but they too were victimized earlier that day when their behind-the-scenes advance work was revealed to a national audience. While the stage set at Invesco was still being erected by work crews, pictures of the "load-in" moved on the *Drudge Report,* spreading quickly across the right-wing blogosphere. Headlines and captions of the photos upbraided the advance team's design as a Greek temple for their celebrity-tagged candidate. The unanticipated exposure led to a last-minute scrubbing of some of the planned bells and whistles, including an expensive fireworks display planned for the end of the speech.

Looking at the early pictures from Invesco, I interpreted the stage design as part homage to the Los Angeles Coliseum, where Kennedy was crowned, part nod to Soldier Field in Obama's hometown of Chicago and, for the "tight shot," part suggestion of the colonnade of the Rose Garden in the White House. The advance team had gone to the effort of creating a likeness of the French doors that led from the anteroom of the Oval Office to the Rose Garden steps, the pulpit from which the president often speaks. The subliminal suggestion to the 38.4 million people who watched his speech that night was that Obama, upon his formal nomination, was actually addressing the nation from the steps of the President's House. Notwithstanding the premature outing and ridicule by the *Drudge Report,* the Democrats had savvy instincts about how to market their nominee.

One week later, back in St. Paul, the green theme that haunted McCain throughout the summer returned in a new form. It came just as the senator was hoping to put the last few months in the rearview mirror and look ahead to the final eight weeks of campaigning.

The Xcel Energy Center, which two months before had been home to the clamorous rally celebrating Obama's clinch of the nomination, had been refashioned into a more intimate setting. Technology replaced people in the backdrop, with a video wall measuring fifty-one feet wide by thirty feet tall, made up of 561 Hibino four-millimeter Chroma LED panels. A GOP news release boasted that the video wall would give "everyone in the convention hall a perfect view of the speeches and videos that will be part of the program of events."[23]

It was visible all right, but it violated one of the first rules of good advance work: don't screw up the tight shot. For the first nine minutes of McCain's speech, the backdrop that framed the speaker's head—generated by an image uploaded onto the video wall—inexplicably showed a sprawling green lawn. To the TV viewer, it looked exactly like McCain's backdrop in Kenner, minus the "A Leader We Can Believe In" text. This was supposed to be a reset, but the convention producers repeated the costly mistake.

If anyone was keeping tabs on Steve Schmidt's promise that the campaign would never again embarrass its candidate, the curtain-raising stanza of McCain's convention acceptance speech, before the image was switched out on the video wall, was one more excruciating example. The bigger head scratcher, beyond the fundamental question of what the green tight shot was trying to accomplish, was what was swirling in the imaginations of production designers when they picked the image of a verdant lawn leading up to a white building as the establishing shot behind the speaker's head. Mount Vernon, perhaps?

It turned out that the attractive edifice was, in fact, a photo of the Walter Reed Middle School in North Hollywood, California. The middle school is known in Los Angeles for its gifted and talented program. It also has a well-maintained and manicured front yard.

That's probably not why the shot was selected. Major Walter Reed, who is buried in Arlington National Cemetery, was an Army physician who, in 1901, led the team that identified transmission by mosquito as the source of yellow fever, thus saving untold lives. For his inroads into epidemiology, Reed had a number of places named in his honor, including the army medical center in Washington, D.C., as well as the middle school in Los Angeles. But nowhere in his speech does Senator McCain refer to Reed, yellow fever or a school in North Hollywood. The backdrop decision became a mysterious sideshow of what was supposed to be the Republican nominee's shining moment. An article in the *New York Times* the next day noted a consensus that "the Republicans committed an act of sloppy stagecraft."[24]

A McCain spokesman, Tucker Bounds, disagreed, telling the *Times* that it was part of the campaign's efforts to share a slideshow of "images of Americana" during the speech. Pushing his case, Bounds said, "The changing image-screen was linked to the American thematics of the speech and the public school was simply part of it."[25]

In North Hollywood, the locals took issue. John Heaner, who worked for the Democratic Party in California and had two daughters who attended the school, told the *Times*, "It's a big mistake, and it's something that John McCain should take ownership of," adding, "I want him to admit the mistake and if it's not a mistake, he should apologize for using my child's school for partisan purposes."[26] Considerably less aggrieved, one of the school's students, sixth-grader Joshua Popue, proved himself a clear-eyed advance man-in-training. "McCain messed up," he told a reporter for the *Los Angeles Times*. "He was talking about Walter Reed hospital, and he used our picture by mistake."[27]

The fuss gained so much notoriety back in Los Angeles that Donna Tobin, Walter Reed's principal, posted an official statement on the school's website saying, in part, *"Permission to use the front of our school for the Republican National Convention was* not *given by our school nor is the use of our school's picture an endorsement of any political party or view."* The word "not" was bolded in the principal's statement.[28]

John McCain may not have intended with his stagecraft to make inroads among voters in North Hollywood or carry California in the general election, but his promotion of one of the city's schools during his convention speech, planned or unplanned, was another distraction for his team. Nine minutes of unidentified, unexplained green screen left viewers confused. Were they watching McCain's acceptance speech or a Stephen Colbert "Make McCain More Interesting" prime-time special?

The 38.9 million viewers of the speech watching at home were left to wonder. I was one of them, critiquing the production staff whose job it was to burnish the nominee's remarks with a backdrop that promoted his message, rather than rekindling unwelcome flashbacks to New Orleans. Coming on the heels of a triumphant finale to the Democratic Convention at a packed Invesco Field in Denver, the curtain fell on McCain's finale at the Xcel Center with a thud.

I had liked the John McCain that I read about in *Faith of My Fathers* and liked the McCain who rode the Straight Talk Express in 2000. But the recurring apparition of his green screen in 2008, while Obama's team commanded exacting control of their theatrics, required those with practiced eyes to conclude that one band had its shit together while the other did not. No matter how likeable a candidate is, he can't afford to be mishandled by his staff or be outgunned by a better-produced and expertly advanced opponent. In 2008, it all added up to a one-sided fight.

FOURTEEN

2012: ROMNEY SINGS
AN AMERICAN TUNE

(Or, How a Patriotic Businessman
Crooned His Way to Caricature)

THE PLAYLIST

What would *Monday Night Football* be without Carrie Underwood, an Ibiza rave party without Cher, or the president of the United States without "Hail to the Chief"?

Ever since cellist Pablo Casals enchanted Jackie Kennedy in the East Room on November 13, 1961, music and the presidency have enjoyed a marriage made for television, with each administration having a distinctive soundtrack. When our advance teams left the Democratic Convention in New York City in 1992 to begin producing events around the country, Fleetwood Mac's "Don't Stop Thinking about Tomorrow" tailed us as our quasi-official theme song, and it enjoyed a strong four-year run until Al Gore put the Macarena on center stage at the 1996 convention in Chicago. Some campaigns have a better ear for music than others.

On the road, between the signature moments on the biggest stages—like conventions and victory nights—advance people create the daily musical playlist of the political power rotation. Campaign rally songs, a standard accessory in the advance person's toolkit, have evolved with technology—and intellectual property law—over the years. In 1988 and

1992, like most fellow advance people unschooled in the formalities of music licensing, I carried around an audio cassette loaded with my favorite tunes to accompany my candidate's public entrances and exits. Later, in 1996, the playlist was transferred onto a CD. For the 2000 cycle, before the first iPod debuted a year later, early MP3 players did the trick. Every advance person running a site needed a playlist.

My tastes, more pedantic than most, ran to Sousa marches and movie scores with big orchestral sound, often John Williams compositions. I also had a thing for Jimmy Buffett, once producing a birthday party on the South Lawn for President Clinton in which I led the White House staff on a sing-along serenade with lyrics adapted from Buffett's "Changes in Latitudes, Changes in Attitudes." The show was going great—my first turn as lead vocalist under the Truman Balcony—until Buffett himself appeared from the Diplomatic Reception Room, grabbed the microphone from my hands and promptly stole the show.

Generally, I veered away from rock and pop at presidential events, not out of fear of litigation, but because I felt lyrics distracted from the crowd's engagement. My colleagues thought me out of touch to turn up my nose at U2, but I believed that if an audience was listening to words, they were less focused on the action on stage. The final moments of rallies were my favorite, when the candidate yelled "thank you" and I, standing at the sound board, would instruct the audio technician to let the music rip, ensuring that we wouldn't miss a beat to end the event on a high note.

A trip to Concord, New Hampshire, on February 2, 1996, was cast as a triumphant return for the "Comeback Kid"—Clinton—who scored an improbable second place to Paul Tsongas in the 1992 primary. The day started at Walker Elementary School, where our team positioned the press within earshot of a computer that barked "You will be reelected!" in a digital voice as Clinton hovered over it. The picture was accentuated by two students at the computer keyboard with their teacher, Steve Rothenberg, looking on. The education-themed day ended with a speech in Concord, where I had Clinton enter his venue at the Capital Center for the Arts to Michael Kamen's score for *Mr. Holland's Opus.* My intentional audio cues were highlighted in the *New York Times* dispatch on the trip, in which correspondent Todd Purdum noted that Clinton liked the computer's prediction and the Concord audience liked the entry music—Purdum enthusiastically reported that the music came from "the three-hankie film starring Richard Dreyfuss."[1]

Music and presidents have a shared heritage that significantly pre-dates the Kennedy administration. In 1786, a new nation rallied around "God Save George Washington," in which the first president's name re-places "the King" in the British anthem. The Whig Party popularized "Tippecanoe and Tyler Too" in the 1840 campaign of William Henry Harrison. In 1960, Frank Sinatra adapted his hit "High Hopes" in ser-vice for Senator Kennedy. And in 2007, Hillary Clinton held a national contest via YouTube to pick her theme song, asking supporters to decide between Celine Dion's "You and I" and offerings from U2, the Dixie Chicks, Smash Mouth and others. (Celine won out.)

Today, early campaign-season scandals are dependable, involving rue-ful artists litigating to prevent candidates from improperly employing their music. Jackson Brown exacted a settlement and apology from John McCain for using "Running on Empty" in 2008, and Survivor sued to stop Newt Gingrich from using "Eye of the Tiger" in 2012. At Donald Trump's cam-paign announcement in June 2015, the candidate descended an escalator at Trump Tower—Stephen Colbert later dubbed it "Stair Force One"—to Neil Young's "Rockin' in the Free World." Trump's campaign even went to the trouble of licensing the song through ASCAP, but failed to get explicit permission from Young, who had pledged his support to Bernie Sanders. Not one to shy away from a publicity opportunity, Trump hit back, tweet-ing out a picture of Young in his office seeking the billionaire's financial backing for a new online music service. The two men were all smiles in the photo; now Trump was calling Young a "total hypocrite" in the tweet.[2]

THE SOLO ACT

Just as riding in a tank provided the imagery for a knockout TV ad against Michael Dukakis in 1988 and windsurfing did the same against John Kerry in 2004, Mitt Romney's own singing voice, and footage of him using it in January 2012, unwittingly created the soundtrack for a pernicious negative ad attacking him.

Romney cut a dashing silhouette on the podium, and his team went to great lengths to use rock show lighting and perfect backdrops to make him look presidential on stage. But when he opened his mouth at The Villages in Sumter County, Florida, on the evening of January 30 and out of his mouth came off-tune musical stylings instead of canned political rhetoric, he sounded like a washout auditioner for a TV talent show that the producers included in the broadcast for comic relief.

The performance was an unforced error of the type that befell Dukakis and Kerry, Romney's fellow Massachusetts politicians, in which public moments in front of the lens reveal too much about the candidate's underlying personality. But while Dukakis was undermined by his staff and Kerry was reckless of his own accord, Romney was simply betraying an old-school patriotic streak that backfired, miserably. It was a self-inflected wound that, having followed Romney across Iowa four years earlier, I didn't expect from him.

In the summer of 2007, I traveled to Des Moines on assignment for *Men's Vogue* magazine. It was the dawn of a new campaign season, and I was conducting an archeological expedition of sorts to document how the species of Democratic and Republican candidates, and their advance people, had evolved as performers and producers in the twenty years since I first roamed the campaign hustings. Two decades spanned an epoch of advance history, from the halcyon days of pay phones, fax machines and Skypagers to the modern era of cell phones, digital cameras and early social media.

Of all the campaigns I watched, I enjoyed spending time with Romney's the most. He was a master marketer, and I catalogued how he adapted his businessman's brand into that of a national politician. Any custodian of the Olympic brand who has wrapped sports venues in the "five rings" motif—as Mitt had in Salt Lake City in 2002—would approach his candidacy with an equally disciplined eye on the visual.

Mitt presented himself in Des Moines as a plaid-shirt-and-khakis man, fitting right in by cheerily flipping patties at the Pork Producer's tent at the Iowa State Fair. His mufti would be the same when he launched his next campaign, four years later in June 2011, at the 300-acre Bittersweet Farm of Doug and Stella Scamman in Stratham, New Hampshire. With a massive American flag draping the Scamman farmhouse, Romney's wife, Ann, ladled out her family's chili recipe to hungry rally-goers, all dutifully captured by the cameras. The visual identity used to present the Romneys was extravagantly Olympian in all respects, right down to the custom-embroidered headrest covers on the candidate's plane.

Among Romney's well-groomed entourage in Des Moines in 2007 was one fellow who, visually, didn't quite fit. Will Ritter, Romney's "body guy," wasn't cut from the same cloth as the Brylcreemed young men who looked just back from Mormon missionary work. A self-described "obnoxious Red Sox fan," Ritter was shorter than the type, with deep-set eyes, thinning hair and a red-tinted beard. His stubble made him prone, as I watched him at the State Fair, to overheating under the scorching Iowa sun. But one thing was clear: Ritter was to his core the hyper-vigilant advance man, keeping an eye out for his boss's every need.

I wasn't surprised when Ritter reenlisted for another Romney tour in 2011–12. This time, he would serve as the director of advance, making a well-earned leap from body guy to management. Ritter had the equivalent of a rock-and-roll stadium tour to produce and had an authoritative voice in where to schedule the main act. Some venues are perfectly suited for marquee troupes. Springsteen plays arenas in the winter. The Stones play stadiums in the summer. Republican candidates play The Villages, "Florida's Friendliest Hometown," in the days leading up to the Florida GOP Primary. At The Villages, a sell-out crowd is almost assured.

THE VILLAGES

In the 2012 GOP primary season, Florida was shaping up as Newt Gingrich's Waterloo. The former House Speaker, once dismissed as an also-ran, had surged in the polls and won the preceding primary in South Carolina. If he could continue his streak in the Sunshine State, he might make it a protracted two-man race that would sap Romney's financial resources. But Gingrich ran into a wave of oppo research about his work for the government-sponsored enterprise Freddie Mac after leaving office and a gauntlet of negative advertising from both Romney and his Super-PAC, Restore Our Future, which together outspent the former Speaker by a margin of four to one. He also found himself outmatched by Romney's talent as a crooner for belting out patriotic standards on the stump.

Built by the late billionaire H. Gary Morse over the course of fifty years on a parcel of about thirty square miles of land between Orlando and Ocala, The Villages is like the nation's largest privately owned wildlife preserve of a flourishing species called aging Republicans. In 2000, the census reported the place having a population of 8,333, giving it only minor impact on the popular vote in the state whose election results precipitated the infamous recount and the U.S. Supreme Court decision in the hotly contested case of *Bush v. Gore.*

But by 2010, the population of The Villages had ballooned 517 percent to 51,442. The expansion allowed Morse to claim the title of fastest-growing "micropolitan" area in the United States. If the evolving political makeup of the U.S. population had mirrored the ecosystem of The Villages, with its unique ZIP code of 32162, Democrats would have long become extinct. Larry Shipley, the president of the local Democratic Club, once said of Morse, "He owns the newspaper, he owns the radio station, and just about all of the businesses have to behave like they're Republicans out of fear that they won't get any more business out of The Villages—and it's a major employer in the area."[3]

According to federal records from 2008, 95 percent of political donations coming from The Villages' residents went to Republicans. Rich Cole, president of The Villages Republican Club, proclaimed that "The road to Washington goes through Tallahassee—you have to win Florida—and the road to Tallahassee goes through The Villages."[4]

On January 30, just before the Florida Primary, Romney was ready to drive nails into the coffin of Gingrich's campaign. He had suffered enough ridicule at the hands of Newt who, five days earlier, told a Univision interviewer in Miami that Romney's immigration policies were "an Obama-level fantasy." During the interview, Gingrich said, "You have to live in a world of Swiss bank accounts and Cayman Island accounts and automatic $20 million income for no work" to be so detached from reality.[5] Extracting Newt's thorn from Romney's side would pave the way for the nomination that eluded him four years earlier.

The Romney campaign would let its negative advertising do most of the work, but to take the high ground and appeal to the state's aging voters, Ritter steered the Romney tour bus toward one of The Villages' three "town squares" where, the community's website maintains, "you'll find plenty of modern day fun."[6] The town squares look like Mayberry with free evening entertainment, but on some nights the revelry makes them feel more like the Sunset Strip. The *Los Angeles Times* described the town squares, when they're not in use for political rallies, as places where "boozy dances each night have helped this community of seniors earn a somewhat double-edged reputation as Disney World for the Cialis set."[7]

When the Romney campaign bus pulled in on the evening of January 30, Will Ritter was on the coach with "the Guv," as he called his boss. The energy level was high, just as it was when the Clinton/Gore bus pulled into the event that Paul Meyer and I created at the Ocala, Florida, rodeo arena in 1992. Campaign rallies at places like Ocala and The Villages, even twenty years apart, will draw crowds with a common thread of patriotism knitted through them, no matter if the audience is Republican or Democrat. The draw has to be strong to get older voters off their couches, and love of country is the ticket. "If the mood was right," Ritter told me, Romney would serenade large crowds bleeding red, white and blue by putting his hand over his heart and leading those gathered in his rendition of "America the Beautiful."[8]

AMERICA THE BEAUTIFUL

"America the Beautiful," with lyrics written in 1893, is long out of copyright protection. Besides, it was unlikely that ASCAP or any other entity would bring a lawsuit against a sixty-five-year-old former governor for belting out three or four verses of the tune in front of a few thousand fellow senior citizens on a warm Monday night in Florida.

The song meant a lot to Romney. His father, George, a governor of Michigan and himself a presidential candidate in 1968, had grown up poor in a Mormon colony in Mexico. Fleeing the Mexican Revolution in 1912, America, the beautiful, was a haven for the Romney clan, eventually endowing it with privilege and the opportunity to run for president in two different generations. When Romney wasn't distancing himself from his dad's progressive legacy, an observer could easily discern deep gratitude for all that the United States had bestowed on him and his family. It was a form of gratitude that expressed itself in pride, and in song.

The mood was right for music on January 30, with the primary the next day. "It was a beautiful night," Ritter told me. "We had thousands of people who had packed that town square. The sun had just set. The residents were all riled up and they were swarming the bus." The moment was almost foreordained. As the bus rolled toward its chalks, "the governor could see people were lined up, waiting to get in," Ritter remembered, "and they were very enthusiastic, and he said, 'maybe I'll sing a little bit tonight.'"[9]

The town square clock at The Villages, resting over Romney's shoulder in the tight shot, stood at 7:02 p.m. Behind it hung a huge white banner proclaiming "Florida is Romney Country." Between the clock and the stage, a resident held high a handmade sign that said "Romney Rocks," but Romney was not about to rock. Warble was a more apt description. With his left hand planted in the front pocket of his pressed blue jeans, wearing an open-collared blue shirt and navy blazer with obligatory flag lapel pin, the would-be singer introduced his ditty like a crooner at a hotel lounge off the Vegas strip.

"When I was a boy, my mom and dad put us in their car and took us around the national parks," he told the attentive gathering. "They wanted us to see the beauty of the land. We came here and saw Cyprus Gardens and the oceans, went west and saw the canyons, rivers and mountains, and fell in love with the land in America. There's a song that captures that for me." He asked the crowd plaintively, "Can you sing that song?"[10]

Watching the video, I saw crowd members moving their lips in synch with the lyrics, but Romney suffered from the same technological limitation that turned Howard Dean's speech at the Val Air into a screaming solo act—the microphone couldn't pick up the crowd sing-along. When he got to "above the fruited plain," it sounded like fingernails scraping across a chalkboard.

Later that night on CNN, Piers Morgan booked Jack and Suzy Welch, the former General Electric CEO and his wife, to come on his show from Florida. They were promoted on air as leading voices of the business community, but Welch was essentially a Romney surrogate from "the establishment," performing the ritual kabuki of spouting talking points of Romney being a "pull-teams-together and get-the-right-answer guy." Welch conceded to Morgan that Romney might be "a little bit dull," but comparing him with Gingrich, he said, "Most Americans would rather have a bore than a bumble bee."[11]

A good part of the segment, however, turned into a CNN version of *American Idol,* with Piers, Jack and Suzy as Simon Cowell, Randy Jackson and Paula Abdul, respectively. Jack and Suzy looked squeamish as Morgan teed up a minute of airtime to screen Romney belting out his song. As the TV screen split between the Welches in one box and Mitt singing in the other, Morgan said, "This could cost Romney the entire election." At its essence, cable TV moves as quickly as engineers in a control room can toggle switches to balance soliloquys of talking heads with flashes of visual catnip to elongate viewer attention spans.

Morgan returned to air following the clip to declare that Romney "murdered" the song and warned that "I think this could become an issue." Mrs. Welch defended the candidate, saying, "Mitt Romney didn't exactly do a beautiful job on that song, but think about what he's singing, okay?" She said Romney sounded "like my dad when he sings it," and theorized that Americans living well removed from the coasts might feel the same way.

An Obama fan, at least as it relates to music appreciation, Morgan wasn't buying it, framing the election more in terms of singing talent and stage presence than a duel of political philosophy. Ten days earlier, also in front of a packed house, this time at the Apollo Theater in Harlem, the mood was right for President Obama to sing. At the close of his remarks, he channeled his inner Al Green with a brief rendition of "Let's Stay To-gether" at a Democratic fundraiser. Morgan described the performance as "brilliant."[12]

Morgan wasn't alone. Obama's debut doing Al Green went viral on YouTube and the video was repeated on every network with airtime to fill. It was about 10:30 p.m. at the Apollo—as opposed to 7:00 p.m. at The Villages—and Obama remembered his senior advisor, Valerie Jar-rett, offstage imploring him not to sing, making a slashing motion across her throat. "You don't think I can do that onstage?" he said to Jarrett. As he recounted the episode for *Rolling Stone,* "I looked at [press secretary] Jay Carney, and he was tired too, and he said, 'Yeah, go for it.' So I went up there and we did it."[13]

The on-air debate over Obama at the Apollo versus Romney at The Villages would peter out once the Florida results were tallied and Romney became the presumptive nominee. But in the offices of Obama's media team, the video from The Villages was filed away for future use by Rich Davis and David Dickson, two of the campaign's ad men, modern-day descendants of Sig Rogich and Jim Weller. Davis and Dickson knew that Romney's performance might someday be worthy of an encore. The poten-tial wasn't yet clear, but they saved it to their servers just the same. Maybe Piers Morgan was right. Maybe it could "cost Romney the entire election."

FIRMS

The Obama campaign didn't need to dispatch a tracker to Florida to re-cord Romney's incaution on the stump. Unlike George Allen's "Macaca" moment, the damning footage was right there on C-SPAN, easy fodder for Piers Morgan and the late-night comics.

"Tell me, *tell* me" Jon Stewart implored his studio audience the night after the impromptu concert, "Mitt Romney isn't about to woo elderly voters with the power of song." Mitt sang one verse of "America the Beau-tiful," then a second, and finally a third, more than most staunch patriots can recite by heart. "It was then," Stewart said, "that everyone in the crowd at The Villages pressed their Life Alert button at the same time and faked a stroke."[14]

But besides *Daily Show* nuggets and lefty blog bait, what other cre-ative content could be harvested from the footage? That's what Rich Davis and David Dickson asked themselves, musing on how a paean to patriotism could be exploited further. If Romney's work as head of Bain

Capital, and his accountants' interpretation of the IRS Tax Code, allowed him to earn a greater return through investment vehicles located *outside* the United States, how patriotic is *that?*, they wondered.

The irony was palpable. Jim Margolis, who led the Obama media team, told me that Davis and Dickson piped up on a conference call, saying, "There's something to this. Here he is singing 'America the Beautiful' and he's got his own investments overseas in Swiss bank accounts and in the Cayman Islands." Margolis remembered Davis and Dickson saying, "There's been a pretty significant amount of offshoring of jobs from the companies that he acquired at Bain and then moved a number of the jobs overseas. This is dissonant. There's something wrong here between that picture of Romney [singing at The Villages] and what actually he has done in much of his business career."[15]

But it was too early in the year to spring the dissonance trap. Any money spent on paid media now would be squandered prematurely in the noise of the Republican nomination season. "We all nodded our heads and said, yeah, this isn't really the right time," Margolis remembered.[16]

A few months later, when more voters became engaged in the two-man finals, the time would be right. Lee Atwater used the same calculus when he decided to wait to define Dukakis using Willie Horton—after the primaries, but before the general election. "As we got into the heat of the campaign," Margolis told me, "and as we got to a point where there really was a lot of conversation about Governor Romney's record as governor and as a CEO, it all of a sudden occurred to us that, you know what, that really was a great point that Dixon and Davis made and, ultimately, that spot was put together."[17]

"Firms," as the spot was called, was a triumph of creative editing, knitting audio and visual elements into a thirty-second ad with a profound emotional effect on the viewer. Romney is seen singing on camera at The Villages for about three seconds, just like Dukakis was only visible for a few seconds of the tank ad. For the remaining twenty-six seconds, Romney's off-pitch voice is heard but not seen, strong at first, becoming progressively more hollow and tinny at the end, the result of a manipulated audio track giving the singer's voice a faint echo before it fades. Beyond the president saying, at the outset, "I'm Barack Obama, and I approved this message," no voice other than Romney's own was needed to make the spot lethal.

Visually, the ad kills with carefully cut imagery and graphics. It starts with Romney in his blue blazer on that beautiful Florida night, the crowd enveloping him. The screen reads, "The Villages, 1/20/12." Then news headlines appear overlaid on haunting video clips. The first headline, set against an idle assembly line, credits the *Los Angeles Times* as its source in tiny letters, but screams, "In business, Mitt Romney's firms shipped jobs to Mexico and China." This is followed by a video cut of a chain link fence surrounding a mothballed factory. And all the while, the Romney serenade continues.

The next headline reads, "As Governor, Romney outsourced jobs to India," sourced from a *Boston Globe* story, over an image of an empty boardroom. A third headline, "He had millions in a Swiss bank account," credits ABC News and floats on screen next to a billowing Swiss flag and a pristine Swiss river and hamlet beyond.

The visual action then shifts as "Tax havens like Bermuda" shows on screen (credit: *Vanity Fair,* of all sources), with palm trees and an open ocean visible behind. The last image to arrive on screen is one of a pristine sandy beach with the camera panning left. The beach's accompanying headline, as if a viewer needs any reinforcement of the message, is "And the Cayman Islands" (thanks, ABC News, again).

The singing continues, but the screen cuts to black with white lettering staring the viewer starkly in the face: "Mitt Romney's not the solution. He's the problem."[18]

"We really tested that ad," Margolis told me. "We were nervous that people would think we were being unfair. In fact, as we tested it and talked to people, they were the ones who convinced us to put it on the air." There was, Margolis said, "a disconnect" between Romney's embrace of patriotism, as evidenced in his song, and Romney's past practices. Margolis, who, as a young ad man for Dukakis in 1988, had seen how Sig Rogich exploited the tank footage from Sterling Heights, knew he was playing with fire. "More than usual did we really try to get a good bead on that so that we didn't have people feeling like we were being unfair," he told me.[19]

Five months elapsed between Romney's performance at The Villages and his return engagement in July in a paid TV ad of his opponent. "Firms" aired in nine battleground states—Colorado, Florida, Iowa, North Carolina, New Hampshire, Nevada, Ohio, Pennsylvania and Virginia—and also became a sensation online and embedded into the discussion on cable news shows. For Romney, he was being "defined" by Obama and his ad team while the "undecideds" were just beginning to make up their minds about who to support—the worst possible time.

FALLOUT

Sitting in his office in Boston with another Romney staffer when "Firms" first went online, Director of Advance Will Ritter received an email from a friend with a link to the ad, which quickly registered more than two million views on YouTube. His memory immediately returned to that evening at The Villages and how his boss's genuine sentiment was bastardized in thirty seconds. "You shudder because they had taken something that, in context, was patriotic and heartfelt, and twisted it to be sinister and ironic. It's too bad, but its politics," Ritter told me. "We both looked at it and said, 'That hurts.'"[20]

A fresh volley of news stories got mileage out of The Villages. "Mitt Romney's Terrible Singing Comes Back to Haunt Him as Obama Uses His Rendition of 'America the Beautiful' in New Attack Ad" blared a headline in London's *Daily Mail* on July 16, noting that "a nonpartisan watchdog group says [the ad's] claims are exaggerated or completely false."[21]

Romney's message machine in Boston sprang into action with the same strategy that another Boston-based campaign used twenty-four years earlier. "So now I guess it's time to attack the middle class and patriotism," read an email from Romney's top strategist, Stuart Stevens, which Jill Lawrence reported in the *National Journal*. "This is what campaigns do when anger and frustration replaces hope and change," Stevens added.[22]

Romney's spokeswoman Amanda Henneberg weighed in with a formal statement. "The Obama campaign," she wrote, "appears to be stuck in their own 'Groundhog Day,' repeating the same, debunked charges they've waged for weeks in an effort to distract voters from his administration's failure to fix the economy and create jobs."[23] But just like the tank ad, no amount of spin could wage effective war against what was a brilliantly imagined, easily digestible spot using the candidate's own image and voice.

"Firms" lingered on air in the early weeks of the summer of 2012, settling in for a much longer run than other paid spots that come and go in a week. Asked about the ad buy, an Obama aide told a reporter, "It's a little slower in getting rotated out than broadcast TV, but this is not sort of a case where we're intentionally stretching it out."[24] The ad, which became the most watched spot of the campaign on Obama's YouTube channel, was seen by many as the most memorable piece of paid media in the campaign.

A research project by YouGov and Vanderbilt University did "pre-and-post" testing of "Firms" with independent voters, pitting it against a negative ad produced by the Romney campaign aimed at President Obama. These "mall tests," which I regularly employed in my days as a consultant at a polling firm, take "cells" of 200 or so undecided voters and expose them to one ad or the other—the winning spot is the one that moves the group in "post" attitudinal measurement farthest in a negative direction from its "pre" origin. After watching "Firms," Romney's "favorable" rating fell off a cliff with its test audience, from 16 percent to 3 percent. That's like losing, in thirty seconds, four out of five voters who might have voted for you. By contrast, the cell that saw Romney's anti-Obama ad budged only a little.

"This one breaks through all the clutter," wrote former Democratic congressman Martin Frost in *POLITICO* on July 24. "The hardest thing in politics is to get a message through all the clutter on TV. Romney has given the Obama campaign a big assist in delivering its message."[25]

Looking back at the ad, long after his second enlistment with Mitt Romney had ended, Will Ritter was wistful but realistic. He would go on to become the founder of his own media company, called Poolhouse, that boasts, "We work to win, and build our clients razor sharp spots." He knew from painful experience what it was like to serve a candidate exposed to the cutting edge of a razor-sharp spot. "I think people understood that ["Firms"] sucked," he told me, "but I don't think anyone said, 'Oh God, why did we do that? We shouldn't have done that. It was one of those, 'Yeah, they got us' moments," Ritter conceded.[26]

There's little remedy to this aside from hiding your candidate from anything but the most sanitary settings. What happens in front of the lens is fair game, either for free- or paid-media ridicule. Heading out for a day of politicking or pleasure made a victim of Dukakis, Bush, Dole, Gore, Kerry, McCain and now Mitt Romney, each of whose actions, as recorded in public, came back to haunt them in the Age of Optics.

"It's really easy in our line of work," Ritter told me, "with the rise of trackers and opposition research, to say that the candidate should never say anything or do anything spontaneous because it can always be in an ad. Well, we're getting to the point where you have to choose between two leaders who aren't going to say anything."[27] At the time Ritter and I spoke, he couldn't envision the campaign of a reality-show star like Donald J. Trump.

PART THREE

THE VANILLA PRESIDENCY, 2009–2017

FIFTEEN

OBAMA AND THE BATSMAN

THE BRAND OF HOPE

Barack Obama made his global television debut on July 27, 2004, the night of his electrifying keynote to the Democratic Convention at the FleetCenter in Boston. In the hours before he spoke his way into history, it was an unremarkable day for the Illinois state senator. The centerpiece was an outdoor speech to a lunchtime crowd of 100 people about environmental policy set against the backdrop of Boston Harbor. He was "relaxed and loose, seemingly unconcerned about what was ahead," according to one account.[1] Leaving the venue in a minivan, he told a reporter riding along with him that his routine before his big speech included "a long shower" and "maybe a nap." His blasé bearing when confronting high-stakes moments became a trademark of the Obama brand.

I was impressed by the power and delivery of his keynote—who wouldn't be?—but a boffo convention speech is nothing new in political stagecraft: William Jennings Bryan did it with the "The Cross of Gold" speech in 1896, Barry Goldwater did it with his "Extremism in the Defense of Liberty" speech in 1964 and, in more modern times, Ted Kennedy and Mario Cuomo electrified their convention audiences in New York City and San Francisco, respectively, in 1980 and 1984.

In a dramatic change of scenery, then-senator Obama got my attention again on the evening of Monday, December 11, 2006. He was a likely candidate for president in 2008 and might have his fifteen minutes of fame somewhere along the line, but his odds were long against pros like Hillary Clinton, Joe Biden, Chris Dodd and John Edwards. While his official announcement of candidacy was still two months away, it didn't stop him from stoking the buzz in a powerful way before a massive audience.

I was settling in for a night of football, tuning into ESPN right before 8:30 p.m. to watch the 11–2 Chicago Bears take on the 5–8 St. Louis Rams at the Edward Jones Dome. My plasma screen came to life and, as it did, nighttime video of the St. Louis Arch—the usual local B-roll before the opening of a major sports broadcast—gave way to video of an interior office scene of controlled chaos. Watching this display, I had a momentary flashback to times I found myself in the Oval Office doing final prep for one of President Clinton's prime-time addresses, those anxious few minutes during which crews fussed with lighting, technicians tested teleprompters and our team made final adjustments to ensure the shot was picture perfect. There, on ESPN, a similar presidential pageant unfolded.

"Okay, folks," a stagehand barked as he waved his fingers in front of a camera lens. "We're live in 3, 2 . . ." At that second, the disorder on camera became serene and revealed a suited Senator Obama sitting at a desk, hands clasped before him, against a backdrop of an American and Illinois flag, family photos placed lovingly around him. While the election was still two years away, the scene was set to make Obama look, and give him a backdrop like he was already, the leader of the free world. And the way he authoritatively delivered his lines, staring stoically into the lens, he sounded like it, too.

> Good evening. I'm Senator Barack Obama.
>
> I'm here tonight to answer some questions about a very important contest that's been weighing on the minds of the American people. This is a contest about the future; a contest between two very different philosophies, a contest that will ultimately be decided in America's heartland . . .

The words in his first few sentences were ambiguous. *What the hell is this?* a viewer might wonder, thinking Obama had hijacked national airtime to jump the gun on his candidacy. The only hints that it might be something else were a slowly amplifying musical underlay and use of a dolly camera, a cinematic "beauty shot" floating right to left. He went on in deadpan fashion, confiding to the viewer whispers floated about him by campaign odds-makers.

In Chicago, they're asking, 'Does the new guy have enough experience to lead us to victory?' In St. Louis, they're asking, 'Are we facing a record that's really so formidable, or is it all just a bunch of hype?'

Let me tell you, I'm all too familiar with these questions. So tonight, I'd like to put all these doubts to rest. I'd like to announce, to my hometown of Chicago, and all of America, that I am ready . . .

If he was about to utter something historic, like he was "in it to win it," as Hillary Clinton would say in a video from her living room sofa the next month, the moment was at hand. But at that second, his torso turned to the right to pick up an object sitting off-camera. His hand returned to the frame holding a Chicago Bears ball cap, which he delightedly placed atop his head. The deadpan suddenly gave way to passionate declaration.

. . . for the Bears to go all the way, baby![2]

A broad smile replaced Obama's stern gaze as he mimicked the ESPN fanfare—*Da da da da!* With Obama laughing good-naturedly at himself, the scene faded to black. With the gag over, the genuine MNF theme song picked up where Obama left off and the game's kickoff ensued, with the Bears beating the Rams by a score of 42–27.

Obama's acute eye for stagecraft never let up. On February 10, 2007, at his real announcement of candidacy in Springfield, the campaign engineered a raised walkway to carry him above the crowd of 15,000 to a stage set against the Greek Revival façade of the Old State Capitol. The sun illuminated the locally quarried Sugar Creek limestone in a striking amber glow, the panorama interrupted only by two teleprompter stands in the foreground, their panels using a solid gray backing instead of transparent glass to minimize glare, a detail missed by most who braved the bone-chilling cold or watched on TV and online. U2's "City of Blinding Lights" accompanied the senator's grand solitary walk amid cheering, placard-waving supporters. It was picture perfect. It was the future. It was hope. Obama's advance team knew how to stage an entrance.

I saw their flair for scene-setting in person, six months later, on the same Iowa trip in which I chronicled the advance work of young men and women of both parties for *Men's Vogue* magazine. While my stop with Hillary Clinton brought me to a nondescript community college gymnasium in Sioux City, a drive farther afield took me to the Cass County Fairgrounds, in the little town of Atlantic, where Obama would soon arrive in his RV to be greeted by advance men Rick Siger and J. P. Eby. Sitting in my rental car with a cup of coffee in those early morning hours in Atlantic, watching those advance men work, I found myself transported back to my first stops in politics twenty years prior.

Siger and Eby could have staged the event in a lovely, modern air-conditioned hall at the fairgrounds, but opted instead for a stockyard on the property with a dirt floor and a thin tin roof supported by wooden rafters. Good move, I thought, to go for a picture with character rather than comfort. The mostly all-white audience of several hundred sat attentively on wobbly metal chairs placed in-the-round encircling the candidate. Nothing says grassroots organizing quite like a crowd on a dirt floor normally home to cattle. Filmmaker Amy Rice seemed to relish the scene, too, as she shot footage for what would become HBO's documentary *By the People: The Election of Barack Obama.*

The election of Barack Obama was still fifteen months away, but when it came, on November 4, 2008, it was staged in high style in Chicago's Grant Park for a crowd of 250,000 people. The dirt floors of Atlantic gave way to rented Jumbotron TV screens erected in the heart of the Windy City. Watching the event live, my thoughts went back to a similar moment so many years prior, when I found myself in the mosh pit of a smaller but equally ebullient crowd—our first victory night with President-elect Clinton in Little Rock in 1992.

Obama's victory night bash in Grant Park bore signatures of pristine advance work, and harsh reality. The Obamas enjoyed a long walk-out on a brightly lit blue carpet against a wide crescent of twenty-seven billowing American flags stretching from edge to edge of a colossal stage, behind which six beams of light stretched infinitely skyward. It was a regal setting worthy of the oratory to come. "Tonight, because of what we did on this day, in this election, at this defining moment, change has come to America," President-elect Obama told the masses.[3] Guarding against the chance a would-be assassin lurked among them, those on either side of the stage had their views obscured by six-inch-thick bulletproof glass, a big-event prophylactic that modern presidents now take with the job.

When the speech ended, the site guy cued the music. It wasn't an easily recognizable song—a hit from the Springsteen, U2 or Motown catalogues—but rather the theme from a semi-successful Denzel Washington movie, *Remember the Titans.* The selection had symbolism. *Titans* was based on the true story of African American football coach Herman Boone, who healed his racially divided football team at T. C. Williams

High School in Alexandria, Virginia, and led them to victory. In Grant Park, amid that human mix of words, images and music, the brand of hope scored a huge win under the lights.

PORT OF SPAIN

There was much about Barack Obama—candidate, president-elect and president—that seemed impressive, augmented by a collection of 291 photographs that White House photographer Pete Souza put online at the end of Obama's first 100 days in office. The series began with a shot of Barack and Michelle, accompanied by staff, on a freight elevator at an Inaugural Ball on January 20, 2009. It ended with a picture of Obama and Vice President Joe Biden taken on April 24, their backs to the camera, in classic framing as the pair strolled in shirtsleeves up the flagstone walkway toward the Oval Office.[4]

It was the kind of archive that is usually revealed only in coffee-table books years after a president leaves office. Never before were the American people given access to such an intimate, instantaneous—but curated—view of the presidency. By posting his pictures so quickly and in such quantity, Souza was democratizing government property in a way never done before. The images nourished those craving behind-the-scenes vignettes of presidential life, but for those who earn their keep by training their lens on Obama, it was a direct threat, and the beginning of a controversy about press access and propaganda that would simmer for years, eventually boiling over into a Washington media spectacle.

I'm a bystander in one of Pete's 291 shots, taken in Port of Spain, Trinidad, on April 17. Swept up in the fervor around the new president, I volunteered to lead his advance team at the fifth Summit of the Americas. The trip marked a return engagement for me to the gathering of hemispheric leaders that I first attended in Miami in 1994 as part of the Clinton staff. I had lived in the Caribbean for a few years between the 1988 and 1992 campaigns, so the trip would also be a homecoming of sorts.

In Trinidad, two decades after my first visit there, I could be seen in Pete Souza's picture looking on as Obama greeted Costa Rican president Oscar Arias in a private reception. A few minutes later, the picture of the summit would be snapped by an official Venezuelan photographer, who captured Obama extending his hand to Hugo Chavez, America's longtime nemesis. The provocative photo quickly went viral around the world.

A storm of criticism formed in the United States and ricocheted back to Trinidad the next morning following front-page treatment of the image. Embracing an enemy, or just clasping his hand, was something presidents did at their peril. It was a risk Bill Clinton took when his motorcade pulled over on a Belfast street to greet Gerry Adams during a 1996 trip to Northern Ireland. That handshake was met by cheers in many quarters, but this one had few fans. "Everywhere in Latin America," said former House Speaker Newt Gingrich, "enemies of America are going to use the picture of Chavez smiling and meeting with the president as proof that Chavez is now legitimate, that he's acceptable."[5]

When I told the president that morning of the uproar over his shot, he was nonplussed. "I knew that would get some attention," he quipped, coolly. It would only get worse. Chavez could be counted on to try to steal the spotlight.

Chavez disrupted the 2005 Summit of the Americas, in Mar del Plata, Argentina, when he appeared at a rally of 15,000 people alongside soccer hero Diego Maradona to denounce the U.S. president. Maradona told the crowd he was there "to repudiate the presence of this human trash, George Bush."[6] Chavez looked on, smiling. In Port of Spain, we girded ourselves for similar antics.

The disruption came early. Chavez stood up and hijacked a "pool spray" on the first morning of the summit to present Obama with a copy of Eduardo Galeano's 1971 book, *Open Veins of Latin America,* which chronicles exploitation of the continent by foreign interests. When photographers put shots on the wire of Chavez giving Obama the book, it jumped from number 54,295 to sixth place on Amazon within twenty-four hours.[7]

This trip, which would mark my return as an advance "dinosaur" among the young Obamacans, was turning into a disaster. I needed to turn it into a field of dreams.

FIELD OF DREAMS

The idea hit me days earlier while going through the normal motions of leading an advance team. I had hoped it would be like the old days, when the lead advance could scour the city for people or places to give the president a fun backdrop and a mental diversion from the rote mechanics of a thirty-three-nation summit.

Hemmed in by the function-room formalities and White House micromanaging, it became clear that this administration would steer clear of spontaneity. My week in Port of Spain wasn't 1988, 1992 or 1996, or the years before, when advance people—connected to their "desk" by only a pay phone or a fax machine—were left largely alone to architect the days in country when "the principal" was under their creative direction.

My role in Trinidad was to show up at walk-throughs and report my findings (or lack thereof) back to the White House in perfunctory conference calls with those gathered around a speakerphone in the Situation Room. As we detailed the routine plans, my team and I sat inside a makeshift tent erected in a sleeping room at the Marriott hotel while technicians from the White House Communications Agency blanketed the room with artificial "white noise." The tent was meant to thwart peeping spies, the white noise a deterrent to eavesdroppers—though I wondered as I ticked off the events on the timetable if any of the information I was conveying was worthy of espionage. The risks were real, I knew, but the itinerary was deathly dull.

The summit needed something to make it memorable for Obama and viewers back home. After all, this was Trinidad, "island of the spices," as Jimmy Buffett sings in "Son of a Son of a Sailor," and I tapped my memory of past trips to the region and the options on the ground in Port of Spain to think of things that might spice up the visit. The last time I had visited the Caribbean on White House duty, in April 1995, Buffett himself joined us on Air Force One on a trip to Haiti for the inauguration of President Jean Bertrand Aristide. As I thought about how to inject some similar sense of excitement in Trinidad, I channeled Buffett's passion for adventure but found myself creatively bereft, even in this island paradise. As I studied my notes at the Marriott, I was feeling old, like the character from "A Pirate Looks at Forty," another of Buffett's songs.

Surely there must be some interesting diversion within a short drive of the Marriott for our hope-fueled president to do with his few minutes of downtime. What could we think of that would be emblematic of the island, offer a welcome photo back home and, perhaps, around the world? I started to ask some questions of our embassy staff in search of more local flavor.

I learned that Port of Spain is the home of Brian Lara, a much beloved hero of cricket, one of the world's most popular sports. Cricket is followed fanatically across the West Indies; among our Anglo-Saxon kin, like Britain and Australia; and in places where America has less kinship, like India and Pakistan. Lara, hailed as the best batsman of his era, still holds the record for the highest individual score in first-class cricket, with a "501 not out" for Warwickshire against Durham in 1994. As I queried the locals further and did some quick research, it was clear that Lara was still hailed everywhere, whether by friend or foe of the United States, for his prowess at a batsman on the pitch.

I asked a consular officer at our embassy how to reach Brian, got his phone number (everyone seems to know everyone in Trinidad) and lobbed a call. Within hours, an embassy car ferried me up winding roads in the hills above the Trinidadian capital, dropping me off at the Lara compound. Soon I was sitting face-to-face with Brian in his open-air trophy room filled with memorabilia of his playing days. I was in the presence of the Ted Williams of the West Indies, and Lara couldn't have been more welcoming or humble.

Earlier that afternoon, I reconnoitered the Queens Park Oval, the largest cricket grounds in the Caribbean, located in the center of Port of Spain. The only inhabitants at the empty stadium were the regulars at the bar of the Queens Park Cricket Club who were passing the day over beer and dominos. The locals surely knew that the summit was in town—two cruise ships were docked to provide sleeping rooms to the incoming flood of diplomats, security and others—but to the barflies at the Cricket Club the summit circus was a world away.

I don't know if they thought I was a tourist or with the CIA, but I tried to blend in by buying a Carib, the local brew, and learned the Oval had no upcoming matches. Slipping out of the club via its field entrance, I walked out into the deserted stands. It could have been any iconic baseball stadium in its offseason idyll, but this was a heralded palace of cricket. My imagination brought me back to Phil Alden Robinson's 1989 classic, *Field of Dreams*.

With the film in mind, I started to hatch a plan: *What if, on one of the evenings President Obama was here in Port of Spain, we do an OTR* (or "off the record" movement) *to Queens Park Oval after the official proceedings were done for the day?*

ON WITH THE OTR

The nature of OTRs is that only a handful of staff and Secret Service knows about them until they happen, this spontaneity helping ensure their security. Richard Nixon made a weirdly famous OTR in the early hours of May 9, 1970, venturing from the White House to visit Vietnam protestors at the Lincoln Memorial. Ronald Reagan made a splash in 1983 by dropping in at the Eire Pub in Boston to raise a pint with patrons. George H. W. Bush upped the OTR ante with a secret 1990 trip to visit U.S. troops in Saudi Arabia on the eve of Desert Storm, in which he was pictured flatteringly in a light blue expedition shirt amid a sea of American soldiers wearing desert camouflage. Bill Clinton perfected the practice of the OTR, conducting one in most cities he visited, leaving a store or an ice cream parlor with a gift for Chelsea or a cone for himself and a dozen good photos for the pool to transmit back to their bureaus. If OTRs worked for Nixon, Reagan, Bush and Clinton, surely a quickie with Brian Lara would be okay, I thought.

Executed well, OTRs can be done in fifteen minutes. The president hops out of the limo and the pool snaps a few photos—you're in and out before anyone gets wind. Executed badly, OTRs can incite an unruly mob. In 1994, we thought it would be an easy OTR for President Clinton to buy a slice of pizza from an open-air shop in the narrow streets of Naples, Italy, during the G-7 Summit. He was instantly surrounded by a crush of Neapolitan fans, raising tensions among the president's Secret Service detail for the rest of the trip.

Queens Park Oval was designed perfectly to welcome a brief stop. It would be dark when we arrived, and there was a large, empty parking lot for our motorcade. We'd turn on the stadium lights at the last minute, the press advance person quickly escorting the pool from their van to a front-row seating area. This would afford an unobstructed view for the lenses of whatever might transpire on the field, but a comfortable distance away to deter the pool's questions. I would place a last-minute call to my new BFF Brian Lara and have him arrive at the field, two bats in hand, a few minutes before the motorcade pulled up.

Once on site, the president would greet the international cricket hero. They would walk, just the two of them, to the center of the Oval, with Joe Clancy, the special agent in charge of the Presidential Protection Division of the United States Secret Service, following behind—just out of the camera's shot, to keep Obama safe.

The frame I was imagining was Kevin Costner as Ray Kinsella and Ray Liotta as Shoeless Joe Jackson in *Field of Dreams*. There they would stand, Obama and Lara, bats in hand, visually alone (but not really), a world leader of hope and world leader of sport, heroes united by the dreams they evoked. An impromptu lesson in batsmanship would follow, the men sharing a bond to which millions could relate. It could be front-page material on an otherwise quiet day in diplomacy. *If you build it, he will come,* I thought.

Like the old days, I went back to my hotel room to draw the cinematic scenario on graph paper. The juices were flowing. I shared the idea with my "scheduling desk," my overseer at the White House, who was probably twenty years my junior. Clearly not a member of the *Field of Dreams* generation, he couldn't quite envision the scene. Based on how my paint-by-numbers advance assignment was going so far, I wasn't surprised.

I worked the chain a bit, calling Emmett Beliveau, the director of White House advance, who was responsible for sending me to Port of Spain. He seemed to have a soft spot for "dinosaur" advance people like me with histories of pushing the envelope, but soon realized that his spot was not too soft. Emmett, one of the cadre of campaign staffers who were with Obama from the very start in Springfield, Illinois, in 2007, did little but discourage the idea.

What the hell, I thought. It had been a dozen years since I worked in the White House. Times had changed and the faces were different, but what did I have to lose?

I sent an email outlining the idea, and the underlying message, to Denis McDonough, then the deputy national security advisor for communications and now White House chief of staff. Denis didn't write back, but I did hear from Emmett, unamused. An advance man for Obama's White House, he made clear, and a volunteer one at that, does not lobby up the chain of command of the National Security Council.

I stood down, until the president arrived, and then resumed marketing the pitch. I talked to McDonough, Press Secretary Robert Gibbs, Personal Aide Reggie Love and finally Trip Director Marvin Nicholson, a veteran of John Kerry's 2004 campaign, where he served as Kerry's body man. While the others didn't know what to make of this dinosaur peddling visuals, Nicholson at least seemed to get what I was talking about.

I once had a long leash at the White House to construct visual imagery. It was common practice among advance people for President Clinton: divine an idea, work the angles among the traveling party and execute it, usually with good results. But this was not that freewheeling White House team. Creativity and visual risk-taking were not in their DNA for all the reasons President Obama would outline to the Navy Midshipmen years later as "Politics 101." They knew how history could repeat itself.

On the day of Obama's wheels-up from Trinidad, he held a news conference with his traveling press corps on the roof deck at the Marriott.

The sun was scorching, a replay of the scene I set for President Clinton's news conference in France after the 1996 G-7 Summit, minus the gnats. The president was questioned about fallout over his handshake with Hugo Chavez, the reporter expecting, maybe, that he would get a rise out of Obama. "It's unlikely," the president said, refusing to take the bait, "that as a consequence of me shaking hands or having a polite conversation with Mr. Chavez that we are endangering the strategic interests of the United States."[8] However chagrined I was that the *Field of Dreams* photo op was quashed, I admired the president's cool under the hot sun and pointed questions.

All was not lost, however, with Brian Lara. Marvin Nicholson and I engineered a behind-the-scenes "meet and greet" for Obama and Lara at the Marriott right after the news conference and before the motorcade left for the airport. Both men were dressed in nearly identical blue business suits—not quite the Costner-Liotta cinematic frame in baseball woolens that I imagined, but close enough. As I watched Obama and Lara bond, my zeal for movie-quality storytelling softened enough to welcome this matinee version of the famed two-shot.

Lara brought a cricket bat as a gift for the president, as I hinted he might, which the president accepted gratefully. Then they did before our eyes, quite naturally, what I hoped they might do in the middle of a deserted Queens Park Oval: the president received an impromptu lesson in batsmanship. The picture, of two fit middle-aged men in almost matching angles of athletic pose, conveyed the story I wanted to tell from the outset.

The composition was a workable facsimile of what might have happened under the lights, even if the backdrop was a hallway of the Marriott. I knew the picture's news value would suffer because none of our pool photographers were there to make the image, but I hoped, as a fallback, that it could be released into the cricket-loving world. Pete Souza snapped some good frames and put one on his Flickr feed when he returned to Washington. The photo appeared on the front page of Trinidadian newspapers and in global cricket websites alongside laudatory commentary, plus a few lighthearted critiques of Obama's form at bat.

Looking back on that episode in Port of Spain, now many years later, it was way premature to push the Obama staff for a Reagan-Clinton style photo. Ray Kinsella's cornfield in Dubuque would have to wait. There would be no *Field of Dreams* in Port of Spain.

In 2009, less than a hundred days into his first term, President Obama and his disciplined team wouldn't risk a potential "Dukakis in the tank" visual for an unpredictable OTR photo, no matter how evocative it might be. It tracked with how, for most speeches, Obama relied on a teleprompter. On television, where production mattered most, he appeared to speak in fully formed paragraphs without the benefit of notes. In reality, almost every word was scripted. This summit had gone off script when Obama shook Chavez's hand, and the resulting storm of controversy almost blew up the Internet.

I had tried to double down. After the Chavez snafu, I was rolling the dice for a front-page photo in the *New York Times* rather than a milquetoast podium shot from a function room at the summit that would run somewhere in the A section. The safer route with Brian Lara, rather than flicking on the lights at an open-air cricket stadium and letting the pool fire away, was for the government to own the shot. Pete Souza would take the picture, rather than the press, and the communications office would decide later whether the image should see the light of day.

I came to Port of Spain to rekindle my past but found a White House risk-averse to nostalgia. Who could really blame them? It was no more than half a year removed from the historic moment in Grant Park, when the first African American won the Oval Office. In the early days, Obama's image needed to be carefully controlled. But from my vantage point as an advance man, it was starting to look like a vanilla presidency.

 **SIXTEEN**

CONTROLLING IMAGE

BARE WALLS

One of Pete Souza's 291 pictures from his "First 100 Days" album is remarkable for its unremarkableness. It shows Barack Obama alone on February 3, 2009, two weeks into his administration, on a phone call in his private study off the Oval Office. At that early point in the new term the private study was unadorned, like that of a college student who has just moved into his dorm at the beginning of the fall semester.

Souza's photo is taken from the photographer's discreet vantage point in the narrow hallway adjoining the Oval Office and the study.[1] In a busy West Wing, this is a spot where very few people ever step foot except the president and his intimates. This particularly plain image in Souza's album is shorn of meaning, except if we're reminded through some reporting or a "read out" from aides that Obama's phone call is in some way historic, as when President Kennedy speed-dialed Mississippi governor Ross Barnett from the Oval Office in September 1962, appealing to him to allow James Meredith to enroll at Ole Miss. The archived photos of Kennedy during that crisis all carry companion captions detailing the gravity of those conversations.

Pete's caption of his February 3 photo—coded "P020309PS-0250," meaning it was his 250th snap of the day—doesn't reveal who was on the other end of the line. What is does betray are naked walls, the color of French vanilla ice cream, in the president's suite. When I would fetch President Clinton in that same study for an Oval Office photo op, the walls in that room, in the hallway leading to it, and in the famous office beyond, were garnished with photos, busts of historic figures, military challenge coins, Arkansas kitsch, travel memorabilia and other relics covering almost every square inch from floor to ceiling. Walking through it was like touring a museum of every year of Clinton's life in public service. There was no such color, yet, to define this president.

Still, any independent photographer would have killed for Pete's access, bare walls or not. In those exhilarating early days, that kind of fly-on-the-wall angle on presidential life was can't-miss, front-page material. And a photojournalist would also have salivated over the intimate proximity Pete enjoyed for any of the 290 other frames in the collection.

Pete was a news photographer—a shooter—in a prior life, having covered Clinton and Bush for the *Chicago Tribune.* He was also a young staff photographer in the Reagan White House. His 1984 shot of Ronald and Nancy Reagan in the Diplomatic Reception Room welcoming Michael Jackson to their home, fully regaled in his trademark single glove and sequined coat with epaulets, was rivaled in the annals of White House strangeness only by Ollie Atkins's shot of Richard Nixon's December 1970 greeting of Elvis Presley. The moment came about after Elvis had written Nixon a six-page letter asking for an appointment as a "Federal Agent-at-Large" in the Bureau of Narcotics and Dangerous Drugs. Weirder still, Elvis presented Nixon with a Colt .45 pistol at the meeting.[2] Of all the requests each year to the National Archives for reproductions of photographs and documents, the Nixon-Presley picture remains the most sought-after.[3]

Now, a quarter century after his Michael Jackson shot, Souza was in charge of the White House Photo Office and approached his duties with solemnity and discretion. There would be thousands of pictures of Obama with singers and celebrities to come, but in those first few weeks in the Oval Office, judging by the shots, it was all business. Souza knew his Canon 5D Mark II was a conduit for history. His sole subject was a hot commodity, and the White House was slowly discovering its unique power as an image spigot in a new age of photo sharing.

More and more, news consumers were sourcing information "sideways" rather than through the front page, finding articles or TV segments via Facebook and Twitter intermingled among galleries of cuddly cats in the social networks. Carefully controlled, the pictures posted in spreads on the White House Flickr stream—of Oval Office and Cabinet Room meetings, of East Room dinners and South Lawn hoop games, of family outings and Air Force One globetrotting—could mutate the Executive Branch into a news agency unto itself.

"The moments that I relish in this presidency," Pete told me, "is being the one person that is in the room, whether that be the Oval Office, the Situation Room, or a gymnasium in Chevy Chase, Maryland, that is able to capture some of these private moments."[4] From Obama's First 100 Days to today, Pete would capture those moments elegantly. But in the process, he would also stir resentment among his former colleagues in the press corps, foment controversy between their bosses and the White House press secretary and disrupt a part of the media business model that has always relied on presidential imagery to fill pages of newsprint.

THE BEER SUMMIT

The discipline of sticking to script that Obama's White House brought to Trinidad was in full flower two months after my trip there, manifest at a prime-time East Room news conference on July 22, 2009. Souza was there, but so too was a hoard of credentialed White House shooters covering the action. The choreography was formulaic: a two-minute warning to cue the networks, a walk down the majestic red carpet of the Cross Hall, and fifty minutes or so of dialogue, with the president grimacing, smiling or otherwise gesturing from behind his "Blue Goose" lectern. Only inventive shooters, like Doug Mills of the *New York Times,* might make more of it, firing a remote-controlled camera from a lighting truss in the Cross Hall to make a unique "walking shot" with a wide-angle lens that *Times* photo editors found irresistible.

Interrupting prime-time network programming on a Wednesday night, the president was using his bully pulpit to outline, in broad strokes, his plans for health-insurance reform. The news conference, in which he was framed by matching gilded lamps at the distant end of the Cross Hall and the sealed wooden doors of the State Dining Room, consumed nearly the full eight-to-nine p.m. slot, leaving a few minutes for anchor-to-correspondent chatter at the beginning and end. It was, by any measure, a premium chunk of broadcast airtime.

Using a head-on teleprompter, which afforded the president the luxury of looking directly into American living rooms without consulting notes, he opened with a lengthy monologue about "the progress we're making on health-insurance reform and where it fits into our broader economic strategy."[5] It was a speech in itself lasting eight minutes, the valuable equivalent of sixteen 30-second spots to advocate for his agenda on every channel that carried it. The show was proceeding on script through the first thirteen of fourteen questions. He then called on Lynn Sweet of the *Chicago Sun-Times* for the final question.

Sweet read from her notes, querying Obama on an incident unrelated to health care. Six days earlier, Harvard professor Henry Louis Gates Jr. had been arrested on the steps of his home by a Cambridge, Massachusetts, police officer, Sergeant James Crowley, who arrived at the house responding to a 9-1-1 call. Obama told Sweet he didn't have all the facts. But, he added, "the Cambridge police acted stupidly in arresting somebody when there was already proof that they were in their own home."[6] The evening's health-care script was ad-libbed in real time. In its final minutes, the answer to the last question unleashed a media feeding frenzy over race and police procedure that lasted for days.

The charged issue would become a lightning rod during Obama's second term. The Trayvon Martin case in 2012, the unrest in Ferguson in 2014, and the Freddie Gray case in 2015—among many others—would command attention at many of the president's news conferences. But the Cambridge incident was the genesis, and Obama's awkward first steps in navigating these gray areas thrust him into the spotlight as a principal actor in the drama.

As the Gates case boiled over into the next day, a narrative emerged that the president regretted how his words, in the early months of his administration, inflamed the debate. The debate was important—it had to happen—but it was too soon when weighed against the priorities of his Year One agenda. On Friday, he made a surprise stop in the White House press briefing room to share news that he had telephoned the Cambridge police officer himself, telling reporters that "I could've calibrated those words differently. And I told this to Sergeant Crowley."[7]

The president's posture earned laurels even from Maureen Dowd, a daughter of a police detective, who wrote, "President Obama was right the first time, that the encounter had a stupid ending, and the second time, that both Gates and Crowley overreacted. His soothing assessment that two good people got snared in a bad moment seems on target."[8] To make amends, he employed his bully pulpit in a different way, summoning the professor and the sergeant to what would become known as "The Beer Summit."

Defusing rancor with a beer instead of a brawl is an American ideal, though in matters of race it's rare. To my eye, the Rose Garden shots a week later of two African American men and two white men (Joe Biden made it a foursome) was the first iconic image of Obama's presidency.

Seated at a patio table under a magnolia tree, with silver saucers of nuts between them, each man quaffed from pints of a different brand of brew, but the four men assembled for a common purpose. In a series of frames, a tense situation was smoothed over by imagery to create, as Obama had hoped, "a teachable moment."

No apologies were offered, but both protagonists issued salving post-summit comments. "I think what you had today was two gentlemen agreeing to disagree on a particular issue," Sergeant Crowley said. "I don't think that we spent too much time dwelling on the past. We spent a lot of time discussing the future."[9] For his part, Professor Gates said, "Sergeant Crowley and I, through an accident of time and place, have been cast together, inextricably, as characters—as metaphors, really—in a thousand narratives about race over which he and I have absolutely no control."[10] In forty seconds of stagecraft—the span allotted to the press pool to witness the summit—a forceful message was sent.

In the canon of White House media coverage, it was a teachable moment as well. The Rose Garden is 125 feet long and 60 feet wide, and the Beer Summit was staged on its eastern end. The setup gave space for the official photographer, Souza, to work in harmony with the shooters from the press corps. The pool could "spray" the scene from a distance of fifty feet, a workable "throw" for cameramen to document it for their media outlets, but the span protected the tableau of "three folks having a drink at the end of the day" (as Obama called it)[11] from morphing into a dialogue with reporters thirsting to insert themselves into the story. The story was well told in one frame, it gave everyone a decent shot for the front page, and it left Pete alone to document the rest of the meeting for history.

SITUATION IN THE SITUATION ROOM

Another story that was told well in one frame, but this time only through Souza's lens, unfolded in the White House Situation Room on Sunday, May 1, 2011, perhaps the most viewed image of President Obama's two terms in office. Given the classified status of Operation Neptune Spear, and the cramped confines in which a photographer could work, it was up to Pete alone to capture it, one shot among what Souza estimates were 1,000 pictures that he took that day.

The photo, which served as a freeze frame for endless hours of TV commentary, shows thirteen men and women, collectively the pinnacle of U.S. government, watching night-vision video from a drone over

Pakistan. The public would never see what they witnessed, but it wasn't necessary to show when you could interpret the anguish on every face. "You're looking for the right facial expressions on everybody that makes it work as a cohesive picture," Souza told me later. "You're not blasting away with a motor drive. You're waiting for this moment or that moment, and I think everything came together in that one picture where everybody's facial expression looked appropriate for what was going on in front of them," he added.[12]

Three conference rooms comprise the Sit Room, a warren of offices underneath the West Wing that I knew well from planning foreign trips for Clinton. The smallest of the rooms, which had a hookup to mission commanders at Bagram Air Base in Afghanistan, was the backdrop for the unfolding action. In Souza's shot, the president is hunched in a corner and his vice president sits next to him. His secretary of state sits across the conference table, her hand pressed to her mouth as she eavesdrops on Osama bin Laden's final hour. The other ten principals in the shot, each a political or foreign policy heavyweight in his or her own right, are extras surrounding these three former rivals, now bonded by a life-or-death mission unfolding 7,000 miles away in Abbottabad.

At that moment, things were not going well, but Souza kept working his angles, maintaining a small footprint while he discreetly fired away. As President Obama remembered, the picture "was taken right as the helicopter was having some problems," noting "there's silence at this point inside the room." One of the SEAL team's modified Black Hawk helicopters, operating "hot and high" as it hovered over bin Laden's compound, impacted one of the compound's walls with its tail rotor on descent and managed a controlled crash landing. Secretary Clinton, making light of her apparent dismay in the photo, said later, "That's the way I usually look when my husband drags me to an action movie."[13]

"At the end of that day," Souza told me, "I had a series of images, and it wasn't until the next day that the White House decided, 'Let's release some of these photos,' so I actually did the editing myself, just because of the importance of this." One "problem," as Souza termed it, was that a document in front of Clinton contained classified data. Souza's first instinct was to "scrap the photo" if it couldn't be released as is. But he felt the shot was "really telling of what had taken place" as bin Laden met his doom. He tried to get the document declassified to allow his photo to be made public. When that failed, he opted instead to "pixelate" the image, doctoring it to keep the secret paper undecipherable.

"We had never done that before," Souza remembered, and he knew this step would be met suspiciously by news organizations traditionally harboring an aversion to any kind of censorship.[14]

It had become common for the media to use White House imagery for its own purposes, an unwelcome development for photojournalists. In a cover story for *New York* magazine called "The Obama History Project," one of Souza's original 291 photos from the First 100 Days, a powerful shot of the president, seen from behind as he gazes upward at Aaron Shikler's portrait of John F. Kennedy in the Cross Hall, bleeds across a full page.[15] It is perfect art for a glossy magazine, and only someone with intimate access could have snapped such a solemn moment as the forty-fourth president seemed to seek inspiration from the oil-on-canvas image of the thirty-fifth. In another example from 2009, Souza released an endearing photo of five-year old Jacob Philadelphia touching the president's hair, the intergenerational duet becoming a story in itself in the *New York Times*.[16]

But the Sit Room shot was different. Not only was the White House sharing a shot that no independent lens could get, it was deliberately altering it before making it public.

There was no way around it. Time was wasting, the world wondered what went down in the Sit Room and the frame showed the president's team in a historic prelude to glory. Either the photo would get fixed, or it would be scrapped. When the pixelation was done, Souza wrote the photo caption himself "because I wanted people to know up front: we blurred this document." He would leave it to editorial judgment whether or not to run the image. "The fact that the *New York Times* used it as a six-column photo made me feel good in that I think they realized it was an important photograph," he told me.[17]

OPPOSITE EXTREMES

The Beer Summit and Sit Room photos, taken a few hundred feet and two years apart, were at opposite ends of White House stagecraft, but they framed a debate that would simmer continuously between Obama's White House and the press corps covering it. The issue was access, and whether the White House was controlling it to an extreme that would disseminate images that flattered the president, while limiting his exposure to other members of the pool, intrusive reporters, who didn't shoot pictures for a living.

The Beer Summit didn't test the limits of access because the Rose Garden offered space for official and independent photographers to work side by side. The other poolers could be there, at a comfy distance, their questions handily ignored. Easing tension further, the Beer Summit was held outdoors, on a temperate July afternoon, removing the nuisance of reverberating walls that amplified the volume of reporters' questions or made their extraction more difficult when the time came to shut down the photo op.

Similarly, the Sit Room situation didn't raise hackles because the press corps had no advance word that a nail-biter was unfolding beneath the West Wing. There was no morning "press gaggle" in which Robert Gibbs briefed reporters that "the president will watch the killing of Osama bin Laden live." Had that happened, it's fair to assume that the gaggle would have demanded a "pool spray," or brief photo op, to lob questions at the top of the raid.

When news did break, late on Sunday night on May 1, 2011, no reasonable editor could argue that a pool of photographers should have been present as officials watched in tight confines while SEALs risked their lives to hunt America's archenemy. Pete Souza worked quickly to edit his picture the next day and, when it hit the wires, it was received as a welcome gift for layout editors rather than a piece of government-supplied propaganda.

Between the extremes, there was a wide berth. The advance of technology, and new means of distribution, gave a big advantage to the White House in the Age of Optics.

During the 2008 campaign, the Obama Flickr feed unleashed thousands of images that were not shot by independent photojournalists. They weren't the best shots but, then again, neither were viewers subjected to the distilled taste of photo editors. On any given day, those who laid out newspapers could select an unflattering shot of the candidate from among scores flowing into newsrooms from competing photo agencies and wire services. Instead, the public had plentiful choices online, and those desiring to click through assorted depictions of the Brand of Hope were free to do so, as long as they had an Internet connection.

Once President Obama took office, Souza's initial series of 291 photos from the First 100 Days was a watershed. Thousands more followed, shot artfully by Souza and his staff. Pictures were posted at a pace of roughly 100 to 200 per month, with more curated into online albums commemorating specific events. There was an album of seventy-two shots for a trip to Russia, Italy and Ghana in 2009. A set of ninety-one pictures focused on health-care reform in 2010. In 2011, there was a series of twenty images covering debt negotiations. There are almost 100 albums on the White House Flickr feed, comprising over 6,000 separate images spanning the president's first day in office to the present.[18]

As taxpayers, the public owns the work and can peruse it at their leisure. Each shot also comes with details of the camera type, f-stop, shutter speed and other data craved by photo junkies. Beyond the White House website and Flickr page, Souza set up a Twitter feed, amassing over 190,000 followers by the end of 2015, all of them with access to an intimate window on the president's day without having to buy a newspaper.

Photo editors are taxpayers too, and they scavenged Souza's pictures for their publications when none of their shooters got access. In the election year of 2012, the photo office posted eleven pictures from the G8 Summit at Camp David. One widely used frame showed Obama with British prime minister David Cameron in Laurel Cabin, watching with other world leaders as Chelsea and Bayern Munich dueled in an overtime shootout in the Champions League final. As the disclaimer reads beneath that and every other picture, "This official White House photograph is being made available only for publication by news organizations and/or for personal use printing by the subject(s) of the photograph."[19] Bloomberg, the *Daily Mail*, the BBC, *Hello* magazine and scores of others ran the chummy picture, all crediting Souza, none of them claiming it was propaganda.

Another power user of these power pictures was Davis Guggenheim, the Oscar-winning filmmaker of *An Inconvenient Truth*. After making Al Gore a movie star in 2006, he took his talents to Barack Obama in 2008, producing a campaign infomercial, "American Stories, American Solutions," that filled three of four broadcast networks with thirty minutes of paid hagiography. He returned to the subject in March 2012 when the race against Mitt Romney was taking shape. *The Road We've Traveled*, Guggenheim's seventeen-minute film for the reelection, brought to politics a palette of documentary techniques he used in *Waiting for Superman*. In the film, Guggenheim painted "a picture of a fearless leader tackling seemingly impossible problems," wrote Jordan Zakarian in the *Hollywood Reporter*.[20] To extoll Obama's first-term exploits, Guggenheim enlisted stylized infographics, Hollywood-style scoring, archival news footage, narration by Tom Hanks, testimonials by Bill Clinton and, by my count, sixty-nine behind-the-scenes tension-filled still images, at a rate of four per minute, many of which came from the camera of Pete Souza.

Before Obama took office, most pictures from official photographers were sent to the National Archives, where few were ever seen again. Scholars might file requests for single shots, or a coffee table book might debut years in the future, but it took the Obama White House to figure out how to exploit technology and distribution, using photography as a weapon of communications, to burnish the president's image. "We know photos have tremendous currency online," White House senior advisor Dan Pfeiffer told me in his West Wing office in 2014. "People share them. What we've done with photos, with Pete Souza, on Instagram and Twitter, has been tremendously powerful for this presidency."[21]

Souza discusses the topic warily. When credited with popularizing the president through Flickr and Twitter, he is quick to disown the innovation. "I can't take credit for that," he told me. "That was the administration coming to me, saying, 'This is what we want to do.' If you go back and look, for the first three months of the administration, there were no pictures, hardly at all, on the Flickr photo stream." After the First 100 Days album, Souza said, "The administration said, 'We want to do this all the time.'"[22]

Posting pictures quickly and publicly, beauty shots of the type that lined the walls of the West Wing when I worked for President Clinton—we called them "jumbos"—was a new practice. "I was ambivalent about it," Souza told me. "I grew up in the Reagan administration, where these were pictures you would see twenty years from now, not today. The Obama administration had a different view. They wanted people to see these pictures today." Once they got started, Souza said, his office put their "heart and soul" into choosing the photos, "toning them right" and becoming "somewhat regular about it," posting them in monthly batches. "It's a great way for people to see inside this administration," Souza said, "to see the things that I get to see."[23]

"JUST LIKE TASS"

For members of the press and young staffers in the press office, days in the White House could be like days in a firehouse, with hours of inactivity punctuated by minutes of chaos. In the Clinton years, the routine West Wing schedule would include hourlong meetings with congressional leaders or visiting dignitaries led off by what we would term a "pool spray." The spray was an ungainly two-minute fire drill of swinging open the door to the Oval Office or Cabinet Room and herding reporters and photographers inside for a glimpse of the action. We let two lighting technicians lead the pack to plug in portable "scoops" to illuminate the room, followed by the cameramen, with writers and correspondents trailing the scrum. When all had entered, the president might offer a few welcoming remarks, followed by his guest. Then questions came lobbing in, sometimes on the topic at hand but often not.

The encounters were over as quickly as they began, with me and others interrupting further inquisition with a sequence of high-volume "thankyous" followed by shuffling and shepherding to flush and sanitize the room so the real meeting could begin. It was an awkward physical ballet, but the press corps got what they needed to do their work—and sustain their business model: a brief exchange documented on film and video that could drive the day's news stories, whatever those stories happened to be.

Images from these momentary sightings of the president did less to document his daily agenda than show his ability, or inability, to put his imprint on the current news cycle. The captions on photos from these sessions may have said "Clinton meets with so-and-so," but they really showed his temperament, patient or not, in granting reporters "access" outside the rhythm of speeches, interviews and news conferences. The resulting pictures were rarely flattering—the president possibly a victim of poor room lighting, a photographer's unfavorable positioning in the scrum, the testiness of the exchange or the whim of editors who chose which frames to print, or video to use, with body language advancing their angle for a story in progress.

A truer representation of the actual presidential meeting would be a fly-on-the wall photo of the closed-door session. Taken by a photojournalist, that would be treated as news. Taken by an official White House photographer, it could be classified as propaganda.

I tried during the Clinton years to fight for a "fly-on-the-wall" pool, one rotating independent photographer working with an official counterpart to witness genuine interaction between the president and his guests. With just two extra bodies in the room, they could shoot unobtrusively for a few minutes and leave. At other times, I escorted pool members behind the Oval Office to shoot the goings-on through the rear window. These maneuvers didn't make everyone happy—especially reporters, who couldn't lob questions—but it worked to validate the moments with an independent lens.

When the Obama White House released pictures of the president in closed-off sessions, working reporters could howl in protest, but the official shots continued to make their way into the public domain. They seeped out in social media, but also through traditional news organizations that paid the reporters' salaries. Work was drying up at the firehouse. The divisiveness reached a crescendo in the summer and fall of 2013. On November 21, noting seven stark examples of closed-press events that might have merited a pool spray, thirty-eight news organizations hand-delivered a letter to Press Secretary Jay Carney "to protest the limits on access currently barring photographers who cover the White House."[24]

"As surely as if they were placing a hand over a journalist's camera lens," the letter said, "officials in this administration are blocking the public from having an independent view of important functions of the Executive Branch of government." The letter aired gripes shared privately with Carney in a meeting with the board of the White House Correspondents' Association. At that meeting, Carney's provocateurs showed him a stack of Pete Souza's photos illustrating their complaint. *New York Times* photographer Doug Mills, a member of the WHCA board, compared the situation to Kremlin image control by the old Soviet state news agency. "Jay," he said, "this is just like Tass."[25]

In my opinion, there is no more creative and inventive photographer working in Washington today than Mills, a journalist who constantly finds unique angles to shoot official events and whose work invariably lands on the front page of the *Times*. Mills shot for the AP while I worked at the White House, competing against other greats such as Dirck Halstead and Diana Walker of *Time* and Wally McNamee and Larry Downing of *Newsweek*. Mills always went the extra mile to score the special image.

While covering Obama at the Lincoln Memorial for the fiftieth anniversary of the March on Washington on August 28, 2013, Mills found himself positioned for a signature shot. Crouching low, he captured the president bending down to greet Yolanda Renee King, MLK's only granddaughter, who was clutching a stuffed animal, while former presidents Clinton and Carter filled the background in soft focus. Pete Souza took to Twitter later to compliment Mills on his composition, but his backstage access was fleeting. "Unfortunately," Mills told me, "it has become more and more rare for us to get those nice moments."[26]

Mills had actually spied a better shot, on the steps of the memorial behind the lineup of presidents as they waved to the crowd massed around the Reflecting Pool. If he could get that historic moment, it could bookend the iconic image of MLK standing on that same spot a half century before. That was, Mills told me, "somewhere that Pete Souza, because he has the access that he does, was able to go." Mills asked to stand with Souza but was denied. "I wish we had been able to go up there," he sighed, surrendering in a "losing battle" he and his colleagues were fighting. "Obviously, with Twitter, Instagram and Facebook, and everything that the White House has at its disposal, a lot of those moments are seen by the White House photographer, and not by us," he told me.[27]

A quick visit to South Africa for Nelson Mandela's memorial service on December 10—requiring a long round trip on Air Force One on which former president George W. Bush and former secretary of state Hillary Clinton joined President Obama—promised memorable moments and a chance, perhaps, for the White House to ease its restrictions. Indeed, on the plane, there was an image that went viral, published by many of the news organizations that signed the November 21 letter to Jay Carney. It showed President Bush proudly displaying for Clinton and others his gallery of new paintings on his iPad as they sat in the aircraft's large conference room. The picture was shot by Souza, and no one else. Sitting in the back of the plane was Steve Crowley, Mills's colleague from the *Times,* who could have been invited up for a fly-on-the-wall moment, validating Souza's work. It never happened. Instead, Souza tweeted out his South Africa collection the next day, writing, "Pres Obama attends Mandela memorial service; includes photos from Air Force One."[28]

At his briefing for reporters one day later, Carney was barraged with questions about the trip's lack of access. What would happen if there was a security breach on stage? What about the marathon flight and the historic gathering of presidents? What about a just-published op-ed in the *New York Times* by the AP's director of photography, Santiago Lyon, headlined, "Obama's Orwellian Image Control"? Reporters piled on.[29]

Carney acknowledged that the access problem was "an issue" and promised to be "responsive" and to "listen to those concerns and act on them where we can." But he said firmly that releasing photos was a consistent practice from administration to administration, "and we're obviously going to continue to do that," pinning the difference between past and present on technology and distribution. "This is part of a bigger transformation," he told the press corps in the briefing room, "that's happening out there that's driven by the ability of everyone to post anything on the Internet free of charge, so that you don't have to buy that newspaper, or subscribe to that wire service, to see that photograph."[30]

The questions kept coming and Carney kept parrying. When April Ryan, the correspondent for American Urban Radio Networks, cross-examined him, photographers echoed her protests by revving the motor drives on their cameras. "Did you hear the clicks from these cameras when you started talking about this?" she said. "They were letting you know that they're here." Laughter filled the room. "I always know they're here," came Carney's reply.[31]

Like Souza, Carney was a former journalist, and between the lines his sympathies were readily apparent. Watching the briefing, mine were too. I collaborated with official White House photographers during the Clinton years, including chief photographer Bob McNeeley, even when he frustrated me by blocking a good angle for the photo pool. I wanted the pool photographers to get as many good shots as they could, knowing, selfishly, that the speed and breadth of their distribution dwarfed that of the White House, which was shooting for history rather than the next day's papers.

Now the tables had turned. The photographers weren't indispensable, especially when their presence came with the baggage of their pool brethren, reporters who would turn any intimate moment into an impromptu news conference on a range of unrelated matters. If you take one of us, you take all of us, went the unsaid condition. Still, taking the long view, something vital was lost when the government became a news agency.

Beyond serving as White House photo office chief, Bob McNeely was also a steward of its history. He knew he owed his job, ultimately, to Lyndon Johnson, who replaced military picture-takers with a civilian, Yoichi Okamoto, to polish LBJ's image for history. He also knew that widely accomplished predecessors who held his post, like David Hume Kennerley, who served under Gerald Ford, and David Valdez, who shot for George H. W. Bush, had also become like family to their bosses, far removed from the objectivity of photojournalism.

When I lobbied to have pool photographers accompany Bob as flies on the wall in tight confines with President Clinton, he knew their purpose. "We loved having them with us," McNeely told me, perhaps overstating his affection. "It validated the pictures we took." The letter from thirty-eight news organizations, the charges of hypocrisy in Santiago Lyon's op-ed, the hammering Carney took from the podium—the chorus could have been quieted by a fly on the wall. "This is affecting the historical record," McNeely lamented. "This historical record is being labeled now, 'the historical propaganda record.'"[32]

 **SEVENTEEN**

THE LAST MILE

BREAKING CONVENTION

The reality about most modern presidents is that they struggle to find the right recipe for being president until somewhere into their second term, if they make it that far. For all of the campaign boasting about "being ready on Day One," it's a pipe dream. Money and calories are often burned on a man and his staff learning on the job.

My last full year working at the White House, 1997, coincided with the beginning of President Clinton's second term. Four years of trial and error, and a big win against a weaker opponent, were behind us. There was smooth sailing ahead, or so we thought. I expected a colorful second term. I had no idea how colorful.

The year began for me in January with the rare privilege of riding in the president's Second Inaugural Parade in a glorified position, immediately in front of the president's black armored limousine as it made its way down Pennsylvania Avenue. The vehicle we rode in was a modified flatbed truck, tricked out with three tiers of steel platforms to accommodate multiple rows of photographers looking backward at the limo with their zoom lenses.

Jeremy Gaines, the deputy director of White House press advance, and I served as the official shepherds for the press pool, along with a Secret Service agent. Our job was to keep the pool sanitized from bystanders and ensure that the press had access to key moments along the route. To parade watchers on both sides of the avenue, our oversubscribed flatbed made our flock look like freezing plastic figurines atop a rolling wedding cake.

It was important for two reasons that our pool preceded the limo as it made its way along the one-and-a-half-mile route from the Capitol to its final destination, a heated, glass-enclosed reviewing stand constructed just outside the gates of the North Lawn of the White House.

First, following the same formula as my advance of Senator Bob Kerrey as he skied down Gunstock Mountain in 1992, the best pictures of the parade panorama would come from a position in front of the subject, with the Capitol Dome as the backdrop. When the president and first lady alighted from the limo in an OTR moment to walk a few blocks in the open air, as was tradition, the scene would unfold before us for can't-miss, front-page photos.

Sure enough, in its "Special Inauguration Edition," the *Washington Post* spread a parade shot taken from our flatbed five columns wide at the top of page 1. It showed a smiling Bill, Hillary and Chelsea, waving to onlookers as they walked toward the White House, their Secret Service detail trailing within arm's length and their armored vehicles crawling behind at a pedestrian pace. Immediately below the photo was a monumental headline of equal width reading, "Clinton Urges End to Division."[1] The wide-angle image and the oversized headline perfectly conveyed our intended message of the Second Inaugural.

But more important for the continuity of government, the second reason we were there was to ensure that an independent press had clear line of sight to the goings-on should tragedy strike. The photographers, and the print poolers traveling with us, were mindful that history might call on them to report the worst of news. When John F. Kennedy was struck by Lee Harvey Oswald's bullets while riding in an open-air limo through Dealey Plaza in 1963, the lack of any video—with the exception of the 26.6 seconds of footage from Abraham Zapruder's 8mm Bell & Howell Zoomatic, filmed at a distance of sixty-five feet—fomented conspiracy theories that continue to this day.

There were no bullets on January 20, 1997, just a few middle fingers pointed the president's way. Beyond the scattered upraised digits, the parade ended without incident, marking a successful, if frigid, start to my last year at the White House.

After visiting, by my count, forty-eight states and forty countries in service to Bill Clinton, I would leave my job as director of production at the end of that year, jumping at a chance to produce a pilot for a show called *West Wing* that my writing partner, Robert Wells, and I created for Lifetime Television. After shooting our pilot in Toronto with an A-list cast and director, the show died a quick death, failing to excite viewers screening it in testing sessions. "Washington shows never work," we were lectured by almost everyone to whom we pitched our idea in Hollywood. They were wrong. Our failure was one of execution. Validating our concept, Aaron Sorkin did a far superior job for NBC with the same subject matter, his show debuting a year after ours would have hit the air. Sorkin's drama enjoyed remarkable longevity that spanned 156 episodes beginning in the fall of 1999.

The seven-year run of *The West Wing*, which ended in 2006, was almost as long as a two-term presidency. I spent much of that period repeating my answer to people asking how closely Sorkin's West Wing matched our real thing. With Marlin Fitzwater, Dee Dee Myers and Gene Sperling as consultants on the show, I always said it was remarkably true to life, at least to life during the Clinton years. Sorkin's exquisite writing captured the gallows humor that levitated our spirits in the darkest hours, along with the complexities of elevating our boss's image through the prism of the skeptical press corps. With George W. Bush in office, and a nation at war, I would also add to those who questioned me that those serving Bush faced a much tougher task than we did.

Clinton's White House was the last with the lessened burden of worrying how the president's message was projected through the limited media universe of four national newspapers, three news magazines, three television networks, and CNN. MSNBC and Fox News debuted in 1996 and the *Drudge Report* was launched in 1995, but it took time for them to attract eyeballs. The only long-form writer we truly feared was Bob Woodward. The cable nets and Drudge drove the narrative during the Lewinsky scandal in 1998 and 1999, but we were spared the effects that 24/7 social media would have visited on Clinton through that brutal period, perhaps saving him from being driven from office. From then on, staffers for presidents that followed would face an exponentially tougher time selling their agenda in a sprawling media ecosystem and deflecting attacks from all sides.

Barack Obama will leave office in January 2017, and his staff has echoed our warnings about new challenges greeting succeeding administrations. "We believed from the beginning of our time here that if you're going to communicate in the new media environment of this era, you're going to have to break convention and do things other presidents have never done," Dan Pfeiffer, the president's senior advisor, told me.[2] While they were slow to adopt our simple tricks for message magnification at speeches and bill signings, the Obama White House was more daring and creative about exploiting peripheral outlets that brought easier access to younger voters and other niche demographic segments.

"That is why President Obama is the first president to appear on a late-night comedy show, the first president to appear on daytime talk, and why he does things like fill out his bracket on ESPN," Pfeiffer told me. In interviews, Pfeiffer alluded to predecessors like Michael Deaver and David Gergen—and people like me—when he cast aside old-school tactics of message enhancement. "We take guff from people when we do these things, because it's something different," Pfeiffer told me, "but I'm confident that all of the things we do the next president will do, and some things we didn't do."

With readers' attention diverted to outlets like Gawker and *The Daily Mail*, the choreographed movements and theatrical photo ops ceased commanding the spotlight they once did. The era of the advance man as storyteller was nearing its last mile. "You have to work so much harder in this day and age to get your message out than you did in the days of Ronald Reagan," Pfeiffer told me, "when you could give one nationally televised speech, reach everyone who had a television, and call it a night."[3]

GETTING YOUR MESSAGE OUT

One way that the president got his message out each week, going back to Reagan, was through the five-minute Weekly Radio Address, a communications channel that traced its origins to Franklin Roosevelt's fireside chats. Usually taped in advance during Reagan's years, but often performed live during the Clinton years, the weekly radio address would air on Saturday mornings and shape the weekend news cycle. Audio of the president's voice was a staple of Saturday night news broadcasts, his spoken words packaged with a still image of him reading into a microphone and a graphic of the Presidential Seal, conferring powerful branding on the recording. We used the occasions more creatively than Reagan, filling the Oval Office with visitors to provide an approving audience and occasionally recruiting other speakers to lend their voice to the message.

When Obama took office, the branding of the address changed, as did its format. Initially called the "President's Weekly Address" (dropping "radio" from the title) and then simply, "Your Weekly Address," the productions were shot on high-definition video, enhanced by flattering lighting, from different White House settings. The framing consistently positioned the U.S. and Presidential flags in soft focus over the president's shoulder; it looked presidential, but it didn't always sound presidential. This wasn't Obama's best format. Without an audience to affirm his statements with nodding heads, the weekly address had the hollow quality of a recital. Obama, his voice passionless, seemed to be going through the motions. Video from the addresses rarely made the weekend news, the networks reticent to air canned material shot by government cameras at the expense of their own footage.

A more ambitious effort to distribute government-produced video storytelling came through "West Wing Week," which by the end of 2015 had surpassed 300 episodes. The brainchild of Arun Chaudhary, Obama's 2008 campaign cameraman who became the first official White House videographer, "West Wing Week" was "your guide to everything that's happening at 1600 Pennsylvania Avenue, and beyond," as the narrator teed up each episode. Averaging six to seven minutes and reaping around 30,000 views on YouTube, it was a professionally produced package that offered viewers, curious about the president's comings and goings, enhanced documentary storytelling about many of the events on Obama's schedule that the TV networks no longer covered.

Chaudhary's self-described job was to "follow the president around," logging the moments just before and after his public appearances. It resulted in a lot of quality time with the president on hotel loading docks and freight elevators. In the West Wing, a building where crafting the narrative was the coin of the realm, Chaudhary also was one of the only bona-fide artists, an NYU-trained fiction filmmaker employed at the White House. His job, a new one on staff, was to package the presidency into a reality show. "I was handed the world's best set and the world's best cast of characters, and all I had to do was hit 'record,'" Chaudhary said. "The thing I take away most from my time filming backstage is not all of the amazing glamorous things that happened, or the state dinners, but the ordinary things that become so much more surreal when they're viewed through the lens of the White House," he added.[4]

In Chaudhary's creation of "West Wing Week," Dan Pfeiffer told me, "we noticed the tremendous interest in the video content of the White House that tells not necessarily the newsy story, but the interesting stories about how the sausage gets made here."[5] Halfway through Obama's first term, the message imperative was less about cracking the major newspapers and TV networks as it was energizing and motivating the base of support that would win electoral votes in battleground states like Nevada,

Colorado, Florida and Ohio. That didn't need a nightly news segment, although such coverage was always welcomed. What it really needed was local press, the kind of hometown memory making that resonated until Election Day.

Almost every week, Air Force One would depart from Joint Base Andrews en route to one or several states critical to electoral math. The logistics required millions in taxpayer dollars, but the national press, no longer endowed with unlimited budgets to charter their own aircraft to pursue these stories, followed in fewer numbers. The choreography of these visits—a town hall, a plant visit, an OTR at a local watering hole— rehashed a similar script each week. With official video, official photos, pool reports and transcripts distributed in fast fashion, the need for networks to spend big dollars to sit in a filing tent far from the proceedings and be spoon-fed "background briefings" lost its appeal.

To win Ohio, it was better to have wall-to-wall coverage in Lorain County's *Morning Journal* newspaper than to earn a brief item in the *Wall Street Journal.* In Obama's White House, the intersection of earning "free media" local coverage and the home-grown storytelling about how the sausage gets made, which Chaudhary had raised to a government- sponsored art form, met side by side. It happened on a January 2010 trip to Elyria, a city of 54,000 in Lorain County that sat along the bank of the Black River, about a half hour west of Cleveland.

GOING LOCAL

A two-part, eleven-minute White House–produced mini-movie, *Behind the Scenes of Presidential Advance,* removed the veil on areas we tried to shroud during the Clinton years and laid many of our methods bare. It opens on an advance woman named Carrie Devine, a veteran Obama lead, making calls from her rental car in an Elyria parking lot during a pre-advance trip to check out the local scenery for an Obama visit two weeks away.

Digital camera in hand, Devine notes the gymnasiums and VFW halls along the snowy roads that could serve as sites for a town hall or OTR. "It's really a privilege," she says from behind the wheel. "We get a peek at a lot of different people's lives and businesses. I know people talk about learning America, but it's really true that you get to see things that you would never otherwise see outside your circle and circumstance."[6]

The advance woman was certainly right. Separated in our advance work by over a decade, her grasp of the rare and special perspective that comes with being sent on the road by the White House was exactly like mine.

When her team arrives, Devine leads walk-throughs of Lorain County Community College, a routine site for a standard-looking town hall, and reports her findings to a team of schedulers huddled around a phone in the White House. As Devine goes about her business, the film zeroes in on the stories of a handful of displaced workers from the manufacturing sector who were being retrained for jobs in alternative energy. Among those interviewed in these sympathetic vignettes are Dennis Little, who spent thirty-seven years as a steelworker, and Anthony Whitmore, who lost his job in construction. With government stimulus money, both Little and Whitmore would receive training for fresh career starts and, if Devine's trip comes off as planned, a chance to meet Obama in the flesh. "Friday will be the greatest day in my life to hopefully be in the same room with the president of the United States," Little says into the camera.[7]

Previous White Houses could rely on papers like *USA Today* or broadcasts like the CBS Evening News to share this kind of backstory with a wide audience, as long as correspondents were granted exclusive access to characters like Little and Whitmore. In the Obama era, the newspapers, with fewer pages supported by dwindling advertising, were less reliable, as were the networks. In a bank shot of message-making, *Behind the Scenes of Presidential Advance* tried to accomplish the same goal, using Carrie Devine's week in Ohio as an unscripted drama with multiple storylines to deliver the feel-good story.

The government-produced film had noble intentions, but it also peeled away camouflage from the White House message machine. It shows Devine mapping pool routes through a machine shop floor and consulting with her colleague about the best vantage points for press, leaving a viewer to witness how most presidential trips place publicity above all else. The script would be revealed one event at a time. "We aren't planning to announce this [visit] until the night before or the morning of," she quietly confides to Brad Ohlemacher of EMC Precision Machining. "Just keep it as quiet as you can," she admonishes. "Don't talk to the press about it."[8] When the White House was ready to share the news, the press would find out soon enough.

The film chronicles another stop on the Ohio trip, to a plant owned by Riddell, the football equipment maker. If executed well, the planned presentation to Obama of a helmet bearing his seal and the number 44 on the back would yield a compelling visual. "The press will be staged on one side and we're going to work on lighting a couple of these workstations where [Obama] can talk to people," a member of Divine's team reports on a call with the White House. On the far end of the line, in Washington, trip director Marvin Nicholson nods approvingly at the prospect of squiring his boss through a shrine of football armor.[9]

On Game Day, as depicted in the film, the box office at the community college opens and 1,250 lucky attendees quickly gobble up their tickets for the town hall. In a few minutes, they will fill the gym that site lead Michael Ruemmler has been working for days to transform into a presidential event site.

Repeating the producer's playbook that could have been employed the week prior in Oregon, and might be followed the week after in Virginia, Ruemmler fills the gym with 100 pieces of four-foot by eight-foot stage deck, hangs trusses from the gym's rafters containing 250 feet of TV-quality lighting, lays out 115 power strips and 90 banquet tables for the media filing center, sets up 1,500 chairs for audience members, connects 400 feet of "bike rack" barricades for security, "and last but not least, four porta potties." Time-lapse photography shows all of Reummler's pieces falling into place. It could have been any week in any gym in America.

The final few minutes of the film show the trip underway. Obama breezes past Devine as she narrates: "When he comes to something like a town hall, we'll start to brief him and he'll give us a look like, 'You think I've never done this before?'" In fact, he follows a similar script almost every week. In brief flashes, the local characters introduced earlier receive their handshakes and moments in the spotlight with Obama, pausing afterward to recount their joy over meeting the president. "I'll never forget this moment, never in my life," one says for the ever-present White House camera.[10]

When he arrives at Riddell, Obama takes his shiny new cranial protection in hand. "Now that's a serious-looking helmet," he says, having starred in this movie before, "I could knock some heads with this." If only. That sound bite, dutifully recorded by the pool, would be the breakthrough line in national stories.

To cap the film, like he caps most trips, Obama does an OTR, this time for a burger and fries at Smitty's Place, a renowned seventy-five-year-old local eating establishment that, according to a 1995 news clip pinned to the restaurant's bulletin board, "blows the buns off the competition." With staffers and security mixing in with the regulars for the half-hour stop, the president dines in a corner with Elyria mayor William Grace. It's left to trip director Marvin Nicolson to supply the film's coda. "This is the world-famous Smitty Burger," Nicholson says, showing off its last morsel. "As you can see, I didn't like it at all. I eat a lot of burgers. This is one of the best burgers I've ever had."[11]

Beyond wire coverage and a piece in the *New York Post* (its headline read, "Bam Plays Offense—He's Going to Need That Helmet for Political Knocks"), the Elyria trip got limited national notice. But that wasn't really the point, not when the *Morning Journal* deployed its newsroom staff to cover the president from wheels-down to wheels-up. The trip to Smitty's provided plenty of color as writers marveled at the twenty-four-vehicle motorcade parked outside. Other stories previewed what Obama would say at the town hall; how Jody Hasman, an unemployed thirty-eight-year-old electrician, would introduce him; and a feature on the new presidential limo flown in aboard an Air Force C-17 to ferry Obama in his secure bubble from site to site.

There were other pieces in the *Morning Journal*'s blanket coverage, along with stories from competing print outlets and local TV and radio stations. In total, the coverage bestows upon Obama a bonanza of clippings in a key county of a must-win state for his reelection that only presidents typically generate. The trip, the first by a sitting president to Lorain County since Harry Truman paused on a whistle-stop tour in 1948, may have been vanilla in flavor, but it helped to cement affection for a man who, less than two years later, would carry Ohio over Mitt Romney, winning its eighteen electoral votes by the slim margin of 50 to 47 percent. Obama won the popular vote in only seventeen of Ohio's eighty-eight counties on his way to victory, but he took Lorain handily, his burger at Smitty's surely helping his cause.

IN THE ROUGH

It didn't take long after Obama's 2012 reelection, celebrated at McCormick Place in Chicago in a slimmed-down reprise of his Grant Park extravaganza, for his second-term honeymoon to wane—if there was a honeymoon at all.

Even as early as his inauguration on the West Front of the Capitol, in which the president invoked "Seneca Falls, and Selma, and Stonewall"[12] in a clarion call for equality on all levels, there seemed to be as much news coverage of Beyoncé lip-synching the National Anthem as there was of Obama's new national agenda. Second terms, as the optimistic adviser's strategy memos lay out, are supposed to be consumed with wisely spending down political capital, cementing a legacy for history, creating plans for a presidential library, and taking a well-earned, extended victory lap at home and abroad.

That wasn't Barack Obama's experience. The attack on the U.S. consulate in Benghazi on September 11, just before the election, cast a long shadow on the president's second term, as did the deadly December 12 massacre at Sandy Hook Elementary School.

The bad news continued into the next year, often arriving at the steps of the White House for comment and action. In 2013 there were, among other headlines, the acquittal of George Zimmerman in the death of Trayvon Martin and the failure of healthcare.gov, the website of the president's signature legislative accomplishment, to operate as promised. "There's no sugar coating," Obama said at an October news conference. "The website has been too slow, people have been getting stuck during the application process and I think it's fair to say that nobody's more frustrated by that than I am."[13]

In 2014, the crises continued. In April and May, Obama accepted the resignations of Kathleen Sebelius and Erik Shinseki, his secretaries of health and human services and veterans affairs, respectively. They departed under a cloud, compounded by the torturously public "loss of confidence" from the White House and the president's plodding pace in cauterizing his political wounds. There was also a string of foreign policy predicaments, from Russia's annexation of Crimea in March, to the controversial release of Sergeant Bowe Bergdahl by the Taliban in May, to the beheadings of James Foley and Steven Sotloff by ISIS in August and in September. Making matters worse back home, there was the killing of Michael Brown in Ferguson and the weeks of ensuing unrest there, and the influx of thousands of unaccompanied migrant children stranded at the U.S. border with Mexico. The second-term strategy memo didn't foresee these plot twists to Obama's closing-act script.

Historians will spend decades studying the arc of events of 2013 and 2014, but in the tale of the tape, those years neared their end with Obama at his lowest point in Gallup's daily tracking poll of the president's approval ratings. Over a three-day average from September 2 through September 5, 2014, his rating stood at 38 percent, thirty points below his average at its historic high point, the three days following his 2009 inauguration.[14] Many factors feed these daily snapshots of public mood, but how the president is portrayed in daily newspapers and newscasts is one of them. His actions and reactions were on public display when big news broke. Sometimes, in these moments, he earned praise for his comportment and style, but sometimes his performance was roundly panned.

Still, every workday, Obama put on his presidential costume and took the stage. "At the heart of any kind of story, there needs to be authenticity," Arun Chaudhary reflected in a lecture in Chicago about his work in the White House. "My contention, after having done this for quite a long time, is that authenticity reads on camera, and the American people are particularly adept at squirreling this stuff out. So any politician, if given enough time on camera, will reveal who they are," Chaudhary added.[15]

President Obama revealed who he was when he arrived unannounced at the White House Briefing Room to opine on the Zimmerman verdict at 1:33 p.m. on July 19, 2013. His candid comments briefly quieted the social media and cable TV machinery primed to render "prebuttals" on such matters hours or days before they happen. "You know, when Trayvon Martin was first shot I said that this could have been my son," Obama told reporters. "Another way of saying that is Trayvon Martin could have been me thirty-five years ago."[16] The twenty-minute appearance, orchestrated steps from the Oval Office, created lengthy top-of-the-news segments that reflected well on his leadership, all without spending a dime on travel.

The only stage direction required for this monologue was a two-minute warning to summon reporters to their assigned spots in the rows of seats and camera positions at the back of the room. There was no teleprompter, just raw Obama authenticity. The chattering class, caught off guard on a slow-news Friday, briefly stopped chattering as the president spoke for eighteen minutes from handwritten notes. "Once [the president] told us the day before what he had wanted to express," then–White House communications director Jennifer Palmieri told me, "that's a situation where you understand he has something very powerful to say—don't overthink it." It was a maneuver that the nation's leader, with his attendant trappings, couldn't pull every day. "You want it to be as organic and true as possible, which is very hard to do when you're dealing with the president of the United States, because of all the setup that's required with getting the press to be able to cover something," Palmieri told me.[17]

Though it didn't appear so on video, a lot of setup was also required in March 2014 when Obama filmed a six-minute sketch with comedian Zack Galifianakis for his *Between Two Ferns* web comedy series. The objective was to spike sign-ups for Obamacare at the enrollment deadline, and the sketch showed the president would use any means to reach his goal, including taking comic punches about his bungled website. Obama's deadpan delivery, recalling his 2006 turn on *Monday Night Football,* and his skill at giving as good as he got from Galifianakis, was disarming, but not without critics. "All I can tell ya is Abe Lincoln would not have done it," declared Fox News's Bill O'Reilly to his millions of viewers. "There comes a point when serious times call for serious action."[18]

Obama clearly wasn't intent on winning over O'Reilly's Fox News audience. He was aiming for a younger demographic, just as he did in late 2015 when he trekked up to Alaska's receding glaciers with Bear Grylls on NBC's *Running Wild* or took a spin around the White House grounds in a 1963 Corvette Stingray with Jerry Seinfeld in *Comedians in Cars Getting Coffee.*

The producer of *Between Two Ferns*, Scott Aukerman, anticipated the hectoring from critics like O'Reilly and thought, for that reason, the president's image makers wouldn't let the sketch move forward. "When we sent Obama's team the sample jokes and outline," Aukerman said, "we figured it would be dead immediately. Let's face it: Zach doesn't treat the people in the 'Ferns' chair with a lot of reverence."[19] There was, in fact, no reverence as Obama and Galifianakis traded comedic insults with a higher purpose in the ornate Diplomatic Reception Room of the White House, its precious antique wallpaper dressed down by chintzy blue drape and the ubiquitous two ferns.

Between the barbs, the episode hit its mark, amassing 10 million views on its first day, an audience greater than a nightly news broadcast. It quickly became the top referrer to healthcare.gov and, within a year, notched over 30 million views. "The president understood the medium and the 'Between Two Ferns' shtick, so he was prepared for it," Dan Pfeiffer told me. "We felt good about doing this. We knew we were taking a big risk. We knew that this was going to cause Dave Gergen to potentially have a heart attack."[20]

Gergen, the politically ambidextrous advisor of both Republican and Democratic presidents, did not have a heart attack watching *Ferns*, but other visual moments during those two years were unsettling to ex–White House advisors and many others. When Sergeant Bergdahl was freed from Taliban captivity in a prisoner swap in May 2014, Obama announced his release on the Rose Garden steps, a spot usually reserved for triumphal moments. He was flanked at the remarks by Bergdahl's mother, Jani, and his father, Bob, who used the occasion to address his absent son in Arabic and Pashto, leaving many to scratch their heads about the peculiar blend of stagecraft on display.

A few months later, in July, when calls came for Obama to visit the immigrant children left stranded at the Mexican border, he steered clear. It's never easy to land Air Force One—and the president's security apparatus—in the middle of a crisis. The optics became even more clouded when he traveled west while the story grew and was pictured playing pool and drinking beer with Colorado governor John Hickenlooper at the Wynkoop Brewing Co. in Denver. To make matters worse, he then flew to Texas for fundraisers in Dallas and Austin, bringing him within driving distance of the stranded kids. "He's so close to the border," said Democratic congressman Henry Cuellar on MSNBC. "And let me say this: when I saw, and I hate to use the word bizarre, but under the circumstances, when he is shown playing pool in Colorado, drinking a beer, and he can't even go 242 miles to the Texas border?"[21]

The unhelpful imagery extended into the president's private time, feeding more negative polling numbers. For the president, taking a summer vacation and still performing the duties of president is fraught with political peril, as I experienced often with President Clinton. The depths of Barack Obama's bad optics reached their low point on August 20, 2014, two weeks before Gallup recorded its record swoon for his approval ratings.

At the Edgartown School in Martha's Vineyard, Massachusetts, just before one o'clock in the afternoon, the president appeared before his press corps wearing a blue blazer and open-collared dress shirt. Reading from a prepared text, he delivered a five-minute statement condemning ISIS for beheading journalist James Foley, a horrific act of brutality staged in front of a video camera and uploaded to the world overnight. "One thing we can all agree on," the president said, "is that a group like ISIL has no place in the twenty-first century."[22]

After reading his statement, exhibiting the same insouciance for the visual as John Kerry showed with his windsurfing off Nantucket a decade earlier, Obama quickly swapped his white dress shirt for a white Nike golf shirt. His motorcade then whisked him to nearby Vineyard Golf Club for a foursome with friends, including Silver Lake founder Glenn

Hutchins, former NBA star Alonzo Mourning and Cy Walker, Valerie Jarrett's cousin. It was his vacation, after all. In the *New York Daily News* the next day, a grinning president behind the wheel of his golf cart filled the top half of the front page under the headline, "Bam's Golf War: Prez Tees Off as Foley's Parents Grieve."[23] Amid the widespread derision, even Obama's staunchest allies had little to offer in his defense.

"If Mr. Obama hoped to show America's enemies that they cannot hijack his schedule," wrote Peter Baker and Julie Hirschfeld Davis in the August 21 *New York Times,* "he also showed many of his friends in America that he disdains the politics of appearance."[24] Two days later, Maureen Dowd weighed in with "The Golf Address," one of the harshest presidential takedowns I can remember reading. Using her 1,027-word column to mirror Lincoln's 272-word Gettysburg Address, she framed the Vineyard golf outing against the Foley beheading and the riots in Ferguson. "We are testing whether that community, or any community so conceived and so dedicated, can long endure when the nation's leader wants nothing more than to sink a birdie putt," Dowd wrote.[25]

When he returned from Martha's Vineyard, nearing the 200th golf round of his presidency, according to the meticulous records maintained by CBS News' Mark Knoller, a weary Obama sat down with Chuck Todd for the moderator's debut on NBC's *Meet the Press.*[26] The interview was staged in the ornate Cross Hall of the White House, steps from the Aaron Shikler portrait of John F. Kennedy that featured so prominently in Pete Souza's album of Obama's First 100 Days in office—before the president's hair turned gray and his approval ratings were thirty points higher.

Almost six years and 2,000 days had passed since Souza's picture was taken, a period spanning hundreds of trip stops and millions of pictures snapped of the president by official, independent and private photographers alike. The archive is exponentially larger than any of Obama's predecessors due to the simple fact that anyone who owns a smartphone, anywhere in the world, can instantly become a photojournalist (or a paparazzi, depending on how you define the work) if they are in the right place at the right time and get the right shot. At any rally of 10,000 people, there is a number close to that who are angling for a selfie. For that reason, plus the risk of surreptitious recording, the chore of having people surrender their devices at closed-door presidential events has become the advance person's newest job.

The unrelenting scrutiny, and the ill-fated juxtaposition of James Foley's murder and Obama's golf game, was addressed in Todd's final question of the president. "Do you want that back?" the host asked the president. It was an uncomfortable topic—the "regrets" questions always are—but the answers often "make news" and earn publicity for Sunday morning shows, especially those with brand new hosts eager to score an early ratings win.

Obama wiggled toward his answer, reflecting part of it back on his inquisitor. "You know," he said, "it is always a challenge when you're supposed to be on vacation, because you're followed everywhere. And part of what I'd love is a vacation from the press." Todd interjected at this point, promising Obama that, in two and a half years, when his public service was complete, he would have one. If he needed any reminding, Obama would only be fifty-six years old upon leaving office, and capable of matching the total golf rounds of his two-term presidency in one year, undisturbed by photographers, if he set his mind to it.

But Obama went on, conceding that, after he made his statement at the Edgartown School, he "should have considered the optics" of hitting the links, an admission that turned the clock back to George W. Bush's remorse over "Mission Accomplished."[27]

A vacation day is a terrible thing to waste. But sometimes, when you're POTUS and the world looks to you to set the right example, it doesn't matter that you're in Martha's Vineyard. Weighed against the looming backlash, sometimes it's just a wiser move to put out a spread of chips and salsa, hold an indoor Monopoly marathon with friends and family, and instruct your press advance guy to "give the pool a lid" for the day. "Part of this job is also the theater of it," Obama conceded to Chuck Todd, adding that "it's not something that always comes naturally to me. But it matters. And I'm mindful of that."[28]

As he entered the final quarter of his presidency, the last mile of his long, unparalleled journey from his Hawaii boyhood to his eight years on the world stage—having accomplished much but also having disappointed many—Barack Obama would finally find peace with the theater of his job and become comfortable in his own skin.

COMFORTABLE IN YOUR SKIN

FORE!

As president, Bill Clinton liked to golf a lot, too, but he made better use of the game, politically, than Obama who, pool reports would note, on Saturdays or Sundays spent many of his rounds with old chums and young aides filling out his foursome. In February 1995, with Clinton still bruising from the humiliating midterm elections in which the Democrats lost both the House and Senate, we accompanied the president on Air Force One en route to Indian Wells, California, for a rendezvous on the desert links with former presidents Gerald Ford and George H. W. Bush at the Bob Hope Chrysler Classic.

Ford and Bush offered powerful political cover from a prior era, even though some bristled at the image of the president engaging so publicly in what might be seen as an elitist sport with senior statesmen of the Republican Party. "One day after blistering congressional Republicans for messing with his education and crime proposals," wrote John Broder in the *Los Angeles Times,* "President Clinton apparently threw in the golf towel and became—at least temporarily—one of them."[1] Alongside his predecessors, Clinton could be pictured, however briefly, above the fray that raged inside the Beltway.

Giants of American pop culture like Hope and Billy Graham have served as a human bridge between presidencies. Two years into Clinton's first term, it was Hope's turn to convene three members of the exclusive club. The rare foursome allowed political rivals to begin to heal the wounds of 1992 and forge a friendship that would endure for decades.

There would be casualties from the round, even though Ford warned the gallery before tee-off: "I would advise people they should stay behind us."[2] Bystander Norma Early was hit in the nose by a Bush slice on the first hole and needed ten stitches. Geraldine Grommesh took an errant Ford drive on 17 that clipped her index finger, and John Rynd of Chula Vista was struck on the buttock by a Bush shot on 14. "No blood, no problem," Rynd quipped, taking home the golf ball, signed by the forty-first president, as a souvenir.[3] Notwithstanding the wayward hooks and slices, the powerful, widely run optics of the three presidents standing shoulder to shoulder, with Clinton in the middle, made the four hours in the desert time well spent.

In many ways, that two-day trip to the Coachella Valley of California provided visual evidence that Clinton was ascending to a different plateau as a national leader, less of a partisan Democrat and more a custodian of the nation's highest office. His dinner on the evening before the golf game at Sunnylands, the midcentury modern residence of Walter and Lenore Annenberg (Ambassador Annenberg had been Richard Nixon's envoy to the Court of St. James's), offered old-school atmospherics that put the president in a rarified setting styled more for Ronald Reagan or Dwight Eisenhower than Jimmy Carter or Lyndon Johnson.

Clinton needed to make that pivot. The early months of 1995 had marked a low point in his presidency. The swooning feeling I felt in the West Wing, expressed in meetings in the Roosevelt Room or in off hours at Lauriol Plaza, a popular Mexican eatery in DuPont Circle, was palpable. The new House Speaker, Newt Gingrich, rode cockily into office against the backdrop of the Contract with America, co-opting our brand of photo op with a scene that put him on a pedestal. On every news show and magazine, I couldn't hide from that picture: three words—"Contract with America"—in raised white lettering plastered to a blue map of the United States erected behind Gingrich. He was surrounded by fellow GOP lawmakers, some of them waving American flags to fill the frame. After a long absence, Republican stagecraft was once again *Reaganesque.*

On April 18, Clinton held a formal East Room news conference, requiring us to lay on all the trappings of production. He was asked if his voice could still be heard in a town where the Senate was once again under GOP control and the House of Representatives had fallen from Democratic hands for the first time in forty years. "The Constitution gives me relevance," Clinton rebutted. "The power of our ideas gives me relevance. The record we have built up over the last two years and the things we're trying to do to implement it give it relevance."[4] Clinton had convinced himself of this, but others weren't sure.

AMAZING GRACE

The next day Timothy McVeigh and Terry Nichols detonated a brew of 5,000 pounds of ammonium nitrate, 1,200 pounds of liquid nitromethane and 300 pounds of Tovex in a Ryder truck in front of the nine-story Alfred P. Murrah Federal Building in Oklahoma City.

The explosion left much of the building in rubble, killing 168 people and injuring nearly 700 more, many of them federal workers. Among the dead were nineteen babies and children who had been playing in the Murrah day-care center. A bank employee, Charles Porter, photographed firefighter Chris Fields cradling an infant named Baylee Almon, who later succumbed to her injuries. The heart-wrenching image, which filled front pages of newspapers worldwide, won the 1996 Pulitzer Prize for Spot News Photography.

Watching coverage of children being pulled from the rubble, Clinton said he wanted to "put his fist through the television"[5] and immediately marshaled his administration to respond on all fronts, including ministering to children affected by the horror.

At that moment, less than twenty-four hours after being forced to defend his relevance, only the president had the power to speak for the nation. "The bombing in Oklahoma City was an attack on innocent children and defenseless citizens," Clinton said. "It was an act of cowardice and it was evil. The United States will not tolerate it, and I will not allow the people of this country to be intimidated by evil cowards."[6] The 1993 bombing of the World Trade Center, which killed six people, opened eyes anew to terrorism aimed at Americans, but from that day in Oklahoma City forward, the role of the president as defender of the homeland and consoler in chief ascended to a singular level of relevance.

Nearly a year later, on April 6, 1996, President Clinton returned to Oklahoma City to lay a wreath at the site of the bombing and dedicate a new day-care center replacing the one that was destroyed. As part of the choreography, he and the first lady would escort six children who had survived the blast to the hallowed place where their playmates died. The wreath stood ready to receive the Clintons, the children, and their accompanying parents. I had arrived a few days before to work with the advance team on the final arrangements. When all of our plans were in place, we added one more fixture to the scene: three bagpipers positioned high atop the remains of the Murrah Building.

The pool cameras tracked the hushed procession as they made their way from the motorcade to the awaiting wreath. Once there, the president adjusted its ribbons while Mrs. Clinton held the hand of four-year-old Brandon Denny, who had been severely injured in the explosion, and helped him leave a teddy bear amid the flowers. At that moment, the bagpipers stepped into view and began a rendition of "Amazing Grace" that broke the solemn silence. A few minutes later, at the day-care center dedication, the president reflected on what had just occurred.

"This is, after all, Good Friday," he said, "a day for those of us who are Christians that marks the passage from loss and despair to hope and redemption. In a way, that is the lesson of this little walk we just took with these children and their parents, from a place where we mourn lives cut so brutally short to this place where, thanks to you and all of those who helped, we can truly celebrate new beginnings."[7] For Bill Clinton, Oklahoma City was a new beginning as well, the beginning of the rest of his life, really, when the world's lonely eyes turned to him for consolation. If Clinton's administration had an anthem, it would be "Amazing Grace."

I had heard "Amazing Grace" played in the presence of presidents a number of times in the decades since the Oklahoma City bombing, but never so meaningfully as when Barack Obama sang it as the finale to his eulogy for the Reverend Clementa Pinckney at the College of Charleston on the afternoon of June 26, 2015. The stage had been designed to emulate the pulpit of the Emanuel African Methodist Episcopal Church in downtown Charleston, where Pinckney and eight others were senselessly murdered by a gunman nine days earlier. There was no presidential lectern for the service. It was replaced by a podium bearing the purple draping of the AME church, with Obama surrounded during his remarks by seated church elders and Reverend Pinckney's rose-draped casket below.

For all but the final paragraphs of his thirty-seven-minute eulogy, the elders and the audience expressed their accord with Obama's words through murmured concurrence and sporadic applause, but they remained respectfully seated during the span of his remarks. At the thirty-five-minute mark, Obama honed in on the idea of "that reservoir of goodness" that resides inside every person, the "open heart" that he had witnessed that week by the people in Charleston. Every person's essential goodness, he preached, "must be a manual for how to avoid repeating the mistakes of the past—how to break the cycle, a roadway toward a better world."[8]

The eulogy was nearing its conclusion. It was a beautifully written speech, earning instant comparisons among those simultaneously watching and tweeting to "A More Perfect Union," the name of his March 2008 address on race at the National Constitution Center in Philadelphia. But it hadn't yet reached its crescendo. "If we could find that grace," Obama added, "anything is possible. If we can tap that grace, everything can change."[9] Waiting for the crowd to hush, he uttered the words "Amazing Grace" twice, standing silently after that for fourteen long seconds, allowing his vision for a better world to percolate among the assembled audience. The next sounds from his mouth were not words, but notes, singing a cappella the first lines of the centuries-old hymn.

> Amazing grace, how sweet the sound
> That saved a wretch like me.
> I once was lost, but now am found,
> Was blind but now I see.

As the song came from his lips, the elders, audience and choir rose in unison to their feet to join in.

The Charleston eulogy, accompanied by "Amazing Grace," coming in the middle of Obama's seventh year as president, marked, as with Clinton, a turning point in his time in office that began at his 2009 inauguration with the words of Poet Laureate Elizabeth Alexander's recital of "Praise Song for the Day." In the long years in between, the journey had odd detours, such as the Beer Summit, and weird images, such as the photo released of him shooting skeet at Camp David as he lobbied for gun control legislation. When Obama came to Charleston, Americans saw him at his best—as a teacher—rather than a man who had to maneuver out of a rhetorical corner by participating in "a teachable moment."

Charleston marked a turning point, but it was part of a long arc that began in 2015 instead of a sharp curve. In March, on the fiftieth anniversary of "Bloody Sunday," Obama spoke movingly along the banks of the Alabama River in front of a deserted Edmund Pettus Bridge, a steel span named for a Confederate general that became a symbol of the Civil Rights struggle. When he finished, he led many of the 20,000 gathered for the ceremony across the bridge, including a number of the original "foot soldiers" from 1965, and even his predecessor in the White House,

George W. Bush. Just as Clinton had stood with President Bush's father in Indian Wells, visually burying the hatchet from earlier partisan rivalry, the scene in Selma elevated Obama in a new way and signaled his entry into the rarefied club where ex-presidents have their successor's back and put the nation's principles ahead of politics.

In June, after the Charleston shootings and the eventual removal of the Confederate Battle Flag from the South Carolina Capitol, after the Supreme Court upheld Obamacare subsidies by a six-to-three vote, and after the Court made same-sex marriage a national right, the corps of print and broadcast pundits finally rendered a collective verdict on Obama's presidency as "consequential." Obama's "Best Week," as many called it,[10] paved the way for historians to vault him, eventually, into the top tier of national leaders.

With the theater of the 2016 campaign beginning to take over the national stage, the week also opened the door, gently, to a waning presidency, when a lame duck slowly makes way for a new flock taking flight. But even as the race to succeed him heated up, powerful symbolism doesn't abandon the sitting POTUS until he flies home on Inauguration Day aboard the famous blue-and-white Boeing 747 with all of its usual trappings, except the call sign "Air Force One."

On Friday, June 26, at the end of that illustrious week, Obama allowed his home to be bathed in rainbow lighting to commemorate the Court's landmark decision on same-sex marriage. It was an idea hatched months earlier by Jeff Tiller, a former press advance man who was part of my team on the Port of Spain trip. Tiller spent that Friday night on a lawn chair gazing at the North Portico, along with large crowds beyond the fence on Pennsylvania Avenue. When asked about the powerful symbolic gesture at a Monday news conference, Obama said it was "a moment worth savoring," twice repeating, "That was a good thing."[11] Embracing, at long last, the theater of his job, which he confessed to Chuck Todd six months earlier was something that didn't come naturally to him, stagecraft finally turned from foe to friend.

WTF

When Barack Obama was seven years old, in 1968, living with his mother in Jakarta, Indonesia, it's doubtful he saw any of the Republican and Democratic National Conventions held that summer in Miami Beach and Chicago. What the future president missed was a new strain of televised content born from ABC's struggle to make its mark on broadcast news. The perennial third-place network hired William F. Buckley Jr. and Gore Vidal to appear in ten one-on-one debates to enliven its convention coverage. Both men, one an ardent conservative, the other a flaming liberal, were dazzling thinkers and writers, but their on-screen battles drove ratings not because of the power of their ideas, but because live TV turned their ideological conflict into an addictive visual spectacle.

Nearly half a century after Buckley and Vidal's summer of sparring, a documentary film, *Best of Enemies,* reminded a new generation of viewers how television first turned political disagreement into hypnotic entertainment. Some memorable segments of the verbal brawls were not, in hindsight, either man's finest hour (Vidal calls Buckley a "crypto-Nazi"; Buckley retorts, calling Vidal a "queer").[12] At the closing curtain of their last debate, however, they seem to have a sense of what they wrought.

"I think these great debates are absolutely nonsense," Vidal says into the camera. "The way they're set up there's almost no interchange of ideas, very little, even of personality." Then, putting on the hat of a TV critic, the prolific author of every sort of written word adds, "There's also a terrible thing about this medium that hardly anyone listens. They sort of get an impression of somebody and they think they figured out just what he's like by seeing him on television." No one listens, they only get an *impression.*

For his part, the loquacious Buckley succinctly addresses the cultural conundrum that would distort public discourse for the five decades that followed. "Does television run America?" Buckley asks rhetorically. "There is an implicit conflict of interest between that which is highly viewable and that which is highly illuminating," he adds.[13]

The Buckley-Vidal verbal one-upmanship spawned a dubious progeny of cheap-to-produce programming serving as viewer catnip to digest along with their TV dinners. Like the two-chair, two-man setup of Buckley-Vidal, they started raw and simple, with the "Point-Counterpoint" segments between James J. Kilpatrick and Shayna Alexander on CBS's *60 Minutes* and Ted Koppel's interviews of boxed-in guests on ABC's *Nightline. Crossfire* showed up on CNN in 1982 and, by the end of the next decade, MSNBC and Fox News Channel began to fill their prime-time hours with nonstop ideological ping pong matches, the balance tipped on either side depending on the channel's slant.

As the productions became more slickly produced, the role of the advance person made Vidal and Buckley's warnings more prescient. Catering to declining viewer attention spans, producers in their control rooms un-moored their cameras from their in-studio guests and began to feed B-roll of the day's political events onto the screen while the talking heads prattled on. If it was hard to "listen" in Vidal's day, it was getting impos-sible in the new century as Buckley's "highly viewable" content trumped that which was "highly illuminating" every night. The cable networks had an insatiable appetite for fresh footage, the kind that advance teams manufactured, and TV crews gathered to feed the advertising-supported product that the networks put onto the air. Veteran correspondents might have turned up their noses at the choreographed imagery and photo-ops staged on the road, but their bosses kept airing it just the same.

Sometimes, the B-roll occupied its own superimposed box as hosts and debaters mixed it up in the main frame, and sometimes the footage took over the whole screen, the voices becoming a trifling soundtrack. A viewer's brain had the tough task of descrambling the words and images and making sense of the audio and visual stew that the shows served up. With all of these empty calories consuming so many hours of airtime, the media landscape cried out for a new medium.

I took my own stab at creating something different by removing the visual from the mix. In January 2011, I joined Adam Belmar, a former ABC News producer and later a White House aide who did for George W. Bush what I did for Clinton, in launching a weekly hour-long radio show for SiriusXM's "POTUS" channel called *Polioptics*, a made-up word that mashed up "politics" and "optics." The mash-up captured the essen-tial mission of the advance man, my passionate on-and-off vocation since my first trip for Senator Paul Simon right out of college in 1987. The show lasted 159 episodes, ending in 2014. Though *Polioptics* never earned me a dime—with a day job, I didn't have the time or need to commercialize it—the series was a labor of love.

Each weekend, after the show aired on SiriusXM, I uploaded the MP3 file to Polioptics.com and posted it to iTunes as a podcast. I had become enamored of the audio medium long before shows like *Serial* catapulted podcasts to mainstream popularity. The opportunity to sit in a soundproofed, air-conditioned studio and talk with interesting guests from government, the media and Hollywood and "shine a light on the theater of politics," as our announcer said, was a joy. Mixing our conver-sations with archival sound from the span of White House history gave *Polioptics* a theatrical quality that maybe even Buckley and Vidal would have enjoyed listening to with high-end headphones.

It wasn't a unique discovery, but I found that by stripping the visual out of a broadcast, even one that was focused on political theater, gave the listener a richer appreciation of a guest's perspective. There was no lighting or makeup, no interruptions for commercial breaks, and no hostile grandstanding among guests in the manner that Vidal unleashed on Buckley. The audience streaming a podcast, by the very nature of that act, opted in to focus intently on what was said rather than have their attention distracted by B-roll, pharmaceutical ads and the preening voices of on-air talent. Listening to other podcasts by far more accomplished performers, I was coming to think that the most effective form of communication for a new age might have no image at all.

One show on my regular iPhone podcast listings was Marc Maron's *WTF*, which launched about a year before mine debuted and owed its title to the Internet slang for "What the Fuck?" The earnest, earthy, often profane host was a stand-up comedian in real life, but has increasingly earned his notoriety from the twice-a-week show he produces in a makeshift studio in the one-car garage of his Highland Park, California home.

To appreciate the unique manner in which Maron engages his guests, you have to leapfrog his expletive-laced opening monologues, but at least you're spared the incessant commercials for erectile dysfunction you get on TV. *WTF* is an entertaining listen while you do the dishes, but as much as I enjoyed it, I didn't expect the homespun podcast to be the kind of production that a president of the United States would drop into. But this was the summer of 2015, at the trailing end of the pivot of Obama's presidency, and a man who made himself at home on the set of *Between Two Ferns* might be willing to take a flyer on *WTF* if it meant reaching an audience desensitized to cable donnybrooks.

On the morning of Friday, June 19, 2015, that's exactly what he did, flying on Marine One from his overnight stay in Beverly Hills to Highland Park for an appointment in Maron's garage. Listening to Obama chat with Maron for an hour was to appreciate the president in a new way and, for many, to really hear him for the first time.[14] In the show, which was posted on the following Monday, he talked candidly about his parents, his college years at nearby Occidental, raising his kids and managing his presidency. Obama spoke with an intimacy and authenticity that couldn't be conveyed in edited TV interviews or long-form magazine articles, and certainly not in two-minute packaged news reports on his stream of daily events. From Roosevelt's fireside chats to Reagan's rallies to Clinton's town halls, Obama's encounter in Maron's garage gave those who downloaded the conversation—close to 3 million by the end of that summer—a front-row seat to the newest and, in many ways, best approach to understanding a president's vision for the country he leads. All you had to do was listen.

In sixty minutes of back-and-forth, Maron and Obama covered his frustrations over gun control, his vision for addressing poverty, his ideas about combating terrorism, his skirmishes with Congress and, in the wake of Charleston, the nation's ongoing struggle with racism. It was here that Obama made "news," though to reduce the visit to Maron's garage to the president using the "N-word" was to miss how *WTF* transcended staged events, speeches and news reports emanating from the White House.

"Racism," Obama said about halfway through the podcast, "we are not cured of it. And it's not just a matter of it not being polite to say 'nigger' in public. That's not the measure of whether racism still exists or not. It's not just a matter of overt discrimination. Societies don't, overnight, completely erase everything that happened 200 to 300 years prior."[15] That was interesting, but it only occupied one minute of an "illuminating," to use William F. Buckley's word, hourlong journey that Maron and Obama took together when the microphones were turned on and the cameras remained off.

The visit to Highland Park, enabled by the Secret Service shutting down a residential block in Los Angeles and Maron banishing his litter of cats that usually comprise his live audience to a remote room in his house, went down as Dan Pfeiffer hinted it might, with the White House "breaking convention" to connect with a new audience in new ways. Everything about how the booking went down was out of the ordinary. The communications office reached out to Maron, not through high-level channels, but through a blind inquiry via his website.

On a follow-on podcast recorded a few hours after Obama left the garage, Maron and producer Brendan McDonald detailed the advance work required to allow the encounter to happen. They spoke of counter-snipers on a neighbor's roof, the bomb sweep of Maron's house and the tent erected in his driveway to shroud the president's limo. They didn't mention the other standard items of the advance checklist, including the secure phone drop for emergency communications with the Situation Room, the counter-assault team on standby to win a firefight should an ambush occur, or the planned evacuation route to the nearest ER if the president took ill, or worse. Even for an event in a one-car garage, moving the president anywhere out of the White House requires that level of planning.

McDonald thought the web inquiry was a fake when it arrived more than a year before the presidential visit actually took place. "It was a vague thing," McDonald said of the cryptic outreach from the White House, noting that no politician had appeared on the program in its prior 612 episodes. Obama's people were intrigued by the prospect of doing *WTF*, and the dialogue with McDonald began. "We would have any guest on," McDonald said, "as long as they can do the type of interview that we do, which is talk about life and talk about other things and not have a specific promotional agenda."[16]

Intent on doing whatever it took to make the interview happen, Maron offered to travel to Washington, cancel a vacation or postpone his stand-up tour to accommodate the president. He thought an Oval Office interview would be cool, but as McDonald reminded him, that option was never on the table. "It is my estimation," McDonald said, "based on how they work, that they need, whatever they're doing—promotionally or publicity-wise, media-wise—to be in the context, in the idiom, of that thing."[17]

McDonald was right. A conversation in the Oval Office, with two mics instead of a pen and paper, would differ only on the margins from lengthy sit-downs with long-form writers like Michael Lewis for *Vanity Fair*, David Remnick for the *New Yorker* or Jeffrey Goldberg for the *Atlantic*. Those had been done with good effect, the subscribers of the three journals getting their behind-the-scenes sense of the president through the probing writer's prism. It was time to do something different, to reach a new audience, and a trip to Los Angeles was required to keep it authentic. "It would not have probably looked good," McDonald guessed, "for them to grant a one-hour interview in the East Room or the Oval Office to you, some non-credentialed guy, comedian, non-journalist, when they have a press corps that doesn't get that kind of access."

"That's insane," Maron said, still disbelieving what had just happened to him.[18]

Seven years into his presidency, Obama was finally becoming adept at escaping, however fleetingly, "the bubble" that had become his life. As he told Bear Grylls in 2015 over barbecued bear-gnawed salmon during an episode of the outdoorsman's NBC reality show *Running Wild*, which was shot in cinema verite style on an Alaskan glacier, "I was telling your producers that the bubble is so tight. It's the toughest thing about being president. So every once in a while I'll go off script, and everybody gets very nervous," he said with a chuckle.

After the millions of miles traveled, from Springfield, Illinois, in January 2007 to over fifty countries by 2016; after all of the exhaustively planned trips, laboriously written speeches and carefully orchestrated photo ops; after all of the White House–produced video content and comedy-show appearances doubling as news conferences, Barack Obama showed his constituents something new simply by visiting a garage in Highland Park. Later in 2015, he would do it again in conversation with Bill Simmons for *Sports Illustrated,* with Grylls in Alaska and with Jerry Seinfeld on the South Lawn of the White House, offering compelling evidence that lame ducks could still fly (or at least take a flyer).

By appearing on *WTF,* allowing his host to take him on a journey through his life and answering Maron's questions genuinely, even using "the N word" when it felt natural, Obama became something that often eluded him during his era of the Age of Optics. In an hour of unadulterated conversation, he was, in his own unique way, being *presidential.*

THE NEW AGE OF OPTICS

THREADING THE NEEDLE

For the seven plus years of Barack Obama's presidency, with increasing frequency over the last four, friends would ask me, "Do you think Hillary will run again?"

For me, the question was more loaded than I let on. Though I've now reached fifty, there's a part of me that still thinks I'm in my early twenties, eager to pack my go-bag of advance gear and hit the road. I think of my friend Sam Meyers, who I met in my first days in the White House, a former Jimmy Carter advance man who has made a life of our brand of work. He has served as Vice President Biden's trip director since day one. In the Clinton years, Sam started bringing his young son, Sam Jr., on trips, turning him into a full-fledged advance man. Sam Jr. now has decades of his own adventurous travel under his belt. With friends taking up roles in Secretary Clinton's campaign, I could take my own young son and daughter to big cities and small towns in 2016 and give them the same joyous front-row seat to American history that I was privileged to occupy straight out of college.

But no, I would say, I don't think Hillary will run again, projecting a different personal calculus onto her circumstances. If I was nearing seventy and made $200,000 a stop to take softball questions and pose for pictures before heading home to await the birth of my granddaughter, I'd think, *Life's pretty damn swell*. With every future Democratic aspirant seeking an audience at my court in Chappaqua, I could be a king-maker, I would say, or surely a queen-maker, and happily call it a glorious career. And if I had a private server holding a few gigabytes of quasi-work-related emails from my turn as the nation's top diplomat, I need only look at the rewarding, unfettered retirements of Colin Powell and Condoleezza Rice to conclude that few would really give a rat's ass about how I disposed of them.

"But she can finally break the ultimate glass ceiling," some would counter. "And she'll have a clear path to the nomination," others would say.

"Yes," I would allow, "but look at the actuarial tables."

Averaging every campaign since I worked as an advance man for Bill Clinton in 1992, the age of the winner on Election Day was fifty-one and the age of the loser was sixty-four. That leaves Hillary a half decade older than the average loser even if she crosses the finish line of this eighteen-month marathon. In her husband's 1992 campaign, even with assorted scandalous baggage dragging on it, advance people orchestrated events from dawn to midnight for a telegenic, gregarious forty-six-year-old governor that would stretch any middle-aged man's stamina. And yet Bill Clinton kept asking for more. Every one of the Clinton advance alumni has a war story of working late-night rope lines without end or pulling a bus tour off the road to allow the extroverted candidate to greet a few stray bystanders waving a sign.

"That's *what it takes,*" I tell my inquisitors, alluding to Richard Ben Cramer's epic tome on running for president in 1988. "So if you want a Democratic woman president, then find me a smart, accomplished, charismatic forty-six- to fifty-six-year-old who can withstand nonstop physical and emotional torment and remain comfortable in her own skin, and you've got yourself a winner. Oh, and it would be terrific if she speaks fluent Spanish," I add, mindful of the sweeping demographic trends that have transformed the electorate in battleground states since my first advance trip in 1987 (the same formula works just as well for men, by the way, assuming a woman of equal measure isn't in the race).

It was crass, ageist and superficial to offer my simple formula—I know—but the Age of Optics rewards a combination of youth, charisma and authenticity, and preferably all three. It's possible to defy the odds by possessing any two of the traits in abundance to compensate for a deficit of the third (see "Reagan, Ronald") or when the age gap is *de minimis,* as it was in 2000 and 2004. But even with demographic trends and electoral math on your side, the presidential victor in each general election matchup over the last quarter century has bested his opponent in at least two of those three attributes.

That's not all, of course. Money is table stakes today: full campaign coffers and a well-endowed Super-PAC can help accentuate your positives and inflate your opponent's negatives, especially to survive the nominating process. On the stump, it's better to be untethered to a teleprompter and quick to crack jokes at your own expense, but they should be genuinely funny. And it helps, also, to appear at ease with journalists up and down the media food chain in both on- and off-the-record sessions. You must stroke their egos and feed their professional needs, and those of their bean-counting bosses, with a daily, high-caloric diet of reportable and photographable stuff. At its essence, winning the presidency is about marketing a product, and to win over wholesalers in the newsroom and consumers at home, it's better to go to market with something fresh and new. Hillary Clinton struggled with a number of these prerequisites.

As I watched the Clinton political machinery ramp up to market *Hard Choices,* Secretary Clinton's 2014 memoir of her four years on the world stage, I saw a new legion of young advance people cutting their teeth on the basics of orchestrating a book signing. The fundamental skills of managing a crowd flow of 300 people seeking a signed copy of *Hard Choices* are immediately transferable to orchestrating a fundraiser, and only a little more training qualifies these political cadets to plan a town hall and, eventually, a downtown campaign rally. It's only a matter of time, I thought. Notwithstanding the stats that argued for a contented grandmotherly retirement, Hillary was going to reach for the big prize again, and many of my old friends and comrades-in-arms were already suited up for another run, or were sure to soon sign up.

With a home office packed with memorabilia from a lifetime of world travel, I'm ever mindful of what I owe the Clintons, starting with the fact that I met my wife while working in the White House, just as so many other couples have over the years in both Democratic and Republican administrations. With Hillary's 2016 die cast—embodied by her blue "H" logo with the red arrow pointed onward printed on a range of items for sale on her website—I would become a supporter too. In May 2015, I cut my own check for the maximum allowable amount to support Secretary Clinton, admonishing her solicitor not to waste my donation on embroidered fleeces for advance people, one of my pet peeves. (I created custom jackets for the Clinton-Gore national advance team in 1992 but made everyone pay for them out of their own pocket.)

After writing my check, I remained otherwise uninvolved, but hopeful about what Secretary Clinton's candidacy represented. If she could thread the needle—defying the odds of age, of succeeding a two-term president in her own party and of selling a dynastic product to a new segment of buyers ready for someone with a surname other than Clinton or Bush—she could fill a rare and attractive niche unrelated to gender. Upon taking office on January 20, 2017, like George H. W. Bush in 1989, she would be immediately familiar with, and broadly experienced in what the role really takes, avoiding, hopefully, the misspent months and years that her three prior predecessors spent learning on job.

But first there's one thing the former first lady, senator and secretary of state had to do first: get elected. The initial cautious steps in 2015 were calculating and calibrated to maximize favorable coverage and minimize unplanned exposure. On Sunday, April 12, she released via social media a two-and-a-half-minute video, retweeted 3 million times in the first hour, to announce her candidacy. The video used Madison Avenue storytelling and editing to touch every demographic segment of a winning coalition: moms, blue-collar workers, retirees, blacks, whites, Spanish-speakers, gays, even dog owners—"everyday Americans," as Clinton would call them. Ninety seconds in, the video cuts to Hillary, wearing the blue and red of her logo, in an outdoor setting that looks like her Chappaqua home, making a pitch that "I'm hitting the road to earn your vote, because it's your time. And I hope you'll join me on this journey."[1]

THE SCOOBY VAN

The coalition wasn't invited on the first 1,000-mile leg of that journey. While the media blanketed the airwaves for two days with that fleeting, fawning footage of the freshly announced candidate, Secretary Clinton was already in the seat of her black Chevy Express Explorer Limited SE conversion van with dark tinted windows, built by UAW workers at a plant in Wentzville, Missouri. Dubbed the "Scooby Van," it wended its way at the speed of traffic from Chappaqua to Monticello, Iowa—a trip that would take seventeen hours or so nonstop.

"Road trip! Loaded the van & set off for IA. Met a great family when we stopped this afternoon. Many more to come," Clinton shared in a Sunday night tweet, adding a snapshot of her posing with a smiling family of four from somewhere along the Rust Belt.[2] The road trip included a Sunday overnight in Pittsburgh, where she called down for room service, and a Monday afternoon detour off I-80 in the Toledo suburb of Maumee, where a security camera caught her and Huma Abedin at a strip-mall Chipotle ordering a chicken burrito bowl with black beans, guacamole, and a blackberry Izzy drink.

The *New York Daily News,* among many other outlets, spread the security cam shot across the front page. In the *Daily News,* the headline read "WHO THE HIL ARE YOU?" along with a jumbo insert of the Chipotle logo, sure to please its corporate marketers. The kicker headline added, "'People's Champion' Hillary Pops into Chipotle—But No One Recognizes Her."[3] Former Obama chief speechwriter Jon Favreau tweeted that Hillary's road trip to Iowa was a "really great" idea, worthy of Alyssa Mastromonaco, a reference to President Obama's longtime head of scheduling and advance.[4] Jennifer Palmieri, who left Obama's White House to assume the role of Clinton's communications director, tweeted back that while it was Mastromonaco-worthy, it was the candidate's idea.[5]

Whoever deserves credit, it was a shrewd masterstroke of image control. The Chipotle shot, inelegant as it was, fit the image Clinton was trying to project. By staying otherwise cloistered in the Scooby Van en route from New York to Iowa, the monkish Clinton avoided the many moments when cameramen could have spied her in a setting other than the backyard backdrop from her video, such as disembarking from a private jet or surrounded by a phalanx of Secret Service agents. Such images were anathema to a campaign packaging itself as by and for "everyday Americans." For two days, media outlets looking for B-roll for their programs or layout editors seeking still shots of the candidate on the move contented themselves with footage from the video or of picking up lunch from a fast-food joint.

The "jet stairs" images would inevitably come after the fervor of her debut died down, but for the first forty-eight hours of her campaign, Clinton remained concealed until the Scooby Van arrived Tuesday morning at the Jones Street Java House in LeClaire, Iowa. There, sitting around a square red table, while other patrons sipped coffee at high tops around her, she joined three Iowa voters for a chai tea that the *New York Times*'s ace photographer Doug Mills shot and promptly tweeted out. The picture looked as if Hillary had just interrupted a casual coffee break among three friends, but those at her table—Austin Bird, Carter Bell and Sara Sedlacek—were hand-picked by the campaign, driven from nearby Davenport to complete the scene. With real reporters witnessing the chat with their own eyes, instead of through a security camera, the advance work involved in fabricating Hillary's version of the standard OTR came as no surprise.

From there, it was onto Kirkwood Community College, eighty-two miles away in Monticello, where a machine shop floor, just like the one Obama visited in 2010 in Elyria, Ohio, served as the backdrop for an "intimate" conversation with students and teachers on the need for more affordable higher-education options. The staged intimacy was only on Secretary Clinton's side of the press stanchion. Behind it, scrunched to-gether like sardines, stood a large pool of journalists snapping pictures, holding recording devices aloft and waiting patiently for an opening to lob questions the secretary's way.

This will be her routine for every public event until her political ca-reer comes to a close. It would manifest itself again at a July 4 parade in Gorham, New Hampshire. Using a page from the advance manual of past campaigns, two members of Hillary's team unfurled a rope to establish a buffer zone between the parading candidate and the pool tracking her ev-ery step. Liz Kruetz, a young digital journalist covering the campaign for ABC News, tweeted out a photo of the scene ("Reporters following Hill-ary Clinton dragged behind on actual ropeline," she posted, along with the image). An online uproar ensued. Media types and other retweeters were "shocked, shocked" that their freedom was being restricted by a rope.

Many times in the past, my hand has been on one end of that rope. While no reporter likes being corralled, the practice has a purpose that, in bygone days, the pool understood. Not every moment in a candidate's day is a news conference, even if questions about emails hadn't been fully addressed. Often, as it was at Kirkwood Community College, the me-dia's role is to observe, not interject. The objective in Gorham was to give small-town citizens standing along the parade route a view of the candidate. The rope was, in this case, nothing more than a moving line, paralleling the secretary a few steps in front of her and establishing parity among the pool for decent photo coverage. The alternative would have been an ugly, unruly rugby scrum that enveloped the woman at its center and left no one satisfied with the result.

At this rate of media umbrage-taking, it would be a long campaign. Back in Iowa, as the Scooby Van pulled away from Kirkwood, with the candidate safely behind her tinted windows, another video segment spread virally through social media. It showed dozens of reporters—carrying cameras, ladders and other gear—chasing after Hillary across the park-ing lot as if they were running with the bulls in Pamplona, Spain. Living inside that inescapable fishbowl is the price she has to pay for the chance to break that ultimate glass ceiling.

ROOSEVELT ISLAND

Watching the gluttonous hoard in hot pursuit of the Scooby Van, starving for another glimpse of the candidate or the chance to bark one more question ("What about the emails?!"), brought me back twenty-three years to Thursday, April 2, 1992. Governor Bill Clinton, working to right his campaign after losing the Connecticut primary to Jerry Brown, came to New York City a few days before the Empire State's primary to stage an outdoor lunchtime rally at the intersection of Wall and Broad Streets, steps from the New York Stock Exchange. It was a logistical and security nightmare that I doubt I'll see again for any presidential candidate in my lifetime. Taking on hecklers and plunging into the mosh pit as only he could, he flung his body into the crowd in search of every last vote. It wasn't a pretty visual.

"It was vintage Clinton," reported Gwen Ifill for the *New York Times,* "a candidate who is as practiced in the atmospherics of a campaign day as he is in describing the minutiae of his economic proposals. And for the first time in nearly a week, the candidate seemed prepared to embrace the unpredictability of New York crowds, which have alternately jeered him, heckled him and greeted him like a Hollywood celebrity."[6] In taking on all comers on Wall Street that day, Clinton made himself at home in that milieu.

A generation later, on June 13, 2015, with the Scooby Van back in Chappaqua and a few months of "conversation-style" events under her belt, Secretary Clinton prepared to hold another massive rally in New York City. The venue wasn't Wall Street, a den of capitalism, but rather Roosevelt Island, a site applauded by Democrats for its ties to its namesake progressive icons and panned by Republicans for the same reason. Hard to access, reachable most easily by subway or cable car, the island site could be sealed off with relative ease from those who might disrupt the rally or, worse, potential terrorists, who long ago designated Manhattan an attractive target. The Federal Aviation Administration even issued a "NOTAM," or "Notice to Airmen," that the island would become "national defense airspace" on the day of the rally, rendering a vast virtual corridor around the site a no-fly zone.

It was, in reality, one of the only practical spots that Clinton could gather thousands of her reliable Senate constituents en masse in an open-air setting. Madison Square Garden or the Barclays Center, massive monoliths with four walls and a roof, couldn't offer a comparable visual.

Even if she had chosen one of those sites, the NYPD might have cordoned off streets for blocks in each direction, snarling city traffic and raising the ire of New Yorkers in the process, already made irritable by the summer heat. Watching the plans for Roosevelt Island fall into place, Bill Clinton's unruly 1992 rally on Wall Street never seemed farther in the rearview mirror.

Four Freedoms Park, the actual patch of island real estate used for the rally, was rather small by big event standards, large enough to accommodate a few thousand, but compact enough to be shrunk if crowds didn't materialize. It was hemmed in on two sides by a triangle of 120 small-leaf linden trees set in allées, and on the third by a one-time smallpox hospital, a Gothic landmark built in 1854 that sits on the site, in front of which the campaign erected two long tiers of press risers. With the new 1,776-foot One World Trade Center in the distance, a reminder of Hillary's service in the Senate during 9/11, and the United Nations just across the East River, recalling her days as secretary of state, the site was awash with symbolism intended to buttress her remarks.

In constructing their site, the Clinton advance team opted for "the bowl effect," with security-screened supporters surrounding the stage on all sides. Creating a bowl of people, an old site guy trick, always makes crowds look bigger and the sites that contain them more boisterously claustrophobic then they really are. Those in the crowd who were positioned at Clinton's rear in large, temporary, stadium-style bleachers could be seen waving flags and taking selfies, but they were far enough behind her that they appeared blurry in the viewfinders of video and still cameras that zoomed in on the candidate at her podium. Only the sign affixed to the front of the podium, advertising the campaign's logo and web address, and the retractable panes of teleprompter glass, which rose on demand from the stage floor, remained in crisp focus along with the secretary.

As the rally started, Clinton's grand entrance was staged from the edge of the backdrop bleachers. As cable networks cut to live coverage of the event, Hillary entered the site to the rhythm of Sara Bareilles's megahit "Brave" blaring from the speakers. She waded through the crowd along a raised walkway, an elevated gladiator, just like Obama's 2007 campaign launch in Springfield, Illinois. To the cameras in the rear press positions, the height boost would show her floating above the crowd as she made her way to an H-shaped stage. The *Times*'s Doug Mills, always in the right place at the right time, snapped an upward angle of Hillary on the catwalk that revealed how the visual effect was created. The unique

H-shaped stage design, the first time I ever saw a letter of the alphabet become a platform for a presidential candidate, was hidden to the live TV audience, but enhanced the tableau when captured by "high shots" from photographers soaring above the site in a campaign-supplied scissor-lift.

In a speech clocking in at forty-five minutes and interrupted often for applause, Secretary Clinton laid out the vision for her candidacy at this "official launch" in a more fulsome way than April's kick-off preludes— the two-and-a-half-minute video or the "intimate conversations" in Iowa or New Hampshire—would allow. Nowhere but in New York would she command such wall-to-wall global news coverage on a sunny Saturday afternoon. If the speech was staged in Des Moines or Manchester at that point in the campaign, far fewer press credentials would have been issued. She owned the day and became the central focus on the Sunday morning news shows that aired twenty-four hours later. John Podesta, Clinton's campaign chairman, compared the rally to the start of baseball season. "We've had the spring training," he said, "and now it's opening day."[7] John Dickerson, the new host of CBS's *Face the Nation*, had his own perch on the press riser and observed, "The event was the Broadway opening of a show that's been off-Broadway."[8]

The remarks, worked over exhaustively by Clinton, speechwriter Dan Schwerin and other guest wordsmiths, were more of a State of the Union address than a stump speech. Like an extended cut of her video, it devoted passages calibrated to appeal to each demographic segment that would comprise a winning coalition in 2016. The policy meat of her speech was sandwiched by slices of her life experience designed to highlight attributes given short shrift in her first presidential run in 2008. Sharing a portrait of the tough stock from which she was bred, the rally gave Clinton another opportunity, on live TV, to align herself with the resilience of her mother, Dorothy Rodham, who was forced to work as housemaid at age fourteen. She also tried to inoculate herself on the age issue. "I may not be the youngest candidate in this race," she declared, "but I will be the youngest woman president in the history of the United States! And the first grandmother as well."[9]

No commentator that I watched or read in the hours or days that followed would nominate the speech to enter the canon of political rhetoric, but nor would they separate the substantive from the superficial in their analysis. In the Age of Optics, it's always about the spectacle.

Glenn Thrush of *Politico* wrote that "it had the discursive and intimate quality of a Facebook stream."[10] Molly Ball of the *Atlantic* chimed in that "in keeping with the campaign so far, Saturday's speech was quite substantive and quite liberal. It was also quite flat. Clinton read it slowly off the teleprompter, articulating every word, sometimes with odd emphasis, in a near-monotone."[11] Peggy Noonan, someone exquisitely practiced in the art of speechmaking, used her column in the *Wall Street Journal* to note that "Mrs. Clinton doesn't seem to enjoy crowds, which is odd since she's in the crowds business."[12]

The armchair commentary omitted some underlying truths about the Age of Optics. The speech, in its entirety, was available for viewing on almost every news website along with galleries of images cataloguing every angle of Clinton looking presidential and being adored by her massive crowd. The critiques, by comparison, amounted to noise. You could criticize the site, the symbolism and the substance of the event, but in a gladiatorial business you couldn't overestimate a campaign's power to draw 5,500 people to an island in the East River sixteen months before an election. No other candidate, in either party, could muster a legion of that size or produce a show with that level of rock concert professionalism.

There were even larger truths, beyond unmatched crowd size and blanket news coverage, hidden in the strategics by which the Clinton campaign would leverage the speech to connect with niche segments more likely to vote in the battleground states. In effect, this "official launch" was a macro event designed for micro targeting. "An event like this is not about the audience," wrote John Dickerson for *Slate*. "It isn't an argument of the kind Bill Clinton used to make. It is a buffalo that is cut up and passed around in social media. So anyone who cares about the environment will see her committed to that in a gorgeous setting. So too, those who are moved most by promises to provide paid family leave. In the age of precise narrowcasting, Clinton offered something that can be shipped to people of all interests."[13] That was Roosevelt Island.

In the old days, an advance person at a wheels-up party for such an event might crow that "it was general election–sized crowds in primary season." Assuming no scandal devoured the campaign, or no bigger phenomenon appeared on the horizon, that level of excitement might be sufficient to cruise to the nomination and sail on to the general election in November.

Four days later, at a far smaller rally staged across the East River in the atrium lobby of a tower bearing his name, Donald J. Trump descended a gilded escalator and announced his candidacy for president of the United States.

THE SUMMER OF TRUMP

Among my yellowing archive of *Time* magazines from the 1980s, back when issues regularly topped 100 pages and Hugh Sidey's columns taught me all I needed to know about the theater of the presidency, sits the issue from January 16, 1989. On the cover of the issue, at the top corner opposite from the publication date, was the newsstand price: $2.00.

The magazine is a time capsule. Ronald Reagan was in his final weeks as president. It was five months since Dukakis rode in his tank, and an item noted he wouldn't seek reelection as governor. Also among the articles was coverage of the shoot-down of two Libyan MiGs by U.S. F-14s, the failing efforts to prosecute Oliver North in the Iran-Contra scandal, a story about hyperactive kids, and Richard Corliss's review of Stephen Frears's new movie *Dangerous Liaisons* with John Malkovich as the Vicomte de Valmont. Corliss wrote of Malkovich's performance, "The lizard eyes crease with desire; tiny curlicues of smirk rise from the corners of his mouth. . . . He embodies the cynical wisdom of this excellent film: life is one big performance art."[14]

With his inauguration days away, *Time*'s cover that week could have pictured President-elect Bush. Instead, it featured another character, like Valmont, quick to brandish curlicues of smirk at the corners of his mouth and to living life as one big performance art: Donald J. Trump.

The cover portrait was shot by Norman Parkinson, showing the then-youngish real estate developer brashly holding an ace of spades between his thumb and forefinger. In the magazine's standard art direction of that era, most of the headline was in smaller white lettering, with the subject's surname in bright yellow capital letters five times larger than the rest. It read: "This Man May Turn You Green with Envy—or Just Turn You Off. Flaunting It Is the Game, and TRUMP Is the Name."

To thumb through the issue today is to go back to the future. The Trump photo by Ted Thai that opens the seven-page spread on page forty-nine shows him in pinstripes and red tie, standing at the foot of the same resplendent escalator that delivered him to his presidential campaign announcement twenty-six years later. The quotes by Trump in Otto Friedrich's 1989 profile read as if they could have been uttered at the 2015 Iowa State Fair. "I love to have enemies," the forty-two-year-old Trump told Friedrich. "I fight my enemies. I like beating my enemies into the ground." Of Trump's aspirations for high office, Friedrich noted, "There has been artfully hyped talk about his having political ambitions, worrying about nuclear proliferation, even someday running for president."[15] Friedrich apparently didn't query him on the nuclear triad.

Fast forward to the summer of 2015. The August 31 issue of *Time* weighed in at a light sixty pages, a shadow of its former heft, and *Time*'s cultural influence had similarly faded. But the figure on the cover was the same—a "winner," a political heavyweight of the first order, making the magazine worth parting with $5.99 for the privilege of adding it to my archive. Staring at me, with an extra yodel of flesh beneath the chin and a few less layers of hair atop his head than in 1989 was, in an overdue encore, Mr. Trump. His eyes now leered more narrowly in Martin Schoeller's 2015 cover portrait, like the lizard in Corliss's description of Valmont, but no one could deny he looked just fine at sixty-nine. If he went head to head with Hillary Clinton, the age gap would be a wash, leaving charisma and authenticity, in my calculus, as the deciders of popular appeal. *I'll need to find a few more key attributes,* I thought. In so many ways, the Donald was threatening to upend my presidential formula.

Time's headline that week cut to the chase quicker than in 1989. Superimposed across the bit of Trump's forehead free from his hairy brim were three words: "Deal with It."[16] That was the stubborn message to pundits and prognosticators—and me—after a summer of surprises approaching Labor Day, five months before the Iowa Caucus, with Trump far ahead in the polls among his sixteen other rivals for the GOP nomination.

He could call Mexicans "rapists,"[17] could defame John McCain's heroism, and could start a one-sided brawl with Fox News's popular anchor Megyn Kelly. Candidates have fizzled by doing less. In 1968, George Romney said he was "brainwashed"[18] by the military brass in Vietnam; in 2015, Trump said he got military advice from "the shows." Romney faded from the national stage from that remark. Trump only gained prominence.

The verbal faucet gushing from Trump's mouth spewed insults at everyone in the race, but he also drove ratings whenever he joined a broadcast, including the Fox News GOP debate, which drew an audience of 24 million. That show tripled the viewership of any previous primary debate and topped numbers for the NBA finals, the World Series and the finale of *The Walking Dead*. Trump delighted in treating senators and governors on his stage like zombies, recalling his 1989 quote in *Time*: "I like beating my enemies into the ground."[19] Viewers, cheering such entertainment during their couch time, rooted for Trump as they did Norman Reedus's *Walking Dead* character Daryl Dixon doing the same thing. One by one, the zombies went down.

As obnoxious as his broadsides were, media outlets valued bellicose bluster over prosaic substance. From August 6, the night of the Fox News debate, to August 23, the closing night of the Iowa State Fair, the newscasts of ABC, NBC and CBS gave Trump a combined thirty-six minutes and thirty seconds of coverage, exceeding all of his rivals combined. A new NASA global warming report noting that July was the hottest month on record going back to 1880 was mentioned on the major cable networks— CNN, MSNBC and Fox News—ten times between August 20 and August 23; in the same span, "Donald Trump" was mentioned more than 750 times. And that was just the start of the Trump phenomenon.

Beyond the nightly news packages, to nab Trump for on-air interviews, bookers of the morning, cable and Sunday news shows capitulated to his demand to appear by phone, sparing him the wasted time of schlepping to the studio and the nuisance of hair and makeup. The off-camera appearances gave Trump another advantage as well, allowing him the option of eyeballing notes, all while the networks candy-coated the TV screen with graphics of his dominant poll numbers or flattering B-roll over his voice that replayed recent footage of his triumphs on the road. The spectacle had crossed into an uncharted dimension.

Trump could even brazenly defy the first rule of advance, that politicians shouldn't wear hats in public. His retro-style, ruby-colored golf cap, with its trademarked "Make America Great Again" slogan, kept his hair grounded during windy outings and self-captioned every photo snapped in his direction. He wasn't a politician, he protested when answering a jury duty questionnaire, he was in "real estate."[20] Whatever he did that summer, wherever he went, his mixture of authenticity and anger kept his polls aloft. Giving the kids a free ride in the Trump helicopter at the Iowa State Fair didn't hurt, either.

David Axelrod, President Obama's longtime media advisor and confidante, cast Trump in a Maureen Dowd column as "the proverbial strongman," the extreme point of the pendulum from Obama's "thoughtful and deliberative" turn as commander in chief.[21] Taking a cue from Hollywood, where Trump owed his fame, the strongman casting fit him like a glove. Sharing one trait with Václav Havel, the playwright who ascended to become the first president of the Czech Republic, Trump was, at the core, a man of theater, scripting his own drama in which old rules didn't apply.

Michael Scherer's eight-page Trump cover story in *Time* was a cooperative product of author and subject. Scherer's sit-down interview with his subject, in Trump's twenty-fifth-floor office of his namesake tower, would be jazzed-up by a full-on photo shoot. To maximize this "get" for the magazine, *Time* needed that extra art-directed *something* to make it fly off newsstands.

"Fly" was the operative word, with the magazine procuring a twenty-seven-year-old bald eagle from Texas, named Uncle Sam, to perch for a portrait with the candidate. With the quintessential "wingman," the avian embodiment of the presidential seal, perched by his side on his desk, Trump fingered a few sheets of paper and sneered into Martin Schoeller's lens for the money shot. The image was reproduced on pages 26 and 27 as a "double-truck," magazine parlance for a pair of facing pages with a single image stretching across both. The front section of the last of America's famed newsweeklies became yet one more parcel of real estate to which Trump could claim ownership.

Every advance person craves seeing their boss pictured flatteringly in a *Time* double-truck. In 2015, Schoeller's portrait of the power couple of Uncle Sam and Donald Trump had no peer. "He's very difficult to photograph," Schoeller said of his assignment. "If you ask him to look up a little bit, he says no or he just doesn't do it. He literally has one angle. If I ask him to smile, he puts on a big grin and then he goes back to his Zoolander 'blue steel' look."[22] Once you've seen Trump's "blue steel" in a double-truck, you don't need to read Scherer's 3,000-word story to get the message: "Deal with it."

With planes, helicopters and branded golf caps at his disposal, Trump was his own scheduler and advance man (and fundraiser, speechwriter, pollster, and oppo researcher). The choreography rarely looked "clean," the gold standard for event production that Steve "Rabbi" Rabinowitz taught my generation of advance people. But when Trump flew over Ladd-Peebles Stadium in Mobile, Alabama in his 757 on the evening of August 21 for the biggest rally to date, by far, of the 2016 campaign, cleanliness didn't much matter. Thirty thousand people—six times more than turned out to welcome Hillary to Roosevelt Island—looked to the sky and beckoned him down for the political edition of *Friday Night Lights*. Once he took the stage, which was erected in the end zone of Ladd-Peebles with thousands of supporters standing behind him, he'd lob one rhetorical bomb after another downfield. That was how Trump became the country's top quarterback that summer.

Despite opponents and pundits of every stripe predicting his imminent downfall following one unleashed fusillade or another, the summer of Trump gave way to the fall of Trump. He trotted roughshod over his opponents and debate moderators alike and treated the hosts of the high-minded Sunday morning news shows like drive-time radio talk jocks waiting for the weekly call-in of "Donald from Queens." There seemed to be nothing to stop his speed-dialing free media juggernaut, in part because his every appearance spiked their ratings. Like him or not, Donald Trump was good for business.

On the very week in mid-November that Trump was assigned protection by the United States Secret Service, conferring upon him a new status as a national candidate, guarded at taxpayer expense by the country's elite law enforcement agents, he approached the extreme edge—at that point—of his unique brand of on-stage performance art. He spoke for ninety-five minutes before a packed house of 1,500 people in Fort Dodge, about ninety miles north of Des Moines.

Trump's podium at Iowa Central Community College was suitably dressed to an advance man's perfection with a placard bearing all of the requisite particulars: "TRUMP" in all capitals, his website URL, his Twitter handle, the locale of "Fort Dodge, Iowa" and his motto, "Make American Great Again." It was a textbook visual diorama, with the exception of the crowd behind him. Unlike Hillary's speech on Roosevelt Island, the Fort Dodge audience was positioned too close to the candidate's posterior, betraying the onlookers' distracting fidgets as Trump's monologue stretched past the hour mark. When the address reached an hour and twenty minutes, even the stoutest of their number elected to fill seats and settle in for the remainder of the show.

What came out of Trump's mouth that night in Fort Dodge was anything but textbook Iowa politicking, featuring jabs at each of the candidates most recently standing in the way of his march toward the nomination. Carly Fiorina was "Carly whatever-the-hell-her-name-is." Marco Rubio was "weak like a baby." Ben Carson was the target of a ten-minute diatribe all his own, including Trump's on-stage reenactment examining whether, in fact, Carson could have really tried to stab a friend as a young man (as Carson claimed in his autobiography), only to have been spared the resulting injury by a heroic belt buckle which parried the full force of the thrust.[23] Trump proved to his satisfaction that it was impossible.

The performance might not have won Trump new supporters in Iowa ("How stupid are the people of Iowa," he asked rhetorically about Carson's supporters in the Hawkeye state), but his frothy excretion of verbal venom toward his opponents earned him prime coverage on the next morning's network and cable news shows. On MSNBC's *Morning Joe* program, the clip played at the top of the broadcast, uninterrupted, for several minutes. When the cameras came back live to the studio, panelist and advertising legend Donny Deutsch uncharacteristically stood up from his chair and gave the clip an extended standing ovation. His colleagues on the set seemed aghast at the apparent display of approval for what they had just witnessed. "It's theater of the absurd," Deutsch said.[24]

In the *Washington Post* that morning, George Voinovich, the former mayor of Cleveland, governor of Ohio and United States senator—a man who had made politics his career and earned the respect of those beyond his state in both parties—spoke for a broad cross-section of America powerless to stop the Trump onslaught, at least until the voters had their say at the polls. "This business has turned into show business," he said.[25]

In succeeding weeks leading up to Christmas, Trump's televised burlesque would be amplified louder still by his call to close America's borders to Muslims, before turning the spotlight on his next target. Near Grand Rapids, Michigan, on December 21, standing before a crowd of 7,500 at the DeltaPlex, the aspiring leader of the free world raised the subject of Secretary Clinton's bathroom break during a commercial pause of a Democratic debate. "I know where she went," Trump said. "It's disgusting. I don't want to talk about it. It's too disgusting." Not too disgusting, in Trump's estimation, was sharing his impression that Mrs. Clinton was "schlonged" by Barack Obama in the 2008 nominating contest. Leaving the podium, which carried a customized "Merry Christmas" Trump placard, the loudspeakers blared Andy Williams's seasonal tune "It's the Most Wonderful Time of the Year." Reflecting on it all on the *Today Show*, host Matt Lauer said, "I can't remember a campaign that needed a holiday break more than this one." As Lauer knew, holiday breaks are blissful but short. The campaign would resume in a week, as would the battle for morning-show ratings.

George Voinovich was right in his assessment but mistaken in his chronology. The business of politics had turned into show business at the dawn of the Age of Optics, if not before. In Fort Dodge and Grand Rapids, as it had before and certainly would again, the show had just gone off script. Still, the show must go on. Trump may not "Make America Great Again," but should fate ever land him on the west front of the U.S. Capitol to take the oath of office from the chief justice of the United States Supreme Court, the four years that follow will be anything but a vanilla presidency.

WEARING MANY HATS

There's something wonderfully perpetuating about publishing a book on the modern era of presidential stagecraft in the spring of an election year: there will surely be a new afterword for the paperback edition.

I started imagining this book in 2009, just back from my Obama trip to Port of Spain, thinking about the many parables advance people learn on the road. There is no practicum like it in any syllabus, and I thought sharing these lessons with "everyday Americans" to decipher the byzantine brew of sights, sounds and mediums—"the theater of politics"—was a worthwhile exercise. While it can be a hard language to learn, with regular study it's like iambic pentameter, a rhythm that repeats itself from beginning to end, with a few new variations added to the traveling spectacle every four years.

Leaving the material aside as my work and home life took priority, my imagination fired again in 2013, approaching the twenty-fifth anniversary of Dukakis and the tank. I had Matt Bennett's diary in my desk and it seemed negligent to keep its revelations buried or ignore the untold, multilayered, tale of an event gone horribly wrong a quarter century ago. This book began with the simple question: "Why did a candidate wear a helmet with 'Mike Dukakis' stenciled on it?" It ended with an epiphany, as I watched Donald Trump wear a golf cap with "Make America Great Again" emblazoned on it.

It was never about the headwear, I realized, but rather the person underneath it. Dukakis—brilliant, cerebral and modest—tried to symbolize someone he wasn't when he rode aboard the M1A1 Abrams in Sterling

Heights wearing his helmet. Trump—patriotic, brash and bombastic—showed exactly who he was when he strode across his raised walkway in Mobile wearing his hat. Trump's journey may never take him to the Oval Office as president, but he successfully created a corollary to the first rule of advance: headwear may be worn in campaigns, as long as it doesn't cover your authenticity.

Starting from the tank ride in Sterling Heights, I had no idea how far my own journey in this book would take me through the Age of Optics. This story eventually included stops in Orlando, Chico, the Connecticut River, the Pacific Ocean, Des Moines, Nantucket, New Orleans, St. Paul, The Villages, Normandy, Trinidad, the Rose Garden, the Situation Room, Elmyra, Martha's Vineyard, Oklahoma City, Charleston, Highland Park, Monticello, Roosevelt Island, Mobile, Fort Dodge and Grand Rapids (*Yeaaggh!*), and so many points in between and beyond. When the events are done, when the boss is wheels-up, we advance people call them war stories. To have these places flood back into my consciousness was, in the course of remembering and retelling them, to become young again.

Our odd, elongated, exasperating spectacle of electing leaders has endured, with minor modifications, for 240 years and repeats itself every four. It is a chance for the country, its citizenry—and the advance people who travel from city to city to introduce candidates to voters—to become young again with each new president we elect. The outcome, ultimately, is for the voters to decide. No other nation has been so successful through such a regular regenerative process. It's not something to waste. It is, instead, something worth cherishing.

If you've enjoyed this book, find some war stories of your own to tell your grandkids. Go out and buy a tape measure, a pad of graph paper, a ruler, protractor and a mechanical pencil and hit the road. It doesn't matter what party you belong to or what ideology you espouse. There's a campaign going on. It's a big country and there are still many states in play. There are tales to be told, there is history to be made, and you won't want to miss it.

ACKNOWLEDGMENTS

My humble admiration, first and foremost, to twelve politicians—Mike Dukakis, George H. W. Bush, Bob Dole, Al Gore, George W. Bush, Howard Dean, John Kerry, John McCain, Mitt Romney, Barack Obama, Hillary Clinton and, yes, even Donald Trump—six Democrats and six Republicans whose days in the public spotlight pursuing office while courting political suicide are chronicled in this book.

Many sit on the sidelines of political change. This determined dozen put themselves *in the arena,* as Theodore Roosevelt said in 1910, vying for the ultimate prize of the presidency but also exposing themselves to ridicule and humiliation every time their motorcade pulled up to a curb. Their careers in military and public service and in business are deserving of genuine respect, and they have mine.

My additional gratitude goes to a thirteenth politician, Bill Clinton, whose stories overlapping mine are woven throughout the book. Governor Clinton and his 1992 campaign staff let me board their bandwagon for an unexpected multiyear journey that brought me around the world many times over. As my friends will attest, my carefully curated relics of those years reflect how much my time in Clinton's shadow is deeply cherished.

One of the hardest things in life is admitting, and revisiting, failure. This book's origin is a war story of political failure retold to me in a barroom in 2012 by my longtime friend Matt Bennett. Matt entrusted me with his 1988 campaign journal and bestowed me with his patience over the years as he reopened his wounds of battle for my forensic examination of the worst event in American political history.

I am grateful to the other witnesses with whom I spoke about the many angles at play on September 13, 1988. They shared their memories and helped me paint as complete a picture as I could of that day, mindful as I am that there are still deeper caverns of truth to mine. My sincere thanks to Madeleine Albright, Rich Bond, Joyce Carrier, David Demarest, Gordon England, Neal Flieger, Mark Gearan, Don Gilliland, Arthur Grace, Joe Lockhart, Mindy Lubber, Nick Mitropoulos, Sig Rogich, Jack Weeks and Jim Weller. My friend Steve Silverman, another 1988 veteran, gave me invaluable assistance as this project was just getting off the ground and conducted a number of the interviews for Part One of the book. For narrative purposes, Steve's interviews and mine are commingled in the body of the book but noted as Steve's in the endnotes.

My sources for Part Two of the book brought me on a time-warping journey across a quarter century of American politics. Marlin Fitzwater's *Call the Briefing* started by giving me a deeper understanding of the supermarket scanner incident than is known through lore. Kent Gray showed me his painful scars of 1996, for which I'm grateful. Mike Feldman, Matt Bennett, Chris Lehane and Nathan Naylor added first-person recollections to my research on Al Gore's trip down the Connecticut River.

On my Sirius XM radio show, *Polioptics,* Beau Willimon gave me a behind-the-scenes look at the Dean Scream, and Scott Sforza brought me on board for President Bush's trip to the USS *Abraham Lincoln.* Mark McKinnon, Russ Schreifer and David Morehouse helped me better understand the linkage between the Kerry windsurfing expedition and Bush's windsurfer ad. Will Ritter brought me into the entourage for Mitt Romney's stop at The Villages, and on my radio show Jim Margolis helped me understand how the Obama ad team worked to exploit it. Steve Schmidt offered to share his thoughts about John McCain's tough summer of 2008.

Part Three of the book is derived from my firsthand experience as a volunteer advance man for President Obama in 2009 and my armchair observations of the years that followed. During four of those years, 2011 to 2014, I had a special perch from which to watch as the host of *Polioptics,* where our hundreds of guests brought fresh insights and analyses of White House stagecraft to our studio. Adam Belmar, who held a job like mine during the administration of George W. Bush, had the vision to get the show off the ground, and Katherine Caperton produced it creatively and valiantly, week after week, during its enduring run of 159 episodes. The show's high production quality and unique sound belied its thin skeletal makeup, a pathfinder for political podcasts that followed.

While they may not fully appreciate their influence on me and how my life evolved, my early advance mentors—Redmond Walsh, Noel

Boxer, Mitchell Schwartz, Andy Frank, Steve Barr, Steve Rabinowitz and the crusty old master himself, Mort Engleberg—taught me how to treat all the world as a stage.

My intrepid colleagues during the Clinton years: directors of advance Paige Reefe and Dan Rosenthal; trip directors Wendy Smith and Andrew Friendly; director of communications Don Baer; personal aides to the president Stephen Goodin, Kris Engskov and Doug Band; and press secretaries Dee Dee Myers, Mike McCurry, Joe Lockhart and Jake Siewert—and every advance man and woman with whom I served—taught me how to tell human stories and withstand heat from presidents and prime ministers. They also conspired with me to create a lifetime of indelible memories in a few short years working together at 1600 Pennsylvania Avenue and on epic trips to innumerable points on the compass.

This book began with an article in *POLITICO* magazine of which then-editor Susan Glasser, now the editor of *POLITICO,* was a champion from day one. My agent, Lauren Sharpe of Kuhn Projects, believed unflinchingly that the dark chapters of the Age of Optics could be a worthwhile chronicle of our political era and stuck with me through multiple iterations of proposals and pitching. My editor and publisher, Karen Wolny of St. Martin's Press, had boundless faith that a first-time author could tell the tale. The team at St. Martin's, Laura Apperson, Donna Cherry, Christine Catarino and Gabrielle Gantz, carried me the last mile in bringing the book to life.

Shrewd political observers, like my friends Jonathan Prince, Jeremy Gaines and Jacob Weisberg, were enlisted as extra eyes on the final page proofs, and Brian Steel serves as my extra set of eyes on life.

My oldest friend, Mark Leibovich, is also the most entertaining writer I've ever read. We tried to write our first book, *Boston: Sports Hub of the Universe,* on his dad's typewriter when we were seven. While that project never got off the ground, his unparalleled genius as a journalist and storyteller has provided me with a role model ever since. My best friend, Adam Rosman, has been a constant rock of support since 1976 and remains my counselor in all things. My mentor, Joe Plumeri, showed me how passion and stage presence can be both compelling and motivating in business as well as politics. Working with Joe allowed me to open a new chapter as a practitioner of political stagecraft, one that continues to this day.

My parents, Howard and Phyllis King, gave unconditional support to my creative streak at an early age and without end, no matter which tangent it took. My in-laws, Ed and Donna Theobald, and my sister-in-law, Laura Theobald, gave me a warm hearth, hot food and cold drinks to support my writing on many weekends when I would steal away from parenting duties to churn out a few thousand more words late into the night.

Better than all of my sometimes exotic travel over the past many years, three simple trips, taken umpteen times between 1997 and the present, have been my favorite. The first was in Washington, D.C., a walk from near the White House, up Connecticut Avenue, to an apartment in DuPont Circle. The second was a five-minute drive from my office in Hartford, west on Asylum Avenue, to a home in the city's West End. The third consists of three stops on the E line of the New York City subway system, from the World Trade Center to Greenwich Village. On each trip, the destination was always the same: home, to my wife, Amy, and kids, Toby and Annabelle. A dinner and movie with them in our living room, with our dog, Huck, lying nearby, is the best event of all.

NOTES

PREFACE: THE AMERICAN SPECTACLE

1. Jim Lehrer, *Tension City: Inside the Presidential Debates, from Kennedy-Nixon to Obama-McCain* (New York: Random House, 2012), 52.
2. Jon Stewart, *The Daily Show,* Comedy Central, "Sigh Language," October 4, 2000, http://www.cc.com/video-clips/s1p0eg/the-daily-show-with-jon-stewart-indecision-2000—sigh-language.

PROLOGUE: THE TROPHY PRESIDENT

1. Reid Epstein, "Obama: 'You Don't Put Stuff on Your Head If You're President,'" *Politico44* (blog), April 12, 2013, http://www.politico.com/blogs/politico44/2013/04/obama-you-dont-put-stuff-on-your-head-if-youre-president-161546.
2. Brian Williams, *Nightly News,* NBC, April 12, 2013, http://www.nbcnews.com/video/nightly-news/51523163#51523163.

INTRODUCTION: POLITICS 101

1. Andrew Rosenthal, "Bush Encounters the Supermarket, Amazed," *New York Times,* February 5, 1992, http://www.nytimes.com/1992/02/05/us/bush-encounters-the-supermarket-amazed.html.

CHAPTER 1: THE ADVANCE MAN

1. Philip Lentz, "Dukakis Picks Bentsen as No. 2," *Chicago Tribune,* July 13, 1988, http://articles.chicagotribune.com/1988-07-13/news/8801140840_1_dukakis-aides-michael-dukakis-new-hampshire-democratic-chairman.
2. Nielsen, "Highest Rated Presidential Debates 1960 to Present," October 6, 2008, http://www.nielsen.com/us/en/insights/news/2008/top-ten-presidential-debates-1960-to-present.html.
3. Maureen Dowd, "The Presidential Debate; 2 Rivals in Red Ties Speak Softly, Looking for Jabs and the TV Cameras," *New York Times,* September 26, 1988, http://www.nytimes.com/1988/09/26/us/presidential-debate-2-rivals-red-ties-speak-softly-looking-for-jabs-tv-cameras.html.
4. A full transcript and video of the debate are available from C-SPAN at http://www.c-span.org/video/?4256-1/presidential-candidates-debate.
5. Morgan Whitaker, "The Legacy of the Willie Horton Ad Lives on, 25 Years Later," MSNBC, October 21, 2013, http://www.msnbc.com/msnbc/the-legacy-the-willie-horton-ad-lives.
6. The "Weekend Passes" ad can be seen at Museum of the Moving Image, "The Living Room Candidate: Presidential Campaign Commercials 1952–2012," online

exhibition, http://www.livingroomcandidate.org/commercials/1988/willie-horton;
the "Revolving Door" ad can be seen at Museum of the Moving Image, "The Living
Room Candidate: Presidential Campaign Commercials 1952–2012," online exhibition, http://www.livingroomcandidate.org/commercials/1988/revolving-door.

7. Bret Schulte, "Michael Dukakis: The Photo Op That Tanked, QA with Michael
Dukakis," *U.S. News & World Report,* January 17, 2008, http://www.usnews.com
/news/articles/2008/01/17/the-photo-op-that-tanked.

8. Times Wire Services, "Reagan on Dukakis: 'I Won't Pick on Invalid': 'Just Trying
to be Funny,' President Later Says of His Answer to Question on Medical Records,"
August 3, 1988, http://articles.latimes.com/1988-08-03/news/mn-6862_1_medical
-records.

9. Steven V. Roberts, "Bush Intensifies Debate on Pledge, Asking Why It So Upsets
Dukakis," *New York Times,* August 25, 1988, http://www.nytimes.com/1988/08/25
/us/bush-intensifies-debate-on-pledge-asking-why-it-so-upsets-dukakis.html.

10. UPI, "Kitty Dukakis, Wife of Democratic Presidential Nominee Michael Dukakis . . . ," August 25, 1988, http://www.upi.com/Archives/1988/08/25/Kitty-Dukakis
-wife-of-Democratic-presidential-nominee-Michael-Dukakis/3260588484800/.

11. Ibid.

12. Mark Gearan, interview by the author's assistant, Steve Silverman, August 25, 2013.

13. Ibid.

14. Ibid.

15. E. J. Dionne Jr., "Dukakis Campaign Fights Slump with New Look and Sharper
Edge," *New York Times,* September 9, 1988, http://www.nytimes.com/1988/09/09
/us/dukakis-campaign-fights-slump-with-new-look-and-sharper-edge.html.

16. Mark Gearan, interview by the author.

17. E. J. Dionne Jr., "Dukakis Campaign Fights Slump."

18. Madeleine Albright, interview by the author, July 17, 2013.

19. Matt Bennett, interview by the author, July 18, 2013.

20. Matt Bennett, "Sterling Heights, MI *Tank Event*" (unpublished journal), November
1988, 6.

21. Jerry Bruno with Jeff Greenfield, *The Advance Man* (New York: William Morrow,
1971), 15.

22. Box Office Mojo, "Smokey and the Bandit," http://www.boxofficemojo.com/fran
chises/chart/?id=smokeyandthebandit.htm.

23. Josh King, "Notes for Advanced Teams" (unpublished tract, 1996); Josh King, "Creating Visuals and Presidential-Style Communications" (unpublished tract, 1998).
Copies of both tracts are available at the author's website, www.polioptics.com.

24. "Dukakis Advance Manual Title" (unpublished tract, 1988), 4.

25. David Rosenbaum, "Dukakis, at Coal Mine, Calls for Energy Policy," *New York
Times,* May 6, 1988, http://www.nytimes.com/1988/05/06/us/dukakis-at-coal-mine
-calls-for-energy-policy.html.

26. Joyce Carrier, interview by the author, September 23, 2013.

27. "Dukakis Advance Manual Title," 3.

28. Bennett, "Sterling Heights, MI *Tank Event.*"

CHAPTER 2: PLAYING WITH FIREPOWER

1. Robert Shogan, "Bush, Dukakis Victors in N.H.: Gephardt 2nd and Simon 3rd for
Democrats," *Los Angeles Times,* February 17, 1988, http://articles.latimes.com/1988
-02-17/news/mn-29372_1_paul-simon.

2. Robin Toner, "Lucky Dukakis Sits above the Fray," *New York Times,* February 15,
1988, http://www.nytimes.com/1988/02/15/us/lucky-dukakis-sits-above-the-fray
.html.

3. Ibid.

4. Bob Drogin, "Says He's Toughest on Defense: Dukakis Carries New Message to the South," *Los Angeles Times,* February 18, 1988, http://articles.latimes.com/1988-02-18/news/mn-43695_1_michael-dukakis.

5. Ibid.

6. E. J. Dionne Jr., "New York Gives Dukakis a Crucial Victory; Jackson Far Ahead of Gore, Who May Quit," *New York Times,* April 20, 1988, http://www.nytimes.com/1988/04/20/us/new-york-gives-dukakis-a-crucial-victory-jackson-far-ahead-of-gore-who-may-quit.html.

7. "Transcript of the Keynote Address by Ann Richards, the Texas Treasurer," *New York Times,* July 19, 1988, http://www.nytimes.com/1988/07/19/us/text-richards.html?pagewanted=all.

8. Ibid.

9. Video of the speech is available at "Bill Clinton's Democratic Convention Speeches," *New York Times,* September 5, 2012, http://www.nytimes.com/interactive/2012/09/05/us/politics/clinton-dnc-speeches.html?_r=0.

10. NBC, *Nightly News,* July 19, 1988, YouTube video, "Clinton Booed at Convention 1988 ElectionWallDotOrg.flv," posted by "ElectionWall.org," June 2, 2011, https://www.youtube.com/watch?v=J5FpRg3Tf9Y.

11. Ibid.

12. Harry Thomason, "Clinton's Carson Appearance," video and transcript, http://www.pbs.org/wgbh/americanexperience/features/bonus-video/clinton-carson/.

13. ABC, *World News,* July 21, 1988, YouTube video, "ABC World News July 21, 1988 Atlanta Democratic Convention Part 1," posted by "Bob Parker," May 22, 2010, https://www.youtube.com/watch?v=EDH3U8tpOSg.

14. Ibid.

15. Ibid.

16. Ibid.

17. "1988: When Bill Clinton Wouldn't Stop Talking," *National Journal,* September 3, 2012, http://news.yahoo.com/1988-bill-clinton-wouldn-t-stop-talking-162037711—politics.html.

18. A transcript of the speech, "A New Era of Greatness for America," is available from the American Presidency Project at http://www.presidency.ucsb.edu/ws/?pid=25961.

19. David Blomquist, "Dukakis Recalls a Simpler Army Life: He's in Favor of Conventional Arms," *Record* (Bergen), August 12, 1988.

20. Ben Bradlee Jr., "Dukakis Reiterates Defense Stance, Backs Conventional Systems Candidate Visits 2 Military Bases after Delivering a Speech at NYU," *Boston Globe,* August 12, 1988.

21. Ibid.

22. Bob Drogin, "Revisits Army Basic Training Site: Dukakis Seeks to Blunt GOP Defense Charges," *Los Angeles Times,* August 12, 1988.

23. Ibid.

24. Ibid.

25. Miller Center, "Interview with James P. Pinkerton," University of Virginia, February 6, 2001, http://millercenter.org/oralhistory/interview/james-pinkerton.

26. Ibid.

27. Michael Oreskes, "Bush Overtakes Dukakis in a Poll," *New York Times,* August 23, 1988, http://www.nytimes.com/1988/08/23/us/bush-overtakes-dukakis-in-a-poll.html.

28. Ibid.

29. Jim Steinberg, interview by the author, July 24, 2013.

30. Edward Walsh, "Dukakis Would Swap SDI for 'Conventional Defense Initiative,'" *Washington Post,* November 14, 1987, http://www.washingtonpost.com/archive/politics/1987/11/14/dukakis-would-swap-sdi-for-conventional-defense-initiative/52e87a80-c14e-4cc6-afde-d8f0823fdae2/.

31. Jim Steinberg, interview by the author.
32. Lewis Sorley, "The Way of the Soldier: Remembering General Creighton Abrams," Foreign Policy Research Institute, May 2013, http://www.fpri.org/articles/2013/05 /way-soldier-remembering-general-creighton-abrams.
33. Ro McGonegal, "First Test: M1 Abrams Tank," *Motor Trend,* April 1982, http://www .motortrend.com/classic/roadtests/8204_first_test_m1_abrams/viewall.html.
34. Ibid.
35. Gordon England, interview by the author, August 27, 2013.
36. Ibid.
37. Ibid.
38. Ibid.
39. Ibid.
40. Ibid.

CHAPTER 3: THIS WHOLE IDEA STINKS

1. William J. Clinton, "The President's News Conference in Lyons," June 29, 1996, online by Gerhard Peters and John T. Woolley, The American Presidency Project, http://www.presidency.ucsb.edu/ws/?pid=53011.
2. Don Baer, in discussion with the author, December 9, 2015.
3. "Dukakis Advance Manual" (unpublished tract, 1988), 2, 10.
4. Matt Bennett, "Sterling Heights, MI *Tank Event,*" unpublished journal, November 1988, 1–2.
5. Bennett, "Sterling Heights, MI *Tank Event,*" 2.
6. Joyce Carrier, interview by the author, September 23, 2013.
7. John Eades, interview by the author's assistant, Steve Silverman, September 22, 2013.
8. Bennett, "Sterling Heights, MI *Tank Event,*" 2.
9. Steven V. Roberts, "Moscow Summit; President Charms Students, but His Ideas Lack Converts," *New York Times,* June 1, 1988, http://www.nytimes.com/1988/06/01 /world/moscow-summit-president-charms-students-but-his-ideas-lack-converts .html.
10. Jim Steinberg, interview by the author, July 24, 2013.
11. Madeleine Albright, interview by the author, July 17, 2013.
12. Mindy Lubber, interview by the author's assistant, Steve Silverman, August 24, 2013.
13. Susan Estrich, interview by the author's assistant, Steve Silverman, August 24, 2013.
14. Ibid.
15. Robin Toner, "Dukakis Rehires Aide Who Left after Role in Ending Biden Drive," September 3, 1988, *New York Times,* http://www.nytimes.com/1988/09/03/us /dukakis-rehires-aide-who-left-after-role-in-ending-biden-drive.htm.
16. Mindy Lubber, interview by Steve Silverman.
17. George Skelton, "The Times Poll: Presidential Nominees in 47%-47% Dead Heat," *Los Angeles Times,* September 14, 1988, http://articles.latimes.com/1988-09-14/news /mn-1902_1_times-poll.
18. Bennett, "Sterling Heights, MI *Tank Event,*" 3.
19. Ibid.
20. Bennett, "Sterling Heights, MI *Tank Event,*" 3–4.
21. Mindy Lubber, interview by Steve Silverman.

CHAPTER 4: THE TROUBLESHOOTER

1. Matt Bennett, "Sterling Heights, MI *Tank Event,*" unpublished journal, November 1988.
2. Ibid., 3.

3. Don Gilleland, interview by the author's assistant, Steve Silverman, September 1, 2013.

4. Ibid.

5. Nick Mitropoulos, interview by the author's assistant, Steve Silverman, August 29, 2013.

6. Neal Flieger, interview by the author, July 18, 2013.

7. Andrew Rosenthal, "Dukakis Focusing on Military Policy," *New York Times,* September 12, 1988, http://www.nytimes.com/1988/09/12/us/dukakis-focusing-on-military-policy.html.

8. Kenneth J. Cooper, "National Defense Focus of Dukakis," *Philadelphia Inquirer,* September 12, 1988, http://articles.philly.com/1988-09-12/news/26232352_1_michael-s-dukakis-campaign-schedule-defense-plants.

9. Bob Drogin, "Dukakis Steps Up Attack on Bush Camp-Bahamas Ties," *Los Angeles Times,* September 11, 1988, http://articles.latimes.com/1988-09-11/news/mn-2821_1_bush-campaign.

10. Maureen Dowd, "Adviser to Bush Quits G.O.P. Post amid Anti-Semitism Allegations," *New York Times,* September 12, 1988, http://www.nytimes.com/1988/09/12/us/adviser-to-bush-quits-gop-post-amid-anti-semitism-allegations.html?pagewanted=all.

11. James Gerstenzang, "Bush Aide Who Probed 'Jewish Cabal' Resigns: Nominee Condemns Bigotry, Says He Believes Official Who Investigated for Nixon Does Too," *Los Angeles Times,* September 12, 1988, http://articles.latimes.com/1988-09-12/news/mn-1352_1_bush-campaign.

12. Robert Schnakenberg, *Crazy Sh*t Presidents Said: The Most Surprising, Shocking, and Stupid Statements Ever Made by U.S. Presidents, from George Washington to Barack Obama* (Philadelphia: Running Press, 2012), 139.

13. William M. Welch, "Reporters Call His Plane 'Sky Pig' but Dukakis Likes the Thing," Associated Press, October 1, 1988, http://www.apnewsarchive.com/198/Reporters-Call-His-Plane-Sky-Pig-But-Dukakis-Likes-the-Thing/id-00a564598fddb662122bf5b56d5e423b.

14. Andrew Rosenthal, "Dukakis Stresses Defense, Ridicules Bush and Quayle," *New York Times,* September 13, 1988, http://www.nytimes.com/1988/09/13/us/dukakis-stresses-defense-ridicules-bush-and-quayle.html.

15. John Nolan, "Pro-Bush Hecklers Drown Dukakis in a Sea of Boos," Associated Press, September 13, 1988, https://news.google.com/newspapers?nid=1696&dat=19880913&id=GioeAAAAIBAJ&sjid=BpgEAAAAIBAJ&pg=2972,2680019&hl=en.

16. Philip Lentz, "Defense Workers Jeer Dukakis," *Chicago Tribune,* September 13, 1988, http://articles.chicagotribune.com/1988-09-13/news/8801290879_1_anti-dukakis-michael-dukakis-foreign-policy.

17. Joe Lockhart, interview by the author, July 18, 2013.

18. Ibid.

19. Ibid.

20. George Condon, "Dukakis Booed—Cincinnati Defense Workers Hoot at Democrat Nominee," Copley News Service, September 13, 1988.

21. Joe Lockhart, interview by the author.

CHAPTER 5: GAME DAY

1. Matt Bennett, "Sterling Heights, MI *Tank Event*," unpublished journal, November 1988.

2. Matt Bennett, interview by the author, July 18, 2013.

3. Jack Weeks, interview by the author, August 6, 2013.

4. Ibid.

5. Ibid.
6. Bennett, "Sterling Heights, MI *Tank Event*," 3.
7. Ibid., 4.
8. Ibid.
9. Ibid.
10. Bob Drogin, "Dukakis Calls for Use of Economic Leverage on Soviets," *Los Angeles Times,* September 14, 1988, http://articles.latimes.com/1988-09-14/news/mn-19 32_1_soviet-leader.
11. Arthur Grace, *Choose Me: Portraits of a Presidential Race* (New England: University Press, 1989).
12. Arthur Grace, interview by the author, May 26, 2015.
13. Ibid.
14. Ibid.
15. Bennett, "Sterling Heights, MI *Tank Event*," 5.
16. Jack Weeks, interview by the author.
17. Bennett, "Sterling Heights, MI *Tank Event*," 5.
18. Ibid.
19. Arthur Grace, *Choose Me,* 94.
20. Madeleine Albright, interview by the author, July 17, 2013.
21. Ibid.
22. Joe Lockhart, interview by the author, July 18, 2013.
23. Nick Mitropoulos, interview by the author's assistant, Steve Silverman, August 29, 2013.
24. Bennett, "Sterling Heights, MI *Tank Event*," 5.
25. One notable example of the protocol being suspended was in 2003, when George W. Bush flew from San Diego to the deck of the USS *Abraham Lincoln* in the copilot's seat in the cockpit of an SB-3 Viking.
26. Arthur Grace, *Choose Me,* 100.
27. Jack Weeks, interview by the author.
28. Ibid.
29. Bennett, "Sterling Heights, MI *Tank Event*," 6.
30. Arthur Grace, interview by the author.
31. Bennett, "Sterling Heights, MI *Tank Event*," 6.

CHAPTER 6: A STORY WITH LEGS

1. Ronald Reagan, "The Boys of Pointe du Hoc," speech, June 6, 1984, YouTube video, posted by "ReaganFoundation," April 16, 2009, https://www.youtube.com/watch?v=eEIqdcHbc8I.
2. Bill Clinton to Colonel Eugene Holmes, December 3, 1969, http://www.pbs.org/wgbh/pages/frontline/shows/clinton/etc/draftletter.html.
3. Congressional Medal of Honor Society, citation for Walter D. Ehlers, December 19, 1944, http://www.cmohs.org/recipient-detail/2724/ehlers-walter-d.php.
4. Karen Ball, unpublished pool report in author's collection, June 6, 1994.
5. Ibid.
6. Ibid.
7. Maureen Dowd, "On Washington; Beached," *New York Times Magazine,* June 19, 1994, http://www.nytimes.com/1994/06/19/magazine/on-washington-beached.html.
8. Michael Kelly, "The President's Past," *New York Times Magazine,* July 31, 1994, http://www.nytimes.com/1994/07/31/magazine/the-president-s-past.html?pagewanted=all.
9. Matt Bennett, "Sterling Heights, MI *Tank Event*," unpublished journal, November 1988, 6.

10. Joe Lockhart, interview by the author, July 18, 2013.
11. Jim Irwin, "Dukakis Jockeys Tank, Vows to Beef Up Conventional Weapons," Associated Press Political Service, September 13, 1988.
12. Ibid.
13. Ibid.
14. Bob Drogin, "Dukakis Calls for Use of Economic Leverage on Soviets," *Los Angeles Times,* September 14, 1988, http://articles.latimes.com/1988-09-14/news/mn -1932_1_soviet-leader.
15. Bob Drogin, "How Presidential Race Was Won and Lost: Michael S. Dukakis," *Los Angeles Times,* November 10, 1988, http://articles.latimes.com/1988-11-10/news/mn -299_1_dukakis-lost-reelection.
16. Drogin, "Dukakis Calls for Use of Economic Leverage on Soviets."
17. Ibid.
18. Bernard Weinraub, "Campaign Trail; Loaded for Bear and Then Some," *New York Times,* September 14, 1988, http://www.nytimes.com/1988/09/14/us/campaign -trail-loaded-for-bear-and-then-some.html.
19. Ibid.
20. Pew Research Center, "Network TV: Evening News Overall Viewership since 1980," http://www.journalism.org/media-indicators/network-tv-evening-news-overall-view ership-since-1980/.
21. Tom Brokaw, *Nightly News,* NBC, September 13, 1988. All further references to this segment are drawn from a video of the broadcast in the author's private collection.

CHAPTER 7: TANK YOU VERY MUCH

1. Mindy Lubber, interview by the author's assistant, Steve Silverman, August 24, 2013.
2. Ibid.
3. Rich Bond, interview by the author, September 11, 2013.
4. Ibid.
5. David Demarest, interview by the author, September 12, 2013.
6. David Demarest, "Line of the Day," September 14, 1988.
7. David Demarest, "Line of the Day," September 15, 1988.
8. Bill Peterson, "Bush Says Rival Can't 'Fool' Voters on Defense," *Washington Post,* September 17, 1988, https://www.washingtonpost.com/archive/politics/1988/09/17/bus h-says-rival-cant-fool-voters-on-defense/5e84110e-3df1-4209-bcde-697f6409edb1/.
9. Ibid.
10. Christine Chinlund, "Bush Takes Aim at Dukakis' Message on Defense," *Boston Globe,* September 17, 1988, http://www.highbeam.com/doc/1P2-8079424.html.
11. Editorial, *State-Journal Register* (Springfield, IL), September 18, 1988.
12. Ibid.
13. Rowland Evans and Robert Novak, "Why Dukakis Is Down," *Washington Post,* September 19, 1988, https://www.washingtonpost.com/archive/opinions/1988/09/19 /why-dukakis-is-down/8743d0c8-d101-4a9e-a01b-0b52bd7dc5c0/.
14. Associated Press, "Poll Indicates Dukakis Lost Ground with Tank Ride," September 20, 1988.
15. Maralee Schwartz, "An Image-Making Flop," *Washington Post,* September 21, 1988.
16. Lois Romano, "Chris Edley, Issues and Images," *Washington Post,* September 21, 1988, https://www.washingtonpost.com/archive/lifestyle/1988/09/21/chris-edley-issues -and-images/1af32485-f75e-4be4-bd46-094b0bc2ca11/.
17. Kiku Adatto, *Picture Perfect: Life in the Age of the Photo Op* (Princeton, NJ: Princeton University Press, 2008), 89.
18. Museum of the Moving Image, *The Living Room Candidate: Presidential Campaign Commercials: 1952–2012* (online exhibition), "Revolving Door," 1988, http://www .livingroomcandidate.org/commercials/1988/revolving-door.

19. Sig Rogich, interview by the author, September 10, 2013.
20. Ibid.
21. Rich Bond, interview by the author.
22. Museum of the Moving Image, *The Living Room Candidate: Presidential Campaign Commercials: 1952–2012* (online exhibition), "Tank Ride," 1988, http://www.living roomcandidate.org/commercials/1988/tank-ride.
23. Sig Rogich, interview by the author.
24. David Hoffman, "Bush Pushes 'Peace through Strength,'" *Washington Post,* October 19, 1988, https://www.washingtonpost.com/archive/politics/1988/10/19/bush-push es-peace-through-strength/787c50e2-c4c2-4c82-a768-ce2a3d940681/.
25. Jeremy Gerard, "All-California World Series Poses Difficulties for NBC," *New York Times,* October 15, 1988, http://www.nytimes.com/1988/10/15/business/all -california-world-series-poses-difficulties-for-nbc.html.
26. Chris Black, "Tank Gives Dukakis No Protection in Bush's Latest Commercial Attack," *Boston Globe,* October 19, 1988.
27. Jill Lawrence, "Bush to Use Dukakis' Tank Ride in Commercials; Dukakis Counters with Drug Ad," Associated Press, October 18, 1988.
28. Lloyd Grove, "TV News, Ad Images Melding," *Washington Post,* October 20, 1988, https://www.washingtonpost.com/archive/politics/1988/10/20/tv-news-ad-images -melding/5d9ddea9-c6ac-4fa7-84d5-001c51144442/.
29. Ibid.
30. Museum of the Moving Image, *The Living Room Candidate: Presidential Campaign Commercials: 1952–2012* (online exhibition), "Counterpunch," 1988, http://www .livingroomcandidate.org/commercials/1988/counterpunch.
31. Bret Schulte, "Michael Dukakis: The Photo Op That Tanked; QA with Michael Dukakis," *U.S. News & World Report,* January 17, 2008, http://www.usnews.com /news/articles/2008/01/17/the-photo-op-that-tanked.
32. Matt Bennett, interview by the author, July 18, 2013.
33. Michael Dukakis, email message to author, July 9, 2013.

CHAPTER 8: HISTORY REPEATS ITSELF

1. Sarah Watts, *Rough Rider in the White House: Theodore Roosevelt and the Politics of Desire* (Chicago: University of Chicago Press, 2003), 169.
2. Margaret Garrard Warner, "George Bush Battles the 'Wimp Factor,'" *Newsweek,* October 19, 1987, http://www.newsweek.com/bush-battles-wimp-factor-207008.
3. George W. Bush, *Decision Points* (New York: Crown Publishers, 2010), 44.
4. Jeff Greenfield, *Then Everything Changed: Stunning Alternate Histories of American Politics* (New York: G. P. Putnam's Sons, 2011). Citation retrieved from Google Books.
5. Matt Bai, *All the Truth Is Out: The Week Politics Went Tabloid* (New York: Knopf Doubleday Publishing Group, 2014), 88–90.
6. George Santayana, *The Life of Reason,* vol. 1, *Reason in Common Sense* (New York, Charles Scribner's Sons, 1905), 284.
7. Mike Moore, "Water Boarding: History Repeats Itself," *Green Valley News* (AZ), December 13, 2014, http://www.gvnews.com/opinion/columns/water-boarding-history -repeats-itself/article_7bc4d874-8318-11e4-860c-1b60a91b2f69.html.
8. "Reagan-Carter Oct. 28, 1980 Debate—'There You Go Again,'" YouTube video, posted by "MCamericanpresident," September 25, 2012, https://www.youtube.com /watch?v=qN7gDRjTNf4.
9. "Debate between the President and Former Vice President Walter F. Mondale in Kansas City, Missouri," Ronald Reagan Presidential Foundation and Library, video, http://www.reaganfoundation.org/reagan-quotes-detail.aspx?tx=2238.
10. Glenn Garvin, "Hatchet Job: Roger Stone's Edgy Takes on History and Politics," *Miami Herald,* October 14, 2014, http://www.miamiherald.com/news/local/com munity/miami-dade/article2766816.html.

11. Rachel Muir, "Saving the President," *George Washington Today,* June 30, 2010, https://gwtoday.gwu.edu/saving-president.

12. PBS, "Carter's 'Crisis of Confidence' Speech," http://www.pbs.org/wgbh/american experience/features/general-article/carter-crisis-speech/.

13. Howell Raines, "Party Nominates Rep. Ferraro; Mondale, in Acceptance, Vows Fair Policies and Deficit Cut," *New York Times,* July 20, 1984, https://partners.nytimes.com/library/politics/camp/840720convention-dem-ra.html.

14. Kathleen Hall Jamieson, *Packaging the Presidency: A History and Criticism of Presidential Campaign Advertising* (New York: Oxford University Press, 1984), 448.

15. Tim Craig and Michael D. Shear, "Allen Quip Provokes Outrage, Apology," *Washington Post,* August 15, 2006, http://www.washingtonpost.com/wp-dyn/content/article/2006/08/14/AR2006081400589.html.

16. Julie Millican, "In Reporting Allen's Use of Derogatory North African Word 'Macaca,' Most Major Media Outlets Ignored Allen's Familial Ties to Region," Media Matters for America, August 16, 2006, http://mediamatters.org/research/2006/08/16/in-reporting-allens-use-of-derogatory-north-afr/136408.

17. Jonathan Martin, "Senator's Thesis Turns Out to Be Remix of Others' Works, Uncited," *New York Times,* July 23, 2014, http://www.nytimes.com/2014/07/24/us/politics/montana-senator-john-walsh-plagiarized-thesis.html?_r=2.

18. Chris Matthews, *Hardball,* MSNBC, July 24, 2014, video and transcript, https://grabien.com/file.php?id=22036.

19. Yahoo News, "Sen. John Walsh Responds to Plagiarism Revelations," July 25, 2014, http://news.yahoo.com/video/exclusive-sen-john-walsh-responds-211044638.html.

20. Marisa Schultz, "GOP Researcher Responsible for Exposing Montana Senator," *New York Post,* October 30, 2014, http://nypost.com/2014/10/30/gop-researcher-responsible-for-exposing-montana-senator/.

21. Jon Terbush, "14 Things Shorter Than Chris Christie's Epic Press Conference over Bridgegate," *The Week,* January 9, 2014, http://theweek.com/article/index/254922/14-things-shorter-than-chris-christies-epic-press-conference-over-bridgegate.

22. Liz Kreutz, "Hillary Clinton Defends High-Dollar Speaking Fees," *ABC News,* June 9, 2014, http://abcnews.go.com/Politics/hillary-clinton-defends-high-dollar-speaking-fees/story?id=24052962.

23. Jorge Ramos, "Hillary Clinton Regrets Saying She Was 'Dead Broke,' Feels Blessed by Success," *Fusion,* July 28, 2014, http://fusion.net/video/3268/hillary-clinton-regrets-saying-she-was-dead-broke-feels-blessed-by-success/.

CHAPTER 9: 1992: BUSH AND THE SUPERMARKET SCANNER

1. Colonel Jerald H. Narum to Justin McCarthy, December 8, 2014, Judicial Watch, http://www.judicialwatch.org/document-archive/obama-california-cover-letter/.

2. Andrew Rosenthal, "Bush Encounters the Supermarket, Amazed," *New York Times,* February 5, 1992, http://www.nytimes.com/1992/02/05/us/bush-encounters-the-supermarket-amazed.html.

3. Rachel Maddow, *The Rachel Maddow Show,* MSNBC, February 11, 2015, transcript, http://www.nbcnews.com/id/56990292/ns/msnbc-rachel_maddow_show/t/rachel-maddow-show-wednesday-february-th/.

4. Associated Press, "Former President George H. W. Bush Marks 90th Birthday with Parachute Jump," June 12, 2014, http://www.foxnews.com/politics/2014/06/12/0-year-old-ex-president-to-make-parachute-jump/.

5. Naval History and Heritage Command, "George Herbert Walker Bush, 12 June 1924–," biography, http://www.history.navy.mil/research/histories/bios/bush-george-h-w.html.

6. Michael Kramer, "George Bush: A Republican for All Factions," *New York,* January 21, 1980.

7. Associated Press, "Former President George H. W. Bush Marks 90th Birthday with Parachute Jump," June 12, 2014.

8. Kevin Bohn, "George H. W. Bush on Bonding with Bill Clinton," CNN, March 5, 2013, http://politicalticker.blogs.cnn.com/2013/03/05/george-h-w-bush-on-bond ing-with-bill-clinton/.

9. Maureen Dowd, "The 1992 Campaign: News Analysis; A No-Nonsense Sort of Talk Show," *New York Times,* October 16, 1992, http://www.nytimes.com/1992/10/16 /us/the-1992-campaign-news-analysis-a-no-nonsense-sort-of-talk-show.html.

10. Associated Press, "Bush, Clinton Tour Tsunami-Hit Areas of Sri Lanka," February 21, 2005, http://usatoday30.usatoday.com/news/world/2005-02-21-presidents -tsunami_x.htm.

11. Michael Wines, "Bush Toll: Memories Lost to Sea," *New York Times,* November 3, 1991, http://www.nytimes.com/1991/11/03/us/bush-toll-memories-lost-to-sea .html.

12. Lauren Sullivan, "George H. W. Bush: Shaving Head Was 'Right Thing to Do,'" *Today,* July 26, 2013, http://www.today.com/news/george-h-w-bush-shaving-head-was -right-thing-do-6C10760866.

13. Michael Kelly, "The Democrats—Clinton and Bush Compete to Be Champion of Change; Democrat Fights Perceptions of Bush Gain," *New York Times,* October 31, 1992, http://www.nytimes.com/1992/10/31/us/1992-campaign-democrats-clinton -bush-compete-be-champion-change-democrat-fights.html.

14. George Herbert Walker Bush diary, January 9, 1992; ATB 545, as noted in Jon Meacham, *Destiny and Power: The American Odyssey of George Herbert Walker Bush,* 495.

15. Adam Clymer, "Little on Its Agenda, Congress Plays Wait-and-See as New Session Starts," *New York Times,* January 3, 1992, http://www.nytimes.com/1992/01/03/us /little-on-its-agenda-congress-plays-wait-and-see-as-new-session-starts.html.

16. U.S. Constitution, Article II, Section 3, http://constitutioncenter.org/interactive -constitution/articles/article-ii#section-2.

17. Marlin Fitzwater, "Regular Press Briefing," Federal News Service, February 2, 1992.

18. Jonah Goldberg, "The Supermarket Scanner Story Cont'd," *National Review,* August 22, 2008, http://www.nationalreview.com/corner/167613/supermarket-scanner -story-contd-jonah-goldberg.

19. Marlin Fitzwater, *Call the Briefing!: A Memoir: Ten Years in the White House with Presidents Reagan and Bush* (Xlibris, 2000), 328.

20. William Neikirk, "No More Racial Conflict, Clinton Implores," *Chicago Tribune,* June 13, 1996, http://articles.chicagotribune.com/1996-06-13/news/9606130291_1 _church-burnings-new-church-president-clinton.

21. Goldberg, "The Supermarket Scanner Story Cont'd."

22. Ibid.

23. Fitzwater, *Call the Briefing!,* 329.

24. Ibid.

25. Andrew Rosenthal, email message to author, April 14, 2015.

26. Joel Brinkley, "On Tape, a President Intrigued by Scanner," *New York Times,* February 13, 1992, http://www.nytimes.com/1992/02/13/us/on-tape-a-president-itrigued -by-a-scanner.html.

27. Ibid.

28. Brit Hume, "The Bush Crack-Up," *American Spectator,* January 1993, http://www .unz.org/Pub/AmSpectator-1993jan-00022.

29. Andrew Rosenthal, email message to author.

30. Fitzwater, *Call the Briefing!,* 330.

31. Ibid., 331.

32. Christopher Connell, "White House Has Media Rescanning the Scanner Caper," Associated Press, February 11, 1992, http://www.apnewsarchive.com/1992/White-Ho

use-Has-Media-Rescanning-the-Scanner-Caper/id-cc3b1c1ec1b56bfe1b96af7a90
bda19b.

33. Goldberg, "The Supermarket Scanner Story Cont'd."
34. Howard Kurtz, "The Story That Just Won't Check Out," *Washington Post,* February 19, 1992, https://www.washingtonpost.com/archive/lifestyle/1992/02/19/the-story -that-just-wont-check-out/65ede30f-9469-4205-9745-c646208c372f/.
35. Robert Scheer, "So Long, Poppy," *Playboy,* November 1, 1992.
36. Hume, "The Bush Crack-Up."

CHAPTER 10: 1996: DOLE'S PRECIPITOUS FALL

1. Kent Gray, interview by the author, February 21, 2015.
2. Ceci Connolly, "Age Question Growing Old for Bob Dole," *Washington Post,* July 22, 1995.
3. Kent Gray, interview by the author.
4. Ibid.
5. Spencer S. Hsu and Susan B. Glasser, "FEMA Director Singled Out by Response Critics," *Washington Post,* September 6, 2005, http://www.washingtonpost.com/wp -dyn/content/article/2005/09/05/AR2005090501590.html.
6. Michael Wines, "'Hatchet Man' Image Must Stay Buried: Dole Walks Fine Line in Attacking Bush,'" *Los Angeles Times,* January 10, 1988, http://articles.latimes.com/19 88-01-10/news/mn-34762_1_hatchet-man.
7. Carl M. Cannon, "Clinton, Strauss Lay on Charm at Dole Dinner," *Baltimore Sun,* July 2, 1993, http://articles.baltimoresun.com/1993-07-02/news/1993183037 _1_bob-strauss-bob-dole-clinton.
8. Susan Page, "The Kiddie Corps; Critics Say Youthful Clinton Staff Lacks Savvy, Stature," *Newsday* (New York), May 23, 1993.
9. Ruth Shalit, "Uncle Bob," *New York Times Magazine,* March 15, 1995, http://www .nytimes.com/1995/03/05/magazine/uncle-bob.html?pagewanted=all.
10. Mike Feinsliber, "Loyal Lieutenant Tries Again to Be President," Associated Press, March 28, 1995.
11. Tom Raum, "Dole Accuses Clinton of Making Light of Drug Use, Proposes New Slogan," Associated Press, September 18, 1996.
12. Ibid.
13. Ibid.
14. Tom Raum, "Dole Urges Media to Help Focus Attention on Drug Abuse," Associated Press, September 19, 1996.
15. Adam Nagourney, "Attacking Drugs, Dole Takes on Entertainment Industry," *New York Times,* September 19, 1996, http://www.nytimes.com/1996/09/19/us/att acking-drugs-dole-takes-on-entertainment-industry.html.
16. Ken Bazinet, "Dole Jokes about Fall, Knocks Clinton," United Press International, September 19, 1996, http://www.upi.com/Archives/1996/09/19/Dole-jokes -about-fall-knocks-Clinton/7572843105600/.
17. Kent Gray, interview by the author.
18. Ibid.
19. Bazinet, "Dole Jokes about Fall, Knocks Clinton."
20. Maria L. La Granga, "Dole Balances Virtue, Vice between the Valley, Vegas," *Los Angeles Times,* September 19, 1996, http://articles.latimes.com/1996-09-19/news/m n-45320_1_bob-dole.
21. Kent Gray, interview by the author.
22. Ibid.
23. Raum, "Dole Urges Media to Help Focus Attention on Drug Abuse."
24. Curt Anderson, "Dole Jokes about Fall; Says He Was Trying to Do Macarena," Associated Press, September 19, 1996.

25. Peter Wilson, "Dole's Campaign Takes a Tumble," *Australian,* September 20, 1996.

26. Mark Dowdney, "It's Dole Over Now; Fall Dashes Poll Hopes; Bob Dole in Election Campaign Stage Fall," *Daily Mirror,* September 20, 1996.

27. Maria L. La Ganga and John Broder, "Dole's Tumble Sends His Aides Spinning," *Los Angeles Times,* September 20, 1996, http://articles.latimes.com/1996-09-20 /news/mn-45687_1_bob-dole.

28. Iver Peterson, "Get the Picture?; Sometimes, Being a News Photographer Is No Snap," *New York Times News Service,* September 21, 1996.

29. Ibid.

30. Lloyd Grove, "The Fall Guy," *Washington Post,* September 20, 1996, https://www .washingtonpost.com/archive/lifestyle/1996/09/20/the-fall-guy/e6fa79be-981d-47f b-8b1f-e2cb046ffdc0/.

31. Ibid.

32. Ibid.

CHAPTER 11: 2000: GORE FLOATS INTO "FLOODGATE"

1. Joe Klein, *Politics Lost: From RFK to W: How Politicians Have Become Less Courageous and More Interested in Keeping Power Than in Doing What's Right for America* (New York: Broadway Books, 2006), 141.

2. Evgenia Peretz, "Going After Gore," *Vanity Fair,* October 2007, http://www.vanity fair.com/news/2007/10/gore200710.

3. Ibid.

4. "Transcript: Vice President Gore on CNN's 'Late Edition,'" CNN, March 9, 1999, http://www.cnn.com/ALLPOLITICS/stories/1999/03/09/president.2000/tran script.gore/.

5. Peretz, "Going After Gore."

6. Eric Boehlert, "The Press v. Al Gore," *Rolling Stone,* December 6, 2001, http://www .angelfire.com/indie/pearly/htmls/gore-nightmare.html; Peretz, "Going After Gore."

7. Paul Waldman, "Gored by the Media Bull," *American Prospect,* December 17, 2002, http://prospect.org/article/gored-media-bull.

8. Michael Feldman, interview by the author, April 4, 2015.

9. Ibid.

10. Ann Devroy, "Bush, Clinton Begin Finish Line Sprint," *Washington Post,* October 30, 1992, https://www.washingtonpost.com/archive/politics/1992/10/30/bush-clinton -begin-finish-line-sprint/54661c19-2cfa-4230-8c3c-65928ca69fe9/.

11. Al Gore, introduction to *Silent Spring,* by Rachel Carson (Boston: Houghton Mifflin, 1994); Al Gore, *Earth in the Balance: Ecology and the Human Spirit* (Boston: Houghton Mifflin, 1992).

12. Michael Feldman, interview by the author.

13. NOAA National Centers for Environmental Information, "State of the Climate: Drought for Summer (JJA) 1999," September 1999, http://www.ncdc.noaa.gov/sotc /drought/199916.

14. Abigail Radnor, "A Toddler in the Oval Office," *The Times* (UK), February 2, 2013, http://www.thetimes.co.uk/tto/magazine/article3670510.ece.

15. The White House, Office of the Vice President, "Vice President Gore Announces $819,000 to Enhance Connecticut River, Surrounding Communities," press release, July 22, 1999, http://clinton4.nara.gov/CEQ/990722.html.

16. Ann S. Kim, "Gore Points to Rivers as Environment-Economic Link," Associated Press, July 22, 1999.

17. Nathan Naylor, interview by the author, August 14, 2015.

18. Matt Bennett, interview by the author, March 11, 2015.

19. Katharine Webster, "Agency Says No Extra Water Released for Gore," Associated Press, July 26, 1999.

20. Matt Bennett, interview by the author.

21. "Al Gore's Candidacy Speech in Full," *Guardian,* June 16, 1999, http://www.the
     guardian.com/world/1999/jun/16/uselections2000.usa1.

22. Katharine Q. Seelye, "Gore Terms Clinton Affair 'Inexcusable,'" *New York Times,*
     June 16, 1999, http://www.nytimes.com/1999/06/16/us/gore-terms-clinton-affair-in
     excusable.html.

23. Maureen Dowd, "Liberties; Here Comes the Son," *New York Times,* October 6, 1999,
     http://www.nytimes.com/1999/10/06/opinion/liberties-here-comes-the-son.html.

24. Maureen Dowd, "Liberties; Freudian Face-Off," *New York Times,* June 16, 1999,
     http://www.nytimes.com/1999/06/16/opinion/liberties-freudian-face-off.html.

25. Ibid.

26. Michael Feldman, interview by the author, April 4, 2015.

27. Nathan Naylor, interview by the author.

28. Ann S. Kim, "Gore Says Environmental Concerns and Economic Progress Go To-
     gether," Associated Press, July 22, 1999.

29. Susan Feeney, "Gore Seeks Edge in Campaign with Environment Issue; He Says
     Protections, Growth Linked," *Dallas Morning News,* July 23, 1999.

30. Sandra Sobieraj, "Gore Picking 'Green' Fight in Presidential Race," Associated Press,
     July 22, 1999.

31. Bill Sammon and Laura R. Vanderham, "New Hampshire Opts to Float Gore's Boat;
     4 Billion Gallons Released for Photo Outing," *Washington Times,* July 23, 1999.

32. Ibid.

33. Nathan Naylor, interview by the author.

34. Sammon and Vanderham, "New Hampshire Opts to Float Gore's Boat."

35. Ibid.

36. Ibid.

37. Ibid.

38. Michael Feldman, interview by the author.

39. Ibid.

40. Associated Press, "Special Dam Release to Keep Gore's Canoe Afloat," July 23, 1999.

41. "Controversy Muddies Gore Float Trip," *Atlanta Journal and Constitution,* July 24,
     1999.

42. Melinda Henneberger, "Gore Takes Aw-Shucks Tour (and Hits a Bump)," *New York
     Times,* July 24, 1999, http://www.nytimes.com/1999/07/24/us/gore-takes-aw-shu
     cks-tour-and-hits-a-bump.html.

43. Jill Zuckman, "Gore's N.H. Canoe Trip Leaves Questions in Wake," *Boston Globe,*
     July 24, 1999.

44. Henneberger, "Gore Takes Aw-Shucks Tour (and Hits a Bump)."

45. Brian Blomquist, "Critics Paddle Gore in 'Dam' Rowing Row," *New York Post,* July
     24, 1999, http://nypost.com/1999/07/24/critics-paddle-gore-in-dam-rowing-row/.

46. Webster, "Agency Says No Extra Released for Gore."

47. Ann S. Kim, "New Hampshire GOP Chairman Files FEC Complaint Against Gore,"
     Associated Press, August 5, 1999.

48. Bill Sammon, "Raising of River Is News to Gore; Was Told at Scene Official Coun-
     ters," *Washington Times,* July 24, 1999.

49. Webster, "Agency Says No Extra Released for Gore."

50. Dan Balz, "Gore, Bradley and the Soft-Money Shootout," *Washington Post,* July
     25, 1999, https://www.washingtonpost.com/archive/politics/1999/07/25/politics/c9
     8a2e8b-e425-4a8f-bbeb-eb7f16696df7/.

51. Howard Fineman, "A War Over Who Controls the Left," *Newsweek,* August 8, 1999,
     http://www.newsweek.com/war-over-who-controls-left-165820.

52. Republican National Committee, "Team Gore Keeps Water Story Flowing; 'It Was
     Only 27,000 Gallons Every Second—Not 180,000,' Say Veep's Defenders," PR
     Newswire, July 29, 1999.

53. Bill Sammon, "N.H. Dam Worked Overtime, Papers Say; Gore Can't Shake 'Flood-gate' Story," *Washington Times,* August 2, 1999.

54. Ibid.

55. Peretz, "Going After Gore."

56. Matt Bennett, interview by the author, March 11, 2015.

57. Michael Feldman, interview by the author.

CHAPTER 12: 2004: BUSH, DEAN AND KERRY

1. Pew Research Center, "In Changing News Landscape, Even Television Is Vulnerable: Trends in News Consumption: 1991–2012," September 27, 2012, http://www.people-press.org/2012/09/27/in-changing-news-landscape-even-television-is-vulnerable/.

2. Bob Woodward, *Bush at War* (New York: Simon & Schuster, 2002). Citation retrieved from Google Books.

3. "One Nation, Indivisible," *Time,* September 24, 2001, http://content.time.com/time/magazine/0,9263,7601010924,00.html.

4. "Senator John Kerry Meets with Veterans at Marshall University," *ABC News,* March 16, 2004, video and transcript, http://www.aparchive.com/metadata/Senator-John-Kerry-meets-with-Veterans-at-Marshall-University/a7b459101bbd46089dcdcfe9f04a8d27?query=MIDDLE+EAST.

5. I had a similar experience during a two-night stay aboard the *USS George Washington* in 1993 while on a site-scouting trip for future presidential visits.

6. M. L. Lyke, "Commander in Chief's Visit Sets Aircraft Carrier's Crew Abuzz," *Seattle Post-Intelligencer,* May 1, 2003, http://www.seattlepi.com/news/article/Commander-in-chief-s-visit-sets-aircraft-1113821.php.

7. Maureen Dowd, "The Iceman Cometh," *New York Times,* May 4, 2003, http://www.nytimes.com/2003/05/04/opinion/the-iceman-cometh.html.

8. Brian Williams, *The News with Brian Williams,* MSNBC, May 2, 2003, video in author's private collection.

9. Ibid.

10. Ibid.

11. Elisabeth Bumiller, "Two Words on a Banner That No Author Wants to Claim," *New York Times,* November 3, 2003, http://www.nytimes.com/2003/11/03/national/03LETT.html.

12. "Press Briefing by Ari Fleischer," July 1, 2003, online by Gerhard Peters and John T. Woolley, *The American Presidency,* http://www.presidency.ucsb.edu/ws/?pid=61118; White House, Office of the Press Secretary, "Press Briefing by Scott McClellan," October 29, 2003, http://georgewbush-whitehouse.archives.gov/news/releases/2003/10/20031029-2.html.

13. "Bush's 'Bannergate' Shuffle," *Time,* November 1, 2003, http://content.time.com/time/nation/article/0,8599,536170,00.html.

14. "Secretary of Defense Donald Rumsfeld Interviews with Mr. Bob Woodward—July 6 and 7, 2006," transcript, October 2, 2006, https://cryptome.org/bob-v-don.htm.

15. Scott Sforza, interview by Adam Belmar and Josh King, *Polioptics,* podcast, episode 26, September 17, 2011, http://www.polioptics.com/2011/09/episode-26-the-producers-part-1-steve-rabinowitz-and-scott-sforza-directors-of-productions-for-presidents-clinton-and-bush/.

16. Jon Stewart, *Daily Show,* Comedy Central, May 5, 2008, http://www.cc.com/video-clips/4f2vjl/the-daily-show-with-jon-stewart-intro—apology-de-mayo.

17. George W. Bush, interview by Heidi Collins, "Bush Recalls Regrettable, Proudest Moments," CNN, November 11, 2008, http://edition.cnn.com/2008/POLITICS/11/11/bush.transcript/index.html?iref=24hours.

18. Howard Dean, "The Great American Restoration," June 23, 2003, http://www.gwu.edu/~action/2004/dean/dean062303/dean062303spt.html.

19. Beau Willimon, interview by Josh King, *Polioptics,* podcast, episode 92, March 9, 2013, http://www.polioptics.com/2013/03/episode-92-with-guests-beau-willimon-and-r-j-cutler/.

20. "The Dean Scream: Howard Dean's Infamous Scream Following the 2004 Iowa Caucus," C-SPAN, August 1, 2012, http://www.c-span.org/video/?c3602686/dean-scream.

21. Blake Morrison, "Dean Scream Gaining Cultlike Status on Web," *USA Today,* January 21, 2004, http://usatoday30.usatoday.com/news/politicselections/nation/2004-01-22-dean-usat_x.htm.

22. "Howard Dean's Scream—The Original," YouTube video, posted by "Save DemocracyNow," March 5, 2010, https://www.youtube.com/watch?v=-3Meg3CEyUM.

23. Beau Willimon, interview by Josh King, *Polioptics.*

24. Ibid.

25. Ibid.

26. Ibid.

27. Howard Dean, interview by Dave Weigel, *WeigelCast,* podcast, episode 1, March 16, 2014, http://www.slate.com/articles/podcasts/weigelcast/2014/03/dave_weigel_interviews_howard_dean_for_slate_s_new_weigelcast_podcast.html.

28. "2004: The Scream That Doomed Howard Dean," YouTube video, posted by "CNN," July 31, 2013, https://www.youtube.com/watch?v=l6i-gYRAwM0.

29. Howard Dean, interview by Dave Weigel, *WeigelCast.*

30. David Martosko, "Howard Dean Re-Enacts His Infamous 'I Have a Scream' Speech in Support of New York City Mayoral Candidate," *Daily Mail,* July 23, 2013, http://www.dailymail.co.uk/news/article-2375414/Howard-Dean-enacts-infamous-I-scream-speech-support-New-York-City-mayoral-candidate.html.

31. "Democratic National Convention, Day 4 Afternoon," C-SPAN, video and transcript, September 27, 2012, http://www.c-span.org/video/?c3986448/clip-democratic-national-convention-day-4-afternoon.

32. Thomas Oliphant, "I Watched John Kerry Throw His War Decorations," *Boston Globe,* April 27, 2004, http://www.boston.com/news/globe/editorial_opinion/oped/articles/2004/04/27/i_watched_kerry_throw_his_war_decorations/.

33. "First Read," *NBC News,* daily memo, August 30, 2004, http://www.nbcnews.com/id/5860672/ns/politics-first_read/.

34. Ibid.

35. David Morehouse, interview by the author, August 24, 2013.

36. James Hebert, "Comedians Elect to Skewer Candidates," *San Diego Union-Tribune,* November 1, 2004, http://legacy.utsandiego.com/uniontrib/20041101/news_1c1jokes.html.

37. "Comedy on the Campaign Trail," Associated Press, September 1, 2004, http://archive.11alive.com/news/article/51318/0/Comedy-on-the-Campaign-Trail.

38. Stephen Robinson, "Gloves Come Off as Renegade Senator Picks Up Bludgeon," *Telegraph,* September 3, 2004, http://www.telegraph.co.uk/news/worldnews/northamerica/usa/1470919/Gloves-come-off-as-renegade-senator-picks-up-bludgeon.html.

39. *Crossfire,* CNN, transcript, September 2, 2004, http://www.cnn.com/TRANSCRIPTS/0409/02/cf.01.html.

40. Kate Zernike, "Who Among Us Does Not Like Windsurfing?" *New York Times,* September 5, 2004, http://www.nytimes.com/2004/09/05/weekinreview/who-among-us-does-not-love-windsurfing.html?_r=1.

41. R. W. Apple Jr., "Conditions in Ohio Point to Kerry, but Bush Runs Strong," *New York Times,* September 12, 2004, http://www.nytimes.com/2004/09/12/politics/campaign/conditions-in-ohio-point-to-kerry-but-bush-runs-strong.html.

42. Maureen Dowd, "Westerns and Easterns," *New York Times,* September 12, 2004, http://www.nytimes.com/2004/09/12/opinion/westerns-and-easterns.html.

43. Anne E. Kornblut, "Bush Ad Plays on Kerry Windsurfing; Senator's Camp Calls Commercial 'Shameful,' Responds with Its Own," *Boston Globe,* September 23, 2004, http://www.boston.com/news/nation/articles/2004/09/23/bush_ad_plays_on _kerry_windsurfing/?page=full.

44. Mark McKinnon, interview by the author, April 9, 2015.

45. Karl Rove, *Courage and Consequence: My Life as a Conservative in the Fight* (New York: Simon & Schuster, 2010), 380.

46. Mark McKinnon, interview by the author.

47. Ibid.

48. Ibid.

49. Russ Schriefer, interview by the author, April 17, 2015.

50. Museum of the Moving Image, *The Living Room Candidate: Presidential Campaign Commercials 1952–2012,* online exhibition, "Windsurfing," 2004, http://www .livingroomcandidate.org/commercials/2004/windsurfing.

51. Mark McKinnon, interview by the author.

52. Ibid.

53. Russ Schriefer, interview by the author, April 17, 2015.

54. Howard Kurtz, "Presidential Attack Ads Move from Land to Water—and Back," *Washington Post,* September 23, 2004, http://www.washingtonpost.com/wp-dyn /articles/A43098-2004Sep22.html.

55. Vince Morris, "Bush A-Tack Ad; Sailing TV Spot Calls Foe Flip-Ant," *New York Post,* September 23, 2004, http://nypost.com/2004/09/23/bush-a-tack-ad-sailing-tv -spot-calls-foe-flip-ant/.

56. Mark McKinnon, interview by the author.

57. Jake Miller, "John Kerry on His Boat during Egypt Upheaval, State Dept. Concedes," *CBS News,* July 6, 2013, http://www.cbsnews.com/news/john-kerry-on-his -boat-during-egypt-upheaval-state-dept-concedes/.

CHAPTER 13: 2008: MCCAIN GOES GREEN

1. John McCain with Mark Salter, *Faith of My Fathers* (New York: Random House, 1999), 3.

2. McCain, *Faith of My Fathers,* 9.

3. "NH Primary Vault: Architect of John McCain's Blowout Win in 2000 NH Primary," WMUR-9, YouTube video, posted by "WMUR-TV," July 9, 2015, https:// www.youtube.com/watch?v=03geHDhzAqQ.

4. Peter Beinart, "Why Karl Rove Uses Dirty Tricks: They Work," *Atlantic,* May 13, 2014, http://www.theatlantic.com/politics/archive/2014/05/why-karl-rove-uses-dir ty-tricks-they-work/370811/.

5. Dan Balz and Haynes Johnson, *The Battle for America: The Story of an Extraordinary Election* (New York: Penguin Books, 2010). Citation retrieved from Google Books.

6. Dan Balz and Michael D. Shear, "McCain Puts New Strategist atop Campaign," *Washington Post,* July 3, 2008.

7. Ibid.

8. John McCain, speech in Kenner, Louisiana, June 3, 2008, transcript, http://www .politico.com/story/2008/06/transcript-of-mccain-speech-010820.

9. https://my.barackobama.com/page/s/stpaulrally/.

10. Bob von Sternberg and Mark Brunswick, "Obama Speech in St. Paul Ends Primary Season, Kicks Off Presidential Race," *Star Tribune* (Minneapolis), June 4, 2008, http://www.startribune.com/obama-speech-in-st-paul-ends-primary-season-kicks -off-presidential-race/19485059/.

11. Ibid.

12. Marc Ambinder, "McCain's Speech," *Atlantic,* June 3, 2008, http://www.theatlantic
.com/politics/archive/2008/06/mccains-speech/53388/.
13. Andrew Sullivan, "McCain's Speech," *Daily Dish* (blog), *Atlantic,* June 3, 2008,
http://www.theatlantic.com/daily-dish/archive/2008/06/mccains-speech/215765/.
14. Stephen Colbert, *Colbert Report,* Comedy Central, June 4, 2008, http://www.cc.com
/video-clips/hfq15q/the-colbert-report-john-mccain-s-green-screen-challenge.
15. Ibid.
16. Stephen Colbert, *Colbert Report,* Comedy Central, June 12, 2008, http://www.cc
.com/video-clips/nsgvgc/the-colbert-report-stephen-colbert-s-make-mccain-exci
ting-challenge-.
17. Stephen Colbert, *Colbert Report,* Comedy Central, June 25, 2008, http://www.cc
.com/video-clips/tog220/the-colbert-report-green-screen-challenge—vogue.
18. Stephen Colbert, *Colbert Report,* Comedy Central, September 2, 2008, http://www
.cc.com/video-clips/gmnlx9/the-colbert-report-green-screen-challenge—last-shot.
19. Ezra Klein, "The Obama-McCain Age Gap That Matters," *Los Angeles Times,* June 1,
2008, http://www.latimes.com/la-op-klein1-2008jun01-story.html.
20. Melissa Dahl, "Youth Vote May Have Been Key in Obama's Win," *NBC News,*
November 5, 2008, http://www.nbcnews.com/id/27525497/ns/politics-decision_08
/t/youth-vote-may-have-been-key-obamas-win/#.VaK02hHbI-V.
21. Robert Draper, "The Making (and Remaking) of John McCain," *New York
Times Magazine,* October 22, 2008, http://www.nytimes.com/2008/10/26/maga
zine/26mccain-t.html?pagewanted=all.
22. Jim Rutenberg and Adam Nagourney, "An Adviser Molds a Tighter, More Aggressive McCain Campaign," *New York Times,* September 7, 2008, http://www.nytimes
.com/2008/09/07/us/politics/07schmidt.html?pagewanted=all.
23. Republican National Convention, "A First Look at the 2008 Republican National Convention Podium," press release, August 21, 2008, http://www.gwu.edu
/~action/2008/chrnconv08/rconv082108pr.html.
24. Michael Falcone, "McCain and the Green Screen," *The Caucus* (blog), *New York Times,*
September 5, 2008, http://thecaucus.blogs.nytimes.com/2008/09/05/walter-reede/.
25. Ibid.
26. Ibid.
27. Bob Pool, "School Goes from Backdrop to Center Stage," *Los Angeles Times,* September 6, 2008, http://www.latimes.com/local/la-me-walterreed6-2008sep06-story
.html.
28. Kate Linthicum, "John McCain's Walter Reed Puzzle," *Top of the Ticket* (blog),
Los Angeles Times, September 5, 2008, http://latimesblogs.latimes.com/washing
ton/2008/09/mccain-walter-r.html.

CHAPTER 14: 2012: ROMNEY SINGS AN AMERICAN TUNE

1. Todd S. Purdum, "Clinton Takes a Trip up North and Down Memory Lane,"
New York Times, February 3, 1996, http://www.nytimes.com/1996/02/03/us/pol
itics-the-president-clinton-takes-a-trip-up-north-and-down-memory-lane.html.
2. Oliver O'Connell, "Trump Calls Neil Young a 'Total Hypocrite' and Claims the
Musician Asked Him for Money before Complaining about Use of Track in Campaign Announcement," *Daily Mail,* June 25, 2015, http://www.dailymail.co.uk
/news/article-3139454/Trump-calls-Neil-Young-total-hypocrite-campaign-music
-row-says-came-office-asking-money-called-invite-concert.html.
3. Alex Seitz-Wald, "The Villages: Where Republicans Rule," *Salon,* July 11, 2012,
http://www.salon.com/2012/07/11/the_villages_where_republicans_rule/.
4. Ibid.
5. Sarah Huisenga, "Gingrich: Romney Lives in World of 'Swiss Bank Accounts' and
$20 Million Income," *CBS News,* January 25, 2012, http://www.cbsnews.com/news
/gingrich-romney-lives-in-world-of-swiss-bank-accounts-and-20-million-income/.

6. "Quaint Town Squares," https://www.thevillages.com/lifestyle/hometown.htm.
7. Paul West, "Why Paul Ryan Chose The Villages for First Florida Stop," *Los Angeles Times,* August 18, 2012, http://articles.latimes.com/2012/aug/18/news/la-pn-paul-ry an-republican-stronghold-first-florida-trip-20120818.
8. Will Ritter, interview by the author, July 31, 2013.
9. Ibid.
10. "Mitt Romney Sings 'America The Beautiful,'" YouTube video, posted by "ElectAd," January 31, 2012, https://www.youtube.com/watch?v=x4eLx_V5Xkg.
11. Piers Morgan, *Piers Morgan Tonight,* CNN, January 30, 2012, YouTube video, "Mitt Romney Sings America The Beautiful," posted by "Neuroticy," February 2, 2012, https://www.youtube.com/watch?v=W7hmycVKDiU.
12. Ibid.
13. "Obama: 'I Wasn't Worried' about Singing Al Green: Inside the President's Decision to Perform 'Let's Stay Together,'" *Rolling Stone,* April 25, 2012, http://www.rolling stone.com/music/news/obama-i-wasnt-worried-about-singing-al-green-20120425.
14. Jon Stewart, *Daily Show,* Comedy Central, January 31, 2012, http://www.cc.com /video-clips/z954w3/the-daily-show-with-jon-stewart-indecision-2012—pander -express.
15. Jim Margolis, interview by Josh King, *Polioptics,* podcast, episode 97, April 13, 2013, http://www.polioptics.com/2013/04/episode-97-with-guests-jim-margolis-and-ron -klain/.
16. Ibid.
17. Ibid.
18. Museum of the Moving Image, *The Living Room Candidate: Presidential Campaign Commercials 1952–2012,* online exhibition, "Firms," http://www.livingroomcandi date.org/commercials/2012/firms.
19. Jim Margolis, interview by Josh King, *Polioptics.*
20. Will Ritter, interview by the author.
21. "Mitt Romney's Terrible Singing Comes Back to Haunt Him as Obama Uses His Rendition of 'America The Beautiful' in New Attack Ad," *Daily Mail,* July 16, 2012, http://www.dailymail.co.uk/news/article-2174327/New-Obama-ad-mocks-Ro mney-singing-America-Beautiful.html.
22. Jill Lawrence, "New Obama TV Ad Hits Romney on Outsourcing, Offshore Tax Shelters," *National Journal,* July 14, 2012, http://news.yahoo.com/obama-tv-ad-hits -romney-outsourcing-offshore-tax-113811028.html.
23. Michael D. Shear, "Obama Ad Continues Effort to Tie Romney to Outsourcing," *The Caucus* (blog), *New York Times,* July 14, 2012, http://thecaucus.blogs.nytimes .com/2012/07/14/obama-ad-features-a-singing-romney/.
24. Aaron Blake, "The Most Memorable Ad of the 2012 Campaign?" *Washington Post,* August 6, 2012, https://www.washingtonpost.com/blogs/the-fix/post/america-the -beautiful-the-most-memorable-ad-of-the-2012-campaign-so-far/2012/08/06/676 d32f4-dfdc-11e1-8fc5-a7dcf1fc161d_blog.html.
25. Martin Frost, "As Romney Sings, Obama Takes Note," *Politico,* July 24, 2012, http:// www.politico.com/story/2012/07/after-romney-sings-obama-takes-note-078904.
26. Will Ritter, interview by the author.
27. Ibid.

CHAPTER 15: OBAMA AND THE BATSMAN

1. Todd Leopold, "The Day America Met Barack Obama," *CNN,* November 5, 2008, http://www.cnn.com/2008/POLITICS/11/05/obama.meeting/index.html?iref=we recommend.
2. "Barack Obama on Monday Night Football," YouTube video, posted by "Barack Obama.com," December 12, 2006, https://www.youtube.com/watch?v=OmWlrtpq p40.

3. "Obama: Victory Speech," video and transcript, *New York Times,* November 5, 2008, http://elections.nytimes.com/2008/results/president/speeches/obama-victory-spe ech.html.

4. Pete Souza, *First 100 Days,* Flickr, 2009, https://www.flickr.com/photos/whitehouse /albums/72157617357737487/with/3483994997/.

5. Steve Holland, "What's in an Obama-Chavez Handshake?" Reuters, April 20, 2009, http://uk.reuters.com/article/2009/04/20/us-obama-handshake-analysis-idU KTRE53J6EK20090420.

6. Julian Borger and Uki Goni, "Bush Feels Hand of God as Poll Ratings Slump," *Guardian,* November 4, 2005, http://www.theguardian.com/world/2005/nov/05 /usa.argentina.

7. Andrew Clark, "Chávez Creates Overnight Bestseller with Book Gift to Obama," *Guardian,* April 19, 2009, http://www.theguardian.com/world/2009/apr/19/obama -chavez-book-gift-latin-america.

8. Peter Nicholas, "Obama Defends Greeting Hugo Chavez," *Los Angeles Times,* April 20, 2009, http://www.latimes.com/la-fg-obama-americas20-2009apr20-sto ry.html.

CHAPTER 16: CONTROLLING IMAGE

1. Pete Souza, "President Barack Obama Takes a Phone Call in His Private Study off the Oval Office," *First 100 Days,* Flickr, February 3, 2009, https://www.flickr.com /photos/whitehouse/3484820530.

2. National Security Archive, "The Nixon-Presley Meeting 21 December 1970," http:// nsarchive.gwu.edu/nsa/elvis/elnix.html.

3. Elvis Presley to Richard Nixon, undated, https://www.archives.gov/exhibits/nixon -met-elvis/page-1.html.

4. Pete Souza, interview by Adam Belmar and Josh King, *Polioptics,* podcast, episode 50, March 24, 2012, http://www.polioptics.com/2012/03/episode-50-with-guest -pete-souza-official-white-house-photographer-for-president-barack-obama/.

5. "Transcript: Obama Pleads Health Care Case," CNN, July 22, 2009, http://www .cnn.com/2009/POLITICS/07/22/transcript.obama/.

6. Ibid.

7. Huma Khan, Michele McPhee, and Russell Goldman, "Obama Called Police Officer Who Arrested Gates, Still Sees 'Overreaction' in Arrest," *ABC News,* July 24, 2009, http://abcnews.go.com/Politics/story?id=8163051&page=1.

8. Maureen Dowd, "Bite Your Tongue," *New York Times,* July 25, 2009, http://www .nytimes.com/2009/07/26/opinion/26dowd.html.

9. Philip Elliott, "Beer O'Clock at the White House: Let's Move On," Associated Press, July 30, 2009, http://www.nbcwashington.com/news/local/NATLObama-A -Beer-is-Just-A-Beer-Not-a-Summit-52100062.html.

10. Chris Good, "No Apologies, but Constructive Words," *Atlantic,* July 31, 2009, http://www.theatlantic.com/politics/archive/2009/07/no-apologies-but-constructi ve-words/22491/.

11. "After Beers, Professor, Officer Plan to Meet Again," CNN, July 31, 2009, http:// edition.cnn.com/2009/POLITICS/07/30/harvard.arrest.beers/.

12. Pete Souza, interview by Adam Belmar and Josh King, *Polioptics.*

13. Brian Williams, "Inside the Situation Room: Obama on Making OBL Raid De-cision," *Rock Center,* NBC, December 27, 2012, http://www.nbcnews.com/video /rock-center/47218575#47218575.

14. Pete Souza, interview by Adam Belmar and Josh King, *Polioptics.*

15. "The Obama History Project: 53 Historians Weigh In on Barack Obama's Legacy," *New York,* January 11, 2015, http://nymag.com/daily/intelligencer/2015/01/53-hist orians-on-obamas-legacy.html.

16. Jackie Calmes, "When a Boy Found a Familiar Feel in a Pat of the Head of State," *New York Times,* May 23, 2012, http://www.nytimes.com/2012/05/24/us/politics /indelible-image-of-a-boys-pat-on-obamas-head-hangs-in-white-house.html.

17. Pete Souza, interview by Adam Belmar and Josh King, *Polioptics.*

18. The White House Flickr feed, https://www.flickr.com/photos/whitehouse/.

19. Pete Souza, "Prime Minister David Cameron of the United Kingdom, President Barack Obama, Chancellor Angela Merkel of Germany, José Manuel Barroso, President of the European Commission, and Others Watch the Overtime Shootout of the Chelsea vs. Bayern Munich Champions League Final, in the Laurel Cabin Conference Room during the G8 Summit at Camp David, Md.," *G8 at Camp David,* Flickr, May 19, 2012, https://www.flickr.com/photos/whitehouse/7229949982/in /album-72157629803869054/.

20. Jordan Zakarin, "Obama Documentary 'The Road We've Traveled' by Davis Guggenheim Reveals Trailer," *Hollywood Reporter,* March 8, 2012, http://www.holly woodreporter.com/news/obama-documentary-road-weve-traveled-davis-guggen heim-297667.

21. Dan Pfeiffer, interview by Josh King, *Polioptics,* podcast, episode 143, March 21, 2014, http://www.polioptics.com/2014/03/episode-143-guest-dan-pfeiffer-senior-ad visor-president-obama/.

22. Pete Souza, interview by Adam Belmar and Josh King, *Polioptics.*

23. Ibid.

24. Coalition of press organizations to Jay Carney, November 21, 2013, http://asne.org /blog_home.asp?Display=1649.

25. Mark Landler, "Photographers Protest White House Restrictions," *New York Times,* November 21, 2013, http://www.nytimes.com/2013/11/22/us/politics/photograph ers-protest-white-house-restrictions.html.

26. Doug Mills, interview by Josh King, *Polioptics,* podcast, episode 117, September 6, 2013, http://www.polioptics.com/2013/09/episode-117-with-guests-samuel-m-ka tz-and-doug-mills/.

27. Ibid.

28. Pete Souza, "Slide show: Pres Obama attends Mandela memorial service; includes photos from Air Force One," Tweet, posted by "@petesouza," December 11, 2013, https://twitter.com/petesouza/status/410736425382866944.

29. Santiago Lyon, "Obama's Orwellian Image Control," *New York Times,* December 11, 2013, http://www.nytimes.com/2013/12/12/opinion/obamas-orwellian-image -control.html.

30. Office of the Press Secretary, "Briefing by Press Secretary Jay Carney, 12/12/13," December 12, 2013, https://www.whitehouse.gov/the-press-office/2013/12/12/press -briefing-press-secretary-jay-carney-121213.

31. Ibid.

32. Bob McNeely, interview by Josh King, *Polioptics,* podcast, episode 131, December 13, 2013, http://www.polioptics.com/2013/12/episdoe-131-guests-doris-kearns-good win-bob-mcneely-chuck-todd/.

CHAPTER 17: THE LAST MILE

1. John F. Harris and Peter Baker, "Clinton Urges End to Division," *Washington Post,* January 21, 1997, http://www.washingtonpost.com/wp-srv/national/longterm/inaug /tues/speech.htm. The image can be viewed at http://pics.amres.com/p_JPG/N286 .jpg.

2. Dan Pfeiffer, interview by Josh King, *Polioptics,* podcast, episode 143, March 21, 2014, http://www.polioptics.com/2014/03/episode-143-guest-dan-pfeiffer-senior-a dvisor-president-obama/.

3. Ibid.

4. Franz Strasser and Daniel Nasaw, "Arun Chaudhary on Life as White House Videographer," *BBC News*, October 8, 2012, http://www.bbc.com/news/magazine-19767164.
5. Dan Pfeiffer, interview by Josh King, *Polioptics*.
6. "Behind the Scenes of Presidential Advance: Part 1," YouTube video, posted by "The White House," January 21, 2010, https://www.youtube.com/watch?v=YYEfhW5W KBM.
7. Ibid.
8. Ibid.
9. Ibid.
10. "Behind the Scenes of Presidential Advance: Part 2," YouTube video, posted by "The White House," February 2, 2010, https://www.youtube.com/watch?v=SEukwa TqY_A.
11. Ibid.
12. Barack Obama, "Inaugural Address," January 21, 2013, https://www.whitehouse .gov/the-press-office/2013/01/21/inaugural-address-president-barack-obama.
13. Office of the Press Secretary, "Remarks by the President on the Affordable Care Act," transcript, October 21, 2013, https://www.whitehouse.gov/the-press -office/2013/10/21/remarks-president-affordable-care-act.
14. Gallup, "Gallup Daily: Obama Job Approval," poll, http://www.gallup.com/poll /113980/gallup-daily-obama-job-approval.aspx.
15. "Arun Chaudhary: Political Narratives: From State Fairs to State Dinners," YouTube video, posted by "ChicagoIdeasWeek," March 18, 2013, https://www.youtube.com /watch?v=7MWOp_Taeio.
16. Office of the Press Secretary, "Remarks by the President on Trayvon Martin," transcript, July 19, 2013, https://www.whitehouse.gov/the-press-office/2013/07/19/re marks-president-trayvon-martin.
17. Jennifer Palmieri, interview by Josh King, *Polioptics*, podcast, episode 115, August 17, 2013, http://www.polioptics.com/2013/08/episode-115-with-guest-jennifer-pal mieri-and-charlie-pearce/.
18. Bill O'Reilly, "Using Comedy to Promote ObamaCare," *O'Reilly Factor*, March 11, 2014, http://www.foxnews.com/transcript/2014/03/12/bill-oreilly-using-comedy-pr omote-obamacare/
19. T. L. Stanley, "How Between Two Ferns Landed Obama," *Adweek*, June 22, 2014, http://www.adweek.com/news-gallery/advertising-branding/how-between-two -ferns-landed-obama-158496.
20. Dan Pfeiffer, interview by Josh King, *Polioptics*.
21. Andrea Mitchell, *Andrea Mitchell Reports*, MSNBC, July 9, 2014, YouTube video, posted by "GOP War Room," July 9, 2014, https://www.youtube.com/watch?v =y8Za_SkMa0s&feature=youtu.be.
22. Office of the Press Secretary, "Statement by the President," transcript, August 20, 2014, https://www.whitehouse.gov/the-press-office/2014/08/20/statement-president.
23. Larry McShane, "Prez Tees Off as Foley's Parents Grieve," *Daily News*, August 21, 2014, http://www.nydailynews.com/news/politics/obama-returns-golf-green-art icle-1.1910781?cid=bitly.
24. Peter Baker and Julie Hirschfeld Davis, "A Terrorist Horror, Then Golf: Incongruity Fuels Obama Critics," *New York Times*, August 21, 2014, http://www.nytimes .com/2014/08/22/us/politics/a-terrorist-horror-then-golf-incongruity-fuels-obama -critics.html?_r=0.
25. Maureen Dowd, "The Golf Address," *New York Times*, August 23, 2014, http:// www.nytimes.com/2014/08/24/opinion/sunday/maureen-dowd-the-golf-address .html.
26. Chuck Todd, *Meet the Press*, NBC, September 7, 2014, http://www.nbcnews.com /meet-the-press/president-barack-obamas-full-interview-nbcs-chuck-todd-n197 616.

27. Ibid.
28. Ibid.

CHAPTER 18: COMFORTABLE IN YOUR SKIN

1. John M. Broder, "The Green Party: Clinton, Ford and Bush a Fearsome Threesome at Golf," *Los Angeles Times,* February 16, 1995, http://articles.latimes.com/1995-02-16 /news/mn-32775_1_golf-cart.
2. William J. Clinton, *Public Papers of the Presidents of the United States, William J. Clinton, 1995, Book I—January 1 to June 30, 1995* (Washington: Government Printing Office, 1996), 215.
3. Broder, "The Green Party: Clinton, Ford and Bush a Fearsome Threesome at Golf."
4. Clinton, *Public Papers of the Presidents of the United States, William J. Clinton, 1995, Book I—January 1 to June 30, 1995,* 547.
5. Mark S. Hamm, *Apocalypse in Oklahoma: Waco and Ruby Ridge Revenged* (Boston: Northeastern University Press, 1997), 54.
6. William J. Clinton: "Remarks on the Bombing of the Alfred P. Murrah Federal Building in Oklahoma City, Oklahoma," April 19, 1995, online by Gerhard Peters and John T. Woolley, *The American Presidency Project,* http://www.presidency.ucsb .edu/ws/?pid=51239.
7. William J. Clinton, *Public Papers Public Papers of the Presidents of the United States, William J. Clinton, 1996, Book II* (Washington: Government Printing Office, 1997), 546–47.
8. Office of the Press Secretary, "Remarks by the President in Eulogy for the Honorable Reverend Clementa Pinckney," June 26, 2015, https://www.whitehouse.gov /the-press-office/2015/06/26/remarks-president-eulogy-honorable-reverend-clem enta-pinckney.
9. Ibid.
10. Chris Cillizza, "This Was the Best Week of Obama's Presidency," *Washington Post,* June 26, 2015, https://www.washingtonpost.com/news/the-fix/wp/2015/06/26/this -was-the-best-week-of-obamas-presidency/.
11. Juliet Eilperin, "For Obama, Rainbow White House Was 'a Moment Worth Savoring,'" *Washington Post,* June 30, 2015, https://www.washingtonpost.com/news/post -politics/wp/2015/06/30/for-obama-rainbow-white-house-was-a-moment-worth -savoring/.
12. Morgan Neville and Robert Gordon, *Best of Enemies,* Magnolia Pictures, 2015, http://www.magpictures.com/bestofenemies/.
13. Ibid.
14. Barack Obama, interview by Marc Maron, *WTF,* podcast, episode 613, June 22, 2015, http://www.wtfpod.com/podcast/episodes/episode_613_-_president_barack _obama.
15. Ibid.
16. Marc Maron, "The President Was Here," *WTF,* podcast, episode 614, June 25, 2015, http://www.wtfpod.com/podcast/episodes/episode_614_-_the_president_was_here.
17. Ibid.
18. Ibid.

CHAPTER 19: THE NEW AGE OF OPTICS

1. "Getting Started | Hillary Clinton," YouTube video, posted by "Hillary Clinton," April 12, 2015, https://www.youtube.com/watch?v=0uY7gLZDmn4&feature=you tu.be.
2. Hillary Clinton, "Road trip! Loaded the van & set off for IA. Met a great family when we stopped this afternoon. Many more to come.-H," Tweet, posted by

"@HillaryClinton," April 12, 2015, https://twitter.com/hillaryclinton/status/5874 19742505426944.

3. "'People's champion' @HillaryClinton pops into @Chipotletweets—but no one recognizes her. http://nydn.us/1FKJIlx," Tweet, posted by "@NYDailyNews," April 14, 2015, https://twitter.com/NYDailyNews/status/587950950293319680/photo/1 ?ref_src=twsrc%5Etfw.

4. Jon Favreau, "Hillary driving to Iowa is an @AlyssaMastro44 worthy idea. Really great," Tweet, posted by "@jonfavs," April 12, 2015, https://twitter.com/jonfavs/stat us/587419553019203584?lang=en.

5. Jennifer Palmieri, "@jonfavs @AlyssaMastro44 it is a Mastro worthy idea, but in this case it actually was @HillaryClinton's idea. She loves her Scooby van," Tweet, posted by "@jmpalmieri," April 12, 2015, https://twitter.com/jmpalmieri/status/587 429754510401536?lang=en.

6. Gwen Ifill, "Clinton Braves an Unruly Crowd in Courting Wall Street Doubters," *New York Times,* April 3, 1992, http://www.nytimes.com/1992/04/03/us/1992-cam paign-clinton-clinton-braves-unruly-crowd-courting-wall-street-doubters.html.

7. Molly Ball, "Hillary's Uninspiring Agenda," *Atlantic,* June 13, 2015, http://www .theatlantic.com/politics/archive/2015/06/hillary-clinton-speech/395813/.

8. John Dickerson, "A Fighter Takes Center Stage," *Slate,* June 13, 2015, http://www .slate.com/articles/news_and_politics/politics/2015/06/hillary_clinton_s_roosev elt_island_speech_the_democratic_frontrunner_holds.html.

9. Sam Frizell, "Transcript: Read the Full Text of Hillary Clinton's Campaign Launch Speech," *Time,* June 13, 2015, http://time.com/3920332/transcript-full-text-hillary -clinton-campaign-launch/.

10. Glenn Thrush, "5 Takeaways from Clinton's Relaunch Rally," *Politico,* June 13, 2015, http://www.politico.com/story/2015/06/5-takeaways-from-clintons-relaunch -rally-118976.

11. Ball, "Hillary's Uninspiring Agenda."

12. Peggy Noonan, "Hillary Will Glide Above It All," *Wall Street Journal,* June 19, 2015, http://www.wsj.com/articles/hillary-will-glide-above-it-all-1434667768.

13. Dickerson, "A Fighter Takes Center Stage."

14. Richard Corliss, "Cinema: Lust Is a Thing with Feathers," *Time,* January 16, 1989, http://content.time.com/time/magazine/article/0,9171,956742,00.html.

15. Otto Friedrich, "Flash Symbol of an Acquisitive Age: Donald Trump," *Time,* January 16, 1989, http://content.time.com/time/magazine/article/0,9171,956733,00.html.

16. Olivier Laurent, "Behind TIME's Cover Shoot with Donald Trump and an American Bald Eagle," *Time,* August 20, 2015, http://time.com/4003904/donald-trump -bald-eagle/.

17. Jonathan Capehart, "Donald Trump's 'Mexican Rapists' Rhetoric Will Keep the Republican Party out of the White House," *Washington Post,* June 17, 2015, https://www.washingtonpost.com/blogs/post-partisan/wp/2015/06/17/trumps -mexican-rapists-will-keep-the-republican-party-out-of-the-white-house/.

18. George Romney, interview by Lou Gordon, WKBD-TV, 1968, "George Romney Brainwash interview on WKBD-TV 50," YouTube video, posted by "Pete Harwick," June 4, 2008, https://www.youtube.com/watch?v=fSdSiBehQpI.

19. Friedrich, "Flash Symbol of an Acquisitive Age: Donald Trump."

20. Jon Blistein, "Donald Trump Reports for Jury Duty, Calls Experience 'Really Good,'" *Rolling Stone,* August 18, 2015, http://www.rollingstone.com/politics/news /donald-trump-reports-for-jury-duty-calls-experience-really-good-20150818.

21. Maureen Dowd, "Donald Trump Struts in His Own Pageant," *New York Times,* August 22, 2015, http://www.nytimes.com/2015/08/23/opinion/sunday/maureen -dowd-donald-trump-struts-in-his-own-pageant.html?_r=0.

22. Tierney McAfee, "Inside Scoop: That Time Donald 'Zoolander' Trump Shared the Stage with a Bald Eagle," *People,* August 20, 2015, http://www.people.com/article /donald-trump-bald-eagle-time-photo-shoot.

23. Jenna Johnson, "Donald Trump Begs Iowans Not to Believe Ben Carson: 'Don't Be Fools, Okay?'" *Washington Post,* November 13, 2015, https://www.washington post.com/news/post-politics/wp/2015/11/13/donald-trump-begs-iowans-not-to-bel ieve-ben-carson-dont-be-fools-okay/.

24. Joe Scarborough and Mika Brzezinksi, "The Real Reason Trump Went Hard After Carson," *Morning Joe,* MSNBC, November 13, 2015, http://www.msnbc.com /morning-joe.

25. Philip Rucker and Robert Costa, "Time for GOP Panic? Establishment Worried Carson or Trump Might Win," *Washington Post,* November 13, 2015, https://www .washingtonpost.com/politics/time-for-gop-panic-establishment-worried-carson -and-trump-might-win/2015/11/12/38ea88a6-895b-11e5-be8b-1ae2e4f50f76_story .html.

INDEX